GLOSSARY
OF THE
THIRD WORLD

GLOSSARY
OF THE
THIRD WORLD

Words for Understanding
Third World Peoples &
Cultures

George Thomas Kurian

Facts On File
New York • Oxford

Glossary of the Third World

copyright © 1989 by George Thomas Kurian

Library of Congress Cataloging-in-Publication Data

Kurian, George Thomas.
    Glossary of the Third World.

    1. Ethnology—Dictionaries.   2. Developing countries—
Dictionaries.   I. Title.
GN307.K87   1989   306'.03   88-31092
ISBN 0-8160-1842-1

British CIP data available on request
Printed in the United States of America
10 9 8 7 6 5 4 3 2 1

INTRODUCTION

Humani Nihil Alienum
(Nothing Human Is Alien to Me)
—Terence

The *Glossary of the Third World* is a companion to the *Encyclopedia of the Third World,* presenting over 10,000 words dealing with the politics, culture, arts, society, religions, languages, ethnic groups, foods, history, dress, festivals, legal systems, military, agriculture, transportation, commerce and customs of the Third World.

As in the *Encyclopedia,* the Third World is defined as all countries of Latin America, Asia (excluding Japan, China, Mongolia, and Israel) and Africa (excluding South Africa).

The purpose of the Glossary is to survey, explore and illustrate the rich variety of Third World cultures. Unfortunately, it is a variety that is dying out. The world is becoming a monoculture dominated by Western traditions and cultures, particularly of Anglo-Saxon vintage. In a global village there is no need for diversity and heterogeneity is considered as an impediment to progress. Customs and social institutions are becoming homogenized under the mandate of economic development. *Pari passu* with such homogenization are the extinction of smaller and weaker cultures and the disappearance of the diversity that characterized human society until about the end of World War II. All areas of Third World life have been affected by this process but some more critically than others. Languages are perhaps the most endangered. At the turn of the century, there were an estimated 9,000 languages in the world, the majority of them in Africa and Asia. By 1980, according to the Wycliffe Translators, there were only 5,445 languages, more than half of them without a script. Within the next hundred years, more than 4,000 of these languages are expected to die out, suffocated or debilitated by the growth of such global lingua francas as English. Weights and measurements provide another example. A 1920 dictionary listed more than 700 units of weights and measurements, but only the SI (metric) system seems destined to survive into the 21st century. The story is similar in the case of dress. Until about 50 years ago more than 1,400 costumes and dresses were listed in major dictionaries, but since then the African has given up his *dashiki,* the Indian his *dhoti* and *jubbah* and the Arab his *burnoose,* and the Western style suit has become all but universal. Religious practices and customs also are becoming fossilized through the growing pressures of secularization. What imperialism failed to achieve in wiping out the teeming variety and profusion of Third World cultures has been achieved through pressures of a different order: industrialization, urbanization, and above all, media and communications.

The Third World is thus becoming denuded of its diversity. It is not inconceivable that within the next century all educated Third Worlders will speak one of the major European languages, dress alike in European dress, receive the same form of Western education, and eat the same kind of food. Such a prospect makes this *Glossary* even more important as an inventory of customs, artifacts and institutions that are slowly passing into oblivion.

The *Glossary* is not designed as a contribution to linguistics but rather as a guide and aid to area studies, country studies, cultural studies, ethnic studies and global studies. For this reason, I have dispensed with some common lexical practices, such as diacritics, which may not be essential for the audience for whom the book is intended. Further, diacritical marks are uncommon among and inconsistently used in translations of the languages of the Third World.

The transliteration of foreign names, especially from Asian and African languages, is a source of unending despair for lexicographers. The reason is twofold: First, because English is not a phonetic language, there are special problems in transliteration from phonetic languages. Second, there are no standard rules or norms for transliteration from Oriental and African languages, and writers have considerable freedom in choosing the forms with which they are most comfortable. The *Observer* of London once identified 56 ways in which the name Qaddhafi is spelled in English (Kaddafi, Gadafhi, Qudhafi, etc.). The names of most ethnic groups may be spelled in at least a dozen ways, and further most languages and ethnic groups have different alternate names. Native speakers may use one name while outsiders may use others. French speakers spell names differently from English speakers. Some names may be considered offensive by those to whom they apply but may sound innocuous to non-natives. A standard nomenclature has never been adopted and could never be enforced. That being so, I have used the spellings most commonly found in English language books published in the United States. Cross references also have been avoided for the same reason since to list all possible permutations and combinations and variations would require a work at least 20 times the size of this work.

The 10,000 words in the *Glossary* are derived from a broad catchment area covering over 70 languages and 120 countries. For obvious reasons, I had to be very selective. The basic purpose had been to choose the most representative words and also to achieve a balance among the various regions and countries and the subject fields and subfields.

My list of acknowledgments is short, but, nevertheless, the debt of gratitude is substantial: to Edward W. Knappman for his unfailing support and inspiration and to Kate Kelly for her editorial guidance and unflagging encouragement. A word of thanks is due also to Mike Valenti for his skillful copyediting.

George Thomas Kurian

GLOSSARY
OF THE
THIRD WORLD

Aanza *Zaire.* Ethnic group.

aba *Arab countries.* A square, ankle-length cotton dress, made of wool or camel's hair, with an open front and two holes at the sides for the arms.

abaan *Somalia.* Patron; host; protector.

Ababdan *Sudan.* Arab tribe of Baja origin in the north.

ababvubyi *Rwanda.* Rainmaker among the Bashara clan.

abaca *Spanish America.* Hemp plant whose tough fibers are made into ropes and coarse cloth.

abacero *Mexico.* Manager of a small grocery store.

abacikizwa *Rwanda and Burundi.* Cattle herders invited by a chief to establish themselves in a new area.

abackire *Burundi.* Cattle herders who establish themselves in a new area through payment of a female calf to the owners.

Abacwuzi *Rwanda and Burundi.* Wandering trader.

abafumu (plural: umufumu) *Rwanda and Burundi.* A magico-medical practitioner who can communicate with the dead, ward off misfortunes and diseases, interpret dreams and predict the future.

abagererwa *Rwanda and Burundi.* Sharecroppers.

abahanza *Rwanda and Burundi.* An important HUTU clan.

abahenyi *Rwanda and Burundi.* A magic practitioner who specializes in curses and incantations.

abaja *Rwanda and Burundi.* A female servant who is kept as a concubine.

abajuru *Rwanda and Burundi.* Elder.

abakonikoni *Rwanda and Burundi.* HUTU bandits.

abamenja *Rwanda and Burundi.* Rebels against the king.

abanga *Indonesia.* 1. Heterodox or nominally Muslim Javanese. 2. *India.* Devotional song. See PADA.

abanyaruguru *Rwanda and Burundi.* TUTSI lineage of 43 noble families.

abapfakazi *Rwanda and Burundi.* Woman who marries a man of lower rank.

abapfasoni *Rwanda and Burundi.* Nobles descended from GANWA lineages who lose their rank when a new king ascends the throne.

abara *Brazil.* Afro-Brazilian dish of beans cooked in pepper and palm oil.

1

Abarambo *Zaire.* Ethnic group.

abarca *Spanish America.* Leather sandal whose sole is cut from the tread of a used truck tire.

abarosi *Rwanda and Burundi.* Witches.

abasapfu *Rwanda and Burundi.* TUTSI noble clan.

abashingantahe *Rwanda and Burundi.* Literally, those who use the stick. Judges. Thus, *abashingantahe bo ru rurimbi,* royal judges.

abashitsi *Rwanda and Burundi.* Practitioners of magic who specialize in catching thieves.

abashumba (plural: umushumba) *Rwanda and Burundi.* Servant paid in kind and not in money.

abasisi *Rwanda and Burundi.* Royal cook.

abasoshi *Rwanda and Burundi.* Young attendant at the royal court.

abatererezi *Rwanda and Burundi.* Gift.

Abavumu *Rwanda and Burundi.* Prestigious HUTU clan.

abavurati (singular: umuvurati) *Rwanda and Burundi.* Rainmaker.

abayah *Islamic countries.* An opaque black, voluminous cloak with batlike dolman sleeves worn by women.

Abbe *West Africa.* One of the LAGOON CLUSTER.

abd *Islamic countries.* Slave of.

Abdali *Yemens.* Ethnic group.

Abe *West Africa.* Niger-Kordofanian language.

abee *Afghanistan.* System of agriculture using irrigation.

abegaz *Ethiopia.* Governor of a frontier province.

abele *West Africa.* A dance of Nigerian origin.

abenhla (singular: enhla) *Zimbabwe.* Middle caste among the NDEBELE.

aberu *Iran.* Face saving.

abezansi (singular: zensi) *Zimbabwe.* Upper caste among the NDEBELE.

Abgal *Somalia.* Clan of the HAWIYE family. See SAMAAL.

abid *West Africa.* Literally, captives. Islamized tribes who were conquered and assimilated by Muslim invaders.

Abidji *West Africa.* 1. One of the LAGOON CLUSTERS. 2. Niger-Kordofanian language.

abiru *Rwanda and Burundi.* Guardians of customs.

abkari *India.* Tax or excise duty on sale and production of alcoholic liquors.

abolengo *Spanish America.* Social position defined by birth rather than by individual ability or achievement.

abosom *Ghana.* Higher gods of the AKAN tribe.

Abou Charib *West Africa.* Nilo-Saharan language.

abou san *Ivory Coast.* Sharecropping system in which produce is shared between the owner and the peasant.

Aboure *West Africa.* One of the LAGOON CLUSTERS. Also, *Essouma, Akapless, Issinois.*

About Charib *West Africa.* Ethnic group of the SAHEL.

abraco *Brazil.* A hug, as a ritual greeting.

Abron *West Africa.* 1. AKAN-speaking ethnic group. Also, *Brong.* 2. Niger-Kordofanian language.

Abu *Oman. See* BU.

Abua *Nigeria.* Niger-Kordofanian language.

Abujmaria *India.* DRAVIDIAN language.

Abulas *Papua New Guinea.* Papuan language.

abuna *Ethiopia.* Title of patriarch of the Ethiopian Orthodox Church.

abuna *West Africa.* Subclan of the TEMNE.

Abure *West Africa.* Niger-Kordofanian language.

Aburune *Spanish America.* Amazon Indian tribe.

abusua *Ghana.* AKAN matrilineal clan.

acabralhado *Brazil.* Descendant of a MULATO and a black.

acaparado *Mexico.* Speculator in foodstuffs.

acapteales *El Salvador.* Heavy mats.

accion civica *Spanish America.* Literally, civic action. Employment of the armed forces in public works projects.

accion communales *Spanish America.* Local community development group.

accommodesan *Sri Lanka.* Land grant in lieu of salary.

Aceh *Indonesia.* Austronesian language.

Achagua *Spanish America.* Indian ethnic group in Bolivar, Guarico and Barinas in Venezuela.

Achang *Burma.* Tibeto-Burmese ethnolinguistic group along the Yunnan border.

achar *Cambodia.* Lay assistant who serves as temporal intermediary between monks and the community.

acharn *Thailand.* Teacher.

acharya *India.* Literally, one who observes the rules. A Vedic teacher.

acheik htamein *Burma.* Intricately patterned open skirt worn by women on ceremonial occasions.

achheotritiya *Nepal.* Powdered spice served with drinks to family and passersby in the month of Baisakh.

Achi *Guatemala.* Mayan language.

Acholi *Central Africa.* 1. Western Nilotic ethnic group. 2. Nilo-Saharan language.

achut *Nepal.* Untouchables; collective name for low castes.

acudes *Brazil.* Storage dam or reservoir.

acuerdo *Spanish America.* Executive regulation having the force of law.

Aculo *West Africa.* GRUSI-speaking ethnic group.

Ada *West Africa.* ADANGBE ethnic group.

adaherta *Malaysia.* The middle class. *See* PERTENGAHAN.

adalat *Indian subcontinent.* Provincial council having both civil and criminal jurisdiction.

Adangbe *Ghana.* GA-related ethnic group along the coast and in Accra Plain.

Adangbe *West Africa.* Ethnic group belonging to GA-ADANGE-KAW family.

adat *Indian subcontinent.* Customary law in Muslim communities.

abat perpatch *Indonesia.* Customary law that recognizes matrilineal descent.

adbar *Ethiopia.* Protective spirits of a community.

Addis Amet *Ethiopia.* In AMHARIC calendar, New Year around September 11.

adelantado *Spanish America.* In colonial times, agent charged with promoting colonization of frontier regions.

Adele *West Africa.* Central Togo ethnic cluster.

Adelos *Venezuela.* Members of Accion Democratico Party.

adentro *Spanish America.* Literally, within. Interior lowlands.

adhikari *India.* A rural headman in the south.

adhl *Morocco.* Lawyer or notary.

Adhola *Central Africa.* Nilo-Saharan language.

Adi *India.* Sino-Tibetan language.

Adi Granth *India.* The SIKH holy scriptures.

adinkra *Ghana.* Cotton cloth stamped with various designs from a dye made from the bark of the badie tree.

Adiou Krou *West Africa.* Ethnic group of the LAGOON CLUSTER.

adivasis *India.* Aboriginals.

Adja *West Africa.* Ethnic group of EWE cluster.

adjanikon *Haiti.* Male assistant in a Voodoo cult.

adma *Mauritania.* The traditional Arabic upper class of warriors.

Adnani *Yemens.* Northern Arab.

adoba *Spanish America.* Clay used in building houses.

adonten *Ghana.* Main body of an AKAN army under the command of an *adontenhene.*

adosa *West Africa.* Annual KOTOKOLI festival, also known as *yeke-yeke.*

Adouma *Gabon.* MBEDE-speaking people in the upper Ogooue.

Aduana *Ghana.* One of the principal AKAN clans.

aduana *Spanish America.* Customs house.

Advaita *India.* Monistic system of epistomology and ontology that holds the universe as *maya,* or illusion.

Adyegey *Turkey.* Caucasian ethnic group.

Adyukru *West Africa.* Niger-Kordofanian language.

Adyumba *Gabon.* MYENE-speaking BANTU group, a part of the MPONGWE clan.

afaqi *Tunisia.* Sedentary rural dwellers.

Afar *Horn of Africa.* 1. Ethnic group, also known as *Danakil.* 2. Afro-Asiatic language.

afectacion *Bolivia.* Expropriation of land for agrarian reform.

afe negus *Ethiopia.* Literally, mouth of the emperor. Former title of the chief justice.

afersata *Ethiopia.* Custom, when a crime is committed, of rounding up all local inhabitants in an enclosure until the guilty person is revealed.

affranchis *Haiti.* Free men.

Afghani *Afghanistan.* Monetary unit.

afilhado *Brazil.* Godson.

afin *Nigeria.* Royal palaces of the YORUBA.

aflaj *Arab countries.* Man-made underground channels.

aforo *Spanish America.* Assessment for tax purposes.

Afridi *Afghanistan.* Warlike tribe on the Pakistani border.

Afshar *Iran.* Turkic group in Khorasan, around Zanjan and south of Kerman.

afuerino *Spanish America.* Migrant farm laborer.

agadir (plural: igudar) *Morocco.* Fortified granary shared by several families.

Agajani *Iran.* Indo-Iranian ethnic group in Gilan.

Aga Khan *Islamic countries.* Religious head of the Bora Ismaili Muslim community.

agal *Arab countries.* Black ropelike hoop holding the KAFFIYAH in place.

agal *Somalia.* Transportable beehive hut with flexible branches forming the rounded skeleton.

agama *Philippines.* Moro judicial courts.

Agarabi *Papua New Guinea.* Papuan language.

Agariya *India.* Austro-Asiatic language.

Agave *Ghana.* EWE group in eastern Accra Plain.

agdal *Morocco.* Pastureland held privately by a single owner.

Agew *Ethiopia.* 1. Important ethnic group in the north and central Ethiopian plateau. 2. The language of this group.

agha *Middle East.* Title of KURD tribal leaders.

aghalik *Algeria.* Jurisdiction of an AGHA.

aghazazit *Mauritania.* Salt mines.

Aghem *West Africa.* Niger-Kordofanian language.

agiotista *Mexico.* Usurer.

agla *Western Sahara.* Well, between one and five meters deep.

Aglipayanism *Philippines.* Nationalistic Christian movement and church founded by Gregorio Aglipay.

Agni *West Africa.* An AKAN group.

Agnikula *India.* Literally, firstborn. Term applied to any or all of the four Rajput clans: *Pawar, Parihar, Chuhar* and *Solanki.*

agogo *Brazil.*   Bell-like musical instrument struck with a metal stick, used in CANDOMBLE and macumba ceremonies.

Agrabi *Yemens.*   Ethnic group.

agregado *Spanish America.*   Literally, attached. Member of a community who was born outside.

agregado *Brazil.*   Landless peasant who pays rent by working free for the landowner for a certain number of days.

agropolis *Brazil.*   A group of 20 AGROVILAS.

agrovila *Brazil.*   A basic colony in the Amazon region consisting of 50 farm plots or 100 hectares.

agrupacion *Cuba.*   Administrative unit consisting of a number of state farms.

Aguacatec *Central America.*   MAMEAN linguistic group in Huehuetenango.

aguadulce *Central America.*   Sweetened water.

aguamiel *Ecuador.*   See CHAHUARMISHQUE.

aguardiente *Spanish America.*   Liquor made from distilled sugarcane juice.

Aguaruna *Spanish America.*   Native Indian language.

aguayo *Spanish America.*   Handwoven square cloth for carrying children or produce among highland Indians.

aguinaldo *Spanish America.*   Christmas bonus.

aguita *Spanish America.*   Herb tea.

Agutaynon *Philippines.*   Minor Christian group in Calimiane.

Agwagurane *West Africa.*   Niger-Kordofanian language.

Agwe Woyo *Haiti.*   Voodoo god of the sea.

agyi *Burma.*   Title of village headman in KACHIN-GUMLAO community.

Ahafo *West Africa.*   TWI ethnic group.

Ahanta *West Africa.*   Ethnic group.

ahel *Western Sahara.*   People or tribe.

ahema (singular: ohema) *Ghana.*   Queen mother among the ASANTE.

ahene (singular: ohene) *Ghana.*   Courtesy title of an ASANTE noble or royal agent.

ahenemma *Ghana.*   ASANTE princess of the golden stool.

ahiafo *Ghana.*   The poor class among the AKAN.

ahijadero *Spanish America.*   Pastureland.

ahimsa *India.*   Noninjury to living things.

Ahiri *India.*   Indo-European language.

ahl *Egypt.*   Extended families.

ahl al suq *Arab countries.*   Resident tradesman of a market.

ahli *Ethiopia.*   Kinship network among the HARAN.

Ahmadiya-Idrisiya *Somalia.*   SUFI order founded by Sayyid Ahmad Ibn Idris (1760–1837).

Ahmadiyyah *Islamic countries.*   Heretical Islamic sect founded by Mirza Ghulam Ahmed (1835–1908).

Ahmadzai *Afghanistan.* GHILAZAI tribe.

ahmudan *Burma.* Palace guards.

ah-nah-de *Burma.* Restraint in the exercise of power, as a political virtue.

ahopoi *Paraguay.* Handmade embroidered textiles, customarily made in the town of Villarrica.

Ahoulan *West Africa.* EWE-speaking ethnic group.

aiga *Western Samoa.* Extended family headed by a MATAI.

aile *Turkey.* Family.

Aimaq *Afghanistan.* Indo-European language.

aini *Spanish America.* Reciprocal labor whereby members of a community work together by turn on each other's lands. Also, *forna vuetta.*

aipim *Brazil.* Sweet cassava root.

ait *Morocco.* Literally, sons of. Generic tribal name, the BERBER equivalent of the Arabic BENI or BANU.

ait arbain *Western Sahara.* Tribal council in time of war.

ait atman *Western Sahara.* One of the two rival blocs of the TEKNA tribe.

ait jmel *Western Sahara.* One of the two rival blocs of the TEKNA tribe.

ait lahsen *Western Sahara.* The main TEKNA group.

ait oussa *Western Sahara.* A TEKNA group.

Aizo *West Africa.* Coastal ethnic group of EWE family.

Aja-Gbe *West Africa.* Niger-Kordofanian language.

Ajami *Ghana.* Arabic script for writing HAUSA.

ajit *Spanish America.* A young shaman.

ajlaf *Bangladesh.* Low-born, or belonging to a menial caste.

ajman *Arab countries.* Large tribe in East Nejd in Saudi Arabia.

ajon *South Korea.* A subgroup of the CHINGIN.

ajoujo *Brazil.* Canoe lashed together to transport cattle along the Amazon in Spanish times.

ajuran *Swaziland.* A clan or confederation.

Akali *India.* A SIKH zealot. Also *Nihang.*

Akan *West Africa.* 1. KWA ethnic group comprising ANYI-BAWLE, NZEMA, TWI-FANTE, EWE, GA-ADANGBE-KAW, GUAN and CENTRAL TOGO. 2. Niger-Kordofanian language.

Akaselem *West Africa.* Niger-Kordofanian language.

Akash Deep *Nepal.* NEWARI festival in the month of KARTIK-ASHWIN. Also, *Ala mata.*

Akawaio *Guyana.* CARIB-speaking Amerindian tribe.

Akebu *West Africa.* Niger-Kordofanian language.

Akha *Southeast Asia.* 1. Tibeto-Burmese ethnic group. 2. Sino-Tibetan language.

akhammes (plural: ikhammessen) *Morocco.* Tenant farmer in central region paid one fifth of the crop.

akhdam *Arab countries.* Servile class of mixed African descent.

akidas *Tanzania.* Under German rule, chiefs who collected taxes and administered justice.

akil *Somalia.* Headman.

Aklan *Philippines.* Minor ethnic group in Visayan.

Aklanon *Philippines.* 1. Christian ethnic group in north Panay. 2. Austronesian language.

Akoose *West Africa.* Niger-Kordofanian language.

Akpafu *West Africa.* CENTRAL TOGO ethnic group.

Akposso *West Africa.* Ethnic group in the Plateaux region.

Aku *West Africa.* Ethnic group.

akua ba (plural: akuamma) *Ghana.* AKAN fertility doll carved of wood with flat oval head, long neck and small round body.

Akuapem *West Africa.* TWI ethnic group.

akutho *Burma.* In Buddhism, demerit accruing from violation of religious or moral codes.

Akwa *Cameroon.* A clan of the DOUALA peoples.

Akwamu *West Africa.* TWI ethnic group.

Akyem *West Africa.* TWI ethnic group.

Akyem Abuakwa *Ghana.* Senior and largest AKYEM division.

Akyem Abuaswa *West Africa.* TWI ethnic group.

Akyem Basome *West Africa.* TWI ethnic group.

Akyem Bosume *Ghana.* Southernmost and smallest AKYEM division.

Akyem Kotoku *Ghana.* Middle AKYEM division.

Akyem Kotoku *West Africa.* TWI ethnic group.

Alaba *Ethiopia.* 1. EAST CUSHITIC ethnic group. 2. Afro-Asiatic language.

Alacitas *Bolivia.* Festival, held on March 4, honoring Ekeko, the AYMARA god of good fortune.

Aladian *West Africa.* Niger-Kordofanian language.

alagado *Brazil.* 1. Shantytown in Fortaleza. 2. Area or district consisting predominantly of mud hovels.

alagbe *Brazil.* Drum player during a CAMDOMBLE ceremony.

Alago *West Africa.* Niger-Kordofanian language.

Alak *Laos.* Austro-Asiatic language.

alakadar *Afghanistan.* Administrator of an ALAKADARI.

alakadari *Afghanistan.* Subdivision of a province.

alamain *Saudi Arabia.* The marker, a few miles from Mecca, beyond which a non-Muslim may not enter.

a la partida *Spanish America.* Sharecropping.

al asif *Arab countries.* Lineage.

Ala Mata *Nepal.* Variant name for AKASH DEEP.

alamma *Western Sahara.* Symbol branded on livestock.

Alawite *Islamic countries.* Heretical Muslim sect that believes in the divinity of Ali. Also, *Nusayris.*

Albaia *Paraguay.* Branch of the CHACO GUAYCURU INDIANS.

albarda *Honduras.* Saddle consisting of two cylindrical bundles of reeds tied tightly.

albazo *Spanish America.* MESTIZO music with syncopated melodies.

albino *Spanish America.* Child of a MORISCO father and a Spanish mother.

al calde *Spanish America.* Mayor.

alcaldia *Spanish America.* Office of an AL CALDE.

aldea *Spanish America.* Small hamlet or village.

aldeamento *Portuguese Africa.* Fortified village system under Portuguese rule.

aldeanos *Spanish America.* Indian villagers.

aleka *Ethiopia.* Administrative head of a local church, chosen from among the monks.

aleqa *Ethiopia.* Tribal chief who also was administrator of local churches and monasteries.

Alevi *Turkey.* Heretical Muslim sect that believes in the divinity of Ali.

Alewi *Yemens.* Ethnic group.

alfabetizacion *Cuba.* Literacy training.

alfabetizadores *Cuba.* Literally, teachers of the alphabet. Teachers in mass literacy campaigns.

alfandoque *Spanish America.* Rattle with pebbles inside a hollow cane, used with music of African origin.

alferez *Spanish America.* Sponsor of a fiesta. Also *carguero.*

alguacil *Central America.* Constable or municipal official.

Ali *Central African Republic.* Ethnic group of BANTU origin.

alifa *West Africa.* Variant of *caliph.*

ali'i *Western Samoa.* Chief of a village council.

Ali Khayl *Afghanistan.* GHILAZAI tribe.

alisan *Indonesia.* Literally, stream. Any one of the major religious or social ideological groups.

alize *West Africa.* Cool wind blowing from the northeast from November through January.

Aljamiahtol Wadaniyal *Somalia.* The former National Assembly.

aljeria *Spanish America.* Sales outlet in a town for the produce of a hacienda.

Alladian *West Africa.* One of the LAGOON CLUSTERS. Also, *Jack-Jack.*

almamy *West Africa.* Military, political and religious leader of the PEUL Muslims.

almocreve *Brazil.* Muleteer.

almud *Spanish America.* Unit of weight equal to 32 lb.

alpana *India.* Floor designs of colored rice paste with abstract floral or geometric patterns.

alpargatas *Paraguay.* Fiber sandals used as house slippers.

alpha *West Africa.* Muslim scholar.

altozanero *Spanish America.* Laborer who waits around church entrances for odd jobs.

Alur *Central Africa.* 1. Western Nilotic ethnic group. 2. *West Africa.* Nilo-Saharan language.

alza *Spanish America.* MESTIZO music with syncopated melodies.

amadhlozi (singular: idhlozi) *Zimbabwe.* NDEBELE spirits representing souls of departed ancestors.

amah *India.* Wet nurse.

amaholi (singular: holi) *Zimbabwe.* Lower caste among the NDEBELE.

amal *India.* Work.

aman *Bangladesh.* Rice planted in spring and harvested in November through January.

amanat al-asimah *Iraq.* The governorate of Baghdad.

Amangwane *Swaziland.* Collective name for the Swazi nation.

amanhene (singular: omanhene) *Ghana.* 1. Chiefs of state who made up the ASANTI CONFEDERATION. 2. AKAN paramount chief.

Amarani *Somalia.* Mixed Arab-Persian-Indonesian ethnic group inhabiting coastal areas.

Amarar *Sudan.* BEDAWIYA-speaking BEJA ethnic group.

amarelo *Brazil.* Literally, yellow. People of Oriental background.

amarillo *Cuba.* People of Oriental, especially Chinese, descent.

amarozi *Rwanda and Burundi.* Charms and amulets made of horns of animals.

amashinga *Burundi.* Judicial system under the former MWAMIS.

amasiado *Brazil.* Literally, friendship. A common-law union or illicit relationship, especially concubinage.

amat *Burma.* Council of ministers in pre-colonial times who received no salaries but enjoyed extensive perquisites.

amat *Laos.* Middle grade of the civil service.

Amavundle *Lesotho.* NGUNI-speaking people in Qutthing district.

amazine *Rwanda and Burundi.* Praise poems.

amba *Ethiopia.* Level-topped mountain used as site of a monastery, prison or fortress.

Amba *Uganda.* 1. Western BANTU ethnic group. 2. *Uganda and Zaire* Niger-Kordofanian language.

Ambo *Southern Africa.* Congolese LUANDA tribe in Luapula Valley, part of the NGUNI cluster.

Ambonese *Indonesia.* Austronesian language.

Ambundu *Angola.* Subgroup of the MBUNDU tribe.

Ambundu or **Akwaluando** *Southern Africa.* A dialect of MBUNDU.

amghar *Morocco.* Chief of a BERBER tribe.

Amhara *Ethiopia.* Dominant ethnic group, mostly Christian.

Amharic *Ethiopia.* 1. Member of the AMHARA. 2. Afro-Asiatic language of the AMHARA.

amil *Yemens.* District governor.

amin *India.* Inspector and process server employed by civil courts.

amin al asimah *Iraq.* Governor of Baghdad.

amir (plural, umara) *Arab countries.* Prince or commander.

amir al muaminin *Morocco.* Literally, commander of the faithful. Traditional title of the kings of Morocco.

Amiri *Yemens.* Ethnic group.

amm *Arab countries.* Paternal uncle who plays an important role in the upbringing of a child.

amo *Spanish America.* Master or boss.

amole *Ethiopia.* Salt money, legal tender until the 19th century.

ampah *Nepal.* Four clay vessels used for ritual purposes by the NE-WARIS in the festival of Pachali-Bhairava.

amparo *Spanish America.* Legal writ, similar to habeas corpus, designed to safeguard constitutional guarantees of human rights by ensuring prompt and equitable judicial treatment.

Ampesh *Papua New Guinea.* Papuan language.

amphoe *Thailand.* District.

amsom *India.* Smallest territorial unit for revenue purposes.

Amuzgo *Central America.* Oto-Manguean language.

an *Somalia.* Title of a WADDAD or saint. Also applied to magistrate of water disputes.

Ana *West Africa.* Ethnic group of YORUBA cluster.

Anaang *West Africa.* Niger-Kordofanian language.

anak dagang *Malaysia.* Foreign Malays, especially immigrants from Indonesia who have been assimilated into Malay society.

Anayzah *Saudi Arabia.* Northwestern tribe to which the Saudi royal family belongs.

anchal *Nepal.* Zone or province.

anda *Spanish America.* A wooden frame for carrying images of saints in processions.

Andar *Afghanistan.* GHILAZAI tribe.

Andevo *Madagascar.* MERINA slave class.

Andino *Colombia.* Highlander of the Andes Mountains.

andriana *Madagascar.* Class of MERINA nobles.

andullo *Spanish America.* Leaf tobacco wrapped in leaves, similar to a cigar.

Ane *West Africa.* Elite ethnic group related to GA.

Anejo *Spanish America.* Literally, annex. Village inhabited exclusively by Indians.

Anga *India.* Indo-European language.

Angal *Papua New Guinea.* Papuan language.

Angas *West Africa.* Afro-Asiatic language.

angklung *Indonesia.* Bamboo musical instrument, part of GAMELAN.

Angonian *Southern Africa.* NGUNI people living in the highlands.

anicut *India.* Dam.

ankobea *Ghana.* Personal bodyguard of an ASANTAHENE.

An-lich *Vietnam.* Chinese lunar calendar dating from 2647 B.C.

Anlo *West Africa.* EWE group along the coast to the east of the Volta river.

anna *India.* Under British rule, ¹/₁₆th of a RUPEE.

ansar *Arab countries.* Band of supporters.

ansar *Bangladesh.* Part-time village constable.

Antailfasy *Madagascar.* Eastern ethnic group.

Antaimoro *Madagascar.* Eastern ethnic group.

Antaisaka *Madagascar.* Eastern ethnic group.

Antakarana *Madagascar.* Northern ethnic group.

Antambahoaka *Madagascar.* Eastern ethnic group.

Antandroy *Madagascar.* Southern ethnic group.

Antanosy *Madagascar.* Southern ethnic group.

anti *Nepal.* Long-necked jug used in drinking rice wine.

Antioqueno *Colombia.* Resident of Antioquia.

antiyanquismo *Spanish America.* Opposition to and distrust of Americans, especially in politics.

Antumba *Southern Africa.* Non-NGUNI ethnic group.

Anuak *Ethiopia and Sudan.* 1. Nilo-Saharan ethnic group. 2. Nilo-Saharan language.

anukhet *Cambodia.* Subprovince.

Anum-Boso *West Africa.* GUAN ethnic group.

Anyang *West Africa.* Niger-Kordofanian language.

Anya Nya *Sudan.* Major southern guerrilla group in the civil war of the 1970s.

anyeint pwe *Burma.* A kind of folk burlesque performed with clowning and dancing.

Anyi-Bawle *West Africa.* KWE-AKAN ethnic group.

Anyin *West Africa.* Niger-Kordofanian language.

aobaia *Central America.* Folk dance performed in a circle in MOSQUITIA.

ao dai *Vietnam.* Literally, long dress. National female attire consisting of a contoured full-length dress over black or white loose-fitting trousers. The dress splits into front and back panels from the waist down.

ao o le malo *Western Samoa.* Title of the head of state.

Aowin *Ghana.* ANYI-BAWLE ethnic group of the western region.

ap *Vietnam.* Hamlet, subdivision of a XA, or village.

apachita *Spanish America.* Roadside shrine for votive offerings.

Apagibeti-Boa *Zaire.* Ethnic group of the Central Rain Forest.

apanjaht *Guyana.* Literally, vote for your own kind. Political slogan of the East Indian groups during elections.

aparceria *Spanish America.* Sharecropping.

aparcero *Spanish America.* Sharecropper who is allotted land for cultivation in return for half the harvest.

a partir *Spanish America.* Sharecropper.

Apatani *India.* Sino-Tibetan language.

Apayao *Philippines.* Pagan IGOROT ethnic group in north Luzon.

a phyo *Burma.* Literally, spinsters. Unmarried girls in a village, 15 years and older, who participate in social festivities.

api *Tonga.* One parcel of land, 3.33 hectares in extent, to which a Tongan is entitled on reaching adulthood.

Apindje *Gabon.* Ethnic group of the OKANDE linguistic family.

Apolista *Spanish America.* ARAWAKan-speaking Indian ethnic group around La Paz department in Bolivia.

aposento *Spanish America.* Sleeping room in a ranch-style house.

apu *Spanish America.* Intermediary between the Indians, the parish priest and the political bosses.

aqabe se'at *Ethiopia.* Chief ecclesiastic of former imperial court.

Aqamir (singular Amiri) *Arab countries.* A large tribe of eastern Arabia.

aqsam *Libya.* Ward or quarter of a town.

aquid *Saudi Arabia.* Rank of colonel in the Saudi army.

'ar *Morocco.* Literally, shame. Action requiring atonement by a religiously sanctioned sacrifice.

Ara *Indonesia.* Austronesian language.

Arab *Arab countries.* Semitic people of the Middle East, properly of Saudi Arabia, but by extension applied to all Arabic-speaking people and those conquered by Arabs since the 7th century.

Arabi *Tunisia.* Nomadic and seminomadic people in the central and southern regions.

arado egipicio *Bolivia.* Literally, Egyptian plow. Wooden plow on a long pole drawn by a team of oxen.

Arains *Pakistan.* Ethnic group in the Punjab.

Arakanese *Burma.* 1. A Muslim minority ethnic group. 2. Sino-Tibetan language.

Arakawan *South America.* Linguistic stock widely but discontinuously distributed throughout western Brazil, lowland Colombia, Venezuela, Guyana, Ecuador, Bolivia, Paraguay and the Antilles.

Aramaic *Middle East.* Afro-Asiatic language, believed to be the language in which Christ spoke. Used as a liturgical language in some of the lesser Eastern churches.

aranyaka *India.* Class of VEDIC writings containing speculative texts for meditation by monks and anchorites.

Araona *Bolivia.* Indian group of TACANAN languages around central Beni department.

araq *Arab countries.* Alcoholic liquor distilled from dates.

Arasa *Bolivia.* Amazon Indian group speaking a TACANAN language around northwest Pando department.

arathi *Kenya.* KIKUYU seers or prophets.

Araua *Bolivia.* Amazon Indian group speaking a PANOAN language around north Pando department.

Arawak *South America.* Collective term for a large number of Indian tribes distributed widely but discontinuously throughout the continent. 2. One of the major South American linguistic stocks spoken by this people.

arbab *Afghanistan.* MALIK or local chief in UZBEK and TURKMEN areas.

arbitrio *Spanish America.* Scheduled tax levied by local boards.

arch *Algeria.* Customary type of landholding under Islamic law.

ardeb *Egypt.* Unit of weight varying from 132 lb to 352 lb, according to the produce.

ardo *Senegal.* Pular term for a leader of a transhumant community.

ardo *West Africa.* Head of lineages among the M'bororo.

Are'are *Solomon Islands.* Austronesian language.

areca nut *India.* *See* BETEL NUT.

Arekuna *Guyana.* CARIB-speaking Amerindian ethnic group.

arendamento *Cape Verde.* Land lease to peasant farmers.

arfaj *Arab countries.* Desert shrub usually two feet tall.

argha *Nepal.* Seven copper vessels used in NEWARI rituals.

Argoba *Ethiopia.* Muslim ethnic group.

arhat *India.* Buddhist or JAIN saint who has attained NIRVANA in this life.

ari *Somalia.* Collapsible tent.

Ari *Ethiopia.* Afro-Asiatic language.

arif *Saudi Arabia.* Rank of corporal in the Saudi army.

Arifa *Somalia.* Strangers adopted as clients by a host clan.

arifa (plural: arifat) *Western Sahara.* Head of a cell of the Polisario Front.

arikis *Cook Islands.* MAORI chiefs making up traditional leadership.

aris *Burma.* Early BRAHMIN teachers who were SHAMANS.

arish *Somalia.* Ordinary dwelling house of several rooms on the coast. It is a rectangular structure with sloping roofs, thatched with palm leaves or grass, and walls of slender posts covered with daubs of soil, ashes and dung.

aristocracia, la *Spanish America.* The aristocracy.

Arma *Niger.* Descendants of the MOORS and SONGHAY women.

Arma *West Africa.* SONGHAY people, descended from Moroccan invaders and their Sudanese wives.

armador *Brazil.* Supplier of arms, especially to bandeirante expeditions.

Armenian *West Asia.* Indo-European language.

arnar *Burma.* The authority of the state.

arnarde *Burma.* Reluctance to correct others or put them down.

Aros *Nigeria.* IGBO subgroup, mostly traders.

Arosien *Western Sahara.* Ethnic group.

arpa *Paraguay.* Small native harp.

arrack *India.* Strong liquor made from toddy.

arraiais *Brazil.* Mining camps established by bandeirantes in the hinterland.

arrendatario *Spanish America.* Small renter who works the land himself, without hired help. Also, *arriendo.*

arrendero *Spanish America.* Indian landowner.

arret *Haiti.* Charm worn to ward off evil.

arriendo *Spanish America.* Variant of ARRENDATARIO.

arriero *Central America.* Muleteer.

arrimadas *Spanish America.* Farm workers who perform special chores on a large estate in return for the privilege of cultivating a part of it.

arrivismo *Spanish America.* Use of underhanded means to obtain public employment.

arrivista *Brazil.* Upstart.

arrobe *Cuba.* Unit of weight equal to 25 lb.

arrondissement *Francophone Africa.* District.

arsch *Algeria.* Property that may be inherited but not alienated.

Artane *Bolivia.* Amazon Indian group in north Beni department.

artistica *Spanish America.* Performing arts.

Arusha *Tanzania.* Tribe of MASAI origin.

Arusha Declaration *Tanzania.* Socialist policy manifesto issued by the National Executive Committee of the CHAMA CHA MAPINDUZI PARTY in 1967.

Aryamehr *Iran.* Literally, light of the Aryans. Title conferred on former SHAH of Iran, Reza Shah, by Iranian parliament in 1963.

Arzal *India and Pakistan.* Lowest caste of Muslims.

asaba *Western Sahara.* Pact between individuals or groups by which the benefits and responsibilities for the payment of DIA are shared.

asabiya *Algeria.* Clannishness or esprit de corps.

asado *Uruguay.* Barbecue. Thus, *asado con cuero,* barbecued heifer.

asafo *Ghana.* Traditional male association among the AKAN peoples of the southern region.

asafohone *West Africa.* Nominal chief of an EWE clan.

Asante or **Ashanti** *Ghana.* TWI ethnic group.

asantehene *Ghana.* 1. Traditional title of the kings of ASANTE. 2. Head of the Asante Union and Keeper of the Golden Stool.

Asantemanhyiamu *Ghana.*   High council or assembly and highest tribunal of the Asante Union.

Asase Yaa *Ghana.*   Earth goddess of the ASANTE.

asel *Western Sahara.*   Lineage.

Asen *Ghana.*   TWI ethnic group.

Asenie *Ghana.*   One of the principal AKAN clans.

asentamientos *Chile.*   Group of farmers in a new settlement.

ashab *Mauritania.*   Members of the TIJANIYA BROTHERHOOD.

ash'b *Yemens.*   Sedentary tribal groups.

ashiko *West Africa.*   Dance of Nigerian origin.

ashirah *Arab countries.*   A subtribe.

ashiret *West Asia.*   Chief clan among the KURDS.

ashraf *Pakistan.*   Highborn or noble.

ashram *India.*   Hindu monastery or religious community under the aegis of a RISHI or MAHARISHI.

Ashura *Islamic countries.*   Death of Husayn on the 10th of MUHARRAM, celebrated among the SHIITE Muslims.

ashura *Senegal.*   New year's celebration.

asentante *Spanish America.*   Liquor drunk to celebrate a business deal or a piece of good news.

asiento *Spanish America.*   Literally, seat. In colonial times, contract for the supply of slaves.

asikafo (singular: is sikani). *Ghana.*   Wealthy ASANTE notables who had an elephant tail carried before them as a mark of status.

asilin (singular: asil) *Saudi Arabia.*   Socially prominent families.

askari *Islamic countries.*   Soldiers.

Asmat *Papua New Guinea.*   Papuan language.

asociacion civil *Mexico.*   Voluntary group engaged in the promotion of public welfare and education.

asofor *Haiti.*   Nine-foot Voodoo drum.

Asoka Chakra *India.*   Wheel motif in the Iron Pillar at Sarnath, national emblem of India.

Asokora *Ghana.*   One of the AKAN clans.

asomfo *Ghana.*   AKAN bureaucrats.

Asona *Ghana.*   One of the AKAN clans.

Asongori *West Africa.*   SAHEL ethnic group.

a-so-ya min *Burma.*   Bureaucratic class in colonial period.

aspirante *Central America.*   Uncertified teacher.

asrat *Ethiopia.*   Form of land taxation consisting of ¹⁄₁₀th of the crop.

Assamese *India.*   Indo-European language.

assegai *Southern Africa.*   Spear.

assimilados *Lusophone Africa.*   Africans granted privileges of Portuguese citizenship until 1961.

Assir *Ghana.*   AKAN group of the central region.

Assumbo *West Africa.*   Niger-Kordofanian language.

Assyrian *Iran and Iraq.*   Small remnant of ancient Assyrian peoples around Lake Rezaiyah in Iran and Mosul in Iraq. Entirely Christian, they have been heavily persecuted in both countries.

Asu *Tanzania.*   Niger-Kordofanian language.

aswaddumized *Sri Lanka.*   Rice grown on flooded flatland.

at *Laos.*   Monetary unit, ¹⁄₁₀₀ths of a KIP.

Ata *Philippines.*   Pagan ethnic group in southeast Mindanao.

atabal *Central America.*   Indian drum played with flexible sticks.

a tabaque *Brazil.*   Conical drum with a single head at the wide end, played in sets of three.

Atacame *Bolivia.*   Indian language spoken in west Potosi department.

Ataiba *Bahrain.*   Tribe from which the ruling family is descended.

Atakpame *West Africa.*   YORUBA ethnic group.

atan *Afghanistan.*   Variant of ATTAN.

Ataturkism *Turkey.*   Manifesto issued by Kemal Ataturk in 1931 proclaiming the "six arrows" of his political philosophy: republicanism, nationalism, populism, etatism, secularism and reformism.

atbia dania *Ethiopia.*   One-judge rural court of first instance.

atchaza *Philippines.*   Pickled fruit or vegetables.

ate kalaye *Ethiopia.*   Group of KEFETEGNAS, or urban dwellers.

athi *Burma.*   Group of servants of local officials.

atila *Western Sahara.*   Rental for a camel.

atilillo *Central America.*   Drink made of dry corn.

Atjehnese *Indonesia.*   Sumatran ethnic group.

atiradores *Brazil.*   Marksmen, members of the civilian TIROS DE GUERRA.

Atjumba *Mozambique.*   Ethnic group of NGUNI cluster.

Atl *Central America.*   NAHUA god of water or ocean.

atman *India.*   Soul.

ato *Ethiopia.*   Mr. as a term of address.

ato *Philippines.*   Community organization in Lepanto and Bontok based on division of villages into wards.

atole *Central America.*   Hot cornmeal drink made from green corn.

atoll varin *Maldives.*   Atoll chief.

atraf or **ajlaf** *India.*   Lowborn convert to Islam.

atta *India.*   Flour.

attan *Afghanistan.*   Properly, *atan-i-milee.* The national dance, believed to have been introduced by Macedonian Greeks during Alexander's invasion.

Attic *West Africa.*   Ethnic group of the LAGOON CLUSTER.

Attie *West Africa.*   Niger-Kordofanian language.

atumpan *West Africa.*   Talking drum.

Atuot *Sudan.*   Nilotic ethnic group.

atwin-Wun *Burma.*   Royal privy councillor in pre-colonial times.

Atwode *Ghana.*   GUAN ethnic group in the Volta region, related to the EWE.

Aucas *Spanish America.*   Primitive Indian tribe in Oriente Province of Ecuador.

Audhali *Yemens.*   Ethnic group.

audiencias *Spanish America.*   Regional and provincial courts with appellate jurisdiction.

auditeur *Francophone Africa.*   Civil servant who assists a court in preparing cases for trial.

Aulagi *Yemens.*   Ethnic group.

Aumba *Angola.*   Ethnic group.

aumildar *India.*   Manager, from AMAL.

aune *Haiti.*   Unit of length equal to 47 inches.

aus *Bangladesh.*   Rice planted in April and harvested from July through August. Compare AMAN.

Aushi *Central Africa.*   Ethnic group of southern Savanna.

Australe *Argentina.*   New monetary unit which replaced the peso.

autarquia *Brazil.*   Quasi independent government agency.

authenticity *Central and West Africa.*   Dewesternization of politics and society, especially Africanization of personal and place names.

autogestion *Algeria.*   Partial autonomous management of farms and factories.

Avadhi *India.*   Indo-European language.

avalou *Haiti.*   Voodoo dance characterized by vigorous movements of the arms and shoulders.

avatar *India.*   Incarnation, especially any incarnation of VISHNU.

Avatime *West Africa.*   1. CENTRAL TOGO ethnic group. 2. Niger-Kordofanian language.

Avikam *West Africa.*   Ethnic group of the LAGOON CLUSTER, including Brignan, GBANDI, and Kouakoua.

Avokaya *Sudan and Zaire.*   Nilo-Saharan language.

Avore *Bolivia.*   Amazon Indian group speaking ZAMUCOAN language in central Beni department.

Avutu *West Africa.*   Niger-Kordofanian language.

Awan *Afghanistan and Pakistan.*   PATHAN agriculturists.

Awandji *Gabon.*   MBEDE-speaking people in the upper Ogooue.

Awatu *West Africa.*   GUAN ethnic group.

Awazim *Saudi Arabia.*   A low-class tribe.

Awi *Ethiopia.*   AGEW-speaking ethnic group.

Awlad (singular: walad) *Arab countries.*   Male offspring of a noble family.

Awlu Be (singular: Gawlo) *Senegal.*   Caste of GRIOTS among the TOUCOLEURS.

Awngi *Ethiopia.*   Afro-Asiatic language.

awqaf (singular: waqf) *Arab countries.*   Religious foundations.

awraja *Ethiopia.*   Province.

Awuna *Ghana.*   Northern group identified as GRUSI, between Kasena and Sisala.

Awuna *West Africa.*   Ethnic group of the GOUROUNSI cluster.

Awutu *Ghana.*   GUAN group in the Gomoa area.

Awya *Indonesia.*   Papuan language.

awza *Burma.*   Authority derived from personal attributes of leadership.

ayah *India.*   Nursemaid.

ayahuasca *Spanish America.*   LIANA, from the leaves of which Indians make an hallucinogenic tea.

Ayamaru *Indonesia.*   Papuan language.

Ayampaco *Spanish America.*   Kind of tamale made of green banana with fish and condiments.

ayan *Morocco.*   Notables, especially the urban upper class.

ayatoolah *Iran.*   Title of the highest ranking Shiite Islamic clergy. Also, ayatollah.

ayla *Algeria.*   Small lineage group, members of which claim descent through the male line from a common ancestor.

ayllu *Bolivia.*   Social unit of Andean Indians based on collective farming.

Aymara *Bolivia.*   1. Oldest Indian ethnic group and the second largest after the QUECHUA. 2. Language of the Aymara Indians.

aynoka *Bolivia.*   Land cultivated in a strict pattern of rotation and fallowing.

ayuntamiento *Central Africa.*   Local or municipal council composed of heads of leading property-owning families.

ayurveda *India.*   Literally, science of life. Ancient Hindu system of medicine relying heavily on medicinal herbs and plants.

Ayurvedic *India.*   Of or belonging to the AYURVEDA.

ayyam al Arab *Saudi Arabia.*   The day of the Arabs.

Azacca *Haiti.*   Voodoo god of agriculture.

azad *India.*   Free.

azadon *Spanish America.*   Hoe with a large blade and an ax-like handle.

azaj *Ethiopia.*   Supervisor of the former imperial palace.

azan *Islamic countries.*   Muslim call to prayer made by a MUEZZIN.

Azanda *Sudan.*   Ethnic group in Equatorial province.

Azer *Mauritania.*   One of the main BERBER dialects.

Azera *Papua New Guinea.*   Austronesian language.

azamari *Ethiopia.*   Minstrels.

Azerbaijani *Iran.*   1. Turkic ethnic group. 2. Ural-Altaic language.

azib *Morocco.*   Type of farm house.

azmach *Ethiopia.*   Military commander.

Aztec *Central America.* Nahua Indian people of the central plateau of Mexico.

Azteco-Tenoan *Spanish America.* Linguistic and racial stock of the Aztecs in Tenochtitlan.

ba *Vietnam.* Count, a rank of nobility.

baal *Somalia.* Natural basin on communal lands, where rainwater collects for the use of livestock belonging to all members.

Baali *Zaire.* Niger-Kordofanian language.

Baathism *Middle East.* Arab socialist and nationalist ideology and movement founded in Syria in 1953, identified with Akram Hourani and Michel Aflaq.

Baba *West Africa.* Niger-Kordofanian language.

baba chaise *Singapore.* Descendant of a marriage between a Chinese man and a Malay woman.

babandwa *Rwanda and Burundi.* A politico-religious fraternity.

baba suja *Brazil.* Scum formed in the process of boiling raw sugar cane juices.

babgay *Cameroon.* Head of a GAY, or family unit.

babouche *Morocco.* Pointed, open-heeled slipper.

Baboute *West Africa.* Southern forest ethnic group.

Babuissi *Gabon.* ESHIRA group in the upper Nyanga River basin.

Babungo *West Africa.* Niger-Kordofanian language.

bachaga *Algeria.* Governor of a CAIDAT during the French administration.

Bachama *West Africa.* Afro-Asiatic language.

bacharel *Brazil.* University graduate.

Bac-Tong *Vietnam.* MAHAYANA, or Greater Wheel school of Buddhism. Also, *Dai Thua.*

bada *Central African Republic.* Initiation camp among the MANDIJA.

Bada *West Africa.* Niger-Kordofanian language.

Badaga *India.* Literally, northern. DRAVIDIAN ethnic group.

bada hakim *Nepal.* District governor or judge in the TARAI region.

badal *Afghanistan.* Social code requiring blood revenge for offenses involving family honor.

Badan Perentjanaan Pembangunan Nasional *Indonesia.* National Development Planning Council.

Bade *West Africa.* Afro-Asiatic language.

Badiaranke *West Africa.* Ethnic group related to Conaigui and BAS-SARI.

Badjao *Philippines.* Pagan and Muslim ethnic group in Sulu archipelago. Also *Sea Gypsies.*

badli *Indian subcontinent.* Substitute.

badolo *Senegal.* Poor or low-caste WOLOF.

badu *Arab countries.* Nomadic Arab.

badui *Indonesia.* Of or relating to Java and its peoples.

Badyara *West Africa.* Niger-Kordofanian language.

Badyaranke *Guinea.* Subgroup of TENDA in Middle Guinea around Youkounkoun.

baeta *Brazil.* Cotton flannel cloth used to make outer garments for slaves in the Paraiba Valley.

Bafia *West Africa.* 1. Highland ethnic group. 2. Niger-Kordofanian language.

Bafokeng *Lesotho.* One of the BASOTHO clans.

Bafut *West Africa.* 1. Tikar tribe. 2. Niger-Kordofanian language.

Baga *Guinea.* Largest of the minor ethnic groups in lower region.

Bagata *India.* Indo-European language.

bagendanyi *Burundi.* Formerly, young attendants at the royal court.

Baggara *Sudan.* Cattle nomads of the GUHAYNA tribe.

baghalah *Oman.* Large DHOW or boat.

Bagheli *India.* Indo-European language.

Bagirmi *West Africa.* Nilo-Saharan language.

Bagobo *Philippines.* 1. Pagan ethnic group in southeast Mindanao. 2. Austronesian language.

bago-or *Philippines.* Fermented fish sauce.

Bagri *India and Pakistan.* Indo-European language.

Baguirmi *West Africa.* SAHELian ethnic group.

bahadur *India and Pakistan.* Literally, great master. Term of respect and rank, often used as part of a name.

bahal *Nepal.* House of a Buddhist priestly sect.

bahareque *Spanish America.* Kind of wattle-and-daub construction in which sticks tied laterally to upright poles are smeared thickly with straw-tempered mud.

baha riya *Saudi Arabia.* The Saudi navy.

bahasa Berirama *Indonesia.* Sonnet-like, often mystical, poem.

Bahasa Indonesia *Indonesia.* National language, a member of the Austronesian group.

Bahasa Malaysia *Malaysia.* Official language and lingua franca of Malaysia, writtten in either the Rumi (Roman) or the Jawi (Arabic) script. Also, *Bazar Malay* or *Malaya Pesar.*

bahiano *Brazil.* Resident or inhabitant of the Bahia.

Bahi Deo Boyegu *Nepal.* Buddhist festival in the month of Asadh.

Bahima *West Africa.* Partly HAMITIC ethnic group.

Bahnar *Vietnam.* 1. Highland ethnic group, the largest MON-KHMER-speaking group including Alakong, Bonam, Hrui, Konko, Roh, Tolo, Monam, and Rongan. 2. Austro-Asiatic language.

Baht *Thailand.* Monetary unit.

bahtaur *Ethiopia.* Hamlet attached to an Orthodox monastery.

bahuzi *Rwanda and Burundi.* Magician who specializes in curing poisoning and treating persons struck by lightning.

bai *Sierra Leone.* Chief of TEMNE group.

baia *Bangladesh.* Drum.

baiao *Brazil.* Popular music used as a setting for a story.

baiboho *Madagascar.* Literally, cultivated plot. Dry-season cultivation.

bai chong *Thailand.* License to use a piece of land.

Baiga *India.* Indo-European language.

bailgari *India.* Bullock cart.

Bailundu *Angola.* OVIBUNDU subgroup.

Baiotes *Guinea-Bissau.* DIOLA group, related to FELUPES, of the Senegambian littoral.

bairagi *India.* Hindu mendicant.

bairro *Lusophone Africa.* Ward in a large town.

baixada fluminense *Brazil.* Coastal lowlands.

baiza *Oman.* Corruption of Indian PAISA. Smallest monetary unit.

bajareque *Spanish America.* See BAHAREQUE.

Bajau *Indonesia and Sabah.* Austronesian language.

Bajau *Philippines, Malaysia and Sabah.* MORO group in Sulu and Zamboanga.

bajio *Mexico.* Literally, flatland. Series of interconnecting basins in the central region.

bajra *India and Pakistan.* Millet.

Bajuni *Somalia.* Non-Somali ethnic group, mostly fishermen and sailors, living on Bajuni Islands.

Baka *West and Central Africa.* 1. Nilo-Saharan ethnic group. 2. Nilo-Saharan language.

bakamyi *Rwanda and Burundi.* Formerly, person credited with supernatural powers who milked the royal cows.

bakele *Central Africa.* See BONGAM.

Bakele *Gabon.* Group of hunters and traders.

bakevvi *Rwanda and Burundi.* Formerly, the royal cook.

Bakgatla *Botswana.* Ethnic group of HURUTSHE stock.

Bakhtiari *Iran.* Ethnic group related to the KURDS.

Bakoena *Lesotho.* Royal clan.

Bakoko *Cameroon.* 1. Subgroup of the FANG. 2. Niger-Kordofanian language.

bakoma *Rwanda and Burundi.* Person, credited with supernatural powers, employed as soothsayer and magician.
Bakongo *Congo.* Ethnic group comprising the LALI, CONGO and SUNDA.
Bakossi *Cameroon.* Ethnic group of the Mungo Valley.
Bakota *Gabon.* Ethnic group in the northeast.
Bakouele *Gabon.* People of the upper Ivindo River.
baksh *Iran.* Subdistrict.
bakshdar *Iran.* Lieutenant governor of a BAKSH.
bakshi *India and Pakistan.* Military paymaster.
bakshish *India and Pakistan.* Customary gratuity or tip.
Bakunde-Balue *West Africa.* Niger-Kordofanian language.
Bakwena *Botswana.* Ethnic group of HURUTSHE stock.
Bakweri *Cameroon.* 1. Coastal people related to the DOUALA. 2. Niger-Kordofanian language.
bakya *Philippines.* Low sandal consisting of a flat wooden sole with a single strap made of rubber from the sidewall of old tires.
bal *Haiti.* Creole term for Western dance.
balabat (plural balabatod) *Ethiopia.* Person with a claim to RIST. Local chiefs who were assigned low-level administrative positions and allocated small landholdings.
bala Chinese *Malaysia.* Assimilated Chinese who speak Malay and adopt Malay customs.
baladiyyah (plural: baladiyyat) *Arab countries.* Municipality.
balafon *Guinea.* Wooden xylophone.
bala hissar *Afghanistan.* High fort.
Balaju Jatra *Nepal.* Buddhist festival in the month of CHAITRA held in Kathmandu.
balak *Philippines.* Poem recited to the accompaniment of a guitar.
balan *Somalia.* Among the SAAB, a pact or promise.
Balanta *Senegal.* 1. Ethnic group. 2. Niger-Kordofanian language.
Balantak *Indonesia.* Austronesian language.
Balantas *Guinea-Bissau.* Largest ethnic group of Senegambian stock.
Balbi *Saudi Arabia.* Tribe on the Red Sea coast.
Balboa *Panama.* Monetary unit.
baldi *Tunisia.* The urban aristocracy.
Bali *Cameroon.* Tribe living in the Bamenda highlands, related to CHAMBA.
Bali *Zaire.* Ethnic group of the Central Rain Forest.
Balinese *Indonesia.* 1. Of or relating to Bali Island; Hindu ethnic group living on Bali. 2. Austronesian language.
Balise *Zaire.* Ethnic group.
balitaw *Philippines.* Visayan serenade.
baloley *Somalia.* Song of short verses.

balopwe *Zaire.* BANTU-speaking peoples who conquered Zaire around 1500.

Balotes *Guinea-Bissau.* Small DIOLA group related to FELUPE.

Baloundou Mbo *Cameroon.* SOUTHERN FOREST ethnic group.

balq *Ethiopia.* The little rainy season.

balsa *Brazil.* Flat shuttle ferry propelled by outboard motor.

Balseria *Panama.* Annual festival of the GUAYMI Indians.

Balti *India and Pakistan.* Sino-Tibetan language.

Baluchi *Pakistan, Iran and Afghanistan.* Ethnic group, principally in Baluchistan province in Pakistan.

Baluchi *Pakistan.* Indo-European language.

Balundu-Bima *West Africa.* Niger-Kordofanian language.

balza *Panama.* Gathering of GUAYMI Indians, including dance contest or tournament in which contestants try to trip each other with a long, curved stick.

ba mai *Vietnam.* Matchmaker or go-between who arranges marriages.

Bamalete *Botswana.* Ethnic group related to NDEBELE.

Bamangwato *Botswana.* Ethnic group of HURUTSHE stock.

Bambalang *West Africa.* Niger-Kordofanian language.

Bambara *West Africa.* 1. Major ethnic group of the MANDINGO family. 2. Niger-Kordofanian language.

Bambara *Mauritania.* Negroid ethnic group.

bamboche *Haiti.* Secular celebration or festivities.

Bamboko *West Africa.* BANTU-speaking ethnic group.

bambuco *Spanish America.* Folk dance, a derivation of the waltz, in moderately quick tempo.

Bambuko *West Africa.* Afro-Asiatic language.

Bamendjou *West Africa.* Niger-Kordofanian language.

Bamessing *West Africa.* Niger-Kordofanian language.

Bamileke *Cameroon.* Ethnic group, living in the highlands southeast of Bamboutos Mountains.

Bamoun *Cameroon.* 1. Western highland ethnic group. 2. Niger-Kordofanian language.

Bamunka *Cameroon.* Niger-Kordofanian language.

ban *Laos.* Village.

Bana *West Africa.* Afro-Asiatic language.

bancada *Brazil.* State delegation of deputies or congressmen.

Banda *Central Africa.* 1. Sudanic people in Bahr el Ghizal province in the Sudan. 2. Niger-Kordofanian language.

banda *Haiti.* Dance common at funerals and carnivals.

banda mocha *Spanish America.* Group of musical instruments, including flute and drum.

bandar *Arab countries.* Port.

Bandawa-Minda *West Africa.* Niger-Kordofanian language.

bandeira *Brazil.* In Colonial times, an armed expedition into the interior to capture slaves and seek gold; thus *bandeirante,* member of a bandeira.

bandeirante *Brazil. See* BANDEIRA.

Bandi *West Africa.* 1. MENDE-speaking people. 2. Niger-Kordofanian language.

Bandia *Central African Republic.* Caste who founded former kingdoms in Nazakara and Chinko.

bandjar *Indonesia.* Hamlet association.

bandoleon *Spanish America.* Mandolin-type musical instrument.

banduk *India.* Musket.

Banen *Cameroon.* 1. Highland ethnic group. 2. Niger-Kordofanian language.

Bang *Cambodia.* Dialect group.

Bangala *Zaire.* Niger-Kordofanian language.

Bangara *India.* Indo-European language.

Bangba *Zaire.* 1. Ethnic group. 2. Niger-Kordofanian language.

Banggai *Indonesia.* Austronesian language.

Bangi *Zaire and Congo.* Niger-Kordofanian language.

bangle *India.* Ring of colored glass worn on the wrist by women.

Bango *Zaire.* Ethnic group.

bango *Philippines.* Commercial fish pond.

Bangu *Zaire.* Ethnic group.

Bangwe Ketsi *Botswana.* Ethnic group of HURUTSHE stock.

banh ba *Vietnam.* Rice wafer made from rice paste covered with sesame seeds dried in the sun and then toasted over an open fire.

banh chung *Vietnam.* Special cake made for the TET celebration.

banh duc *Vietnam.* Rice cake made from white rice ground into flour paste.

banh gray *Vietnam.* Rice cake made from glutenous rice.

bani (singular ibn) *Arab countries.* Sons of.

Bani Hajir *Saudi Arabia.* A major tribe.

bani khoms *Yemens.* Literally, sons of the five. Practitioners of five despised trades of barber, bloodletter, butcher, bath attendant and tanner.

baniya or **vaniya** *India.* VAISYA subcaste of traders.

banja *Mozambique.* Smaller extended family among the NGUNI within one geographical locality.

Banjar *India.* Muslim sect of carriers and itinerant traders.

Bankam stool *Ghana.* Beaded stool, symbol of the DENKYIRA royalty.

bankshall *India.* 1. Warehouse. 2. Office of a harbormaster.

bansik or **kading** *Philippines.* Jew's harp made of bamboo or grass.

bansri *India.* Bamboo flute. Also *murali, venu.*

bantaba *Gambia.* Meeting place, usually a raised platform under a shade tree.

bantfanenkosi *Swaziland.* Tribal chiefs as members of the LIBAN-DHLA.

ban tho gia tien *Vietnam.* Family altar located in the middle of the house and used to worship the ancestor spirits of a nuclear family.

ban tho ho *Vietnam.* Household altar used to worship the ancestor spirits of an extended family or clan.

banting *Burma.* Wild ox.

banto faro *Gambia.* Land areas above river levels that remain dry in the arid season but are flooded during the rainy season.

Banton *Philippines.* Christian ethnic group of Banton and Simara Islands.

Bantu *Africa.* Large and homogeneous group of related African languages spoken, with the exception of KHOISAN in southwest Africa, throughout south, east and central Africa. One of the 15 subfamilies of the Niger-Congo family of languages.

Bantuanon *Philippines.* Austronesian language.

Bantu Ba Kwa Ngwana *Swaziland.* Name of the Swazi tribe in SIS-WATI language.

Banun or **Bainuk** *Senegal.* Ethnic group in lower Casamance.

banyan *India.* Undershirt.

banyange *Rwanda and Burundi.* Guardians of the royal tombs. Also, BIRU, *baterekerezi.*

banyenama *Rwanda and Burundi.* Catholic counselors whose task is to assemble the local congregation for visits by itinerant priests.

Banyum *West Africa.* Niger-Kordofanian language.

Banyuns *Guinea-Bissau.* Senegambian group related to the CASSAN-GAS and COBIANAS.

Banziri *Central African Republic.* Ethnic group of the Ubanguian family.

Baoule *West Africa.* AKAN ethnic group.

bap *Thailand.* Demerit caused by nonobservance or neglect of religious duties.

Bapedi *Swaziland.* SOTHO group living to the north and east of Transvaal.

Baphetla *Lesotho.* One of the oldest tribes living in Quthing, Qacha's Nek, and Mohale's Hock districts. Also, *Maphetla, Baphuti.*

Baphuti *Lesotho.* See BAPHETLA.

Bapounou *Gabon.* Ethnic group in upper N'Gounie and Nyanga Rivers.

Baqqara *Sudan.* Ethnic group including *Rizayqat, Homr,* and *Messiriyyah.*

baquianos *Uruguay.* Gaucho scout.

Bara *Madagascar.*   Southern ethnic group.

baraa *Islamic countries.*   Hostility toward infidels.

Barabang *Tanzania.*   Ethnic group.

Baraguyu *Tanzania.*   Ethnic group whose warriors are noted for their necklaces and earpieces.

barak *Afghanistan.*   Heavy woolen cloth woven in Hazarjat, used as a blanket.

baraka *Islamic countries.*   1. Charisma, especially in MARABOUTS. 2. Blessing or divine grace indwelling a holy person.

Barambu *Zaire.*   Niger-Kordofanian language.

barangay *Philippines.*   Communal settlement, the lowest political unit.

barani *Mali.*   Migrant seasonal agricultural workers.

barasti (plural: barastiyat) *Arab countries.*   Dwelling made of date palm fronds and reed mats over a frame of wooden poles.

baraza *East Africa.*   Public meeting or meeting place.

Barazani *Iran.*   BALUCHI tribe.

Barbari *Iran.*   Indo-Iranian ethnic group in Khorasan.

barbeiros *Brazil.*   In former times, slave musical group, usually made up of barbers.

barcarola criolla *Central America.*   Sentimental serenade.

Bare *Nepal.*   Brahmin caste of Buddhist NEWARIS.

Bareli *India.*   Indo-European language.

Bargue *Mozambique.*   Ethnic group of SHONA-Karanga cluster.

bari *Bangladesh.*   Village consisting of a cluster of homesteads.

Bari *Central Africa.*   1. Nilotic ethnic group in Equatoria Province in Sudan. 2. Nilo-Saharan language.

Bariba *West Africa.*   1. Voltaic ethnic group, related to Yoruba. 2. Niger-Kordofanian language.

barime *Guyana.*   The elder brother's wife as the submatriarch of a family.

barines *Venezuela.*   Wind blowing across lowlands into the southeast.

Barka *West Africa.*   Small MANDE ethnic group.

Barma *Chad.*   Muslim people who founded the BAGUIRMI kingdom in the 16th century.

barnos *Ethiopia.*   Tailored cape made of black wool. Compare BURNOOSE.

Baroa or **San** *Lesotho.*   Pre-BANTU people with pale brown or golden hair.

Barolong *Botswana.*   HURUTSHE ethnic group.

Barong Tagalog *Philippines.*   National male dress consisting of a square, richly embroidered and nearly transparent shirt, made popular by President Ramon Magsaysay.

Baron Samedi *Haiti.*   Voodoo god.

barou *Comoros.*   Smallest unit of local government.

barra *Panama.* Claque.

barraca *Bolivia.* Literally, barracks. Jungle settlement in the northeast.

barracan *Libya.* Tentlike garment, resembling a Roman toga, worn by men and women.

barracao *Brazil.* Trading post or company store.

barraco *Brazil.* Shack of mud, brick or wood, typical of squatter settlements.

barriada *Peru.* Neighborhood squatter settlement.

barrio *Philippines.* Settlement consisting of primary villages or BARANGAYS and hamlets or SITIOS.

barrio *Spanish America.* Working-class residential neighborhood.

barrio clandestino *Spanish America.* Slum or shantytown.

barsino *Central Amercia.* Child of a LOBO father and MULETA mother.

Baru *West Africa.* Niger-Kordofanian language.

Barwe *Southern Africa.* BANTU-speaking ethnic group.

Basant Panchami *Nepal.* Spring festival in the month of MAGH dedicated to the goddess of learning.

Basara *Ghana.* GURMA ethnic group.

Basari *Senegal.* Ethnic group of TENDA origin.

Basari *West Africa.* Niger-Kordofanian language.

basha *Ethiopia.* Commander of a rifle corps.

basha *Burma.* Woven split bamboo used to build house walls.

Bashar *West Africa.* Niger-Kordofanian language.

Bashara *Rwanda.* Ethnic group.

Bashgali *Afghanistan.* Indo-European language.

Bashikongo *Angola.* A division of KONGO tribe.

basi *Philippines.* Beverage of fermented sugarcane juice.

Basia *Lesotho.* One of the original LESOTHO clans.

basilique *Haiti.* Tree, the leaves of which are soaked in water and used for ritual cleansing.

basmati *India and Pakistan.* Fine grain rice.

Basotho *Lesotho.* People of LESOTHO including *Bafokeng, Basia, Bataung,* and *Batlokoa.*

Basotho hat *Lesotho.* Shallow cone hat ornamented with circles; used as a national emblem.

Bassa *Liberia.* KRUAN-speaking people in Marshall, Grand Bassa, and River Cess territories.

Bassa *West Africa.* 1. KRU branch of KWA-speaking peoples. 2. Niger-Kordofanian language.

Bassa Kwomu *West Africa.* Niger-Kordofanian language.

Bassari *West Africa.* Ethnic group of Katokoli cluster.

bastenero *Philippines.* Cane-wielding foreman of a team of workers.

basti *India.* Slum.

basuti *Uganda.* Floor-length wraparound dress.

bat *Burma and Thailand.* Begging bowl used by Buddhist monks.

Bata *West Africa.* Afro-Asiatic language.

bata-coto *Brazil.* War drum of YORUBA origin, banned in 1835.

batai *Nepal.* Land tenure system under which the tenant and share-cropper share the produce.

Batak *Indonesia.* 1. Sumatran ethnic group. 2. Austronesian language.

bataka *Uganda.* Hereditary chief of the BAGANDA clan.

batalhoes *Brazil.* Cooperative labor group in Bahia, especially in building or repairing houses.

Batalokwa *Botswana.* HURUTSHE ethnic group.

Bataung *Lesotho.* Tribe descended from the BAROLONG.

Batawana *Botswana.* HURUTSHE ethnic group.

bat-cu *Vietnam.* Form of classical poetry with eight lines of which five rhyme.

bateas *Central America.* Wooden dishes.

bateia *Brazil.* Concave pan used by GARIMPEIROS to filter out sediment from gold nuggets in river water.

Batera *Pakistan.* Unclassified language.

baterekerezi *Rwanda and Burundi.* *See* BANYANGE.

batey *Cuba.* Urban community around a sugar mill.

Bathepu *Lesotho.* Ethnic group of NGUNI origin.

batik *Indonesia.* Art method of making designs on cloth by dyeing only part at a time, the rest being protected by a removable coating of wax.

batik sarong *Cambodia.* Dress worn by the CHAU.

Batlokoa *Lesotho.* Ethnic group.

batta *India.* Advance or extra allowance paid to officials for performance of extra duties.

batterie maconnique *Haiti.* Slow, measured beating of drums and clapping of hands at the beginning of a Voodoo ceremony.

batuque *Brazil.* Afro-Brazilian CARNAVAL dance.

baugi *Guyana.* Elder brother's wife.

Baule *West Africa.* Niger-Kordofanian language.

Baure *Bolivia.* Amazon Indian group speaking an ARAWAKAN language in eastern Beni department.

Bawi *Burma.* Hereditary CHIN headman.

Bawle *West Africa.* ANYI-BAWLE ethnic group.

baya *Morocco.* Document signed by the ULEMA confirming the accession of a new sultan.

Baya *Central African Republic.* Second largest ethnic group related to the LOBAYE and MANDIJA.

bayadir (singular: bidar) *Oman.* Persianized ethnic group.

bayasirah (singular: baysari) *Oman.* Pre-Arab ethnic group.

bayete *Zimbabwe* and *Swaziland.*   NDEBELE salutation to a king.

bayeton *Colombia.*   Poncho-like cloak that falls almost to the ankles.

Bayingti *Burma.*   Term applied to Europeans.

bayt *Arab countries.*   Individual couplet in an ode, or QASIDAH.

bayt *Oman.*   House. Also, a clan.

bayt al-mal *Arab countries.*   Literally, house of wealth. Public treasury.

bazar *India and Arab countries.*   Permanent market.

bazinguer *Central African Republic.*   Armed militias of the merchant lords of the Upper Nile, 1860–75.

Bbadha *Central Africa.*   Nilo-Saharan language.

Bdyogo *West Africa.*   Niger-Kordofanian language.

Beafadas *Guinea-Bissau.*   Senegambian group.

Bebele *West Africa.*   Niger-Kordofanian language.

bedaja *Indonesia.*   Classical dance.

Bedawiya *Sudan.*   1. Northern Cushitic language of the BEJA, member of the Afro-Asiatic language family. 2. BEJA ethnic group.

Bedouin *Arab countries.*   Collective term for nomadic tribes.

bega *Ethiopia.*   Hot season.

beganna *Ethiopia.*   Lyre or harp with eight to 12 gut strings plucked with a plectrum.

begenna *Ethiopia.*   Ten-stringed lyre or harp.

begum *India and Islamic countries.*   Wife of a SHAYKH or Muslim nobleman.

Beihan *Yemens.*   Ethnic group.

Beir *Sudan.*   Nilotic ethnic group.

Beja *Sudan* and *Ethiopia.*   1. Group of predominantly Caucasoid people in the northeast, mostly nomadic and seminomadic pastoralists. They are considered by some as Hamitic. Includes the tribes of Abadba, Amarar, Beni Amer, Bisharin, and Hadendowah. 2. Afro-Asiatic language.

bejirond *Ethiopia.*   Treasurer and chief of store.

bekcilar (singular: bekci) *Turkey.*   Night watchmen charged with peace-keeping duties in rural areas.

beke *Trinidad and Tobago.*   White foreigners.

Bekwarra *West Africa.*   Niger-Kordofanian language.

Belanda *Sudan.*   Ethnic group.

Belanda Viri *Sudan.*   Niger-Kordofanian language.

Belcismo *Bolivia.*   Authoritarianism, after dictator Manuel Belzu, caudillo 1808–60.

bele *Trinidad and Tobago.*   Dance of African origin.

belediye *Turkey.*   Municipality.

Bella *Burkina Faso.*   Nomadic herdsmen who live in the Beli River areas.

bellaka *Cameroon.*   Chief of M'BOUM tribe.

Belle *Liberia.*   KRU branch of KWA-speaking peoples.

belwo *Somalia.*   Short lyric poem.

bemanti *Swaziland.*   Literally, people of the water. Priests who control the annual INCWALA RITUAL.

Bemba *Southern Africa.*   1. Ethnic group of Southern Savanna. 2. Niger-Kordofanian language.

Bembi *Congo.*   Subgroup of the KONGO.

Bembo-Nguni *Swaziland.*   Northern NGUNI.

Bemdza buko *Swaziland.*   True SWAZI.

Bena *Tanzania.*   1. Ethnic group. 2. Niger-Kordofanian language.

Benabena *Papua New Guinea.*   Papuan language.

benamee *India.*   Literally, anonymous. Document or contract in which a false name is entered as one or both of the parties.

Bencho *Ethiopia.*   Afro-Asiatic language.

Bende *Tanzania.*   Ethnic group.

bendito *Uruguay.*   Temporary shack made of long branches of pine or willow and tied together with a flexible vine to form two sloping roofs.

beneficiencia *Chile.*   System providing welfare, charity or medical aid.

beneficio *Costa Rica.*   Processing plant for coffee.

Benga *Gabon.*   Fishermen of Cape Esterias.

Bengali *India and Bangladesh.*   Indo-European language.

beni *Afghanistan.*   Term denoting tribe of, family of, or sons of.

Beni Amer *Ethiopia.*   Tribal federation of pastoral peoples living along the Sudanese border.

Beni Sakhr *Arab countries.*   Camel-breeding BEDOUIN tribes.

Berber *Maghreb.*   1. Indigenous ethnic group, subgroup of the HAMITIC race, including *Riffians, Soussis, Kabyles, Shawiyas,* and *M'zabites.* 2. HAMITIC language spoken by the Berbers.

Beretitenti *Kiribati.*   President.

Beri-beri Manga *Niger.*   Ethnic group.

Beretuo *Ghana.*   One of the ASANTE clans whose silver stool is the second most important stool in the Asante Union.

berlinda *Brazil.*   In colonial times, a canopied sedan chair used to carry the sick on the shoulders of slaves.

Berom *West Africa.*   Niger-Kordofanian language.

Berta *Sudan.*   DARFUNG ethnic group.

betasab *Ethiopia.*   Family circle.

Beta Israel   *See* FALASHA.

Bete *West Africa.*   1. Ethnic group of the KROU complex. 2. Niger-Kordofanian language.

betel nut *India.*   Orange-colored nut of the betel palm universally chewed as a mild exhilarant. Also *areca nut.*

Beti *Cameroon.*   Southern Forest subgroup of PAHOUIN.

be-ti-sika *Ivory Coast.*   Bride price paid to the girl's parents.

Betsileo *Madagascar.*   Ethnic group of the Central Highlands.

Betsimisaraka *Madagascar.*   Eastern ethnic group.

Bette-Bende *West Africa.*   Niger-Kordofanian language.

bey *West Asia.*   Governor.

beylerbey *Turkey.*   Chief governor of a province.

Bezanozano *Madagascar.*   Eastern ethnic group.

bgha *Burma.*   Family spirits.

Bhadrawahi *India.*   Indo-European language.

Bhagvad Gita *India.*   Sanskrit sacred poem of Hindus, consisting primarily of a dialogue between Arjuna and Krishna, the most important personages of the *Mahabharata.*

bhaja *Nepal.*   Pot used for carrying various materials, such as vermilion, for worship.

bhajan *India.*   Devotional song.

bhakti *India.*   Devotion expressed to a particular deity.

bhalincha *Nepal.*   Type of pot containing a cake made of mustard oil, rice, etc.

bhang *India.*   Hemp or hashish.

bharandari *Nepal.*   Court of appeal.

Bharat or **Bharat Varsha** *India.*   Official name of India. Historically, the land of the descendants of the sage Bharata.

bharata natyam *India.*   Popular style of Hindu dance, including ritualized pantomime and song.

bhat *India.*   Title of respect for a tribe of poets, bards and genealogists in RAJASTHAN.

bhatiali *Bangladesh.*   Boatman's songs. Also, *bhawaiya.*

Bhatri *India.*   Indo-European language.

bhatta *India.*   Religious teacher.

bhawaiya *Bangladesh.*   See BHATIALI.

Bhele *Zaire.*   Niger-Kordofanian language.

bhikku *Thailand and Burma.*   Buddhist monk.

bhikshu (female: bhikshuni) *India.*   Male mendicant who receives alms from the public.

Bhil *India.*   1. KOLARIAN aboriginal tribe of west central region. 2. Indo-European language.

Bhilala *India.*   Indo-European language.

bhisti *India.*   Water carrier.

Bhojpuri *India and Nepal.*   Indo-European language.

Bhoksa *Nepal.*   THARU ethnic group.

bhoodan *India.*   Movement for redistributing land by gifts of individual holdings to village groups, started by Acharya Vinoba Bhave.

bhoota mali boye-ke-gu *Nepal.*   Buddhist kite-flying ceremony in the month of ASHVIN.

Bhote or **Bhotiya** or **Bhotia** *Bhutan.*   1. Tibeto-Nepalese ethnic group which forms the majority in the kingdom. 2. Language of the Bhotiyas. Also, Bhote.

Bhumji *India.*   1. Tribe in central India. 2. Austro-Asiatic language.

Biafada *Guinea-Bissau.*   Niger-Kordofanian language.

Biak *Indonesia.*   Austronesian language.

Biali *West Africa.*   Niger-Kordofanian language.

Biateh *Indonesia.*   Austronesian language.

bibi *India.*   Term of address to a Muslim woman.

bibingka *Philippines.*   Cake made of ground rice, coconut milk, sugar and eggs baked in a clay oven, topped with cheese and duck egg slices and served with hot tea.

bico *Brazil.*   Literally, faucet. Supplementary jobs or sources of income.

Bicolano *Philippines.*   Austronesian language.

bida *Islamic countries.*   Unorthodox innovation in Islam.

bidan *Mauritania.*   White MAURE of Arab-BERBER origin.

Bideyat *Chad.*   Ethnic group in Fada region of Ennedi.

bidi *India.*   Low-quality cigarette using tobacco leaf wrapper.

Bidio *Chad.*   Subgroup of HADJERAY.

bidonville *Algeria.*   Shantytown.

bidri *India.*   Ornamental metalwork made in the Deccan.

bie *Burma.*   Witch or wizard among the PALAUNGS.

Bieno *Angola.*   OVIMBUNDU subgroup.

Biete *India.*   Sino-Tibetan language.

bie-yau *Burma.*   Spirit of the harvest.

bife a caballo *Argentina.*   Literally, beef on horseback. Steak topped by a fried egg.

bigari *Iran.*   Unpaid labor.

bigha *India and Bangladesh.*   Measure of land equal to 3,025 sq yards or five-eighths of an acre.

Bihari *Bangladesh.*   Muslim refugee from Bihar at the time of partition.

bihon *Philippines.*   Rice noodles.

bijuwa *Nepal.*   Shaman of the RAI group.

Bikdanos or **Vikols** *Philippines.*   Visayan ethnic group.

Bikele-Bikeng *West Africa.*   Niger-Kordofanian language.

Bikol *Philippines.*   Christian ethnic group in southeast Luzon.

Bilaan *Philippines.*   Pagan ethnic group.

bilabandi *India.*   Revenue settlement of a district.

bilad al makhzan *Morocco.*   Literally, land of the central government. Regions where central government authority is fully established.

bilad al siba *Morocco.*   Literally, land of dissidence. Regions where central government authority is weak.

bilal *Islamic countries.*   MUEZZIN who calls the faithful to prayer in a mosque.

Bilala *West Africa.*   1. Subgroup of the Lisi. 2. Nilo-Saharan language.

Bilen *Ethiopia.*   AGEW-speaking ethnic group. 2. Afro-Asiatic language.

Bili *Sierra Leone.*   Secret society among the KONO which conducts circumcision of its members.

bilito *Rwanda and Burundi.*   Melancholic elegy.

Bilochi *Pakistan.*   Ethnic group in the Punjab.

biltong *Zimbabwe.*   Sundried or smoked beef.

Bima *Indonesia.*   Austronesian language.

Bimal *Somalia.*   Largest DIR clan-family group.

Bimbia *West Africa.*   Ethnic group of the northwest BANTU configuration. Also, *Isuwu.*

Bimoba *West Africa.*   1. GURMA ethnic group. 2. Niger-Kordofanian language.

binasuan *Philippines.*   Folk dance in which dancers balance wine glasses. Also, *pandango sa ilaw,* in which they balance lighted oil lamps.

Binga *Congo.*   Pygmy ethnic group.

Bingkokak *Indonesia.*   Austronesian language.

Binh-Xuyen *Vietnam.*   Political organization of bandits, active from 1945 to 1955.

Binja *Zaire.*   Ethnic group of Central Rain Forest.

Binjhwari *India.*   Indo-European language.

Binji *Zaire.*   Niger-Kordofanian language.

binna *Sri Lanka.*   Marriage in which the man moves into the woman's home.

Binukid *Philippines.*   Austronesian language.

Binza *Zaire.*   Ethnic group of the Central Rain Forest.

bir *Western Sahara.*   Well deeper than 12 meters.

Bira *Zaire.*   1. Ethnic group of the Central Rain Forest. 2. Niger-Kordofanian language.

Bira *Indonesia.*   Austronesian language.

biraderi *Pakistan.*   Group of patrilineally related families. Also, *bradri.*

Biri *Sudan.*   Sudanic people related to the AZANDA.

Birifor *West Africa.*   Ethnic group of MOSSI cluster.

Birifor-Wali *West Africa.*   Niger-Kordofanian language.

birike *Sierra Leone.*   Rite of initiation for males in KORANKO subtribe.

biri-mesu *Sierra Leone.*   Rite of initiation for females in KORANKO subtribe.

birmadka poliska *Somalia.*   Riot police.

birr *Ethiopia.*   Monetary unit.

birta *Nepal.* Land from which revenues were allocated to individuals under the regime of the RANAS.

biru *Rwanda and Burundi.* Oral historians who interpret tribal traditions. *See also* BANYANGE.

Birwa *Botswana.* Ethnic subgroup.

Birwa *Zimbabwe.* SOTHO-speaking people around the Tuli River.

Bisa *Zambia.* Congolese LUNDA tribe in Luapula Valley.

Bisaya *Sabah.* Austronesian language.

bish'a *Yemens.* Ordeal by fire.

Bisharin *Sudan.* BEDAWIYE-speaking BAJA group.

bisht *Saudi Arabia.* Long outer cloak, white, black or brown depending on the season, worn over the THAUB.

Bislama *Tuvalu.* English Creole.

Bissa *West Africa.* Niger-Kordofanian language.

Bissagos *Guinea-Bissau.* Ethnic group in the Bissagos archipelago.

bitwoded *Ethiopia.* Literally, beloved. Grants to ex-ministers or special confidants of the emperor under the former imperial regime.

Blaan *Philippines.* Austronesian language.

blackbirders *Samoa.* Unscrupulous 19th-century European labor recruiters who raided the islands and carried away adult males.

Black Carib *Central America.* Descendant of runaway African slaves.

Black Thai *Vietnam.* Ethnic group in the north.

blanco *Spanish America.* Persons of pure Spanish blood or descent.

bla-on-kole *Ivory Coast.* Part of a bride-price.

blatengette *Ethiopia.* Chief administrator of the palace under the former imperial regime.

blatta *Ethiopia.* Former court official.

Ble *West Africa.* MANDE-speaking ethnic group.

bled *Algeria.* Back country.

Boa *Zaire.* Ethnic group.

Babangi *Zaire.* Ethnic group.

bobbin *Jamaica.* Song improvised and sung by work gangs.

Bobo *West Africa.* Ethnic group related to BANDE, divided into White Bobo (Bobo Gbe or Kian), Red Bobo (Bobo Oue or Tara) and Black Bobo (Bobo Fing or Boua). Also Bwanu (singular) and Bwabe (plural).

Bobo Fing *West Africa.* Niger-Kordofanian language.

Bocayes *Nicaragua.* Subtrial group of the Chontales tribe.

bocona *Panama.* Four-string native guitar.

bocor *Haiti.* Voodoo sorcerer.

bodega *Spanish America.* Small grocery store or warehouse.

Bodiman *Cameroon.* Coastal ethnic group.

Bodo *India.* Sino-Tibetan language.

Boeni *Guinea.* Subgroup of TENDA.

boghali *Lesotho.* Bride-price.

Boghom *West Africa.* Afro-Asiatic language.

bogor *Somalia.* Title of chief or elder.

Bogotano *Colombia.* Resident of Bogota.

Bogotazo *Colombia.* Major urban riot in Bogota in April 1948 that marked the beginning of the period known as LA VIOLENCIA.

bogyoke *Burma.* Literally, great commander. Title of Ne Win, virtual dictator from 1962 to 1981.

Bohanes *Uruguay.* An aboriginal group.

bohio *Central America.* Typical rural house with earthen floor, thatched roof and palm bark or wood walls.

bohn shay *Burma.* Long drum used in BONSHE festivals.

bohn shay pwe *Burma.* Theatrical performer in the BONSHE dance.

Bohra *Islamic countries and India.* ISMAILI subgroup headed by the Aga Khan.

Boikin *Papua New Guinea.* Papuan language.

Boiteko *Botswana.* Community venture initiated in 1969.

bojalwa *Botswana.* Traditional beer made from sorghum.

bakor *Somalia.* Literally, a belt. Clan.

Bokyi *West Africa.* Niger-Kordofanian language.

Bola *West Africa.* Afro-Asiatic language.

bolas *Bolivia.* Primitive weapon comprising three stone balls joined with long thongs and thrown with a spring motion.

botan *Bolivia.* Indian grinding stone.

boleadores *Uruguay.* A GAUCHO lasso made by knotting three ropes with stone weights on the free ends.

Bolia *Zaire.* Niger-Kordofanian language.

bolilands *Sierra Leone.* Seasonally flooded low-lying grasslands in the north central areas.

Bolinao *Philippines.* Austronesian language.

bolivar *Bolivia.* Monetary unit.

Bolivianidad *Bolivia.* Literally, Bolivianness. Term stressing development of national identity.

bollo *Panama.* Tamale, a cylindrical cornmeal dough wrapped in sugarcane leaves or corn husks.

bolo *Philippines.* Large curved knife used in harvesting.

Bolon *West Africa.* Small MANDE group in Orodara.

bolsicon *Spanish America.* Full skirt reaching halfway to the ankles made usually of coarse cotton or wool with an embroidered border.

boma *Malawi.* 1. Group performing MALIPENGE dance. 2. Administrative station, usually the office of the district commissioner.

boma *Tanzania.* 1. Ring fence. 2. Administrative center.

Boma *Zaire.* Ethnic group

Boma-Sakata *Zaire.* Ethnic group of southern savanna.

bombacha *Brazil and Paraguay.* Loose baggy trousers.

bombilla *Paraguay.* Metal or straw spoon used in drinking MATE.

bomunzu *Rwanda and Burundi.* Lineages who live as one household.

Bon *Nepal.* Shamanistic Buddhism.

Bon *Somalia.* Low caste among the SAAB.

bonde *Brazil.* Street car or tram.

Bondel *Tanzania.* 1. Ethnic group 2. Niger-Kordofanian language.

boneh *Iran.* Cooperative farming by landlord and tenant or sharecropper.

Bongam *Central Africa.* Ethnic group. Also, *Bakele.*

bongo *Malawi.* Kind of zither with seven strings.

Bongo *Sudan.* Negroid ethnic group in Bah el Ghazal and Equatoria. 2. Nilo-Saharan language.

Boni *East Africa.* Hunter ethnic group south of the Juba River.

Boni *Kenya.* "Sam" or nose-speaking people near the Somali border.

bonnes femmes de bois *Seychelles.* Female magicians and conjurers.

bonshe *Burma.* Folk dance and music of pre-Thai origin performed at harvest times.

bonshommes *Seychelles.* Male magicians and conjurers.

Bontok *Philippines.* 1. Pagan ethnic group in Mountain Province in north Luzon. 2. Austronesian language.

bonze *Burma.* Buddhist clergy.

boon *Burma.* Cleansing ceremony marking end of ritual seclusion following childbirth for LU mothers.

boqueiroes *Brazil.* Narrow gorges in the northeast filled intermittently with water.

Boran *Kenya.* Ethnic group.

borchas *Argentina.* Form of bowling.

bordj *Morocco.* Small hill fort in a dissident territory.

bori bori *Paraguay.* Native soup with chicken and corn dumplings.

Boro *Bangladesh.* Irrigated rice harvested April through May.

Boron *West Africa.* Ethnic group of MANDE cluster.

Bororoan *South America.* 1. Group of Indian tribes near the headwaters of the Paraguay River. 2. The language of this tribe.

Boruca *Central America.* Ethnic group of the Pacific coast.

bosale *Haiti.* Newly arrived slave not yet initiated into Voodoo cult.

bose vakaturaga *Fiji.* Advisory body for the preservation of the rights of indigenous Fijians.

bossa nova *Brazil.* Popular dance.

bot *Thailand.* The most important building in the WAT, or temple compound. Also, *uposatha.*

botas de potro *Uruguay.* GAUCHO's shoes made from hide taken from the hind legs of a colt.

botella *Spanish America.* Literally, the bottle. Bribery as a means of obtaining favors.

Botocudos *Brazil.* Aimore Indians, a ferocious tribe whose men ornamented themselves by driving wooden pegs or BOTOQUES through their lower lips.

Botoques *Brazil. See* BOTOCUDOS.

Bouaka *Central African Republic.* Ethnic group related to the BAYA.

boubou *West Africa and Haiti.* Loose lightweight flowing robe with wide sleeves.

Boudouma *West Africa.* SAHELian ethnic group.

boui *Chad.* Elder or an older person among the TOUBOU.

Boulou *Cameroon.* Subgroup of the PAHOUIN. Also, *Bulu.*

Bouraka *Central African Republic.* Ethnic group of Ubanguian stock.

Bowli *Ghana.* CENTRAL TOGO ethnic group.

bowmung *Burma.* KACHIN headman.

Boyo *Zaire.* Ethnic group.

Bozo *West Africa.* 1. Ethnic group. 2. Niger-Kordofanian language.

braca *Brazil.* Unit of length equal to 2.2 meters.

bracao *Mexico.* Ranch hand.

bracero *Spanish America.* Laborer.

bradri *Pakistan. See* BIRADERI.

Brahma *India.* God in the Hindu pantheon identified as the creator.

Brahui *Pakistan and Afghanistan.* 1. DRAVIDIAN ethnic group in Baluchistan. 2. Dravidian language.

Braj Bhasha *India.* Indo-European language.

brak *Senegal.* Title of the king of WALO.

bra-kos *Chad.* Literally, master of the hoe. Farmer, among the SARA.

brahman *India.* In Hinduism, universal soul.

Brahmanas *India.* Class of Vedic scriptures consisting of interpretations by Brahmins.

brahmin *India.* In the Hindu caste system, the first and priestly caste.

Brames *Guinea-Bissau.* Senegambian group on the right bank of the Mansoa River.

brancarroes *Brazil.* Light-skinned mulattoes.

brancos de Bahia *Brazil.* Literally, whites from Bahia. Near-white people with slight Negro blood.

Brao *Cambodia.* 1. Subgroup of the KHMER LOEU. 2. Austro-Asiatic language.

braza *Central America.* Unit of land measurement, equal to 36 sq ft.

Bribri *Costa Rica.* Dialect derived from HUETAR.

Brinjari *India.* Itinerant dealers in grain and salt.

brochismo *Spanish America.* Political hypocrisy.

Brong *Ghana.*   AKAN group in the Brong-Ahafo region.
Bru *Vietnam.*   Highland ethnic group in Quang-Tri Province and along Laos border.
Bru *Vietnam and Laos.*   Austro-Asiatic language.
brujeria *Cuba.*   Witchcraft.
brujo (female: bruja) *Mexico.*   Wizard or sorcerer.
brukbri *Central America.*   Shamans among the Burucas.
Brunei *Sabah.*   Austronesian language. Also, *kadayan.*
Brunka *Costa Rica.*   Indigenous tribe of CHIBCHA origin.
bu *Oman.*   Variation of ABU. Father.
Bua *West Africa.*   Niger-Kordofanian language.
buat nak *Thailand.*   Ordination ceremony performed at the time a male is eligible to enter Buddhist monkhood.
Bube *Equatorial Guinea.*   Niger-Kordofanian language.
bubud *Philippines.*   Alcoholic drink made from rice in Tinggian province.
bucaklar (singular bucak) *Turkey.*   Subdistrict.
bucak mudur *Turkey.*   Head of a district administration.
budbud *Philippines.*   Glutenous rice mixed with coconut, milk and sugar and boiled in a banana leaf wrapper.
Buddhism *South and East Asia.*   Religion that developed from the teachings of Gautama Buddha in the 5th century B.C. Its two main branches are Mahayana and Hinayana.
budi bahasa *Malaysia.*   Literally, language of character. Elaborate pattern of formal social behavior.
Budjga *Zimbabwe.*   Major SHONA group speaking a dialect of Korekore in the Mtoko district.
budlong *Philippines.*   BISAYAN shell trumpet.
Budu *Zaire.*   1. Ethnic group of Central Rain Forest. 2. Niger-Kordofanian language.
bududira *Rwanda and Burundi.*   Traditional spirit of a family.
Budumas *West Africa.*   Afro-Asiatic language.
Buem *West Africa.*   CENTRAL TOGO ethnic group.
buey acarreador *Nicaragua.*   Water-carrying oxen on Omotepe Island.
bufetes colectivos *Cuba.*   State-controlled attorneys' bureaus.
bufo *Paraguay.*   Kind of draw poker.
Buganda *Uganda.*   Former kingdom of the GANDA people ruled by the KABAKA, now part of Uganda.
buggalow *Maldives.*   Wooden sailing craft similar to a DHOW.
Buginese *Indonesia.*   SULAWESI ethnic group.
Bugis *Indonesia.*   Austronesian language.
Builsa *West Africa.*   MOLE-DAGBANE ethnic group. Also, *kangyaga.*
Buja *Zaire.*   Niger-Kordofanian language.

Bukidnon *Philippines.* Ethnic group in Bukidnon Province in north central Mindanao.

Bukiyup *Papua New Guinea.* Papuan language.

Bukusu *East Africa.* Niger-Kordofanian language.

bukwe *Rwanda and Burundi.* Wedding day.

bula *Haiti.* Smallest of the three drums used in Voodoo ceremonies.

bulaklak *Philippines.* General store.

Bulala *Chad.* Ethnic group of Arab ancestry.

bula materi *Zaire.* Literally, he who can break rocks. In colonial times, native nickname for Belgian governors.

Buli *West Africa.* Niger-Kordofanian language.

bullarengue *Panama.* Regional dance in Darien.

bulopwe *Zambia.* Hereditary ruling quality transmitted in a single descent line.

Bulu *West Africa.* 1. Variant form of BOULOU. 2. Niger-Kordofanian language.

bum *Oman.* Large DHOW or boat.

bumba-meu-boi or **boi surubi** *Brazil.* Dance in the northeast with characters dressed as VAQUEIROS and bois (oxen).

bumiputras *Malaysia.* Literally, sons of the soil. Indigenous Muslim Malays, as distinguished from Indians and Chinese.

bum nat *Burma.* Spirits of the mountains, among the KACHIN.

bun *Thailand.* Merit earned through observing religious practices and doing good works.

Bunak *Indonesia.* Papuan language.

bunde *Panama.* Ceremonial dance generally performed around Christmas time.

Bundeli *India.* Indo-European language.

bundh *India.* General strike involving complete shutdown of all shops, factories, and transport services.

bundobast *India.* Literally, tying and binding. System or means of protection against encroachment or attack.

bundu *Zimbabwe.* Wild bush country.

bunfangfai *Thailand.* Literally, the merit of firing rockets. Rainmaking festival and ceremony with processions, fairs and rockets, held from mid-May to mid-June.

bung *Papua New Guinea.* Executive of a political party.

bungalow *India.* Single-story house, typically with a pyramidal roof.

Bunge *Tanzania.* National Assembly.

Bungku *Indonesia.* Austronesian language.

Bungku-Laki *Indonesia.* SULAWESI ethnic group.

bunglat *Burma.* Among the KACHINS, a feud for which revenge and reprisal are considered justified.

bunques *Nicaragua.* Storage bins for food in Pacific coastal areas.

bun sern phrawed *Thailand.* Major agricultural festival in the northeast in February at the completion of the rice harvest.

Buol *Indonesia.* Austronesian language.

bupati *Indonesia.* Formerly regent, and currently, chief executive of a KABUPATEN.

bur *Gambia.* Title of SERER kings.

bur *Senegal.* WOLOF term for king.

Bura *West Africa.* Afro-Asiatic language.

buraambur *Somalia.* Relatively short semiclassical composition, composed for and by women.

Buran *Afghanistan.* Major subdivision of the GHILZAI.

Burji *East Africa.* 1. Ethnic group in Kenyan Northeast Province. 2. Afro-Asiatic language.

Burmese *Burma.* Sino-Tibetan language.

burnoose *Arab countries.* One-piece cloak with a hood.

burqua *Islamic countries.* Loose embroidered garment covering head and body with latticed eyeholes worn by women in public.

burundaya (plural: maburundaya) *Zimbabwe.* CHISHONA term for person from Malawi.

Burungi *Tanzania.* Ethnic group.

Burushaski *India and Pakistan.* Isolated, unclassified language.

Busa *West Africa.* Niger-Kordofanian language.

Busanga *West Africa.* MANDE ethnic group.

Busansi *West Africa.* Ethnic group of MANDE cluster.

Bushong *Zaire.* Niger-Kordofanian language.

bustee *India.* Slum or shantytown.

butog *Senegal.* Nuclear family among the DIOULA.

Buton *Indonesia.* Austronesian language.

butut *Gambia.* Coin, 1/100ths of a DALASI.

buurmaaBe (singular buurnaajo) *Senegal.* Among the TOUCOLEUR, potters.

Buyo *Philippines.* BETEL NUT, used for chewing.

Buyuk Millet Meclisi *Turkey.* Grand National Assembly.

buyut *Arab countries.* Extended family group comprising several households.

buzkashi *Afghanistan.* Polo-type sport in which horsemen attempt to carry the carcass of a goat or sheep across the opponents' goal.

buzuq *Jordan.* Long-necked mandolin with two strings bound together.

bwa *Zaire.* Niger-Kordofanian language.

Bwamu *West Africa.* Niger-Kordofanian language.

Bwanu (plural: Bwabe) *West Africa.* *See* BOBO.

Bwi *West Africa.* Niger-Kordofanian language.

Bwile *Zambia.* Congolese LUNDA tribe in Luapula Valley.

Bwiti *Equatorial Guinea.* Syncretic religion of 20th century origin among the NTUMU FANG.

byaite *Nepal.* Sacramental marriage.

Byansi *Nepal.* Minor ethnic group.

bye-daik *Burma.* Privy council.

byet *Ethiopia.* Household.

caada *Maghreb.* District governor or tribal chief.

caatinga *Brazil.* Stunted scrub forest in part of northeast sertao and western agreste.

caatingueiros *Brazil.* Transient workers who migrate to the northeast sugarcane plantations during the harvest season but return home after the harvest.

cabacera *Spanish America.* Capital of a MUNICIPIO or department.

caballeria *Spanish America.* Unit of area varying from 111.5 acres in Guatemala to 45.3 acres in Costa Rica and 33.2 acres in Cuba.

caballero *Spanish America.* Gentleman whose behavior and attitudes exhibit such virtues as chivalry, generosity and paternalistic leadership.

cabalqadas *Western Sahara.* In the early modern period, slave raids.

cabeca de porco *Brazil.* Tiny single-room cubicle occupied by an entire family.

cabecar *Costa Rica.* Dialect of the TALAMANCAn Indians.

Cabecares *Costa Rica.* Main group of the TALAMANCAn Indian tribe.

cabide de empregos *Brazil.* Person who holds several jobs in the bureaucracy.

cabide de imprego *Brazil.* Literally, employment ranger. Simultaneous holding of two or more jobs as a means of professional advancement.

cabildo *Cuba.* 1. Prerevolutionary black social club. 2. Government of a MUNICIPIO.

cabildo *Spanish America.* In colonial times, a municipal council. Also applied to the town hall.

cabildo abierto *Spanish America.* Open municipal council meeting.

caboclada *Brazil.* Characteristics of a CABOCLO.

caboclino *Brazil.* Carnaval dance akin to the samba and frevo performed by male dancers wearing grass skirts, bone necklaces and feathers.

caboclo *Brazil.* Literally, copper-colored. MESTIZO.

cabiya *Ecuador.* Plant from the fiber of which twine is made and from the juice of which various beverages are made.

cabra *Brazil.* MESTIZO of African, Amerindian or Caucasian origin.

cabrestillo *Panama.* Long gold chain adorned with trinkets and a pendant brooch.

cabungueiro *Brazil.* Menial servant.

cabure *Brazil.* Darkskinned CABOCLO.

cacaste *Guatemala.* Wooden carrying frame for transporting goods on backs. It has four legs, allowing the bearer to set it down while resting.

cachabia *Algeria.* Heavy, usually woolen, garment worn by men.

cachaca *Brazil.* Crude and powerful light rum.

cachaco *Spanish America.* Plebeian with upper-class pretensions.

cachullapi *Ecuador.* MESTIZO music with syncopated melodies.

cacicazgo *Spanish America.* Territory or domain under a tribal chief, or CACIQUE.

cacimbo *Angola.* Dry season from May to September.

cacique *Spanish America.* Tribal chief.

cacique *Philippines.* Wealthy landowner or member of the aristocracy.

caciquismo *Spanish America.* Boss-rule or control of local political machinery by group or party leaders.

caco *Haiti.* Kingmaker and power broker.

cacoism *Haiti.* Revolutionary or terrorist activities by peasant guerrillas.

Caconda *Angola.* OVIMBUNDU subgroup.

ca-dao *Vietnam.* Folk songs.

cadena chata *Panama.* Collar made of small interlaced gold links.

caderneta *Guinea-Bissau.* Labor passbook in the CONTRATADO system.

cadi *Islamic countries.* Judge. Also *qadi.*

cadjan *India and Sri Lanka.* Palm fronds, used for thatching houses.

cafe con lecha *Uruguay.* Coffee and milk mixed in equal proportions.

cafe zinho *Brazil.* National drink, a demitasse cup of black coffee served with a heaping of cane sugar.

cafuso *Brazil.* Offspring of African and Amerindian parents.

Cagayanes *Philippines.* Christian ethnic group.

ca hue *Vietnam.* Entertainment music.

cai bam *Vietnam.* Person elected by villagers to conduct religious ceremonies and rituals.

caicara *Brazil.* Bamboo fence surrounding TUPI GUARANI settlements.

caid *Morocco.* Administrative head of a local government unit. Also *qaid.*

caidat *Morocco.* Administrative division of a CERCLE.

caille *Haiti.* Creole term for hut.

caille mysteres *Haiti.* Hut where Voodoo gods are worshipped.

cai luong *Vietnam.* Modern musical theater.

caipiras *Brazil.* Rustics.

caites *Mexico.* Sandals.

caja *Spanish America.* Literally, a box. Government fund for a particular purpose of public interest.

caja de retiro y jubilacion *Uruguay.* Pension fund.

cajero *Mexico.* Fiscal officer in a state or local government.

cajon *Spanish America.* Unit of weight equal to 5,000 lb of mineral ore.

Cakchiquel *Guatemala.* MAYAN language.

cakra *India.* Psychic center of the body.

Calagan *Philippines.* MANDAYA ethnic group in Mindanao.

Calenos *Colombia.* Inhabitants of Cali.

caleretes *Venezuela.* Wind which blows northward from June through September, bringing rain.

calico *India.* Cotton cloth of fine texture, originally from Calicut (Kozhikode) in south India.

caliph *Islamic countries.* Religious and political head of a Muslim nation.

caliph *Senegal.* Head of a Muslim brotherhood.

Callagan-Caragan *Philippines.* Papuan ethnic group.

Callahuaya *Bolivia.* Indian tribe, subgroup of the AYMARA.

callampa *Chile.* Mushroom village or urban shantytown.

callejon *Peru.* Inner city or ghetto.

calpulli *Honduras.* Town council under a CACIQUE.

Caluyanum *Philippines.* Austronesian language.

calzones *Ecuador.* Shin-length trousers worn by highland Indians.

camara *Uruguay.* Municipal council.

camara de vereadores *Brazil.* Municipal council.

camari *Ecuador.* Gift of grain, chickens and other produce from Indians to the owners of a HACENDADO.

camarilla *Mexico.* Political clique based on close relationships.

camba *Bolivia.* Relating to lowlands.

Camba *Bolivia.* Highly Hispanicized Indian tribe.

camboy *Sri Lanka.* Woman's dress, a skirt of white CALICO similar to SARONG.

camera muncipais *Angola.* Municipal council.

camino real *Colombia and Peru.* Literally, royal road. Road across the Andes built by the Incas.

camionette *Haiti.* Gaily colored wooden truck for carrying passengers.

Campa *Peru.* Indian language.

campements *Ivory Coast.* Temporary settlements.

campesino *Spanish America.* Rural laborer.

campesinos pobres *Spanish America.* Literally, poor peasants. Term applied generally to the rural poor.

campo *Brazil.* Plot of entirely cleared land.

campo *Paraguay.* Interior rual areas.

campo *Uruguay.* Country outside the capital or metropolitan cities.

camtolee *Seychelles.* Type of square dance.

cana *Paraguay.* Natonal drink made of sugarcane juice.

cana *Uruguay.* Inexpensive white rum.

Canacure *Bolivia.* American Indian group speaking a TACANAN language.

canada *Spanish America.* Chapel.

canada *Nicaragua.* Valley settlements of the MATAGALPAS Indians.

canaris *Haiti.* Vessels for storing or transporting water.

candomble *Brazil.* Cult of African origin related to VOODOO.

candy *India.* Unit of weight equal to 500 lb.

cangaceiro *Brazil.* Bandit of the northeast backlands.

canichana *Bolivia.* Amazon Indian group in east Beni department.

canicula *Guatemala.* Short dry period in late July or August coinciding with heavy rainfall in the highlands.

canjica *Brazil.* Traditional PAULISTA dessert made of green corn meal, butter, coconut milk and sugar.

canoas *Brazil.* Police sweeps of city streets for rounding up potential military conscripts.

canol *Nicaragua.* Large rectangular house resembling a patio house but without corridors.

cantegrile *Uruguay.* Shantytown on the outskirts of Montevideo.

cantimplora *Uruguay.* GAUCHO leather water bottle.

cantina *Spanish America.* Bar.

canton *Spanish America.* Territorial unit or county in rural areas and a ward in urban areas.

cantones *Nicaragua.* Administrative subdivision of a COMARCA.

cantores *Uruguay.* GAUCHO balladeer.

Cao Dai *Vietnam.* Native eclectic religion founded by Ngo Van Chieu in 1919 through a series of "revelations." Victor Hugo and Winston Churchill are among its deities.

Caolan *Vietnam.* Ethnic group in Tuyen-Quang, Ho-bac, and Bac-Mai.

capanga *Brazil.* Personal bodyguard of thugs.

capataz *Uruguay.* Foreman over livestock in an ESTANCIA.

capelao *Brazil.*   Rural chaplain who organizes prayers and litanies in honor of local saints.

capitacao *Guinea-Bissau.*   Head tax.

capitaes mores *Brazil.*   In the early years of the Empire, agents of provincial president who combed the city streets for conscripting recruits for military service.

capitan *Spanish America.*   Person responsible for conducting a FIESTA.

capitan general *Spanish America.*   In colonial times, a high official directly responsible to the king.

capitanias-mores *Lusophone Africa.*   Area of military command under a captain general.

capitao *Guinea-Bissau.*   Military commander of a CAPITANIA or RESIDENCIA under Portuguese rule.

capitao de mata *Brazil.*   In former times, a slave hunter.

capitao-mor *Brazil.*   Military administrator of a captaincy or municipality.

capitulacion *Spanish America.*   In colonial times, royal license granted to a CONQUISTADOR.

capixaj *Spanish America.*   Poncho-like woolen robe fastened at the waist.

capoeira *Brazil.*   Stylized dance and martial art of Angolan origin.

caporal *Spanish America.*   Leader of a group or section in the FINCA.

capotes *Nicaragua.*   Rain capes.

Capuibo *Bolivia.*   Amazon Indian group speaking a PANOAN language in north Beni department.

carabinero *Spanish America.*   Rural policeman.

caracol *Guatemala.*   Bagpipe-like musical instrument made of shell.

cara e caballo *Panama.*   Two-masted sailing vesssel made from a single tree trunk.

caramba *El Salvador.*   Bow with a string struck with a piece of wood. Also, see QUIJONGO.

caramillo *Bolivia.*   Handwritten tracts or flyers distributed by student agitators on campuses.

carana *Costa Rica.*   Aromatic liquor made of copal.

Caranca *Bolivia.*   Subgroup of AYMARA-speaking Indians in west Oruro department.

carbonado *Uruguay.*   Beef stew with rice, pears, peaches and raisins.

carga *Spanish America.*   Unit of weight varying from 200 lb in Bolivia to 1,800 lb in Costa Rica.

cargo *Bolivia.*   In Inca times, a series of ranked offices, each of which had specified duties attached to it.

cargo cult *Oceania.*   Pseudo-religious movement fostered by initial contacts between Europeans and Pacific islanders in the 1800s, based on expectations of Western-style goods or cargo reaching the islands through supernatural means.

carguero *Spanish America.* Variant form of ALFEREZ.

Carib *Central America.* 1. Amerindian tribe believed to be the original inhabitants of the region. 2. Hybrid language.

Caribujo *Honduras.* Child of a LOBO father and Indian mother.

carioca *Brazil.* 1. Native of the city of Rio de Janeiro. 2. Dance similar to the Samba.

Caripuna *Bolivia.* Amazon Indian group of PANOAN language in south Beni department.

carnaval *Brazil.* Lenten carnival marked by nonstop street dancing and music, often accompanied by violence.

carnavalito *Bolivia.* Dance of African origin.

carne asada *Central America.* Beef cut into strips, salted and sundried, hung in the kitchen and roasted on a spit or stick over a fire.

carne de sol *Brazil.* Dried beef made from CHARQUE.

carona *Uruguay.* Leather topping of the GAUCHO saddle.

carreau *Haiti.* Unit of area equal to 3.33 acres.

carregadeira *Brazil.* Poor variety of manioc.

carrera de cintas *Central America.* Sport in which men on horseback try to lance small metal rings suspended on an overhead rope.

carreta *Central America.* Ox cart with solid wooden wheels drawn by a four-oxen team.

carta de doacao *Brazil.* Land grant as part of the charter of a capitaincy.

carta del alforria *Brazil.* Formerly, a letter or certificate attesting the free status of an ex-slave.

carta de usanca *Brazil.* Formerly, a letter of appointment of a local official.

carumbe *Brazil.* Miner's bucket used by GARIMPEIROS to pan gold.

caruru *Brazil.* Afro-Brazilian dish made with okra.

casa *Spanish America.* House.

casa de comodo *Brazil.* Slum tenement.

casa de fundica *Brazil.* Official smelting house for gold.

casa grande *Brazil.* Plantation house or manor in the northeast.

casas aviadoras *Brazil.* Central trading enterprises in the Amazon region.

casas improvisades *Paraguay.* Improvised houses of nomads or seasonal agricultural workers.

casbah *Maghreb.* Native quarters in a town usually surrounded by a fortress or stronghold.

casbah *Morocco.* Fortress or citadel in a city.

cascalho *Brazil.* Gravel subsoil mixed with quartz and gold.

caserio *Central America.* Subdivision of an ALDEA; rural settlement smaller than a village or hamlet.

castas *Spanish America.* Groups of MESTIZOS, MULATTOES and Negroes with some Spanish blood.

castellanizacion *Bolivia.* Emulation of Spanish models, or Hispanicism as opposed to BOLIVIANIDAD.

castizo *Honduras.* Child of a Spanish father and a MESTIZA mother.

catedraticos *Paraguay.* Professor holding a chair at a college or university.

catimbo *Brazil.* Form of Afro-Brazilian spiritism involving use of marijuana and tobacco.

Catio *Colombia.* MACRO-CHIBCHAN language.

Los Catorces Grandes *El Salvador.* The elite families, numbering between five and 10, who control the politics, society and economy of the country.

caudillo *Spanish America.* Head of state viewed as boss or strongman. Caudillos are generally divided into *caudillos barbaros* (ruthless dictators) and *caudillos letrados* (benevolent dictators).

Cauri *Guinea.* Coin, ¹⁄₁₀₀ths of a SYLI.

Cauterie *Bolivia.* Indian group speaking a ZAMUCOAN language.

Cavina *Bolivia.* Amazon Indian group speaking a TOCANIAN language in north La Paz department.

cawng-nak *Burma.* Elaborately embroidered, multicolored blankets among the CHINS.

Cayapas *Ecuador.* Indians of the COSTA.

cay neu *Vietnam.* Bamboo pole stripped of leaves except for a tuft at the top and covered with red paper during TET.

cayuco *Guatemala.* Dugout canoe, 12 to 20 ft long, made from a single log.

Cayuvava *Bolivia.* Amazon Indian group in east Beni department.

Cebuano *Philippines.* Austronesian language.

Cebuanos *Philippines.* Ethnic group dominant in Cebu, Bohol, eastern Negros and west and south Leyte. Also, *Sugbunanon.*

cedi *Ghana.* Monetary unit.

cedo *Senegal.* WOLOF term for crown slaves.

cedula *Bolivia.* Official identification papers.

cedula unica *Ecuador.* Identification card for voters.

cenotes *Guatemala.* Natural wells.

centavo *Argentina.* Coin, ¹⁄₁₀₀ths of an AUSTRALE.

centavo *Brazil.* Coin, ¹⁄₁₀₀ths of a CRUZEIRO.

centavo *Guatemala.* Coin, ¹⁄₁₀₀ths of a QUETZAL.

centavo *Honduras.* Coin, ¹⁄₁₀₀ths of a LEMPIRA.

centime *Algeria.* Coin, ¹⁄₁₀₀ths of a DINAR.

centimo *Costa Rica.* Coin, ¹⁄₁₀₀ths of a COLON.

centinsimo *Panama.* Coin, ¹⁄₁₀₀ths of a BALBOA.

central *Bolivia.* Group of SINDICATOS.

central *Cuba.*   Sugar mill with own plantations.

Central Togo *West Africa.*   Ethnic cluster.

cercle *Francophone Africa.*   Territorial unit, subdivision of a region.

ceremony-yam *Haiti.*   Offerings of the first fruits of the fields to VOO-DOO gods so that they will render the fields productive next season.

cerno *Senegal.*   PULAR term for Muslim teacher and leader.

Ceylon Tamils *Sri Lanka.*   Native-born TAMILS who are less hostile to SINHALEse culture than Indian Tamils who immigrated in the last decades of British rule.

CFAF *Francophone Africa.*   Monetary unit, Communaute Financiere Africaine Franc.

Chaamba *Algeria.*   Nomadic Arab group of the Sahara.

chacara *Brazil.*   Small rural holding.

chacara *Panama.*   Bag made of vegetable fibers.

cha-cha *Haiti.*   1. Seed-filled Calabash used as a musical instrument. 2. *Spanish America* Fast paced dance.

chaco *Bolivia.*   Uncultivated area, especially shrub forest. Also, Chaco, geographical region consisting mostly of shrub lands, much of which was lost to Paraguay in the Chaco War (1933–38).

Chacobo *Bolivia.*   Amazon Indian group speaking a PANOAN language in central Beni department.

chacra *Paraguay.*   Small farm, one to two acres in area.

chadar or **chadari** *Afghanistan.*   Head-to-toe garment for women in accordance with Islamic custom.

chadouf *North Africa.*   Pole-and-bucket method of irrigation.

Chaga *Tanzania.*   1. Ethnic group. 2. Niger-Kordofanian language.

cha gio *Vietnam.*   Popular dish, a mixture of crabmeat, pork, noodle and chopped vegetables rolled in thin rice paper.

chagra *Ecuador.*   Pejorative term for highlanders of little culture and taste.

chagunchip *South Korea.*   The younger in a kinship organization.

Chahar Aimak *Afghanistan.*   Seminomadic tribe of Turko-Mongolian origin comprising *Jamshidi, Firuzkuhi,* and *Taimanni.*

chahuarmishque *Ecuador.*   Beverage, either fermented or unfermented, similar to *aguamiel.*

chai *South Asia.*   Tea.

chai-khana *South Asia.*   Teahouse.

chairo pie *Haiti.*   Shuffling group dance during festivals.

chaitya *Nepal.*   Small STUPA.

Chake *Venezuela.*   Indian group in the Maracaibo Lake region.

chakkraphat *Thailand.*   Literally, wheel-roller. Title of emperor.

Chakma *India and Bangladesh.*   1. Tribal group in the Chittagong tract. 2. Indo-European language.

chakra *India.*   Wheel.

chakravarti *India.* Literally, ruler of all lands over which chariot wheels roll. Title of Hindu emperor in ancient India.

chakwana *Malawi.* Side-blown flute with two finger holes.

Cham *Cambodia and Vietnam.* 1. Muslim ethnic group, also known as Cham-Malay or Khmer-Islam. 2. Austronesian language.

Chamba-Daka *West Africa.* Niger-Kordofanian language.

Cham-Cuu *Vietnam.* Acupuncture.

Chameali *India.* Indo-European language.

chamia *India.* Petticoat.

champa *Honduras.* Thatch-roofed, wattle-walled primitive dwelling in MISKITO coastal areas.

champan *Colombia.* Large, flat-bottomed river boat with enclosed arch-shaped sides open at the ends.

chancaca *Bolivia.* Crude brown handmade sugar.

chandra grahana *Nepal.* Religious celebration on lunar eclipse marked by fasting, communal bathing and gifts.

Chane *Bolivia.* Indian group speaking an ARAWAKAN language in CHACO area.

chang *Nepal.* Home-brewed beer drunk among the RAIS and LIMBUS.

Changa *Mozambique.* Ethnic group. See XANGA.

changwat *Thailand.* Province.

chaniso *Honduras.* Child of an Indian father and MESTIZO mother.

chanod tidin *Thailand.* Title deed.

chao *Thailand.* Guardian spirits.

chao athikan *Laos.* Abbot or head of a WAT.

chao awat *Thailand.* Abbot or head monk of a WAT.

Chaobon *Thailand.* MON-KHMER highland group.

chao fa *Laos.* Chief of the LU ethnic group in Muong Sing Province.

chao khana *Thailand.* SANGHA administrative official who is also an abbot or head monk.

chao khana muong *Laos.* District head of the Buddhist SANGHA.

chao khana tasseng *Laos.* Cantonal head of the Buddhist SANGHA.

chao khana khoueng *Laos.* Head of the Buddhist SANGHA in a province.

chao muong *Laos.* Chief of a district.

chao phap *Thailand.* Lay host of merit-making ceremonies in which monks chant and give blessings.

chaophraya *Thailand.* Title of the highest ranking official in the civil government.

chao raja khana *Laos.* Member of the Buddhist religious council.

chao thi *Thailand.* Literally, lord of the palace. Family tutelary deity.

Chaouis *Algeria.* BERBERS inhabiting the Aures Mountains in southern Constantine Province.

Chaoula *Algeria.* Major Berber group in the Aures mountain range.

chap or **chung** *Thailand.*   Small cymbals.

Chapacura *Bolivia.*   Indian ethnic and linguistic stock comprising many tribes in the Santa Cruz department.

Chapacuran *Bolivia.*   Member of the CHAPACURA.

chapadas *Brazil.*   Mountainous region in the northeast generally drought-free.

chapan *Afghanistan.*   Overcoat or cloak.

chapandaz *Afghanistan.*   Horsemen who play BUZKASHI.

chapar *Afghanistan.*   Simple form of YURT or tent built of flexible reeds which are gathered on top to form a vault. Also, *chapari.*

chapatty *India.*   Unleavened cake or bread patted flat with the hand and baked upon a griddle.

chapeton *Colombia.*   Ultra-conservative or mossback, used pejoratively.

chapras *India.*   Badge or engraved brass plate attached to the shoulder belt of a messenger.

chaprassi *India.*   Messenger or peon.

charak *Iran and Afghanistan.*   Unit of weight equal to 4 lb.

charango *Bolivia.*   Small stringed instrument of the COCHABAMBA, similar to the ukulele, with an armadillo shell as sound box.

Charca *Bolivia.*   Dialect of AYMARA spoken in north Oruro department.

Charjat *Nepal.*   Subgroup of the GURUNGS.

charpoy *South Asia.*   Bed made of rope strung between sideboards.

charque *Brazil.*   Dried or jerked beef.

charqueadas *Brazil.*   Beef drying stations.

charqui *Spanish America.*   Jerked meat, also called *tosajo.*

charreada *Mexico.*   Rodeo.

charro *Mexico.*   1. Gentleman cowboy. 2. Costume worn by *charros.*

chasqui *Spanish America.*   Mail carrier.

Chatino *Central America.*   Oto-Manguean language.

cha tom *Vietnam.*   Dish consisting of sticks of sugarcane around which spiced shrimp paste is rolled.

chatti *India.*   Earthenware pot.

Chattisgarhi *India.*   Indo-European language.

chattras *Thailand.*   Nine-tiered royal umbrella.

chattrum *India.*   House where upper-caste pilgrims and travelers are entertained and fed for a day or two.

chatur varna *India.*   Hindu system of four castes: BRAHMINS, KSHATRIYAS, VAISYAS and SUDRAS.

chau *Cambodia.*   Title of chief, as in *chau athikar rong,* head of the pagoda or *chau vaykhet,* governor.

chau *Vietnam.*   Administrative unit of a TRAN, itself divided into HUYEN.

chaudhurani *Pakistan.*   Wife of a CHAUDHURI.

chaudhuri *Pakistan.* Prosperous landowner, usually the leading man in a village.

chauk *India.* Market or public square.

chaukhi *India.* Rural police station with attached lockup or jail.

chaukhidar *India.* Watchman or patrolman.

Chaungtha *Burma.* Sino-Tibetan language.

chauveykhet *Cambodia.* Governor of a KHET or province.

Chavacano *Philippines.* Mixed Malay-Spanish dialect spoken in Zamboanga and Mindanao.

Chawai *West Africa.* Niger-Kordofanian language.

chawl *India.* Long narrow building divided into separate rooms for families.

chayu minjujuui *South Korea.* Liberal democracy.

che *Vietnam.* Light dessert.

Chechens *Jordan.* Shiite group, originally from the Caucasus. Also, *Shishaus.*

chechia *Algeria.* Woolen cap for men.

chedi *Thailand.* STUPA or shrine for the relics of the Buddha or saints.

chef de section *Haiti.* Sheriff.

chef lieu *Francophone Africa.* Headquarters of a CERCLE.

chefferies *Zaire.* Chiefdoms.

cheka *Ethiopia.* Village official.

chela *India.* Disciple of a GURU.

chena *Sri Lanka.* Slash and burn cultivation system.

chenchu *India.* DRAVIDIAN language.

chenda *India.* Round drum in Kerala.

Chepang *Nepal.* Minor ethnic group.

Cherepons *Ghana.* Guan ethnic group. Also KYERPON.

chergui *Morocco.* Intensely hot wind blowing from the Sahara in the summer.

Chero *India.* Unclassified language.

chetri *Nepal.* KSHATRIYA caste among the PAHARI.

chetrum *Bhutan.* Coin, $\frac{1}{100}$ths of a NGULTRAM.

chettiar *India.* Subcaste of moneylenders in south India.

Chewa *Southern Africa.* Congolese LUBA group in southeast Zambia.

chhau *India.* All-male dance in honor of SIVA, popular in Orissa. So-called from the chhaus, or masks, worn by dancers.

chhing *Cambodia.* Small bell cymbals.

chia *Burma.* CHIN commoner.

chiapanecas *Mexico.* Popular folk dance with hand clapping.

Chiapas *Mexico.* Ethnic group.

chibahai *Nepal.* Small Buddhist monastery on the grounds surrounding a CHAITYA or STUPA.

chibang haeng jong wiwonhoe *North Korea.* Local administrative committee.

chibang imminhoeui *North Korea.* Local people's assembly.

chibang immin wiwonhoe *North Korea.* Local people's committee.

Chibcha *Panama.* Ethnic group including *Comagres, Chiriquis,* and *Cocles.*

chicha *Spanish America.* Fiery Indian corn liquor fermented with human saliva. Formally outlawed in certain countries.

chichak *Afghanistan.* Bowed cordophone with two strings and cylindrical neck.

chicheme *Panama.* Drink made by boiling unground corn and adding milk and sugar.

chicheria *Spanish America.* Place where CHICHA is sold.

chick *India.* Hanging sunblind made of narrow strips of bamboo fastened with a string.

chiclero *Spanish America.* Laborer in a chicle farm.

Chicunda *Mozambique.* Ethnic group of the lower Zambezi cluster.

chidao (plural: zvidao) *Zimbabwe.* Subclan.

Chiga *Uganda.* Niger-Kordofanian language.

chigefu (plural: zvigufe) *Zimbabwe.* Flute.

Chikunda *Zimbabwe* and *Zambia.* Congolese LUBA group speaking a Nsenga or Sena dialect of BANTU.

Chile Barik *India.* Unclassified language.

chilena *Ecuador.* Dance inspired by the Chilean CUECA.

Chilengue *Angola.* NYAKEKE subgroup.

chilot *Ethiopia.* Court of last resort.

chilotes *Nicaragua.* Ears of green corn.

chimarrao *Brazil.* Drink of the GAUCHO.

Chimoio *Mozambique.* Ethnic group.

chimurenga (plural: zvimurenga) *Zimbabwe.* CHISHONA word for resistance or rebellion.

Chin *Burma.* Southern group of the KUKI CHIN people.

Chin *South Asia.* Sino-Tibetan language.

chinamit *Honduras.* Town council under a CACIQUE. Also *calpulli.*

Chinanteco *Mexico.* Oto-Manguean language.

china poblana *Mexico.* Folk peasant costume consisting of a long green skirt with a red yoke, trimmed with sequins, a white embroidered blouse, shawl or reboza and red hair ribbons.

chincharon con yuca *Central America.* Dish of deep-fried pigskin with yucca served on a banana leaf.

chinchibi *Bolivia.* Beverage popular in the Yungas with pineapple juice, cinnamon and honey.

chinchines *Guatemala.* Rattles used in carnivals.

chindunduma *Zimbabwe.* CHISHONA word for uprising or riot.

chingin *South Korea.* Commoners.

Chiniva Lama *Nepal.* Spiritual head of Buddhist lamaism in Nepal, based at Bodnath.

chinlon *Burma.* Game in which teams stand in a circle and kick, butt, or otherwise bat a light wicker ball without touching it with hands or arms.

chinthe *Burma.* Mythical guardian lions.

chipa *Paraguay.* 1. Bread made from MANIOC flour or cornmeal. 2. Delicacy similar to a bun made with mandioca flour and cheese.

Chipaya *Bolivia.* Indian group speaking a PUQUINAN language in the altiplano.

chipendani (plural: zvipendani) *Zimbabwe.* Mouth bow.

Chipeta *Mozambique.* Ethnic group of the NGUNI cluster.

Chipungo *Angola.* NYANEKE subgroup.

chiqa-shum *Ethiopia.* Literally, mud-chief. Representative of rist-holders who acts as an intermediary between the gult holders and other peasants.

chiqueiro *Brazil.* Small ranch.

Chiquitoan *Bolivia.* Indian linguistic and ethnic stock in east Santa Cruz department.

chiremba (singular: zuiremba) *Zimbabwe.* CHISHONA word for doctor or healer, especially herbalist.

Chiriba *Bolivia.* Amazon Indian group in central Beni department.

Chiricoa *Venezuela.* Indian group in the Llanos.

Chiriguano *Bolivia.* Indian group speaking a TUPIAN language in west Santa Cruz department.

chirimia *Central America.* Indian musical instrument shaped like a clarinet and sounding like an oboe.

chiripas *Paraguay.* GAUCHO leather breeches drawn up between the legs.

chirundu *Malawi.* Long wraparound woman's dress among the YAO.

Chishinga *Zambia.* Congolese LUNDA tribe in Luapula Valley.

chisi *Zimbabwe.* Ritual day of rest.

Chisona *South Africa.* Variant of SHONA.

chite *Chad.* Cold dry season from the middle of November to March.

chitimene *Zambia.* Slash and burn cultivation.

chitupa *Zimbabwe.* CHISHONA word for registration certificate.

chiva *Panama.* Small bus with seats along the sides.

chivara *Zimbabwe.* See DARE.

chivero *Panama.* Driver of a CHIVA.

Chiwa *Gabon.* Ethnic group also known as FANG Makina.

chiwoda *Malawi.* Popular woman's dance.

Chi yaka *Angola.* OVIMBUNDU subgroup.

cho *Thailand.* Simple melodic music.

Choa *Cameroon.* Arab subgroup.

chocao *Panama.* Dish of ripe plantain and coconut milk cooked with ginger.

choclotanda *Spanish America.* Tamale made from green corn cut from the cob and ground to a paste.

Choco *Central America.* Indian ethnic group in the southeast and Pacific coastal areas of Panama and Colombia.

Chodhari *India.* Indo-European language.

choei *Thailand.* Being unruffled and unagitated, as a social virtue.

chogyal *Sikkim.* Title of the former ruler.

choi *Thailand.* Traditional solo courting song of northern region.

Chokosi *Ghana.* AKAN group in the north, also called *Ahufo.*

Chokosi *West Africa.* 1. Ethnic group of Mandingo origin famed for their martial skills. 2. Niger-Kordofanian language.

chokpo *North Korea.* Genealogical records.

Chokwe *Zambia and Zaire.* Ethnic group of BANTU origin. 2. Niger-Kordofanian language.

Chol *Mexico.* 1. Ethnic group of the lowlands. 2. Mayan language.

chollima *North Korea.* Work unit and productivity movement in which workers are paid on the basis of team performance, named after the legendary Chinese flying horse.

cholo *Spanish America.* Indian who has acquired some Hispanic characteristics but less so than a MESTIZO.

choloficacion *Spanish America.* Transformation from Indian culture to a MESTIZO one.

chompa *Panama.* Pleated shirt decorated with buttons.

chon or **jun** *North Korea.* Coin, $1/100$ths of a WON.

Chondal *Nicaragua.* Language of the CHONTALES people.

Chondogyo *South Korea.* Indigenous monotheistic religion stressing the unity and equality of man. Formerly, *Tonghak.*

chong *Bhutan.* National drink distilled from rice.

Chong *Cambodia.* Subgroup of KHMER LOEU.

chongbo *North Korea.* Unit of area equal to 2.45 acres.

chongbu *South Korea.* Government.

chongmuwon *North Korea.* State administrative council.

chongni *North Korea.* Premier.

ch'ongsan-ni *North Korea.* On-the-spot guidance as a productivity technique developed by Kim Il Sung in 1960 on a visit to Ch'ongsanni Cooperative Farm in South Pyongan Province.

chonmin *Koreas.* The traditionally despised or lowborn people.

Chontal *Central America.* HOKAN language.

Chontales *Central America.* Tribal subgroup of QUIRIBIES.

Chonyi *East Africa.* Niger-Kordofanian language.

Chopi *Mozambique.* 1. Ethnic group. 2. Niger-Kordofanian language.

chorfa *Western Sahara.* Descendants of the Prophet Muhammad.

choroes *Brazil.* Instrumental bands.

chorten *Nepal.* Mound or monument.

Chorotega-Mangues *Costa Rica.* Ethnic group of Nicoya Peninsula.

Chorti *Central America.* Language group of CHOLAN stock of the proto-CHIAPAS Tabasco family of MAYAN superfamily.

Chorutegan *Central America.* Member of the CHORUTEGANOS.

Choruteganos *Central America.* Indian tribe of NAHUA origin.

Choson *Koreas.* Historic name for region now composed of North and South Korea.

chouhada *Algeria.* Martyr in the revolutionary war.

choul chhnam *Cambodia.* Cambodian new year, celebrated in April.

choultry *India.* Hall or shed as a rest area for travelers.

chowdhry *South Asia.* Headman of a craft guild.

chowk *India.* Open square or wide street in the middle of a town.

chowkhidar *India.* Private watchman.

chrieng *Cambodia.* Angular script used in modern KHMER.

Chroo *Vietnam.* 1. KOHO-speaking ethnic group in the southern part of the central highlands. 2. Austro-Asiatic language.

chrouqi *Arab countries.* Folk music of Lebanese origin.

chua *Vietnam.* Literally, lord or prince. Former hereditary title for nobles.

Chuabo *Mozambique.* Ethnic group of the lower Zambezi cluster. Also, *Maganja, Mahinde.*

chua krao *Thailand.* Buddhist practice whereby young men enter the SANGHA, or monkhood, for a short period of time.

Chuave *Papua New Guinea.* PAPUAN language.

chuch'e sasang *North Korea.* Ideology of self-reliance. Also, *Kim Il Sungism.*

Chuh *Central America.* MAYAN tribe.

Chuhar *India. See* AGNIKULA.

Chuhras *Pakistan.* Low caste of sweepers and scavengers.

Chuj *Central America.* MAYAN linguistic group of the Proto-CHIAPAS Tabasco family.

Chuka *East Africa.* Niger-Kordofanian language.

chukker *India.* Literally, wheel. 1. Circular course for exercising horses. 2. One of the divisions of a polo game.

chularajamantri *Thailand.* Official head of the Muslim establishment.

chulla *Spanish America.* Lower-class person who tries to pass off as an upper-class one. Also *chulla-leva.*

chulla-leva *Spanish America.* See CHULLA.

chullo *Peru.* Men's woolen hat.

Chulupi *Paraguay.* Indian language.

Chumbura *West Africa.* Niger-Kordofanian language.

chung'in *North Korea.* Middle class.

chuno *Spanish America.* Processed form of potato that is as hard as a walnut.

Churahi *India.* Indo-European language.

Churapa *Bolivia.* Amazon Indian group speaking a Chiquitoan language in Santa Cruz department.

churrasco *Argentina.* Grilled steak.

chusok *North Korea.* President.

Chwabo *Mozambique.* Niger-Kordofanian language.

chwage *North Korea.* Sitting drum.

cibongo *Malawi.* Clan name.

cidade flutante *Brazil.* Makeshift huts on clusters of rafts at the confluence of the Amazon and Negro rivers.

cidawo *Southern Africa.* Lineage name among the KARANGA.

cielito *Uruguay.* Dance, usually around campfires.

cifra *Uruguay.* Folk music.

cihad *Turkey.* Variant of JIHAD.

Cil *Vietnam.* KOHO-speaking ethnic group of the central highlands, especially Khanh-Hoa Province.

cilongo *Swaziland.* Brass military trumpet.

cimba *Malawi.* Female society in NGONI and CHEWA tribes consisting of those who have undergone initiation at the same time.

cipo *Uruguay.* Flexible vine used to tie together pine and willow in building shacks.

Circassian *West Asia.* SUNNI Muslim group, originally from Caucasus.

circulo *Mozambique.* Local FRELIMO party unit or cell.

circunscrioes civis *Lusophone Africa.* Rural administrative districts.

ciseaux *Haiti.* Dance in which the feet and legs cross one another in a scissor-like movement.

cisunga *Zambia.* Puberty ritual for girls among the BEMBA.

citimukulu *Zambia.* Title of BEMBA paramount chief.

ciudad *Spanish America.* City.

ciudades perdidas *Mexico.* Literally, lost cities. Slums.

civilized *Liberia.* Term designating Americo-Liberians as distinguished from tribals.

cizwarwa *Mozambique and Zimbabwe.* Three-generation family group among the SHONA-KARANGA.

clairin *Haiti.* Raw white rum, popular with peasants.

clarin *Burma.* Flute made of black wood with seven finger holes.

clase *Bolivia.* Noncommissioned officers.

clase media acomodada *Chile.* The comfortable middle class.

clissage *Haiti.* Wattle used in construction.

Coayqueres *Ecuador.* Colombian Indian group.

coberture *Brazil.* Protection or coverage through good connections or relatives.

Cocama-Cocamilla *Spanish America.* Indian language.

cocida *Paraguay.* MATE, drunk in the morning.

Cocolis *Guinea-Bissau.* Small Senegambian group related to the Bissagos.

Cofan *Ecuador.* Indian tribe.

coff *Algeria.* Political party.

cofono *Chad.* Clan meeting among the TOUBOU.

cofradia *Spanish America.* Religious brotherhood. Among LADINOS it
is a social organization composed of upper classes and among Indians
a group of men charged with preserving traditions.

cogobierno *Bolivia.* Co-government by two or more parties or two
or more presidents.

coivara *Brazil.* Amerindian method of clearing land for planting by
burning heaped brushwood and debris.

Col *Vietnam.* See CUA.

colectivo *Bolivia.* Bus.

colegiado *Uruguay.* Collegiate executive, especially the one introduced by Jose Batlle Y Ordonez in Uruguay.

colegio *Bolivia.* Secondary school.

colegio *Brazil.* Junior high school.

collectivities *Zaire.* Group of rural administrative units, as chiefdoms
and sectors.

collector *India.* Head of a district.

colon *El Salvador.* Monetary unit.

colon *French North Africa.* French colonists, especially in Algeria.

colonato *Bolivia.* Quasi-feudal tenant farming in which a COLONO enjoys usufruct privileges in return for unpaid labor and other obligations to the owner.

colonato *Mozambique.* Agricultural settlement on state-owned land.

colonatos *Angola.* Planned rural settlements in Portuguese times.

colones *Costa Rica.* Squatters.

colonias *Mexico.* Colonials.

colonias proletarias *Mexico.* Literally, proletarian neighborhoods.
Slums.

colono *Spanish America.* Agricultural laborer who resides on a plantation permanently and who receives a small plot of land and usu-
fructs in return for unpaid labor.

Colorado *Ecuador.* Indians of the Costa.

colorado *Spanish America.* Literally, red. Term applied to liberals.

comadre *Spanish America.* Co-mother in the COMPADRAZGO system.

comadrona *Spanish America.* Midwife.

comal *Central America.* Saucer-shaped griddle of fired clay for making tortillas.

comandancia *Spanish America.* Office of the military commander.

comandante jefe *Panama.* Commander in chief of the National Guard.

comarca *Brazil.* Judicial district.

comarca *Spanish America.*   Administrative subdivision.

comarcas *Panama.*   Indigenous territories.

combite *Haiti.*   Working party of rural neighbors summoned by a farmer to assist him in fieldwork.

comisaria *Colombia.*   Administrative unit of the national government of less importance than the department.

comisaria *Chile.*   Second-ranking police station.

comissario *Brazil.*   Coffee broker.

commandant du cercle *Senegal.*   District commandant.

communalism *India.*   Divisiveness resulting from promotion of the conflicting interests of various communities.

commune de plein exercise *Francophone Africa.*   Municipality.

Comorian *Comoros.*   Niger-Kordofanian language.

compadrazgo *Spanish America.*   Literally, co-paternity. System of ritual co-parenthood that links parents, children and godparents.

compadre *Spanish America.*   Co-father in the COMPADRAZGO system. Compare COMADRE.

compadresco *Brazil.*   Ritual extended kinship.

compadrio *Brazil.*   Ritual kinship, including specifically relationship to godparents.

companero *Bolivia.*   Comrade.

compania *Paraguay.*   Rural political subdivision.

comparsa *Bolivia.*   Team of dancers.

Compeche *Mexico.*   MAYA ethnic group.

component *Malaysia.*   Police territorial division in East Malaysia.

comptoir *Guinea.*   State trading agency.

comun *Chile.*   Regular or basic academic curriculum offered in primary or secondary schools.

comunario *Bolivia.*   Indian freeholders.

comuneros *Spanish America.*   Literally, common people. Rebels against Spanish authority in the 18th century.

comunidad *Spanish America.*   Literally, community. Indigenous community.

comunidades *Nigaragua.*   Communal land granted to MATAGALPAS.

con ca *Vietnam.*   Eldest son in a family with specific ritual responsibilities.

concejales *Western Sahara.*   Under Spanish rule, city council member.

concelhi *Lusophone Africa.*   Subdivision of a province consisting of a number of CIRCUNSCRIOES CIVIS.

concertaje *Ecuador.*   Form of debt peonage abolished in 1918.

concunado *Spanish America.*   Brother-in-law relationship, often extended to include nonrelated peers.

confinamiento *Spanish America.*   Punishment without physical restraint involving enforced residence in a specified place or house.

confiteria *Uruguay.* Snack shop.

confradia *Spanish America.* Religious brotherhood.

cong *Vietnam.* Duke, a rank of nobility.

cong bien or cong tho *Vietnam.* Public or communal lands.

cong ngo *Vietnam.* Entrance or gateway to a home or village, of great ritual significance.

congo or congada *Brazil.* Dramatic dance, akin to BUMBA-MEU-BOI, originally a coronation dance in the Congo.

congregacao *Brazil.* Members of a university faculty with professional rank.

congregacion *Spanish America.* In colonial times, nuclear settlement founded by enforced grouping of scattered Indians. Also, *reduccion.*

congruas *Brazil.* In Spanish times, stipends for the clergy.

Conhaques *Guinea-Bissau.* Small Senegambian ethnic group.

Coniagui *Guinea.* Ethnic group in the middle region.

conquistador *Spanish America.* Empire builders in the 15th and 16th centuries especially under Cortes and Pizarro.

consciencia *Cuba.* Political and social awareness, including active commitment to Castroism.

conscientizacao *Brazil.* Educational concept of Paulo Freire stressing self-dignity, self-awareness and dialogue.

conscientizacion *Uruguay.* Political consciousness-raising.

conscildes notables *Senegal.* Council of notables.

conseillers *Senegal.* Associate judges.

consejos superiores *Spanish America.* Higher university governing council.

constitucionalistas *Mexico.* Advocates of constitutional government in the 1910s—Venustiano, Carranza, Alvaro, Obrego and Villa.

constitucion vitalicia *Bolivia.* Literally, lifelong constitution. First constitution of Bolivia drafted by Simon Bolivar.

consulado *Spanish America.* In colonial times, a merchants' guild.

contingent *Malaysia.* Police territorial division in West Malaysia.

continuismo *Spanish America.* Self perpetuation in office by the president beyond normal term of office through political manipulation.

contra *Nicaragua.* Guerrilla engaged in struggle against the SANDINISTA government.

contratado *Angola.* Plantation work.

contratados *Angola.* Contract laborers forced into service.

contregile *Uruguay.* Slum.

conuco *Dominican Republic.* Small farm.

conugueros *Venezuela.* Slash and burn farmer.

conventillos *Uruguay and Argentina.* Inner-city slum consisting of dingy cubicles affording little light or air.

converso *Bolivia.* Jewish convert to Catholicism.

convivenccia *Peru.* Literally, living together. Political cooperation of groups with opposing ideologies.

cooly *India.* Hired laborer.

cooperativo *Spanish America.* Private cooperative school.

cooperativo *Bolivia.* Truck used in rural areas to transport goods as well as people.

coparticipacion *Uruguay.* Sharing of power and the spoils of office between the majority and minority parties.

co phja *Burma.* SHAN prince of Kayah.

copra *India.* Dried kernel of coconuts.

copresidente *Bolivia.* Co-president.

Copt *Egypt.* Member of the Coptic Orthodox Church, descendants of the pre-Arab inhabitants. From *qubt,* Egypt.

Cora *Mexico.* Azteco-Tanoan language.

Corabe *Bolivia.* Amazon Indian group in Santa Cruz department.

Coraveca *Bolivia.* Indian group of Bororoan language in Santa Cruz department.

cordillera *Bolivia.* Range of mountains.

cordoba *Nicaragua.* Monetary unit.

cordonaza *Nicaragua.* Pacific hurricane.

coronel *Brazil.* Political boss.

coronel-coiteiro *Brazil.* Literally, boss. Influential person who extends patronage and dispenses power in a small community.

coronelismo *Brazil.* System by which political bosses control the machinery of local government.

corosso *Honduras.* Variety of palm grown commercially on the north coast.

corregidor *Spanish America.* Local official with judicial and administrative powers in colonial times.

corregimientos *Spanish America.* Municipal zone, as a unit of a district.

cortico *Brazil.* Shantytown in Sao Paulo.

costa *Spanish America.* Coastal plain, especially in Ecuador and Peru, as distinguished from the highlands.

costenos *Spanish America.* Inhabitants of the coast, as distinguished from highlanders.

costumbres *Spanish America.* Traditional way of doing things.

costumbrismo *Venezuela.* Literary genre in which realism and naturalism dominate.

costumbriste *Colombia.* Literary work or author portraying everyday life and prevailing customs.

cota *Venezuela.* Embroidered white blouse worn loose in order to leave the shoulders bare.

cotier *Madagascar.*   Inhabitant of the coastal regions.

Coto-Coli *West Africa.*   Ethnic group of undetermined family.

co-tuong *Vietnam.*   Chess of Chinese origin.

cotwal *India.*   Formerly, police station.

country chop *Liberia.*   Highly spiced traditional cuisine of tribal peoples.

coutume *Ivory Coast.*   Rent paid to native chief for trading rights.

coyol *Costa Rica.*   Wine made from the sap of the palm tree.

creentes *Guatemala.*   Believers, especially as applied to Evangelical Christians.

cremade almendra *Nicaragua.*   Delicious mixed refreshing drink made from almonds and milk.

crimen *Nicaragua.*   Serious crimes.

criollo *Spanish America.*   Person of Spanish America born in the New World as distinguished from one born in Spain, or elsewhere.

Crioulo *Cape Verde.*   Cape Verdean dialect of Portuguese.

crique *Honduras.*   Creek.

Cristeros *Mexico.*   Defenders of Christ, especially those who opposed the anticlericalist and antireligious measures of President Plutarco Elias Calles.

crore *India.*   Ten million.

cruzeiro *Brazil.*   Monetary unit.

Cua *Vietnam.*   1. Highland ethnic group of central Vietnam. Also, *Khua, Kor,* or *Col.* 2. Austro-Asiatic language.

cuadra *Central America.*   Unit of length, equal to 91.9 yards.

cuadrillero *Central America.*   Migrant day laborer.

cuadro *Central America.*   Picture of a saint in a home, often adorned with flowers.

cuando *Chile.*   Dance of Argentine origin.

cuarentino *Guatemala.*   Short two-month growing season for maize.

cuarta *Honduras.*   Unit of length equal to 8.3 inches.

cuartelazo *Spanish America.*   Literally, blow from the barracks. Military coup.

cuatro *Spanish America.*   Four-stringed guitar.

cuchilla *Uruguay.*   Range of hills.

cudo *Guatemala.*   Unit of length equal to 22.1 inches.

cueca *Bolivia.*   Indian highland folk dance.

cueca *Spanish America.*   Dance of Indian origin with singing accompanied by guitar music characterized by lively rhythm and waving of handkerchiefs.

cuerda *Guatemala.*   Unit of area equal to one-fifth to one-sixth of an acre.

cuestion del Pacifico *Bolivia.*   Bolivia's perennial claim to a corridor to the Pacific through Chile's restitution of the coastal region annexed by the latter during the War of the Pacific (1879–83).

Cuges *Nicaragua.* Subtribal groups of CHONTALES tribe.

cuias *Brazil.* Small split gourds used by slaves as utensils.

Cuicateco *Mexico.* Oto-Manguean language.

Cuitlatel *Mexico.* Southern highland ethnic group.

Culhua *Nicaragua.* Dialect of the CHORUTEGAN language spoken in Condega.

culo en tierro *Venezuela.* Percussion instrument, a half coconut shell covered with parchment and placed in a hole in the ground.

cumbia *Spanish America.* Lengthy dance.

Cuna *Panama.* Indian ethnic group in San Blas.

Curaca *Peru.* The political boss or CACIQUE.

curacha *Panama.* Native dance.

curandero *Spanish America.* Folk physician and herbalist, often associated with magic.

Curiboca *Brazil.* Person of Indian and African descent.

curry *India.* Sauce, universally eaten along with rice.

curuchupa *Spanish America.* Religious fanatic in politics, used pejoratively.

cusiquia *Bolivia.* Amazon Indian group speaking a CHIQUITOAN language in Santa Cruz department.

custos rotulorum *Jamaica.* Chief magistrate of a parish.

cususa *Central America.* Distilled liquor made from CHICHA.

cutu *Ecuador.* QUECHUAS who adopt Spanish customs and traits.

cuvette *Zaire.* Literally, basin. Low areas southeast of the great curve of the Zaire River.

Cuyonon *Philippines.* Austronesian language.

cyclo *Vietnam.* Three-wheeled pedicab.

daara *Senegal.* Community of disciples in an Islamic brotherhood.

Daba *West Africa.* 1. Northern ethnic group. 2. Afro-Asiatic language.

dabke *Lebanon.* National folk dance in which performers line up side by side holding hands.

dabshir *Somalia.* New year's day.

dacoit *India.* Robber belonging to an armed gang.

dadi *Ethiopia.* Beer made from millet.

dadia *Indonesia.* Kinship organization among the Balinese.

Dadibi *Papua New Guinea.*   PAPUAN language.

Dadjo *West Africa.*   SAHELian ethnic group.

daerah *Malaysia.*   Subdistrict in Kelantan State.

dafadar *India and Pakistan.*   1. In the police, a minor policeman. 2. In the army, a major.

daff *Jordan.*   Circular tambourine. Also, *riqq.*

Dafing *West Africa.*   Southern MARKA ethnic group, a branch of the MANDI.

Dafla *India.*   Sino-Tibetan language.

daftar *India.*   Public record office or archives where judicial and other documents are kept.

daga *Zimbabwe.*   Mud as building material.

Dagaba *West Africa.*   MOLE-DAGBANE ethnic group. Also *Dagarte.*

dagaba *Sri Lanka.*   STUPA or mound built over the bones of an ancestor.

Dagada *Indonesia.*   Papuan language.

Dagamba *West Africa.*   Ethnic group.

Dagari *West Africa.*   1. Ethnic group of GOUROUNSI cluster. 2. MOLE-speaking people.

Dagbani *West Africa.*   Niger-Kordofanian language.

Dagomba *West Africa.*   MOLE-DAGBANE ethnic group.

dagra *Ethiopia.*   Official slightly lower in rank than the village head.

dah or **dao** *India.*   Heavy knife used as a tool or weapon.

Dahalo *Kenya.*   Ethnic group along the lower Tana River.

dahir *Morocco.*   Edict of the Sultan, royal decree.

dahman *Western Sahara.*   Commander of a tribal army.

dai *Yemens.*   Muslim missionary or propagandist. Also head of the Ismailis in the role of MAHDI.

dair *Somalia.*   Light rainy season from September or October to December.

daira *Afghanistan.*   Single-headed drum played with the rim resting on the extended palm while beaten with the fingers of the other hand.

daira (plural dairaat) *Algeria.*   Administrative district.

Dai Thua *Vietnam.*   *See* BAC-TONG.

Daju *Sudan.*   1. Ethnic group. 2. Nilo-Saharan language.

dak bungalow *India.*   Rest house.

dakshina *India.*   Gift to a deity for favors rendered or asked.

Dakshinachara *India.*   Right-handed Tantrism, a Buddhist occult sect.

Dalad *Somalia.*   Founding stock of the Digil Rahanweyn clan-families.

dalang *Indonesia.*   Puppeteer.

dalasi *Gambia.*   Monetary unit.

Dalatawa *Chad.*   Muslim ethnic subgroup of KANEMBU and KANURI.

dalava *India.*   Commander in chief in a south Indian army from the 17th to 19th centuries.

dali *Pakistan.* Curdled boiled milk.

damai *Nepal.* Class of untouchables consisting of tailors and musicians.

dama-mayu or **mayu-dama** *Burma.* Mate-swapping among the KACHINS.

damballa *Haiti.* Voodoo god of rain.

dambo *Malawi.* Small grassy flood plain.

dam-bop *Vietnam.* Massage therapy.

dambura *Afghanistan.* Stringed instrument tuned in fifths touched only by fingers of the right hand.

damel *Senegal.* Title of the king of Kajor.

damoz *Ethiopia.* Temporary marriage arrangement, usually for pay, between a man away on travel and a woman who is his companion or cook.

Dan *West Africa.* A MANDE ethnic group. Also, *Yacouba Diafoba, Yaboufa.*

Danakil *Horn of Africa.* See AFAR.

Danaqla *Sudan.* Arabized NUBIAN group in Dongola region.

dan bau *Vietnam.* One-stringed musical instrument using a wooden sounding board and a gourd-shaped resonator.

Danda *Mozambique.* Ethnic group of the SHONA-Karanga cluster.

dan dey *Vietnam.* Three-stringed musical instrument to accompany professional singers.

Dangaleat *West Africa.* 1. Subgroup of the HADJERAY. 2. Afro-Asiatic language.

Dangi *India.* Indo-European language.

Dani *Indonesia.* Papuan language.

dan kim *Vietnam.* See DAN NGUYET.

Dankyira *West Africa.* TWI ethnic group.

dan nguyet *Vietnam.* Moon-shaped lute. Also, *dan kim.*

dan tranh *Vietnam.* Traditional zither with 16 strings and movable bridges, which is plucked with finger picks.

Danuwar *Nepal.* Minor ethnic group.

danza de la botella *Paraguay.* Bottle dance in which each dancer balances a flower-filled bottle on his head.

danzante *Ecuador.* Dance in which the participants wear symbolic masks personifying primitive gods.

Dao *Vietnam.* Ethnic group in the north. Also, *Man, Zao, Yai.*

dao *Vietnam.* Administrative and military region.

dao *Burma.* Large all-purpose knife made by the NAGAS.

dara *Senegal.* WOLOF term for a group of disciples attached to a MARABOUT.

darabukka *Jordan.* Long clay drum with a skin drumhead.

Darai *Nepal.* Minor ethnic group.

darat *Burma.* Free-born commoner in KACHIN society.

darawishta poliska *Somalia.* Mobile police operating in frontier and rural areas.

darbar *South Asia.* Royal court.

darbuqa *Morocco.* Funnel-shaped drum.

Dardown *Somalia.* SAAB weaver group.

dare *Zimbabwe.* Open space around a group of houses. Also, *chivara.*

Darfung *Sudan.* Arab people of the Blue Nile region.

Dari *Afghanistan.* National language also known as Farsi or Persian.

Darod *Somalia.* One of the four SAMAAL clan-families.

daroga *India.* 1. Under the Moghuls, governor of a province or city. 2. Under the British, local chief of police.

darshan *India.* Spiritual blessing obtained through beholding a spiritual teacher, or MAHATMA.

darshana *India.* Basic metaphysical viewpoint.

dar-ul-Islam *Islamic countries.* Literally, house of Islam. Term applied to the worldwide community of Islam.

darussalem *Brunei.* Kingdom; used in the official name of the country.

Darwasi *Afghanistan.* Indo-European language.

darwish *Somalia.* Dervish.

dasain *Nepal.* National Hindu festival, lasting 15 days in the month of ASWIN. Also, *durga puja.*

dasa rajadhamma *Buddhist countries.* Literally, 10 duties of a king. They include charity, high moral character, readiness to sacrifice for the good of the people, honesty, kindness, austerity, freedom from ill will, nonviolence, tolerance and nonopposition to the will of the people.

Dasenech *Ethiopia.* Afro-Asiatic language.

dash *Liberia* and *Ghana.* Gift, usually money, in acknowledgment of services rendered.

dashiki *West Africa.* Loose, shirtlike garment, usually embroidered.

dasht *Iran.* Salt flat.

Dashte Margo *Afghanistan.* Vast plain to the southwest bordered by the Khash and Helmand rivers.

dasserah *India.* Festival, also called *durga puja,* celebrated with lights and fireworks.

data de terra *Brazil.* In the 18th century, grant of land.

Dathina *Yemens.* Ethnic group.

dato *Malaysia.* See DATUK.

datu *Malaysia.* See DATUK.

datuk *Malaysia.* Title of distinction. Also *dato, datu.*

datus *Philippines.* Leader of a MORO Muslim community.

daulat *Malaysia.* Authority, power or royalty as an attribute.

dava brahmin *Nepal.* BRAHMIN priestly caste among the NEWARS.

davaweno *Philippines.*   Austronesian language.

daw *Burma.*   Term denoting royal or sovereign applied to kingly institutions.

Daw *West Africa.*   Niger-Kordofanian language.

Dawasir *Saudi Arabia.*   Ethnic group.

dawk *India.*   Formerly, post by relays of men and horses.

dawlat *Islamic countries.*   State; used in official names of countries.

dayah *Jordan.*   Cluster of houses.

Dayak *Indonesia.*   1. Ethnic group of Kalimantan. 2. Austronesian language.

dayr *Somalia.*   Short rainy season from October to December.

Daza *Chad.*   Branch of the TOUBOU people in Bourkou.

De *Liberia.*   *See* DEI.

debiha *Western Sahara.*   Sacrifice of a goat or sheep to establish an alliance.

debtera *Ethiopia.*   Priest-teacher in the Ethiopian Orthodox Church.

decadentism *Colombia.*   Literary movement between 1895 and 1925.

decamisados *Argentina.*   Literally, shirtless ones. Politically militant workers spearheading anti-government demonstrations.

decepcionarse *Spanish America.*   Disenchantment with political leadership.

dechra *Morocco.*   Village.

decima *Panama.*   Type of folk song.

Declaration of Sitges *Colombia.*   Agreement of July 20, 1957, at Sitges, Spain, between the Liberal and Conservative parties providing for alternating terms in office for 12 years. The agreement ended LA VIOLENCIA.

deega *Sri Lanka.*   Marriage in which the woman moves into the man's house. Compare BINNA.

deepavali *India.*   The festival of lights in south India coinciding with the DASSERAH or DURGA PUJA.

Deforo *West Africa.*   HABE ethnic group.

Deg *West Africa.*   Niger-Kordofanian language.

dega *Ethiopia.*   Cool zone, comprising the central part of the western and eastern sections of the high plateau.

Degema *West Africa.*   Niger-Kordofanian language.

degregados *Portuguese Africa.*   Exiled criminals as settlers in former Portuguese colonies in Africa.

deh *Iran.*   Village, used in compound place names.

dehdar *Iran.*   Sheriff.

dehistan *Iran.*   Township.

dehqan *Afghanistan.*   Farmer or peasant.

Deh-Sekyi *Ghana.*   River god of the lower Volta.

Dehu *New Caledonia.*   Austronesian language.

Dei *Liberia.*   KRU branch of KWA-speaking peoples. Also, *De, Dey.*

deim *Sudan.*   Inexpensive new houses.

dejazmach *Ethiopia.*   Literally, general of the king's gate. Title of provincial governors in imperial times.

delegacion *Spanish America.*   Remote and unpopulated territory as a unit of local government. Also, police precinct.

delegado *Brazil.*   Police chief, usually with additional quasi judicial functions.

delegado *Spanish America.*   Administer of a DELEGACION.

delegado de gobierno *Paraguay.*   Government official in charge of public order in a department.

delegation generale *Francophone Africa.*   Capital city as a prefecture.

delegations speciales *Francophone Africa.*   Local advisory councils.

delegue general *Zaire.*   Government supervisor of an industrial or mining enterprise.

delitas *Spanish America.*   Less serious crimes in the penal code.

delroba *Afghanistan.*   Stringed instrument with long handle producing long and gliding sounds.

demis *Polynesia.*   Natives, called Euronesians, who have adopted Gallic life-styles.

demoowo *Senegal.*   Free cultivators among the TOUCOLEURS.

den *Vietnam.*   Village temple or shrine larger than a MIEU and smaller than a DINH.

den *Senegal.*   Literally, community of the breast. Matrilineage among the SERER.

Dende *Togo.*   Nonindigenous MENDE merchants from Songhai.

Dendi *West Africa.*   1. Sudanese ethnic group. 2. Nilo-Saharan language.

dendirigal *Senegal.*   Joking relationship among the PEUL.

Den-jong-ke *Bhutan.*   Language of the BHOTE.

Deno *West Africa.*   Afro-Asiatic language.

deo *Nepal.*   BRAHMIN caste of NEWARS.

deo *Vietnam.*   Mountain pass.

Deori *India.*   Sino-Tibetan language.

depa *Malaysia.*   Unit of length equal to six feet.

departamento *Spanish America.*   Political subdivision of a province.

departement *Francophone Africa.*   Administrative unit.

Dera *West Africa.*   Afro-Asiatic language.

derde *Chad.*   TOUBOU chief of a canton during French rule.

derecho al mar *Bolivia.*   Literally, right to the sea. See CUESTION DEL PACIFICO.

dergue *Ethiopia.* Literally, committee. The ruling junta, officially called Coordinating Committee of the Armed Forces, which seized power in 1974.

derhet *Chad.* Hot, humid season from the middle of September to mid-November.

desa *Indonesia.* Village.

desai *India.* Official in charge of a district in western India.

descimentos *Brazil.* Expeditions to kidnap Indians in the interior.

descrente *Brazil.* Literally, disbeliever. Term used to describe peasants as stubborn, suspicious and uncooperative.

desembargador *Brazil.* In imperial times, appeal court judge.

deshek *Somalia.* Natural basin for collecting water.

deshmukh *India.* Formerly, hereditary official with police and revenue authority in a district.

designado *Spanish America.* President-elect or one delegated presidential authority.

desobriga *Brazil.* Paschal tax paid by communicants during Lent.

despachante *Brazil.* Middleman between the bureaucracy and the citizen.

despachante expedita *Brazil.* Official who handles a variety of minor transactions, including police work, naturalization, auto licensing, etc.

despensa *Mexico.* Home-delivery systems for nonperishable goods.

deva *India.* Any of various Hindu gods.

devadasi *India.* Literally, maid of god. Ritual prostitute attached to a Hindu temple whose services are available to worshippers.

devale *Sri Lanka.* Temple for lesser Buddhist gods.

devaloka *Burma.* The six heavens above the seven mountains surrounding Mount Meru in MON mythology.

Devanagiri *India.* Script in which most north Indian languages are written.

devaraja *Thailand.* Literally, divine king. Term expressing the divinity attached to Thai kingship.

devarshi *India.* Hindu sage who is exalted as a demigod after attaining spiritual perfection.

devassa *Brazil.* In the 17th century, a judicial inquiry.

devata *India.* Minor Hindu god or demigod.

Devesa *Ethiopia.* East Cushitic people.

devi or **devata** *India.* Female deity.

devsirme *Turkey.* Collection of booty.

Dewan Negara *Malaysia.* Senate.

Dewan Pertimbangan Agung *Indonesia.* Supreme Advisory Council.

Dewan Perwakilan Rakjat *Indonesia.* House of People's Representatives.

Dewan Rakyat *Malaysia.* House of Representatives.

dey *Algeria.* Former title of the regent of Algiers.

Dey *Liberia.* See DEI.

Dghwede *West Africa.* Afro-Asiatic language.

dhabit murasha *Saudi Arabia.* Officer cadet in the Saudi army.

Dhaiso *Tanzania.* Niger-Kordofanian language.

dhami *Nepal.* Priest among the TAMANG.

dhammantaraya *Burma.* Monkish slogan, "Buddhism in Danger," to counter encroachments of secularism.

dhammasetkya *Burma.* Festival commemorating Buddha's renunciation of worldly life and marking the official start of the holy season.

Dhammathat *Burma.* Buddhist canon law written on palm leaves.

Dhammayutika *Thailand.* One sect of the SANGHA.

Dhammazedi pyathon *Burma.* Collection of laws made by King Dhammazedi.

Dhanka *India.* Indo-European language.

Dhanwar *India.* Indo-European language.

dhanya purnima *Nepal.* Harvest festival among the NEWARS.

dharma *South and Southeast Asia.* Positive religious obligations of a Hindu or Buddhist, extended often to include all moral laws.

Dharma Chakra *India.* Literally, the wheel of law. Ancient symbol in the form of a many-spoked wheel.

Dharmashastra *India.* Literally, the science of moral law. Body of Hindu law ascribed to Manu, Yajnavalkya and other sages.

Dharmasuksa *Thailand.* Course of Buddhist studies for lay men and women.

dharmsala *India.* In north India, a rest house for wayfarers.

dharna *India.* Literally, to sit. Mode of extracting payment, collecting a debt or enforcing compliance with a demand by the complainant sitting at the offender's door and fasting until his demands are met.

Dhattki *Pakistan.* Indo-European language.

dhatu *Sri Lanka.* Relic of the Buddha preserved in a temple.

dhatuwan *Burma.* Class of MON historical writings that record the history of relic pagodas.

Dhawahir (singular: Dhahiri) *Oman.* Largest tribe of the Buraimi Oasis.

Dhawahir *Saudi Arabia.* Tribe in Buraimi Oasis.

dhenkli *India.* In north India, a swing pole for raising water. *See* PICOTTAH.

dhikr *Arab countries.* Literally, testifying or remembering. Incessant repetition of words or formulas in praise of Allah, often with music and dancing in order to create religious ecstasy, especially among SUFIS.

Dhimal *Sikkim.* Ethnic group.

dhimmi *Islamic countries.* Literally, people of the book. Christians and Jews tolerated in Muslim countries in accordance with the Koran in exchange for payment of special taxes and certain political and social restrictions.

Dhodia *India.* Indo-European language.

dhol *Afghanistan.* Two-headed drum suspended from the neck of a musician.

dholak *India.* Cylindrical double-headed drum played with one hand and a stick.

dhole *Bangladesh.* Country drum.

dhoot *Kenya.* Lineage among the LUO.

dhoti *India.* Long, narrow loincloth worn around the waist by men.

dhow *India.* Coastal sailing craft.

dhrupad *India.* Devotional song or hymn.

Dhyana *Vietnam.* Zen Buddhist sect. See also THIEN.

dia *Somalia.* Blood money paid or received by kin as compensation for homicide.

dia de la raza *Bolivia.* Literally, day of the race. Columbus Day celebrated on October 12.

Diakhanke *Guinea.* Ethnic group.

Dialonke *Guinea.* Ethnic group, probably a branch of SOUSSOU. Also, *Djallonke, Dyalonke, Jallonke.*

Diankhanke *Senegal.* Muslim ethnic group.

Diawara *Mali.* Ethnic group speaking SARAKOLE.

dictablanda *Spanish America.* Soft dictatorship.

dictadura *Spanish America.* Hard dictatorship.

Dida *Ivory Coast.* 1. Ethnic group of the KROU complex. 2. Niger-Kordofanian language.

Didinga *Sudan.* 1. Nilotic ethnic group in Equatoria. 2. Nilo-Saharan language.

Die or **Jeh** *Vietnam.* MON-KHMER ethnic group in Quang-Nam, Quang-Tin and Kontum provinces.

dieri *Senegal.* Rain-fed land suitable for peanut cultivation.

diezmo *Mexico.* Ecclesiastical tithe.

diffa *Morocco.* Tribal or official banquet.

Digambara *India.* Literally, sky-clad. Sect of JAINISM considering clothes as sinful. Its holy people move about totally naked.

Digil *Somalia.* One of the two SAAB clan families.

diglal *Ethiopia.* Paramount chief of the Beni Amer.

dignidad or **dignidad de la persona** *Spanish America.* Inner dignity as a characteristic of worthy people.

Digo *Tanzania.*   1. Ethnic group. 2. Niger-Kordofanian language.

dildevrimi *Turkey.*   Turkish language revolution through the introduction of the Roman alphabet and purification of the vocabulary under Ataturk in 1928.

Dilruba *India.*   Fretted musical instrument.

Dimasa *India.*   Sino-Tibetan language.

dimboeli *Senegal.*   Work group of individuals who spontaneously offer to help anyone in need of assistance among the WOLOF.

dinar *Arab countries.*   Monetary unit of Algeria and Iraq.

Ding *Zaire.*   Ethnic group.

dinh *Vietnam.*   Multi-purpose communal home in a village also serving as a shrine for the patron saint or guardian spirit of the place.

Dinka *Sudan.*   1. Nilotic ethnic group in Bahr al Ghazal. 2. Nilo-Saharan language.

Diola *Guinea-Bissau.*   Senegambian ethnic group related to the Serer.

Diola *West Africa.*   Extensive ethnic group from Senegal to Ivory Coast. Also, *Dioula, Mande, Malinke.*

Dionkor *Chad.*   Subgroup of the HADJERAY.

Dioula *West Africa.*   Ethnic group of MANDE cluster.

dioulakro *West Africa.*   Residential quarters of the DIOLA.

diputado *Spanish America.*   Deputy in a legislature.

diputados de partido *Spanish America.*   Deputy at large.

diqwa *Ethiopia.*   Hymnary of the Orthodox Church.

Dir *Somalia.*   Oldest of the four SAMAAL clan-families.

dirah (plural: diyar) *Oman.*   Territory of a nomadic tribe.

dirham *Iraq.*   Coin, 1/100ths of a DINAR.

dirham *Egypt.*   Unit of weight equal to three grams.

dirigente *Bolivia.*   Director or officer of a SINDICATO.

Diriku *Namibia.*   Niger-Kordofanian language.

Dirim *West Africa.*   Niger-Kordofanian language.

disarticulacao *Brazil.*   Literally, disarticulation. Lack of communication between individuals or groups.

dishdasha *Arab countries.*   Ankle-length white gown similar to a caftan.

disquite *Brazil.*   Legal separation of husband and wife.

dissawa *Sri Lanka.*   Under Portuguese rule, governor.

distensao *Brazil.*   Relaxation of the rigorous political curbs on restoration of democracy in the mid-1980s.

distrito *Spanish America.*   County or parish, as a unit of a province.

Ditamari *West Africa.*   Niger-Kordofanian language.

divan *India and Nepal.*   Chief minister of a native state. Also, *diwan.*

divan *West Asia.*   Council, especially of senior military or political officials.

Divehi *Maldives.* Indo-European language.

Divehi Raja *Maldives.* Kingdom of the islands, a description of Maldives.

divessi *Maldives.* Native of Maldives.

diwan *India and Nepal.* See DIVAN.

diwan (plural: dawwin) *Oman.* Royal advisory council.

diwan khas *Jordan.* Special council that interprets constitutionality of laws.

diwani *Nepal.* Civil courts.

dizimeiros *Brazil.* Tithe collectors.

djellaba *Arab countries.* Garment of pure white or neutral color like a monk's robe but without belt.

djemma *Arab countries.* Council of village or tribal leaders.

djerman *Chad.* Formerly, the first dignitary at court.

Djerma-Songhai *West Africa.* Ethnic group.

djoget *Indonesia.* Folk drama in Sumatra.

Djoheina *Chad.* Large group of seminomadic Arab clans who came from Sudan in the 14th to 19th centuries.

Djuka *French Guiana.* Indian language.

do *Burma.* Blood brotherhood among the KARENS.

do or **to** *Koreas.* Province.

Doab *India.* Fertile land between two rivers, as between the Ganges and Yamuna rivers.

dobat *Burma.* Song, music and dance used by villagers for all occasions except funerals.

dobra *Sao Tome and Principe.* Monetary unit.

docente livre *Brazil.* Faculty member less than a full professor.

doctrina *Spanish America.* Colonial parish.

doctrinero *Chile.* Teacher of church doctrine.

dodai *Afghanistan.* Bread, also known as *nan,* staple of Afghan diet.

Dodoth *Uganda.* Eastern Nilotic ethnic group.

Doe *Tanzania.* Ethnic group.

dogh *Afghanistan.* Watered yogurt with pieces of cucumber and mint. Also known as *shromby* in Pushto.

Dogon *West Africa.* 1. Ethnic group. Also, *Habe, Cadau.* 2. Niger-Kordofanian language.

Dogra *India.* Kshatriya subcaste of partial Hun descent.

Dogri Kangri *India.* Indo-European language.

doho *Kenya.* Lineage council among the LUO.

dohol *Afghanistan.* Heavy, two-faced drum hanging from the neck by a strap.

Doko *Zaire.* Ethnic group.

doli *India.* Litter carried by two or four men.

dolmus *Turkey.*   Private cab operated like a bus on fixed routes.

dom *Nepal.*   Polluting or unclean caste among the PAHARI.

doma *Segenal.*   WOLOF witch.

domador *Uruguay.*   GAUCHO who specializes in broncobusting.

domain *Guinea.*   Under President Sekou Toure, superministry in the cabinet.

domaine de la loi *Ivory Coast.*   Area of legislative activity reserved to the National Assembly by the Constitution.

domaneab *Nauru.*   Meetinghouse.

Dombe *Angola.*   OVIMBUNDU subgroup.

dombo (plural: madombo) *Zimbabwe.*   CHISHONA word for large rock or stone.

Dombondole *Angola.*   OVAMBO subgroup.

domibur *Senegal.*   Nobles of various ranks among the WOLOF.

Dompago *West Africa.*   Niger-Kordofanian language.

donatarios *Angola.*   In the 16th century, Portuguese nobles assigned land in the colony with additional fiscal and administrative powers.

don-dien *Vietnam.*   Military settlement of new lands.

Dondo *Congo.*   Subgroup of the KONGO.

dong *Vietnam.*   Monetary unit.

donga *Swaziland.*   Gullies.

donga *Zimbabwe.*   Ravine or gully, usually dry for most of the year.

don gahn *Vietnam.*   Bamboo carrying pole with baskets hanging at either end.

dong-bang *Vietnam.*   Plains in a delta area.

Donme *Turkey.*   Jewish descendant of the followers of the false messiah, Sabbatai Sebi (1632–75) who converted to Islam toward the end of his life.

dontri puen muang *Thailand.*   Ensemble of instrumental music in the north.

Doohyaayo *West Africa.*   Niger-Kordofanian language.

dooli *India.*   Light litter for transporting people.

Doraces *Panama.*   Indian group of Chiriqui Province.

dori *Nicaragua.*   Seagoing dugout vessel.

dorje *Nepal.*   Representation of the thunderbolt as a symbol of Buddhist priestly authority.

dork *Burma.*   MON slave caste.

Dorli *India.*   DRAVIDIAN language.

Dorobo *Kenya and Tanzania.*   Ethnic group of hunters.

Doroma *Tanzania.*   Ethnic group of MASAI origin.

Dorosie *West Africa.*   Ethnic group of LOBI cluster.

Dorze *Ethiopia.*   OMETO people of Gemu-Gofa highlands.

dou *Togo.*   Clan of EWE origin.

Douala *Cameroon.* Southern forest ethnic group who form the majority in the Douala region.

douar *Morocco.* Hamlet, smaller than a village.

douh *Somalia.* Dry watercourse which turns into a fast-moving stream after every downpour.

doumegawo *Togo.* Assembly of nobles among the EWE.

Dourou *Cameroon.* Northern ethnic group.

doutor *Brazil.* Holder of a doctorate.

dowreh *Iran.* Informal male group.

draa *Western Sahara.* Flowing cotton robe worn by men—white for teachers, MARABOUTS and leaders and blue for others.

Draconianos *Colombia.* More moderate liberals, less doctrinaire than GOLGOTHAS, between 1849 and 1854.

Drak-yul *Bhutan.* Official name of the country.

drame *Mauritania.* MARABOUTS of the second class.

Dravidian *India.* Semi-Negroid people whose ancestors were the pre-Aryan, indigenous inhabitants of the land.

drift *Lesotho.* Unbridged stream.

druk gyalpo *Bhutan.* Title of the MAHARAJA of Bhutan.

druk kargue *Bhutan.* Branch of KAGYUTPA, one of the RED HAT orders of Tibetan Lamaism.

Druze *Syria and Lebanon.* Heretical sect of Islam believing in the divinity of Hakim, the third Fatimid caliph of Egypt, founded by M. Ben Ismail el Daraz in 1020.

du *Burma.* Title of chief of KACHIN GUMSA community.

dua *Iran.* In Shiite religion, short prayers that include the names of SUFI saints or IMAMS, inscribed on rugs and amulets or written down and carried around on a person.

Duala *West Africa.* Niger-Kordofanian language.

Duan *Vietnam.* Highland ethnic group of MON-KHMER origin on the Laos border.

dubash *India.* Literally, two languages. Translator, used by Europeans to transact business with natives in colonial days.

dubat *Somalia.* Irregular fighter.

Dubla *India.* Indo-European language.

duerka taira *Honduras.* Seagoing dugout canoe used in coastal waters.

Duguri *West Africa.* Niger-Kordofanian language.

duha *Syria.* Political expertise.

duhukan *Indonesia.* Hamlet.

duiduias *Philippines.* KALINGA bamboo panpipe.

Duka *West Africa.* Niger-Kordofanian language.

dukan *India.* Small retail shop or grocery store.

dukka *East Africa.*   Retail shop run by East Indians.

dukkawallah *East Africa.*   Retail shopkeeper of East Indian origin.

dukun *Indonesia.*   Any of a variety of folk healers, sorcerers, fortune-tellers, shamans, etc.

dukunam *Indonesia.*   Hamlet.

dulce *Costa Rica.*   Crude brown sugar.

dulce de leche *Argentina.*   Concoction of milk and sugar.

Duma *West Africa.*   1. Ethnic group. 2. Niger-Kordofanian language.

dumboy *Liberia.*   Traditional dietary staple made from cassava by boiling, pounding and straining it into a thick, doughy mass. Also, *fufu.*

dumbuseya *Zimbabwe.*   SHONA group of obscure but apparently recent origin.

Dumpo *Ghana.*   GUAN group in the Brong area.

Duna *Papua New Guinea.*   PAPUAN language.

dungaree *India.*   Blue denim fabric.

dunhu *Southern Africa.*   Ward or political division among the SHONA-KARANGA.

du nja *Burma.*   Literally, fixed sayings. KAYAH proverbs.

dunum *Iraq.*   Unit of area equal to one-fourth of a hectare.

Duobe *Ivory Coast.*   Ethnic group of the KROU complex. Also *Wobe.*

dupatta *South Asia.*   Scarf, $2\frac{1}{2}$ yards long, thrown over the shoulder and sometimes over the head of women.

dura bazi *Afghanistan.*   Whip-racing with two teams.

durai *India.*   In south India, SAHIB, or a title of respect for Westerners.

Durand Line *Pakistan and Afghanistan.*   Border line between Pakistan and Afghanistan drawn by Sir Mortimer Durand in 1893.

Durani *Afghanistan.*   Subgroup of the PUSHTUNS.

durga puja *Nepal.*   See DASAIN, DASSERAH.

Duru (singular: Dara'i) *Oman.*   Nomadic tribe.

Duru *West Africa.*   Niger-Kordofanian language.

Duruma *Kenya.*   Niger-Kordofanian language.

durwan *India.*   Doorkeeper at the gate of an office or mansion.

dustoor *India.*   Any customary practice or mode of doing things.

Duun *West Africa.*   Niger-Kordofanian language.

duwa *Burma.*   Village chief of the KACHINS.

duwwar *Egypt.*   A large home.

dwa *Ghana.*   AKAN symbol of office.

dwifungsi *Indonesia.*   Literally, double mission. Role of the army in military as well as civil life.

Dyan *West Africa.*   Ethnic group of the LOBI cluster.

Dyerma *West Africa.*   Nilo-Saharan language.

Dyola *West Africa.*   Niger-Kordofanian language.

Dyula *Gambia.*   Mandingo people.

Dyulas *Guinea-Bissau.* Mandingo ethnic group from the Soninke branch with some Fulani admixture.

dzivaguru *Zimbabwe.* SHONA spirit medium.

dzong *Bhutan.* Castle-monastery serving as the secular and religious headquarters of a district; by extension, the district itself.

dzongda *Bhutan.* Administrative head of a district.

Dzongkha *Bhutan.* Sino-Tibetan language.

Dzviti (plural: Madzviti) *Zimbabwe.* SHONA term for MFECANE invaders, including the NDEBELE, Gaza and NGONI.

ebeng *Indonesia.* Classical Sumatran dance.

Ebira *West Africa.* Niger-Kordofanian language.

Ebrie *West Africa.* 1. Ethnic group of the LAGOON CLUSTER. 2. Niger-Kordofanian language.

echege *Ethiopia.* Deputy to the patriarch of the Orthodox Church.

eder *Ethiopia.* Voluntary welfare association.

edir *Ethiopia.* Communal funeral association.

Edo *West Africa.* 1. Ethnic group. 2. Niger-Kordofanian language.

educandas *Brazil.* Secular entrants to colonial-era convents.

effendi *Turkey.* Former title of respect, originally applied to officers in the middle and lower grades of the bureaucracy.

Efik *West Africa.* Niger-Kordofanian language.

Efitop *West Africa.* Niger-Kordofanian language.

Efutu *Ghana.* GUAN ethnic group.

Egba *Nigeria.* YOMBA subgroup.

Eggon *West Africa.* Niger-Kordofanian language.

egresado *Ecuador.* Student who has attended classes but has not graduated from a university.

Eguafo *Ghana.* GUAN coastal group.

egyin *Burma.* Historical ballads composed by court poets between 1338 and 1638.

Eile *Somalia.* Hunter group south of the Juba River.

eingyi *Burma.* Long-sleeved and starched jacket worn by both sexes, usually along with the LONGYI and a wraparound skirt.

einshemin *Burma.* Formerly, heir apparent to the Burmese throne.

Ejagham *West Africa.* Niger-Kordofanian language.

ejidal *Spanish America.* System of landownership in which land belongs to the municipalities.

ejidatario *Spanish America.* Worker on an EJIDO.

ejido *Spanish America.* Land held in common by a village or a cooperative farm.

ekadasi *India and Nepal.* Meatless fast days observed two days in each calendar month: on the 11th day of the light half and the 11th day of the dark half of the lunar cycle.

Ekagi *Indonesia.* PAPUAN language.

Ekajuk *West Africa.* Niger-Kordofanian language.

Eket *West Africa.* Niger-Kordofanian language.

ekka *India.* Small one-horse carriage.

Ekpeye *West Africa.* Niger-Kordofanian language.

ektara *India.* One-stringed fiddle played by wandering minstrels.

Ekuana *Ghana.* One of the principal AKAN clans.

ekub *Ethiopia.* Credit society.

ekuele *Equatorial Guinea.* Monetary unit.

Ekumfi *Ghana.* Coastal FANTE group.

el *Somalia.* Well excavated in the rocks or earth as distinguished from natural water basins.

ela *Malaysia.* Unit of length equal to three feet.

Eleme *West Africa.* Niger-Kordofanian language.

El Molo *Kenya.* One of the smallest ethnic groups in Africa with less than 200 people.

elotes *Nicaragua.* Large ears of green corn.

Eloyi *West Africa.* Niger-Kordofanian language.

emabet *Ethiopia.* Title of noble woman.

emafik amuva *Swaziland.* Literally, latecomers. Ethnic subgroups who arrived in the country after the true Swazis. Also, *labofik emuva.*

Emai-luleha-ora *West Africa.* Niger-Kordofanian language.

emajobo *Swaziland.* Loin skins made from the pelts of animals worn by Swazi men over their MAHIYA, one in the front and one behind.

ema khandzambili *Swaziland.* Any one of three categories into which Swazi society is divided.

emancipados *Brazil.* Freed slaves.

embita *Ethiopia.* Fife or flute with no stops.

Embu *Kenya.* 1. Ethnic group of central Bantu speakers, related to MERU. 2. Niger-Kordofanian language.

emir *Arab countries.* Ruler.

empirico *Central America.* Primary school teacher without formal training.

empleado *Spanish America.* Salaried employee.

empleita *Brazil.* Piecework performed by sharecroppers for which they receive cash payments.

empreguismo *Brazil.* Practice of making extensive patronage appointments to enhance the incumbent's hold on power.

enagua *Honduras.* Long garment worn by country women with ruffles at the hem.

en banc *Costa Rica.* Plenary session of the Supreme Court.

encargado *Bolivia.* Representative of landlord's interests in dealing with SINDICATO CAMPESINO.

encilhamento *Brazil.* Period of financial chaos in Brazilian history, 1890–92.

encogido *Spanish America.* Indian who does not participate in social activities.

encomendero *Spanish America.* One in charge of an ENCOMIENDA.

encomienda *Spanish America.* Former system during Spanish rule under which individual colonists were given the right to collect tributes from Indian communities in return for the responsibility of supervision and religious education of Indians.

Endeh *Indonesia.* Austronesian language.

Enenge *Gabon.* Ethnic group.

Enga *Indonesia.* PAPUAN language.

enganchador *Bolivia.* Literally, broker. Labor contractor who organizes work crews on commission basis.

enganche *Spanish America.* Contract-labor paid advances to ensure their regular appearance at work.

engenho *Brazil.* Small sugar mill.

engenhocas or **molinetes** *Brazil.* Small sugar plantation producing distilled alcohol.

Engenni *West Africa.* Niger-Kordofanian language.

Engganese *Indonesia.* Sumatran ethnic group.

enhla (plural: abenhla) *Zimbabwe.* SINDEBELE term for north as distinguished from *zansi,* south.

enjarma *Panama.* Packsaddle of leather or wood for carrying goods.

enkang *Kenya.* MASAI homestead.

ensalada *Nicaragua.* Medley of songs and dances in traditional fiestas.

ensino supletivo *Brazil.* Supplementary education.

entes autonomos *Uruguay.* State corporations, as autonomous entities.

entregista *Brazil.* Literally, one who hands something over to another. Brazilian individual or group who sells out to foreign interests.

entreguismo *Peru.* Surrender of power or national resources to foreigners, especially North Americans.

entron *Ecuador.* Indian social climber.

envueltos *Central America.* Wraparound woman's skirt, usually ankle length.

Epie *West Africa.* Niger-Kordofanian language.

equb *Ethiopia.* Communal savings association.

erg *Mauritania.* Series of sandy dunes in the Sahara Desert.

Erseris *Afghanistan.* Subgroup of TURKMANS.

Erzilie *Haiti.* Voodoo goddess of water.

Esan *West Africa.* Niger-Kordofanian language.

escalafon *Colombia.* Teacher's register or certification.

escravos de servico *Brazil.* Hired slaves.

escudo *Chile.* Monetary unit.

escuela parvularia *Chile.* Preschool.

escuro *Brazil.* Black person of relatively high social class.

Eshira *Gabon.* Ethnic group.

esketa *Ethiopia.* Shoulder dance performed by both men and women, but mostly by women.

Eso *Zaire.* Ethnic group of Central Rain Forest.

espanolo *Honduras.* Child of a CASTISO father and Spanish mother.

esquadrao de morte *Brazil.* Rightwing death squads or police vigilantes.

esquerda festiva *Brazil.* Limousine liberals.

esquilmo *Costa Rica.* Tenancy for a single harvest.

esray *India.* Fretted musical instrument in Bengal.

estado *Guatemala.* Unit of length equal to $5\frac{1}{2}$ ft.

estado del sitio *Spanish America.* Literally, state of siege. Martial law.

estancia *Spanish America.* Large ranch.

estancieros *Spanish America.* Members of the landowning class.

estancos *Nicaragua.* Establishment licensed to sell AGUARDIENTE.

estante *Spanish America.* Posts or columns used as supports for houses constructed on coastal flood plains in order to raise them above the water level.

estra mahkama *Afghanistan.* Supreme court.

etape per etape. *Tunisia.* Literally, step by step. Gradualism, characteristic of former President Habib Bourguiba's pragmatic political philosophy.

etat de siege *Francophone Africa.* State of siege.

etat d'urgence *Francophone Africa.* State of emergency, less critical than a state of siege.

etege *Ethiopia.* Empress.

Ethiopia Tikdem *Ethiopia.* Ethiopia First, national slogan.

etina *Zaire.* Major lineage.

Eton *Cameroon.* 1. BETI subgroup. 2. Niger-Kordofanian language.

Etsi *Ghana.* Small GUAN group.

etuka *Zaire.* Group controlling tribal property.

Evale *Angola.*   OVAMBO subgroup.

evalue *Ghana.*   AKAN group in southwest related to NZEMA.

evangelico *Central America.*   Evangelical Protestant, often a Pente-costal.

evangelista *Bolivia.*   Among QUECHUA-speaking Indians, one who opposes FIESTAS.

Evegbe *Ghana.*   EWE language of which ANLO is a dialect.

Evegbe *Togo.*   EWE language.

Eveia *Gabon.*   Ethnic group.

evkaf (singular: vakif) *Turkey.*   Religious trusts, variant of WAKF.

evolue *Francophone Africa.*   Literally, evolved one. A gallicized native who adopted French customs and life-styles through modern education and who received special privileges in colonial times.

Ewage *Papua New Guinea.*   PAPUAN language.

Ewe *West Africa.*   1. Ethnic cluster, consisting of *Ewe, Ouatchi Mina, Fon* and *Adja.* 2. Niger-Kordofanian language.

Ewondo *Cameroon.*   1. Largest unit of the Beti-Pahouin group. 2. Niger-Kordofanian language.

excedentes *Brazil.*   Students who pass the vestibular examination but who, because of shortage of places, are denied access to universities.

exilados *Bolivia.*   Exiles.

expediente *Bolivia.*   Dossier.

expediente laboral *Cuba.*   Work record maintained by an employer.

eyepass *Guyana.*   Public redress of insult or humiliation in which the avenger requires the offender to reaffirm their bonds or validate his claim to a high status in society.

fa'a Samoa *Western Samoa.*   Literally, the Samoan Way. Customs and traditions of the Samoan people as a desirable alternative to Western life-styles.

facon *Uruguay.*   Long knife used by the *gauchos.*

facultad (plural facultades) *Spanish America.*   College within a university offering degree programs.

fada *Cameroon.*   Ministerial council of the FULANI.

Fadhli *Yemens.*   Ethnic group.

fado *Brazil.* Serenade, a wailing love song.

fady *Madagascar.* Taboo.

faena *Bolivia.* Voluntary community work project.

faghih *Iran.* In the Constitution, spiritual leader of the state and the Islamic Revolution. Title applied exclusively to AYATOOLAH Khomeini.

faiscadores *Brazil.* Itinerant gold prospectors.

fakdah *Arab countries.* Subdivision of a subdivision of a subtribe.

fakhd *Western Sahara.* Fraction of a tribe or patrilineal clan.

faki (plural: fokara) *Chad.* Koranic scholar or literate Muslim.

fakir *Islamic countries.* Dervish or religious mendicant.

falaj (plural: aflaj) *Oman.* Communal water supply system for agriculture consisting of a water channel.

falangismo *Spanish America.* Emulation or admiration of Hispanic traits and culture.

Falasha *Ethiopia.* AGEW-speaking black Jews, said to descend from converts to Judaism in Solomonic times. Also, KAYLA, BETA ISRAEL.

fale *Samoa.* House.

Fali *Cameroon.* 1. Northern ethnic group. 2. Niger-Kordofanian language.

faltas *Spanish America.* Least serious crimes in the penal code.

fama *Mali.* King.

famadihana *Madagascar.* Customary funeral rite in which bodies are exhumed.

Fanakalo *Zimbabwe.* Kitchen Kaffir, a pidgin amalgam of Africaans, Sindebele, Chishona and English.

fanal *Senegal.* Float of wood and paper paraded at Christmas.

fanega *Spanish America.* Unit of weight equal to 640 lbs or unit of area equal to 500 cubic inches.

Fang *Central Africa.* 1. Major southern forest ethnic group, subgroup of PAHOUIN. 2. Niger-Kordofanian language.

Fante *Ghana.* TWI-FANTE ethnic group.

faqih *Maldives.* Lawyer in an Islamic court.

fara (plural: afra) *Western Sahara.* Subfraction of a FAKHD.

fara or **farba** *Senegal.* MALINKE term for viceroy or military governor.

faragua *Panama.* Grass used as fodder.

farang *Thailand.* General term for Westerners, from feringhi or Frank.

faren *Senegal.* PULAR term for lineage head.

fariq *Saudi Arabia.* General in the Saudi army.

farmandari *Iran.* Governorate headed by a *farmandar.*

farofa *Brazil.* Manioc meal mixed with melted butter or lard, chopped eggs and banana.

farsakh *Iran.* Unit of length equal to six km.

Farsi *Afghanistan and Iran.* Indo-European language. Also, *Dari, Persian.*

farsiwan *Afghanistan.* TAJIK dwelling in urban centers.

fashanbur *Somalia.* Literally, pile of shields. Protective alliance of clans.

fasli *India.* Revenue year, as distinguished from a calendar year.

fatidra *Madagascar.* Blood oath.

fatma *Algeria.* Maid servant.

fatwa *Islamic countries.* Authoritative legal interpretation by a MUFTI on a disputed point of Islamic theology or law.

fautua *Western Samoa.* Title of adviser held by heads of certain families.

favela *Brazil.* Jerry-built squatter settlement or slum on the fringe of a major city.

favelados *Brazil.* Inhabitants of FAVELAS.

fazenda *Latin America.* Large ranch or plantation; thus *fazendeiro,* owner of a fazenda.

fazendeiros *Latin America.* Large landowners.

febrerismo *Paraguay.* Socialist movement that grew out of the revolt of February 17, 1936.

fedangma *Nepal.* Among the LIMBU, a shaman.

fedayeen *Arab countries.* Arab commandos or guerrillas, especially in the struggle against Israel.

feddan *Arab countries.* Unit of area equal to 1.038 acres.

fedde *Mauritania.* Social grouping based on age among the TOUCO-LEUR.

Fe'efe *West Africa.* Niger-Kordofanian language.

feijoada *Brazil.* National dish, a stew of dried meat, sausage, tongue, black beans, FAROFA and orange sections, served with rice.

feira *Portuguese Africa.* Market or fair.

fella (plural: fellahin) *Arab countries.* Peasant.

Fellata *Sudan.* West Africans living in Sudan.

Felupe *Guinea-Bissau.* Small Senegambian group related to BALANTAS and Balotes.

Fera *Ghana.* AWUNA group in the upper region.

feria *Spanish America.* Annual fair, especially in honor of a saint.

ferik *Sudan.* Commander in chief.

ferik *Sudan and Central Africa.* Camp that travels together during nomadic transhumance.

Fernandinos *Equatorial Guinea.* Creole community of Fernando Po descended from Liberians, Nigerians, Sierra Leonians and liberated slaves.

Feroge *Sudan.* Ethnic group.

ferrias *Uruguay.* Open-air market.

fertile crescent *Islamic countries.* Semicircle extending from Israel around the Syrian Desert to the Persian Gulf, representing the cradle of Islamic power.

feterita *Sudan.*   Quick-growing millet.

Fetha Nagast *Ethiopia.*   The Law of Kings, the basic document of AM-HARA jurisprudence written in GE'EZ in the 12th century.

feticheur *Ivory Coast.*   Priest of any cult.

fez *Islamic countries.*   Cylindrical hat without a brim, usually red.

Fia *Ghana.*   EWE word for chief.

fidalgo *Brazil.*   Noble.

fidelismo *Cuba.*   Ideology associated with Fidel Castro, stressing communism and opposition to the United States.

fidelista *Cuba.*   Follower of Fidel Castro and his variety of communism.

fiesta *Latin America.*   Festival, usually of a religious nature.

fifos *Brazil.*   Lamp made of small glass bottle with a wick passed through the top.

figa *Brazil.*   Afro-Brazilian amulet in the form of a fist with a thumb inserted in between the middle and index fingers.

fihavanana *Madagascar.*   Ties of kinship, including friendship and tolerance.

Fijian *Fiji.*   Austronesian language.

fil *Arab countries.*   Coin, 1/100ths of a dinar.

Filala *Western Sahara.*   High caste tribe.

filhos de terra *Sao Tome and Principe.*   Literally, sons of the soil. Native-born Sao Tomeans.

filhotismo *Brazil.*   Nepotism, from FILHO, son.

filibuster *Central America.*   Freebooter or pirate.

filipe *Brazil.*   Man supported by the earnings of his wife.

financiera *Spanish America.*   Private development finance company.

finca *Spanish America.*   Intermediate-size agricultural farm.

finquero *Spanish America.*   Owner of a FINCA, or farm.

fiohawo *Togo.*   Assembly of EWE chiefs and notables.

Fipa *Tanzania.*   1. Ethnic group. 2. Niger-Kordofanian language.

fiqh *Bangladesh.*   Positive Islamic law in contrast to Sharia, or moral law.

fiqh *Islamic countries.*   Literally, understanding. Corpus of tradition and interpretation that make up Islamic law.

fiqi (plural: fuqaha) *Islamic countries.*   Koranic teacher.

firman *Islamic countries and India.*   Royal or government order granting a license or pass.

firqah (plural: firaq) *Arab countries.*   Subdivision of a subtribe.

Firuzkuhi *Afghanistan.*   See CHAHAR AIMAK.

fiscal *Spanish America.*   Member of a board of directors.

fiscal auxiliar *Panama.*   Assistant to the procurator general.

fiscal de corte *Uruguay.*   Court prosecutor.

fiscalizada *Peru.* Private school maintained by a large industrial or mining firm.

fitawrari *Ethiopia.* Literally, general of the vanguard. Title of some governors under the imperial rule.

Five K's *India.* Five articles obligatorily worn by each member of the Khalsa, or SIKH religious community. These include: *Kesh* or long hair and beard; *kungha* or hair comb; *kuchcha* or shorts; *kara* or iron bangle; and *kirpan* or sword.

flagelados *Brazil.* Literally, the flagellated. Victims of northeast droughts driven periodically from their homes.

Fnang *West Africa.* Ethnic group related to EFIK.

foco *Latin America.* Guerrilla nucleus in the countryside.

foko *Madagascar.* Descent group or lineage including many extended families.

fokonolona *Madagascar.* Council composed of heads of all households in a village.

foliao *Brazil.* Participant in a CARNAVAL.

fombe *Madagascar.* Customs.

fon *West Africa.* Among the BAMILEKE, a politico-religious chief or dignitary.

Fon *West Africa.* 1. Ethnic group of the EWE family. 2. Niger-Kordofanian language.

fonctionnaire *Francophone Africa.* Cadre of civil servants under French rule.

fonio *Guinea.* Variety of millet.

fon lep *Thailand.* Dance in northern region, also called nail dance.

Fon-Mahi *West Africa.* Collective name for two separate ethnic groups found in Benin and Togo.

fono *Western Samoa.* Governing body of a village.

fono a faipule *Western Samoa.* Traditional consultative assembly.

foo-foo *Ghana.* Basic West African food made from cassava flour or yams, plantains, bananas and rice.

foqra *Mauritania.* Member of the Islamic QADIRIYA Brotherhood.

foqra *Western Sahara.* One of the sub tribes living in Reguibat ech charg.

foquistas *Spanish America.* Urban middle-class guerrillas.

foral *Brazil.* Feudal contract granted by the Crown to the donataries under the captaincy system of the 1530s.

Fore *Papua New Guinea.* Papuan language.

foreiro *Brazil.* Peasant farmer who rents marginal lands to grow marginal crops in exchange for CORVEE labor during planting and harvest seasons.

formulario *Spanish America.* Incantation.

forna vuetta *Spanish America.* See AINI.

Foro *Gambia.* Free-born caste among the Mandingo.

forro *Brazil.* Manumitted slave.

Fotsy *Madagascar.* White MERINAS.

Fouikat *Western Sahara.* A small tribe.

foujdar *India.* Military commander.

foxtrot Incaico *Ecuador.* Literally, Inca foxtrot. Dance.

fraction *Morocco.* Segment of a tribe.

frafra *Ghana.* Mole-Dagbane ethnic group.

Frelimo *Mozambique.* Ruling Marxist party, Frente da Liberatacao de Mozambique founded in 1962.

frentes *Cuba.* Subcommittees within neighborhood vigilance committees.

fresco *Peru.* Cold drink consisting of sweetened fruit juice.

frevo *Brazil.* CARNAVAL dance indigenous to the northeast, and danced alone like the Samba.

freguesia *Brazil.* In the colonial era, a district as part of a TERMO.

frigorifico *Uruguay.* Refrigerated meatpacking plant.

friq *Western Sahara.* Nomad encampment.

fron-tenis *Mexico.* Form of JAI ALAI in which tennis rackets are used in place of cestas, or baskets.

frontera, las *Nicaragua.* Frontier region.

frozen *Cuba.* Dance.

fu *Burma.* Religio-secular leader among the LAHU.

fuba *Brazil.* Cornmeal.

fuero *Venezuela.* Privileges granted to certain classes of people during the colonial period.

fufu *Liberia.* See DUMBOY.

fugara *Iran.* Disciples of a SUFI master.

fukara *Ethiopia.* Military dance, also known as boasting dance, performed by a man with a stick or rifle (formerly a spear) held horizontally above his shoulders with his head moving left and right to the accompaniment of defiant shouts.

Fukudh *Arab countries.* Clan, or small unit of a subtribe.

fulafula *Zaire.* Big truck with boxlike cage in the back for passengers.

Fulakunda *West Africa.* Niger-Kordofanian language.

Fulani *West Africa.* Major ethnic group found scattered in many countries from the mouth of the Senegal River to Lake Chad. They established a historic empire extending from Guinea to northern Nigeria with capitals at Sokoto and Gando. They are almost entirely Muslim. Also, *Fulbe* (singular: Pullo), *Fula, Peul.*

Fulbe Burure *Gambia.* Dialect group of the Fulbe.

Fulbe Firdu *Gambia.* Dialect group of the Fulbe.

Fulfulde *West Africa.* Niger-Kordofanian language of the FULANI.

Fuliru *Zaire.* Niger-Kordofanian language.

Fullah *Sierra Leone.* Ethnic group, a branch of the FULANI.

Fulse *West Africa.* Ethnic group, branch of the NINISI.

fundo *Chile.* Landed estate.

funduq *Morocco.* Warehouse, often with an attached inn, in a port city.

Fungom *West Africa.* Niger-Kordofanian language.

fuqara *Ethiopia.* Boasting songs of warriors.

Fur *Sudan.* 1. Ethnic group of the Darfur. 2. Nilo-Saharan language.

Furiiru *Zaire.* Ethnic group of eastern highlands.

futa *Somalia.* Traditional wraparound sarong-like garment worn by both men and women. Also, *maro, tob.*

Futanke (plural: futankobe) *Senegal.* Native of Futa Toro.

futbol *Uruguay.* Soccer.

futuwal *Egypt.* Paramilitary force of secondary school students undergoing military training.

Fuuta Jalon *West Africa.* Niger-Kordofanian language.

Fuyuge *Papua New Guinea.* Papuan language.

fuzdari *Nepal.* Criminal courts.

Fyam *West Africa.* Niger-Kordofanian language.

Ga *West Africa.* Major ethnic group, related to Ane.

ga *Burma.* Communal lands among the KACHINS.

Ga-Adangbe-Kaw *West Africa.* 1. Ethnic cluster. 2. Niger-Kordofanian language.

gaadi *Afghanistan.* Two-wheeled horse-drawn carriage.

Gaalin *Sudan.* Arab tribe.

Gaanda *West Africa.* Afro-Asiatic language.

gaban *Guatemala.* Man's short jacket made of black wool.

gabar (plural: gabaroch) *Ethiopia.* Tenant.

gabay *Somalia.* Poems, generally between 30 and 150 lines, dealing with serious political or religious themes, chanted solo by men to a slow, simple and dignified melody.

gabbang *Philippines.* Xylophone made of bamboo, metal or wood, having 14 to 20 notes.

Gabbra *Kenya.*   Oromo-speaking people in the northeast.

gabily *Sudan.*   Arabic term for tribe.

gabobi *Niger.*   Negroid SONGHAY.

Gabri *West Africa.*   Afro-Asiatic language.

gacekondu *Turkey.*   Shanty house.

gacetillas *Mexico.*   Paid publicity stories appearing as news items in papers.

gachupines *Mexico.*   Iberian-born Spaniards. Perjorative term for Spaniards.

gada *Ethiopia.*   OROMO system that groups persons of the same generation.

Gadaba *India.*   Austro-Asiatic language.

Gadabursi *Somalia.*   Script for the Somali language devised by Shaykh Abdur Rahaman Nuur in 1933. Also *Borama.*

Gadala *Western Sahara.*   One of the nomadic SANHAJA tribes.

Ga'dang *Philippines.*   Austronesian language.

Gaddang *Philippines.*   Minor ethnic group in Luzon.

Gaddi *India.*   Indo-European language.

Gadi *West Africa.*   Niger-Kordofanian language.

gadi *India.*   Throne of a MAHARAJA.

Gadsup *Papua New Guinea.*   Papuan language.

Gagou *Ivory Coast.*   One of the Mande peoples. Also, *G'ban.*

Gagu *West Africa.*   Niger-Kordofanian language.

Gahuku *Papua New Guinea.*   Papuan language.

Gaine *Nepal.*   Minstrel.

gaing *Burma.*   Party, sect or division in contemporary Buddhism.

gaingdauk *Burma.*   Head of the local village monastery.

gainggyok *Burma.*   Head of a Buddhist ecclesiastical district.

gailoa *Brazil.*   Motorized river boat on the middle Amazon.

gaita *Colombia.*   Music of Indian origin.

Galela *Indonesia.*   Papuan language.

Galla *Ethiopia.*   Cushitic-speaking, predominantly Caucasoid people. Also, *Oromo.*

galle *Senegal.*   Extended family among the TOUCOLEURS.

galleta *Paraguay.*   Biscuit.

Gallinas *Sierra Leone.*   Ethnic group in Yakemo, Kpukumu and Krim chiefdoms.

gallitcha *Ethiopia.*   OROMO magician-priest.

Galoa *Gabon.*   Myene-speaking ethnic group.

galon *Honduras.*   Unit of weight, equal to 0.8 gallon.

Galong *India.*   Sino-Tibetan language.

Gama *Swaziland.*   Ethnic group classified as late arrivals.

ga mancha *Ghana.*   Principal GA chief of Accra.

Gamashie *Ghana.*   GA of Central Accra.

Gambai *West Africa.* Nilo-Saharan language.

Gambage *Chad.* Major SARA subgroup in Moundou.

gambuh *Indonesia.* Ancient dance-drama in Bali.

gamelan *Indonesia.* Javanese or Balinese percussion orchestra.

Gamit *India.* Indo-European language.

gamonal *Colombia.* Local political party boss.

gamoa *Senegal.* Rite of pilgrimage among the Muslims.

Gan *Burkina Faso.* Ethnic group, branch of the LOBI.

Gan *West Africa.* Ethnic group of the LOBI cluster.

Ganda *Angola.* OVIMBUNDU subgroup.

Ganda *Uganda.* Ethnic group.

gandega *Mauritania.* Ruling group among the SONINKE.

Gangam *West Africa.* Niger-Kordofanian language.

Ganguela *Angola.* NGANGUELA subgroup.

gansa *Nepal.* SHERPA temporary settlement, usually located below a main village.

ganwa *Burundi and Rwanda.* Princes of the royal blood.

gara *Sierra Leone.* Handprinted clothes made from cotton. Also *garri, garra.*

garagu *Rwanda and Burundi.* Serf in a ubuhake relationship.

garesa *Somalia.* Stone building of more than one floor, usually a palace.

Garhwali *India.* Indo-European language.

gari *India.* Cart or carriage.

gari *West Africa.* Toasted cassava flour, a staple dish.

garimpeiro *Brazil.* Prospector for gold and minerals.

garmi *Senegal.* WOLOF term for royal offspring.

Garo *India and Bangladesh.* Sino-Tibetan language.

Garo *India and Bangladesh.* Tribal group.

garra *Sierra Leone.* See GARA.

garri *Sierra Leone.* See GARA.

Garreh *Kenya.* Afro-Asiatic language.

garuda *Nepal.* Mythical man-bird with the body of a man and the wings of an eagle.

gasha *Ethiopia.* Unit of land measurement of varying length.

ga shadip *Burma.* KACHIN earth spirit of fertility.

gato *Ecuador.* Merry COSTA dance.

gaucho *Spanish America.* Cowboy of the southern plains, usually skilled in broncobusting.

gaun *Nepal.* Village.

gaung *Burma.* Head, as in *zay-gaung,* bazaar headman or *ywa-gaung,* village headman.

gaung baung *Burma.* Men's turban made up of a strip of brightly colored silk worn around the head.

gaun sevak *Nepal.* Village development worker.

Gawar *West Africa.* Afro-Asiatic language.

Gawari *India.* Indo-European language.

Gawwade *Ethiopia.* Afro-Asiatic language.

gay *Cameroon.* Patrilineal and patrilocal family.

Gayo *Indonesia.* Austronesian language.

Gayo-Alas *Indonesia.* Sumatran ethnic group.

gaz *India.* Unit of length equal to between 18 and 52 inches.

gazbar *Ethiopia.* Sacristan in an Orthodox church.

gazi *Mauritania.* Plundering raid in which at least 40 camels are employed. Compare MEJBUR.

gazi *Turkey.* Warrior in a JIHAD, or religious crusade.

Gbagyi *West Asia.* Niger-Kordofanian language.

Gbandi *Liberia.* MANDE-speaking people. Also, *Gbande, Bandi.*

Gbanya *Ghana.* GUAN language spoken in Gonja.

Gbaya *Central Africa.* Niger-Kordofanian language.

Gbugbla *Ghana.* People of Prampram, an ADANGBE coastal town.

geadas brancas *Brazil.* Light frost in Sao Paulo and Parana.

gebbar *Ethiopia.* Peasant.

gebbi *Ethiopia.* Residence of an emperor or a provincial chief or noble.

geber *Ethiopia.* Tax paid in kind to the provincial government.

gebere *Ethiopia.* Holder of rist land.

gebo *Burma.* Marriage tax.

gebo *Sierra Leone.* God, among the LOKO.

gede *Haiti.* Voodoo god.

Gedeo *Ethiopia.* Afro-Asiatic language.

geelher *Somalia.* Camp of young unmarried herdsmen and their camels.

geerar *Somalia.* Form of classical poetry with six to eight syllables per line recited in a rapid and lively tempo.

Geez *Ethiopia.* Ancient Semitic language which ceased to be the spoken language of the people after the 10th century but continues to be the liturgical language of the Ethiopian Orthodox Church.

Geledi *Somalia.* Clan of the Rahanweyn family.

Gelo *Vietnam.* Kam-Tai language.

gember *Somalia.* Subclan among the SAAB.

Gen-Gbe *West Africa.* Niger-Kordofanian language.

generale *Bolivia.* Popular dice-poker game.

genna *Ethiopia.* Type of field hockey.

genna *India and Burma.* NAGA generic term for village religious ceremonies.

gens de couleur *Haiti.* Mulattoes.

gente buena or **gente docente** *Spanish America.* Literally, good or decent people. The upper class in rural areas.

gente de razon *Mexico.* Literally, reasonable people. Gentry of status and influence.

gente grauda *Brazil.* The good families.

gente pequena *Spanish America.* Humble people.

gente pudiente *Spanish America.* Powerful people.

gente que tem destaque *Brazil.* People of distinction.

gente regular *Spanish America.* Ordinary people.

genya *Senegal.* Literally, belt. Patrilineage among the WOLOF.

Ge Pano Carib *Honduras.* Language of the CARIB family.

ger *Senegal.* WOLOF term for person of noble birth.

Gera *West Africa.* Afro-Asiatic language.

gerad *Somalia.* Chiefly title among the DAROD.

gerant *Haiti.* Farm manager who receives use of part of the land as his salary.

getem *Ethiopia.* Form of poetry recited or sung to music.

gewel *West Africa.* Resident village oral historian belonging to a low caste known as *nenyo* among the WOLOF. See also *griot.*

ghaffer *Western Sahara.* Collective tribute paid by an entire tribe or fraction.

ghaffir *Egypt.* Guards or messengers.

Ghafir, Bani (singular: Ghafiri) *Oman.* Major ethnic group.

Ghamorro *Guam.* Austronesian language.

ghar *Bangladesh.* Nuclear family.

gharbi *Saudi Arabia.* West wind blowing from the Rub al Khali across Muscat and Oman.

gharry *India.* Carriage or cart drawn by a horse or bullock.

ghat *India.* 1. Mountain, as in Western Ghats. 2. Funeral pyre.

ghatasthapana *Nepal.* Festival of 10 days known as nawaratri, beginning the day of the sowing of the sacred barley.

ghaus *Pakistan.* Preceptor in a Sufi order.

Ghawarna *Jordan.* Dark skinned, socially inferior Arab group.

ghawazi *Egypt.* Public dancing girl.

ghazal *India.* Amorous ode in Hindi or Urdu literature.

ghazal *Arab countries.* Oriental love lyric in which the first two lines rhyme with a corresponding rhyme in the second line of succeeding couplets.

ghazu *Arab countries.* Minor armed raid, as a traditional sport.

ghee *South Asia.* Boiled butter, universally used for cooking.

gheyrat *Iran.* Face-saving, as a social imperative.

ghibli *Libya.* Hot scorching wind that blows across the country from the south.

Ghilzai *Afghanistan.*   Subdivision of PUSHTUNS, including Turans and BURANI.

ghoda jatra *Nepal.*   Festival of the horse with sporting events and chariot races.

Ghomala *West Africa.*   Niger-Kordofanian language.

ghuevo *Haiti.*   Small chamber with an altar for VOODOO worship.

ghurry *India.*   Measure of time equal to 1/60th of a day or 24 minutes. By extension, the water clock or the gong on which the hours are struck.

ghyang *Nepal.*   Buddhist temple of the TAMANGS.

ghybate *Iran.*   Literally, occultation. Hiding into which Shiite IMAMS were forced by persecution from Sunni CALIPHS.

gla-pha *Vietnam.*   Family register or genealogy book.

giao-thua *Vietnam.*   Hour of transition between the old and the new year during TET celebrations.

gia-truong *Vietnam.*   Head of a nuclear family.

Gidar *West Africa.*   Afro-Asiatic language.

Gilani *Iran.*   Ethnic group along the Caspian coast. They are related to Persians, but speak a different dialect.

Gimi *Papua New Guinea.*   Papuan language.

ginasio *Brazil.*   Lower middle school.

Gio or **Dan** *Liberia.*   Eastern branch of MANDE-speaking peoples.

gio lao *Vietnam.*   Literally, winds of Laos. Hot and dry summer wind in the plateaus of the central highlands.

gir *Senegal.*   Father among the WOLOF.

Girasia *India.*   Indo-European language.

Giryama *East Africa.*   Niger-Kordofanian language.

Gisu *Uganda.*   Eastern BANTU ethnic group.

gitgit hanunoo *Philippines.*   Three-string lute similar to the Indonesian rebab.

githaka *Kenya.*   Land jointly owned by members of a lineage, among the KIKUYU.

Giziga *West Africa.*   Afro-Asiatic language.

Glavda *West Africa.*   Afro-Asiatic language.

gnana *India.*   Gnosis. Knowledge as an end in itself.

goo *Somalia.*   Noble, among the SAAB.

Gobaweyn *Somalia.*   Small group of Negroid hunters and cultivators in the Juba River area.

gobernador *Bolivia.*   Literally, governor. Colonial district commissioner.

Gobeze *Ethiopia.*   Afro-Asiatic language.

gobi *Guyana.*   Object imbued with magical power placed in the fields to protect the crops from evil spirits.

gobwein *Somalia.*   Elder, among the SAAB.

gobyar *Somalia.* Assistant to a SAAB elder.

godet *Haiti.* Bowl, used as a unit of measure.

Godie *West Africa.* Niger-Kordofanian language.

godown *South Asia.* Warehouse.

Goemai *West Africa.* Afro-Asiatic language.

gogle *Somalia.* Rural armed constabulary.

Gogo *Tanzania.* 1. Ethnic group in the central region. 2. Niger-Kordofanian language.

Gogadala *Papua New Guinea.* Papuan language.

gogol *Indonesia.* System in which the village as a corporate body owns part of the land.

goja *Nepal.* Conical object made of rice paste used in religious festivals.

Gokana *West Africa.* Afro-Asiatic language.

Gola *Liberia.* Southern branch of West-Atlantic-speaking peoples.

Gola *Sierra Leone.* Ethnic group related to KISSI.

Gola *West Africa.* Niger-Kordofanian language.

Golbal *Chad.* Core social unit among the SARA.

golden foot *Burma.* Royal title.

Golden Stool *Ghana.* Symbol of royal power among the ASANTE.

Golgotas *Colombia.* Radical doctrinaire liberals from 1849 to 1854.

Golin *Papua New Guinea.* Papuan language.

Golo *Sudan.* Sudanic people in the Bahr al Ghazal.

golpe blando *Uruguay.* Soft, bloodless coup.

golpe de cuartel *Spanish America.* Literally, barracks stroke. Military coup.

golpe de estado *Spanish America.* Coup d'etat.

golpismo *Spanish America.* Government by frequent coups.

gomati *India.* Member of a trading caste in Andhra Pradesh.

gombwe *Zimbabwe.* Spirit medium similar to MHONDORO.

gomoa *Ghana.* AKAN group in the Winneba area.

gompa *Bhutan.* 1. Buddhist temple or temple school. 2. Small shrine.

Gomshadzai *Iran.* BALUCHI ethnic group.

gon *Burma.* Virtue derived from the moral content of social relationships.

Gond *India.* Kolarian aboriginal tribe in Gondwana in central India, including the *Chandellas.*

Gondi *India.* Dravidian language.

gong aew *Thailand.* Long, cannon drum.

gongoui or **gong yong** *Thailand.* Large-knobbed gongs.

gong wong yai *Thailand.* Musical instrument with 16 gongs arranged in a circular rattan frame.

Gongya or **Gonja** *Ghana.* GUAN ethnic group.

Gonja *West Africa.* Niger-Kordofanian language.

gonpa *Nepal.*   Lamasery, or lamaistic Buddhist monastery.

gopuram *India.*   Literally, city gate. Pyramidal tower over the entrance gate to a Hindu temple.

goraga *Chad.*   Blood price among the TOUBOU, usually 10 camels.

Goroa *East Africa.*   Afro-Asiatic language.

Gorontalo *Indonesia.*   Austronesian language.

Gorowa *Tanzania.*   Ethnic group.

Gosha *East Africa.*   Ethnic group, along the Shabelle River.

gosha *India.*   Seclusion of women in Hindu or Muslim homes; also, women thus secluded.

goswara *Nepal.*   Office of civil administration.

gotong-rojong *Indonesia.*   Mutual aid and cooperation, usually in the form of unpaid labor exchange in rural areas.

gotra *India.*   Vedic community that followed the sacrificial custom of a particular RISHI or patriarch. Gotras are divided into *gotrakulas* or subgotras, and *ganas* or clans. A direct gotra line is *vamsa* and a collateral branch is *varga.*

gougs *Ethiopia.*   Game of horsemen trying to unseat opponents with long staves.

Gouin *West Africa.*   1. SENUFO tribe. 2. Niger-Kordofanian language.

Goulaye *Chad.*   Nilo-Saharan language.

Goulaye Bara *Chad.*   Subgroup in Moyen Chari.

goum *Algeria.*   Body of armed horsemen.

goum *Mauritania.*   Cameleer.

goum *Morocco.*   Armed band of small Berber military units.

goumiers *Morocco.*   Members of the French security forces in colonial times used to maintain peace and order, train irregular troops, and erect schools and hospitals, etc.

Goun *Benin.*   Ethnic group of Ewe family stock.

gourbi *Tunisia* and *Algeria.*   Traditional mud hut.

gourbiville *Tunisia.*   Shantytown or squatter settlement consisting of mud huts.

gourde *Haiti.*   Monetary unit.

Gourma *West Africa.*   Ethnic group on the right bank of the Niger River. Also, *Gourmantche.* 2. Niger-Kordofanian language.

Gouro *Ivory Coast.*   One of the MANDE peoples. Also, *Koueni, Dipa, Lo* and *Gourunbo.*

gourouna *West Africa.*   TOUBARI and MASSA rite in which men retire for several months from ordinary pursuits and restraints and drink prodigious amounts of milk.

Gourounsi *West Africa.*   Large ethnic group including *Sissala, Kasena, Issala* and *Frafra.*

Gova *Zimbabwe.*   Several unrelated SHONA groups.

Govera *Zimbabwe.*   Branch of the Karanga cluster of the SHONA.

Gowa *Zambia.* Bantu tribe in south central region.

goyigama *Sri Lanka.* Sinhalese high caste.

goyol *Indonesia.* Land tenure system in which a few families hold traditional rights to the village land.

gram *India.* Village.

gramdan *India.* Grant of entire village in the BHOODAN movement.

gram sevaka *India.* Village official.

grandes propriedades *Central America.* Large landowner owning from 350 to 1,750 acres.

grand mufti *Arab countries.* Head of the Muslim clerical establishment, usually the chief ULEMA.

grands blancs *Haiti.* Important whites.

gran fino *Brazil.* Upper class behavior.

granja *Paraguay.* Small farm or ranch.

granjas del pueblo *Spanish America.* State farms.

gran moun *Haiti.* Important person.

granthi *India.* Learned person in SIKH religion, especially an authority on the ADI GRANTH.

grapa *Uruguay.* Pure grape alcohol.

grara *Western Sahara.* Basin or depression in which water collects.

gravana *Sao Tome and Principe.* Dry season from June to September.

Grebo *Liberia.* 1. Kruan-speaking people. 2. Niger-Kordofanian language.

Green March *Morocco.* Four-day walk in 1975 by 350,000 unarmed Moroccan volunteers led by King Hasan into Spanish Sahara to dramatize Morocco's claims.

gremiales *Bolivia.* Generic term for semiskilled artisans, such as carpenters and masons.

gremio *Uruguay.* Guild.

griffon *Haiti.* Offspring of a first generation mulatto and a pure black.

griha *Morocco.* Popular music.

grilero *Brazil.* Land speculator and entrepreneur in jungle regions.

griot *West Africa.* One of a hereditary caste of musician-storytellers who specialize in the oral history and genealogies of a tribe.

Griqua *Zimbabwe.* Ethnic group of KHOI and Afrikaner descent.

griquas *Lesotho.* Collective term for mixed African-Europeans, such as Hottentots.

gris-gris *West Africa.* Leather-bound verses from the Koran carried by Muslims as a phylactery.

gros-bouzain *Haiti.* Gyrating dance performed during carnivals.

gros habitant *Haiti.* Wealthy and influential farmer.

groupement de villages *Francophone Africa.* Group of villages.

grumettas *Guinea-Bissau.* Ship crew making up the lowest rank in the navy.

grupo dinamizadores *Mozambique.* Literally, dynamizing groups. Politically militant groups engaged in indoctrination of rural folks.

Grusi *Ghana.* Collective name for numerous small groups in the northern and upper regions, including KASENA, MO, NUNUMA, SISALA, TAMPOLENSE, and VAGALA.

Grusi *West Africa.* Language of the Gur ethnic group.

Gu *Somalia.* Major rainy season lasting from middle or late March to May or June.

guabina *Colombia.* Dance of the interior highlands.

guacanahua *Bolivia.* Amazon Indian group speaking a TACANAN language in north La Paz department.

guacha *Colombia.* Hollow 15-inch-long hardwood pipe filled with seeds that rattle.

guacharaca *Colombia.* Primitive musical instrument consisting of a hardwood palm with shallow grooves over which the player scrapes a piece of dried bamboo.

Guahibo *Colombia.* Indian language.

guajarapo *Bolivia.* Amazon Indian group in north Santa Cruz department.

Guajiquero *Central America.* Indian dialect, one of the LENCA languages.

guajira *Cuba.* Type of indigenous music.

Guajiro *Spanish America.* Indian language.

Guajiro *Venezuela.* Aborigine of the Guajiro Peninsula.

Guambiano *Colombia.* Indian language.

Guan *Ghana.* KWA ethnic group.

guancasco *Central America.* Reciprocal visit of the patron saints of neighboring towns on their respective feast days.

Guanexicos *Nicaragua.* Aboriginal mountain group speaking a Chondal language in the Segovia Mountains.

Guarambarae *Paraguay.* Indian ethnic group of the GUARANI family.

guarande *Ecuador.* Dance in which the participants wear symbolic masks personifying primitive gods.

Guarani *Spanish America.* Collective term for a number of Indian tribes speaking languages of the Tupi-Guarani stock in Paraguay, Brazil, Uruguay and Argentina.

Guarani *Paraguay.* Monetary unit.

Guarani *Paraguay.* Language, part of the Tupi-Guarani stock.

Guarania *Paraguay.* Lilting and rhythmic music introduced by Jose Asuncion Flores.

guarapo *Colombia.* Drink made from fermented PANELA.

Guarayo *Bolivia.* Amazon Indian group speaking a CHAPACURAN language in Beni and Santa Cruz departments.

Guardia Civil *Costa Rica.* Civil Guard.

guaro *Guatemala.* Sweet drink made from cane.

guarumo *Ecuador.* Musical wind instrument, about six feet in length, into the side of which is fitted a reed mouthpiece.

Guato *Bolivia.* Amazon Indian group in east Santa Cruz department.

Guavanaco *Bolivia.* Indian group of Zamucoan language in Santa Cruz department.

guayabera *Spanish America.* Starched white ribbed shirt-jacket of linen or cotton decorated with buttons and large pockets, usually worn outside the trousers.

guayacan *Panama.* Dance of Guaymi Indian group.

Guaycuru *Spanish America.* 1. Indian tribal group including Mbaya, Abipon, and Toba, once widely distributed in the Chaco region. 2. The language of this group.

Guaymi *Panama.* 1. Indian ethnic group. 2. Micro Chibchan language.

gubayl (singular: qabila) *Yemens.* Tribes.

gube *Zaire.* Minor lineage.

Gubhaju *Nepal.* Priestly caste of Buddhist NEWARIS.

Gude *West Africa.* Afro-Asiatic language.

Guduf *West Africa.* Afro-Asiatic language.

guelowar *Gambia.* Matrilineage among the MANDINGO.

guelowar *Senegal.* Royal lineage among the WOLOF.

guenguence *Nicaragua.* Theatrical production during a FIESTA.

guelta *Western Sahara.* Rocky hollow that collects rain water.

Guere *Ivory Coast.* 1. Ethnic group of the KROU complex. 2. Niger-Kordofanian language.

Guerze *Guinea.* Ethnic group in Nzerekore region. Also, Nguerze, Ngere.

Guhayna *Sudan.* One of the Arab tribes.

Guidar *Cameroon.* Northern ethnic group.

Guin *Burkina Faso.* Ethnic group of SENUFO cluster.

guirises *Honduras.* Rural miners who work alone or in small groups.

guitarron *Mexico.* Oversized guitar which serves as a string bass in an orchestra.

Guiziga *Cameroon.* Northern ethnic group.

Gujar *Pakistan.* Ethnic group in the Punjab.

Gujarati *India.* Indo-European language.

Gujun *Afghanistan.* Indo-European language.

Gujuri *South Asia.* Indo-European language.

Gule *Sudan.* Ethnic group in Darfung.

gulelat *Ethiopia.* Clay object mounted on the top of a hut.

gule wa mkulu *Malawi.* Major tribal dance; also *vinyao.*

gult *Ethiopia.* Principle of land tenure among the AMHARA and TIGRAY under which landowners were empowered to collect taxes.

gumastha *India.* Native clerk, agent or accountant.

gumba *Nepal.* Tibetan-style temple.

gumbo *Ethiopia.* OROMO water and butter jar ornamented with simple designs.

gumbolola *Uganda.* Administrative subdivision.

gumlao *Burma.* Sociopolitical organization of the KACHIN.

gumlao mung *Burma.* District where GUMLAO prevails among KACHINS.

gumrawng gumsa du *Burma.* Literally, boasting chief. Among KACHINS, a nonlegitimate claimant to a chiefdom who establishes a new village on uninhabited land.

Gumuz *Sudan and Ethiopia.* Nilo-Saharan language.

gunda *India.* Hired thug.

Gun-Gbe *West Africa.* Niger-Kordofanian language.

gunruk *Nepal.* Mixture of dried leaves of certain vegetables.

Gunu *West Africa.* Niger-Kordofanian language.

guoc *Vietnam.* Wooden shoes worn in the rainy season to prevent the feet from sinking into the mud. They are made of bamboo roots and held on the foot with a strap.

Gur *Ghana.* 1. Ethnic group comprising MOLE-DAGBANE, GURMA and GRUSI. 2. Voltaic language of the GURMA, TEM, MOLE-DAGBANI, GRUSI AND LOBI.

gur *South Asia.* Black or brown sugar made of sugarcane juice.

Gurage *Ethiopia.* 1. Southern SHONA tribe. 2. Afro-Asiatic language.

Gurenne *West Africa.* Niger-Kordofanian language.

Gurensi *Burkina Faso.* Ethnic group related to *Nankensi* and *Tallensi.*

gurgi *Somalia.* Nomadic hamlet of a few closely related families of the same DIA-paying group.

gurh *Nepal.* Staple food of the SHERPAS, a kind of potato pancake made from raw grated potato, GHEE and spices baked over a hot stove.

Gurkha *Nepal.* Term loosely applied to various ethnic groups, especially MAGAR, GURUNG and RAI. Although of small build, they are tough soldiers, and were recruited by the British to serve in colonial armies.

Gurma *Ghana.* People of northern region, including BASARA, KYAMBA, BIMOBA, MOBA, KONKOMBA.

Guro *Ivory Coast.* Niger-Kordofanian language.

Guronaoco *Mozambique.* Ethnic group.

guru *India.* Spiritual preceptor, especially a teacher of Hindu DHARMA.

guru *Indonesia.* Islamic official.

gurudev *India.* Term of address to a GURU, particularly applied to Indian poet Rabindranath Tagore.

gurudwara *India.* Sikh temple, especially the Golden Temple at Amritsar.

Gurung *Nepal* 1. Tibeto-Nepalese ethnic group. Also, TSHONG. 2. Sino-Tibetan language.

Guruntum-Mbaaru *Nigeria.* Afro-Asiatic language.

Gusii *Kenya.* 1. BANTU group in Kisii district in Nyanza Province. 2. Niger-Kordofanian language.

gusthi *Bangladesh.* Group of patrilineal families. See also PARIBAR.

gutana *Rwanda and Burundi.* Divorce.

guthi *Nepal.* Land, as endowment for rest houses and shrines.

guti (plural: makuti) *Zimbabwe.* CHISHONA word for misty, rainy weather.

guttegna *Ethiopia.* Recipient of a GULT or land grant from the emperor.

Gwandara *Nigeria.* Afro-Asiatic language.

Gwarri *Nigeria.* Ethnic group in Niger State.

Gwe *Uganda.* BANTU ethnic group.

gweng *Kenya.* Land owned by a lineage among the LUO.

Gwera *Uganda.* 1. Eastern BANTU ethnic group. 2. Niger-Kordofanian language.

gyasahene *Ghana.* Head of personnel in the ASANTAHENE'S palace.

gyeh *Korea.* Credit union.

gym-khana *India.* Place for athletics and sports.

Ha *Tanzania.* 1. Third largest ethnic group. 2. Niger-Kordofanian language.

habanera *Cuba.* Rhythmic dance, used by Georges Bizet in *Carmen.*

Habanero *Cuba.* Inhabitant of Havana.

Habasho *Somalia.* Formerly BANTU-speaking Negroid groups who live along rivers.

Habe *West Africa.* FULANI term for all non-Fulani people.

habilitadores *Spanish America.* Labor contractors of the 19th century.

Habisha *Ethiopia.* AMHARA and TIGRAY considered together.

habitant *Haiti.* Landowning farmer.

habus *Maghreb.* Islamic religious endowment or trust, usually real estate. Also *habous.*

hac *Turkey.*   Variant of HAJ.

hacendado *Spanish America.*   Owner of a HACIENDA, or large plantation.

hacendero *Philippines.*   Landowner.

hacienda *Spanish America.*   Large ranch or landed estate. Also the main house on such a ranch or estate.

hackney *India.*   Bullock cart.

hadar *Arab countries.*   Urban or sedentary Arabs as distinguished from nomads.

Haddad *Chad.*   Group of clans, formerly slaves, in northern region.

Haddadin *Syria.*   ALAWITE confederation.

Hadendowa *Sudan.*   One of the Bedawiya-speaking BEJA peoples.

Hadhrami *Yemens.*   Native of Hadhramaut region of Southern Yemen.

Hadimu *Tanzania.*   Ethnic group in Zanzibar.

Hadith *Islamic countries.*   Sayings of Prophet Muhammad.

Hadiyya *Ethiopia.*   1. East Cushitic peoples. 2. Afro-Asiatic language.

Hadjeray *Chad.*   Collective name for Muslim peoples between Mongo and Melfi in south central Chad.

hadr *Oman.*   Variant of HADAR.

hadra *Arab countries.*   Liturgical meeting of a SUFI order in a mosque.

Hadroga *Fiji.*   Austronesian language.

Hadzapi *Tanzania.*   Ethnic group, also called KINDIGA or Tindiga.

haeksim tangwon *North Korea.*   Member of a communist party cell.

hafir *Sudan.*   Artificial reservoir.

haft lang *Iran.*   Literally, seven legs. Confederation of BAKHTIARI tribes.

haga *Somalia.*   Season when the southwest monsoon is blowing, from June or July to September.

haik *Algeria.*   Wraparound garment for women.

Haitian creole *Haiti.*   Hybrid language containing elements of French, English, Spanish and African dialects, spoken by the common people.

haj or **hadj** *Islamic countries.*   Pilgrimage to Mecca, as a ritual obligation for a Muslim, considered one of the five pillars of Islam. Thus, *haji,* one who has completed the pilgrimage.

haji *Islamic countries.*   Muslim who has completed the haj.

hajin *Arab countries.*   Song sung by the BEDOUINS to the rhythm of the camels' gait.

hajirond *Ethiopia.*   Treasurer, or guardian of royal property.

Hajong *India.*   Indo-European language.

hakala *Zimbabwe.*   Divining dice among the SHONA.

hakem *Arab countries.*   Governor of a province.

hakim *Nepal.*   Official of a court of appeal.

hakim *South Asia.*   Physician of the UNANI school of medicine.

hakim *Yemens.*   QADI; judge.

hakk *India.*   Lawful claim, just right, or perquisite established by usage.

Hako *Angola.* MBUNDU subgroup.

hakouma *Sudan.* Title of the khedival administrator in the 19th century.

haksoeng undong *South Korea.* Student activism.

halal *Islamic countries.* Permissible or sanctioned by religious law; kosher.

halalah *Saudi Arabia.* Coin, 1/100ths of a RIAL.

Halang *Vietnam.* 1. Mon-Khmer highland ethnic group in southwest Kontum and neighboring Laos. 2. Austro-Asiatic language.

Halbi *India.* Indo-European language.

halfaBe *Senegal.* Slaves among the TOUCOLEURS.

Halic *Papua New Guinea.* Austronesian language.

halus *Malaysia and Indonesia.* Delicate, polite and sensitive behavior, highly prized by Malays. Opposed to *kaser.*

Hamal *Nepal.* KSHATRIYA caste among the PAHARI.

hamasah *Saudi Arabia.* Fortitude and enthusiasm.

Hamer-Benna *Ethiopia.* Afro-Asiatic language.

Hamite *North Africa.* Relatively dark-skinned people of North and East Africa, including the Egyptians and Berbers. Thus, *Hamitic.*

hammada *Morocco.* Rocky plateau in a desert.

hammam *Islamic countries.* Communal bath.

Hamtai *Papua New Guinea.* Papuan language.

hamulah (plural: hamulat). *Arab countries.* Lineage unit consisting of a group of extended families with a common ancestor and usually occupying a specific quarter in a town.

Hamuni *Yemens.* Ethnic group.

han *Vietnam.* Chinese characters or written language. Also, *chu han, han van.*

Han *Vietnam.* Sino-Tibetan speaking ethnic group in Quang Ninh, Habac, Lang-Son and Ha Giang. Also, *Ngai.*

Hanabalite *Islamic countries.* One of the four schools of Islamic jurisprudence founded by Ahmad ibn Hanabal (died 855). Strongly traditionalist, it represented a back-to-the-Koran movement continued in modern times by WAHHABISM.

Hanafite *Islamic countries.* One of the four schools of Islamic jurisprudence founded by Abu Hanifa (died 776). It is based on analogy in the interpretation of the Koran and is the preferred school in Turkey.

hanat *Morocco.* Guild of craftsmen.

Hande *Angola.* NKHUMBI subgroup.

Hangaza *Tanzania.* Niger-Kordofanian language.

hangul *Korea.* Phonetic alphabet for Korean language.

Hanha *Angola.* OVIMBUNDU subgroup.

Hani *Southeast Asia.* Sino-Tibetan language.

hanif *Islamic countries.*   Old Testament prophets and sages, such as Abraham and Moses, included in Muslim Scriptures.

Hanlik *Philippines.*   Christian ethnic group in Panay Islands.

Hantik *Philippines.*   Minor ethnic group in Visaya.

Hanunoo *Philippines.*   Pagan ethnic group.

hanyak *Korea.*   Traditional system of medicine using herbs and acupuncture.

hao *Vietnam.*   Coin, 1/10th of a DONG.

Hara *Zimbabwe.*   SHONA-speaking people, a branch of the ZEZURU.

harah *Arab countries.*   Section or quarter of a town or village occupied by members of a single lineage.

haram *Libya.*   Landed property belonging to a ZAWAIYA.

haram *Saudi Arabia.*   Literally, sacred and forbidden. Area around Mecca closed to non-Muslims.

harambee *Kenya.*   Literally, pull together. National slogan attributed to Jomo Kenyatta calling Kenyans to work together in nation-building.

Harari *Ethiopia.*   1. Afro-Asiatic language. 2. Ethnic group of AMHARA origin.

haratin *Mauritania.*   Slaves.

Harauti *India.*   Indo-European language.

Harb *Saudi Arabia.*   Ethnic group.

Hareri *Ethiopia.*   Ethnic group.

harijan *India.*   Literally, people of god. Term devised by Mahatma Gandhi to designate untouchables, or the menial castes outside the caste system.

hariq *Sudan.*   Burning of grassland for cultivation.

harissa *Tunisia.*   Hot sauce of red pepper, garlic and salt.

harkat (plural: harakat) *Morocco.*   Formal military expedition by the sultan into dissident territory.

harkis *Algeria.*   Muslim irregular force loyal to France during the struggle for independence.

Haroi *Vietnam.*   Austronesian language.

hartal *India.*   Complete suspension of all public activities as either a mode of protest or a mark of respect to a dead person.

hartani (plural: haratin) *Mauritania.*   Freed man.

hasht nafari *Afghanistan.*   Literally, one in eight. Military conscription system, under which every eighth man between the ages of 20 and 40 was called to obligatory military service.

hashuma *Morocco.*   Literally shame. Misbehavior by women.

hassan *Mauritania.*   Arab upper class also called RAB or ADMA.

Hassaniyya *Mauritania.*   Language derived from Arabic.

hassi *Western Sahara.*   Well between five and 12 meters deep.

Hassouna *Chad.*   Arab tribe.

hasta *Malaysia.*   Unit of length equal to 18 inches.

hat *Bangladesh.*   Periodic market held weekly or biweekly.

hat-a-dao *Vietnam.*   Form of poetry sung to the accompaniment of a DAN DEY, or lute.

hat bai choi *Vietnam.*   Form of musical theater with gestures.

hat boi *Vietnam.*   Classical theater based on Chinese opera with scenery, gestures, orchestra and singing.

hat chea *Vietnam.*   Satirical folk theater with sung verses in the Red River Delta region of North Vietnam.

hat noi *Vietnam.*   Form of HAT-A-DAO.

hat quan-ho *Vietnam.*   Form of singing in which boys and girls exchange dialogue in verses.

Hattam *Indonesia.*   Papuan language.

hat trong quan *Vietnam.*   Form of martial singing.

hau *Vietnam.*   Title of marquis, a rank of nobility.

haud *Somalia.*   Wet-season grazing area in the southern part of north Somalia.

Hausa *West Africa.*   1. Major ethnic group converted to Islam by the FULANI found all over West Africa, but primarily in Nigeria. Prior to FULANI conquest in the 19th century, they were divided into seven independent states, or *Hausa Bokwe:* Biram, Daura, Gobir, Kano, Katsina, Rano and Zaria as opposed to seven "upstart states," or Banza *Bokwe:* Kebbi, Zamfara, Jakun, Nupe, Gwari, Yelwa and Ilorin. 2. Sudanic language of the Hausas.

Haushabi *Yemens.*   Ethnic group.

hava *Costa Rica.*   Standard Indian basket among the CABECARES.

havana *Madagascar.*   Kinsmen.

havildar *India.*   Noncommissioned office equal in rank to a sergeant.

Havu *Zaire.*   Eastern highland ethnic group.

Havunese *Indonesia.*   Austronesian language.

Hawiye *Somalia.*   One of the four SAMAAL clan-families.

Haya *Tanzania.*   1. Ethnic group. 2. Niger-Kordofanian language.

hazam *Arab countries.*   Metal belt worn by women.

Hazaras *Afghanistan.*   DARI-speaking tribe of Turko-Mongolian origin.

Hazaragi *Afghanistan.*   Dialect of the HAZARAS.

Hazarajat *Afghanistan.*   Region extending from the highland of the upper Helmand River on the southern slopes of the Hindu Kush to Herat.

Hazareh *Iran.*   Indo-Iranian ethnic group in Khorasan.

Hazim *Saudi Arabia.*   Ethnic group.

hed boun *Laos.*   The earning of merit by doing good works and giving alms to the clergy, among Buddhists.

heello *Somalia.*   Long lyric poem.

heer *Somalia.*   Collective compact, contract or treaty binding all members of a tribe.

hees *Somalia.*   Modern song influenced by Europeanized Arab music.

Hehe *Tanzania.*   1. Ethnic group. 2. Niger-Kordofanian language.

Helai *Somalia.*   1. Non-Somali people of Baydhaba. 2. Most numerous of the Rahanweya clan.

Hembe *Zaire.*   Ethnic group of southern savanna.

heml *Egypt.*   Unit of weight equal to 249.6 kg.

-hene *Ghana.*   AKAN suffix meaning chief or ruler.

her *Somalia.*   Islamic religious teacher.

herbolario *Philippines.*   Folk healer who uses both herbs and magic.

Herero *Southern Africa.*   1. Ethnic group. 2. Niger-Kordofanian language.

hermit kingdom *Korea.*   Historic name for Korea in medieval times, because of its relative isolation from the rest of the world.

heruka *Nepal.*   Fierce aspect of any of the five major Buddhas.

het *Senegal.*   Mother among the WOLOF.

hidalgo *Bolivia.*   Nobleman, as a term of respect.

higbetsotso *Togo.*   Popular EWE festival around September in the south.

higgler *Jamaica.*   Commercial middleman.

highlife *Liberia.*   Traditional music as influenced by Western pop music.

hijo *Ecuador.*   Form of address to Indian by a HACENDADO.

hijra (plural: hijar) *Islamic countries.*   Immigration or flight, particularly the flight of Muhammad from Mecca to Medina on June 20, 622. The Islamic calendar begins from this event, but was fixed by Caliph Omar on July 16.

hijra (plural hajar) *Arab countries.*   Agricultural oasis settlement.

Hiligaynon *Philippines.*   1. Christian ethnic group in Panayti, Negros, Tablas and Sibuyan. 2. Austronesian language.

Hill Nubians *Sudan.*   Ethnic group.

hilm *Arab countries.*   Combination of magnanimity, tolerance and self-discipline.

hima *Burundi.*   Group of lineages including 30 noble families.

Hima *Rwanda.*   Nilotic ethnic group.

Hina, Bani (singular: Hina'i) *Oman.*   Settled IBADI tribe.

Hinawi *Oman.*   Northern Arab tribe.

Hinayana *Buddhist countries.*   Literally, lower vehicle. One of the two main divisions of Buddhism, also called *Theravada,* or the Way of the Elders. It stresses the monastic way of life as the only path to nirvana and idealizes ARHATS, or saints, who have attained salvation.

Hindi *India.*   One of the two official languages in the Constitution designated as national. It is an Indo-European language written in SAN-

SKRITized DEVANAGIRI characters. Its many dialects are grouped into two main divisions: Eastern Hindi and Western Hindi.

Hinduism *India.* Religious and social system that developed from Brahminism and is based on Vedic scriptures.

Hindustan *India.* Literally, land of the Hindus. Proper term for part of India north of the Vindhyas. Also, BHARAT, *Aryavarsha.*

Hindustani *India.* Term applied to standard vernacular forms of both HINDI and URDU, belonging strictly to Western HINDI. 2. Form of North Indian music.

hinka *Burma.* Thin soup of vegetables boiled with pepper and dried shrimp.

al-Hirth (singular: Harithi) *Oman.* Tribe.

Hispanidad *Spanish America.* Spanishness, as a cultural and social ideal.

Historicos *Colombia.* Doctrinaire conservatives of the 1890s.

hivernage *Mauritania.* Rainy season that lasts from July to September or October.

hiya *Philippines.* Shame or loss of face.

hka *Burma.* JINGHPAW KACHIN word for debt, incurred by an offense.

Hkun *Burma.* Dialect of SHAN, spoken in Kengtung.

hkungri *Burma.* Bamboo altar in front of a KACHIN house.

Hlengwe *Mozambique.* Ethnic group of the TSONGA cluster. Also, *Lhengwe, Hlengue.*

Hlutdaw *Burma.* Supreme Council of State.

Hmar *India.* Sino-Tibetan language.

Hmong *Southeast Asia.* 1. Hill people divided into White Hmong, Blue Hmong and Gua M'Ba Hmong. Also *Miao, Meo.* 2. Sino-Tibetan language.

Hmong Daw *Vietnam.* Sino-Tibetan language.

Hne *Burma.* Oboe-like musical instrument with double reeds, a conical bore with seven holes and a large, loosely hung metal bell.

Ho *India.* 1. Aboriginal tribe. 2. Austro-Asiatic language.

Hoa Hao *Vietnam.* Buddhist sect founded by Huynh Phu-So in 1939. Also known as Phat Giao Hoa Hao.

hoang-de *Vietnam.* Emperor.

hoa vang *Vietnam.* Act of burning imitation or paper money as a sacrifice or offering to an ancestral spirit.

hobatoke *Sierra Leone.* God, among the SHERBRO.

Hobson-Jobson *India.* Corruption of Oriental words through transliteration into English. From Anglicized version of YA HASAN, YA HASAN, chanted by Shiite Muslims during MUHARRAM festival, used to denote any melee.

hoc top *Vietnam.* Reeducation and indoctrination program for former members of the government of South Vietnam.

hoeletsa *Lesotho.* System of relaying messages over long distances.

hoi dong-ky-muc *Vietnam.*   Village council.

hoja maxan *Guatemala.*   Leaf of a broad-leaved plant used for wrapping food.

Hokan *Mexico.*   Ethnic group in the northwest.

holi *India.*   VAISHNAVITE festival of colors celebrated in March universally. Also, *Dol Yatra.*

holi *Zimbabwe.*   Sindebele term for people who are neither SHONA nor NGUNI.

Holli *Benin.*   YORUBA subbranch of the Pobe, south of Ketou.

Holoholo *Tanzania.*   Ethnic group.

Holu *Southern Africa.*   Niger-Kordofanian language.

hombre de confianza *Panama.*   Honorable man.

hommes bons *Brazil.*   Good men or leading citizens.

homowo *Ghana.*   A GA-ADANGBE homecoming festival.

hongo *Burundi.*   Family holding of less than 2.5 acres.

honorable *Liberia.*   Title applied to a member of the Americo-Liberian elite.

hookah *India.*   Tobacco pipe with a long tube by which smoke is drawn through water in a vase and cooled.

horm *Morocco.*   Sacred enclosure around mosques and tombs of certain marabouts.

horma *Western Sahara.*   Tribute paid by low caste tribes to powerful warrior tribes in return for protection.

hormiguillo *El Salvador.*   Key of a MARIMBA.

Hornacheros *Morocco.*   MORISCO community, formerly notorious as highwaymen and pirates.

hospedaria *Brazil.*   Flophouse renting beds on a nightly basis.

hota *Ethiopia.*   Loyalty dance, a group dance with much jumping.

Hotak *Afghanistan.*   GHILAZAI *tribe.*

houngan *Haiti.*   VOODOO priest.

houngenicon *Haiti.*   Male assistant to a VOODOO priest.

houngfor *Haiti.*   VOODOO temple.

hova *Madagascar.*   MERINA commoners.

how *Burma.*   KAYAH sacred building.

howdah *India.*   Seat, often with elaborate trimmings, for riding an elephant.

hoyo *Ecuador.*   Basin or valley between mountains.

hpaga *Burma.*   KACHIN ritual wealth objects, such as swords and spears, used in settlement of legal disputes.

Hpon *Burma.*   Literally, power or glory. Group of agriculturists living on the Irrawaddy between Chamo and Sinbo in northern Burma.

hpongyi-chaung *Burma.*   Monastery school.

Hre *Vietnam.*   1. Highland ethnic group in Quong-Ngai Province. Also, *Kre, Kare.* 2. Austro-Asiatic language.

Hroy *Vietnam.* Highland ethnic group in Phu-Yen and Phu-Bon.

Hsa-Ra *Burma.* Among the PALAUNG, a shaman combining the roles of a diviner and physician.

Hsungywe *Burma.* Ceremonial and communal giving of gifts to monks and monasteries.

hti *Burma.* Umbrella atop shrines, posts and pagodas.

Hting u *Burma.* Chief's house among the KACHIN.

Htinggaw *Burma.* Literally, people under one roof. Household in both the nuclear and extended senses.

htinggaw amying *Burma.* Household name or surname among the KACHINS.

hto k'sa kawk'se *Burma.* The great sacrifice of the KARENS.

Huaca-Tocori *Bolivia.* Highland folk dance mimicking a bullfight.

huachicola *Spanish America.* Cheap, but potent, brandy.

huairo *Ecuador.* Gambling device like a die and the game played with it.

Huambo *Angola.* OVIMBUNDU subgroup.

Huanyam *Bolivia.* Amazon Indian group speaking a CHAPACURAN language in central Beni department.

huapango *Mexico.* Very fast dance performed by couples.

huapango *Mexico.* Folk music shifting from a rapid beat to slow rhythm.

huaraches *Mexico.* Mexican sandals with flat soles.

huasipungo *Spanish America.* Literally, house door. Piece of land assigned formerly to an Indian in partial payment for labor and other services. The system was abolished in 1964.

huasipunguero *Spanish America.* Occupant of a HUASIPUNGO as opposed to a free Indian who owns his own land.

huaso *Chile.* Cowboy.

Huastec *Mexico.* MAYAN language.

Huasteca *Mexico.* Indian tribe.

Huasteco *Mexico.* MAYAN language.

Huave *Mexico.* Huevean language.

huayno *Bolivia.* Popular folk dance of the QUECHUAS.

hubi kanbu *North Korea.* Reserve party cadres.

huerta *Spanish America.* Plot of irrigated and cultivated land.

Huetar *Costa Rica.* Aboriginal Indians of the Chibcha region.

Huichol *Mexico.* 1. Indian tribe. 2. Azteco-Tanoan language.

Huila *Angola.* NYANEKA subgroup.

huinapo *Bolivia.* Flour made from sprouted maize used in making CHICHE.

huipil *Mexico* and *Guatemala.* Sleeveless tunic or blouselike upper garment worn by women. Also, *coton.*

hujra *Saudi Arabia.* Square white silk for covering head.

Hukbalahap *Philippines.*   Communist guerrilla force formerly active in central Luzon. Often, *Huk.*

hukin *Senegal.*   Patrilineage among the DIOLA.

hukm *Islamic countries.*   Order or command.

hukm al badu *Yemens.*   BEDOUIN customary law.

hukm al qabila *Yemens.*   Tribal law.

Huli *Papua New Guinea.*   Papuan language.

Hum *Zaire.*   Ethnic group.

huma *Indonesia.* Intermittently cultivated land in Java.

Humbe *Angola.*   NKHUMBI subgroup.

humita *Ecuador.* TAMALE made from green corn ground into meal and cooked in a steam bath with pieces of pork.

humu (plural: vahumu) *Mozambique.*   Elder chosen as village chief among the Maconde.

humul *Sierra Leone.*   Secret society for women among the MANDE.

Hunde *Zaire.*   1. Ethnic group. 2. Niger-Kordofanian language.

hungry season *Gambia.*   Near-famine conditions just before the harvest season.

Hungu *Angola.*   MBUNDU subgroup.

hun krabok *Thailand.*   Humorous marionette show.

hunsi *Haiti.*   Person initiated into VOODOO rituals.

huntor *Haiti.*   Spirit of the VOODOO drum.

huong oc *Vietnam.*   Village charter.

hurkiya *Nepal.*   Drummer class of untouchables.

Hurutshe *Botswana.*   Subgroup of the TSWANA.

hushiyyah *Arab countries.*   Private army maintained by a shaykh.

huta *Indonesia.*   Toba-Batak settlements.

Hutaym *Saudi Arabia.*   Tribe.

Hutu *Rwanda and Burundi.*   Dominant ethnic group in Rwanda and numerically superior group in Burundi of BANTU origin. Properly *Umuhutu* (plural *Bahutu or Abahutu*). Formerly, general term for slave, vassal or serf.

Huwaqah, al *Jordan.*   Subgroup of the BENI SAKHR tribe.

Huwaytat *Jordan.*   BEDOUIN tribe.

huyen *Vietnam.*   District.

huyuk *Turkey.*   Archeological mound.

huza *Ghana.*   Among the ADANGBE, notably the KROBO, a company or group of individuals who pool their resources to acquire large tracts of land for farming.

huzoor *India* and *Arab countries.*   Literally, the presence. Term of respect used in talking to a master or exalted personage.

hwan *South Korea.*   Coin, $1/100$ths of a WON.

Hwana *Nigeria.*   Afro-Asiatic language.

Hwe Togo.   Niger-Kordofanian language.

Hwela *Ghana.*   DYULA farmers along the Black Volta.
Hyam *Nigeria.*   Niger-Kordofanian language.
hyang pipa *North Korea.*   Lute.
hyanngga *North Korea.*   Folklore literature.
hyodo *North Korea.*   Filial piety.
hyongmyong sasang *North Korea.*   Revolutionary ideology.
hyong piri *North Korea.*   Musical instrument resembling a pipe.

Ibadi *Arab countries.*   Moderate group of KHARADJITES, from Abd Allah ibn Ibad al Murr al Tamimi of the seventh century. The ruling family of Omar belongs to this sect.
Ibaloi *Philippines.*   1. Pagan ethnic group in Neguet Province in north Luzon. 2. Austronesian language.
Iban *Indonesia and Sarawak.*   1. Ethnic group, formerly head hunters. Also, *Sea Dyak.* 2. Austronesian language.
Ibanag *Philippines.*   1. Minor Christian group in Luzon. 2. Austronesian language.
Ibani *West Africa.*   Niger-Kordofanian language.
Ibibio *Nigeria.*   1. Ethnic group related to Ibo. 2. Niger-Kordofanian language.
Ibiheko *Rwanda and Burundi.*   Amulets.
Ibiletwa *Burundi.*   HUTU sharecroppers who were virtual serfs of TUTSI landlords.
Ibimanuka *Rwanda and Burundi.*   Literally, those fallen from the heavens. Legendary ancestors of the TUTSI.
Ibo *Nigeria.*   Major ethnic group, largely Christian, inhabiting south Nigeria on both sides of the Niger River from Port Harcourt to Onisha. They are divided into about 500 independent subgroups.
Ibriyyin (singular: Ibri or Abri) *Oman.*   Large tribe.
ibutho (plural: amabutho) *Zimbabwe.*   SINDEBELE term for a group of men roughly the same age organized as a unit.
ichanyo *Burundi.*   Hillock on which a house is built.
ichege *Ethiopia.*   Head of the Orthodox Church appointed from among the monks of Debra Libanos.
ichu *Bolivia.*   Coarse grass grown in the altiplano used as fodder and as thatch.

icibara (plural: ivyibara) *Burundi.* Piece of land granted to one's superior as a form of tribute.

id al fitr *Islamic countries and India.* Muslim festival commemorating Abraham's sacrifice of Isaac and marking the end of the RAMADAN fast.

Idahan Murut *Malaysia.* Ethnic group in Sabah.

Idakho-Isukha Tiriki *Kenya.* Niger-Kordofanian language.

ider *Ethiopia.* Burial society.

idjaza *Mauritania.* Document setting out the rules and doctrines of an Islamic brotherhood.

idlozi (plural: amadlozi) *Zimbabwe.* NDEBELE term for ancestor spirit.

Idoma *West Africa.* Niger-Kordofanian language.

idono *Burundi.* Musical instrument like a hunting bow with a single taut string pulled against the bow by a ring that is also connected to a bowl-shaped wooden chamber.

Idrisiyyah *North Africa.* SUFI order founded by Ahmad ibn Idris.

idu *North Korea.* Korean script devised by Solch'ong.

Ife *Togo.* Niger-Kordofanian language.

ifoga *Western Samoa.* Local custom as distinguished from law.

Ifugao *Philippines.* 1. Pagan ethnic group in Ifugao Province. 2. Austronesian language.

igacabas *Brazil.* Amerindian burial pots.

Igala *West Africa.* Niger-Kordofanian language.

Igbira *Nigeria.* Ethnic group of northern Nigeria.

Igbo *West Africa.* Niger-Kordofanian language.

Igede *West Africa.* Niger-Kordofanian language.

Iggauen (singular: iggiu) *Western Sahara.* Itinerant bards.

Igitutsi *Burundi.* Language of the TUTSI.

ignames *Congo.* Type of yam.

Igorot *Philippines.* Pagan ethnic group in the mountains north of Luzon.

iguales *Mexico.* Monthly gratuities accepted by journalists from the organizations on their beat.

ihansalem (singular: ahansal) *Morocco.* Line of descendants in the male line of Sidi Said Ahansal.

ihram *Arab countries.* Special white garment consisting of two seamless pieces of which one reaches from the waist to the ankles and the other goes over the shoulders, used by Muslim pilgrims on the HAJ.

ijaha (plural: amajaha) *Zimbabwe.* SINDEBELE term for young man.

Ijaw *Nigeria.* Ethnic group in River and Bendel States.

Ijebu *Nigeria.* Subgroup of the YORUBAS.

ijma *Islamic countries.* Consensus on matters of faith and practice as held by the Islamic community as a whole at any given time.

Ijo *West Africa.*   Niger Kordofanian language.

ijtihad *Islamic countries.*   Individual interpretation of the Koran and Islamic traditions and laws by qualified authorities.

ikhiwa (plural: amakhiwa) *Zimbabwe.*   SINDEBELE for European.

ikhwan *North Africa.*   Literally brother. Member of an Islamic order.

ikhwan al Muslimin *Islamic countries.*   Brotherhood of Muslim warriors founded by King Abd al Aziz.

ikihu sehama *Burundi.*   Wooden flute like a clarinet.

ikinama (plural: ibinama) *Rwanda and Burundi.*   Private or public place where cattle are kept and fed.

ikisagara *Burundi.*   1. Several homesteads of the same extended family. 2. Right to pasture during summer or dry season.

Ikiza *Tanzania.*   Ethnic group.

Ikomo *Tanzania.*   Ethnic group.

Ikwere *West Africa.*   Niger-Kordofanian language.

Ila *Southern Africa.*   Niger-Kordofanian language.

Ilagnum *Philippines.*   Muslim ethnic group of southern Mindanao.

ilaka *Nepal.*   District.

Ilanon *Philippines.*   Moro group in Mindanao.

iler *Gambia.*   Tool with short handle and inverted heart-shaped blade.

illalo *Somalia.*   Rural armed constabulary in former British Somaliland.

ilceler (singular: ilce) *Turkey.*   Districts.

ilkhan *Iran.*   Head of a tribe.

iller (singular: il) *Turkey.*   Provinces.

ilm *Islamic countries.*   Theological knowledge.

Ilocano *Philippines.*   1. Christian ethnic group in Luzon. 2. Austronesian language.

Ilongot *Philippines.*   Pagan ethnic group in east central Luzon.

ilustrado *Philippines.*   Socially and politically influential and wealthy land-holding families.

imam *Islamic countries.*   Worship leader in a mosque.

imamabara *Shiite countries.*   Shia enclosure for celebrating MUHARRAM.

imamah *Iran.*   Belief in IMAMS as successors of Prophet Muhammad.

imamal difa *Islamic countries.*   IMAM hidden or concealed in times of danger or persecution.

imam al muminin *Saudi Arabia.*   Literally, IMAM of believers. Title of Saudi king.

imana *Rwanda and Burundi.*   God conceived as life force.

imazighen (singular: amazir) *Morocco.*   Free BERBERS.

imba *Zimbabwe.*   SHONA house.

imbongi (plural: izimbongi) *Zimbabwe.*   Poet or praise singer.

imeraguen *Western Sahara.*   Fishing people on the south coast.

imgawon *Mauritania.* Caste of musicians.

imizira *Rwanda.* Ritual prohibitions and taboos.

imiziro *Burundi.* Traditional taboos.

imma *Egypt.* White turban.

immatriculation *Francophone Africa.* Registration of EVOLUES, or Africans officially recognized as Europeanized.

immigrado *Mexico.* Permanent residents.

immigrante *Mexico.* Immigrant.

impalampala *Swaziland.* Traditional hunting horn of the Swazi.

impanga *Rwanda and Burundi.* Twins.

impi *Swaziland.* NGUNI term for army.

impi (plural: izimpi) *Zimbabwe.* SINDEBELE term for military force.

imposable *Chad.* Farmer subject to a delivery quota of cotton to the authorities.

imposicion *Spanish America.* Manipulation of electoral process to maintain political power, as in Mexico.

imvyino *Burundi.* Type of group song with a strong beat.

inafectabilidad *Spanish America.* Land exempt from expropriation under land reform statutes.

inahediya *Sri Lanka.* Dancing dress made of silk or velvet adorned with silver ornaments.

inam *India.* Gift.

inama *Burundi.* Place of social or political gathering.

inanga *Rwanda and Burundi.* Zither-like musical instrument with six to eight strings strung across a long flat bowl of bark or wood.

indaba (plural: izindaba) *Zimbabwe.* NGUNI term for parley or discussion.

indare *Burundi.* Land left fallow for a season.

indayog *Philippines.* Special style of musical delivery with a high-pitched voice in a ZARZUELA.

indigena *Guatemala.* Term for Indian in polite language.

indigenat *Francophone Africa.* 1. Person who is not an EVOLUE or assimilated person. 2. System of summary discipline designed to keep natives in subjection.

indigenismo *Spanish America.* Philosophy calling for the integration of Indian culture in the national cultures of South America.

indigenista *Spanish America.* Adherent of INDIGENISMO.

indio *Spanish America.* General term for Indian.

indirimbo *Rwanda and Burundi.* Popular song sung by a person or small group.

inditas, las *Central America.* Traditional dance in which masked couples move to the strains of MARIMBA or guitar.

indlunkulu *Swaziland.* Great hut of a tribal chief decorated with the skulls of cattle sacrificed to ancestors, sometimes also used as a shrine.

indoda (plural: amadoda) *Zimbabwe.* SINDEBELE term for adult man.
indra jalia *Nepal.* Festival in honor of Indra, the god of rain.
induna (plural: izinduna) *Zimbabwe.* Chief of the NDEBELE, leader of an IMPI.
indvuna (plural: tinduvna) *Swaziland.* Royal counselor.
Inenga *Gabon.* Ethnic group along the lower Ogooue River.
ingabe *Burundi.* Sacred cows of the MWAMI.
ingassana *Sudan.* Ethnic group in Darfung.
ingenuos *Brazil.* Free children born to slave mothers.
ingoma *Burundi.* Drum as a symbol of authority.
ingoma *Malawi.* War dance.
ingorore *Burundi.* Obligations in cattle owed to chiefs.
ingulile *Malawi.* Villagers of the same age group.
injera *Ethiopia.* Round, limp, slightly sour bread with a sponge-like texture.
inka *Rwanda and Burundi.* Cow, as the focal point of social life.
Inkala *Southern Africa.* South African political movement among the Zulus.
inkangala *Swaziland.* SISWATI word for the high veld.
inkosi *Malawi.* Paramount chief.
inkosi (plural: amakosi) *Zimbabwe.* SINDEBELE term for king or ruler.
inkosikazi (plural: amakosikazi) *Zimbabwe.* Female equivalent of IN-KOSI.
ino *Haiti.* Group of VOODOO gods.
inquilinato *Colombia.* Single-family urban housing unit, subdivided into spaces for two or more families in which cooking and sanitary facilities are shared.
inquilinos *Spanish America and Philippines.* Land lessees under the HACIENDA system.
insanga *Swaziland.* Marijuana or Indian hemp.
inshoreke *Rwanda and Burundi.* Formerly, female royal attendants and servants.
insila (plural: tinsila) *Swaziland.* Person linked with the king in a special blood ceremony.
institutionalizacion *Cuba.* Incorporation of the (Marxist) revolutionary program in the structure of government and society.
intaba (plural: izintaba) *Zimbabwe.* SINDEBELE term for hill.
intendant *Chile.* Administrative head of a province.
intendencia *Colombia.* Sparsely populated territorial unit under the direct administration of the national government.
intendente *Spanish America.* Administrative head of a district or IN-TENDENCIA in colonial times.
internado *Colombia.* Boarding school.
Intha *Burma.* Sino-Tibetan language.

intizar *Arab countries.*   Religious virtue.

intore *Burundi.*   Men between 25 and 30 years of age.

invasion *Colombia.*   Occupation of public lands by landless peasants or workers.

invasiones *Colombia.*   Squatter settlements.

invasoes *Brazil.*   Shanty towns in the northeast.

invernadas *Brazil.*   Winter grasslands in the south.

invierno *Spanish America.*   Winter season from April through September marked more by lack of rain than cold.

invuna lenkulu *Swaziland.*   Great royal counselor in charge of the capital.

inxwala (plural: izinxwala) *Zimbabwe.*   Annual NDEBELE religious festival.

inyambo *Burundi.*   Cattle owned by the MWAMI or *ganza.*

inyanga (plural: tinyanga) *Swaziland.*   Specialist in handicrafts or any of the professions, especially a herbalist.

inyarwa *Burundi.*   Crops raised on confiscated, abandoned or uninherited land that have reverted to the state or tribal chief.

Inyimang *Sudan.*   Nilo-Saharan language.

inzorezi *Rwanda.*   Woman who grants sexual favors in return for gifts.

inzu *Rwanda.*   All persons, both male and female, who can trace their descent from a common ancestor through three or four generations.

iqub *Ethiopia.*   Credit union.

iradah *Jordan.*   Royal decree.

Iramba *Tanzania.*   Ethnic group.

Iraqw *Tanzania.*   1. Ethnic group south and west of Lake Eyasi. 2. Afro-Asiatic language.

Iraya *Philippines.*   Pagan ethnic group on Mindoro Island.

ird *Arab countries.*   Honor as well as avoidance of disgrace.

irdhi *Buddhist countries.*   In Buddhism, ability to travel through the air.

irifi *Western Sahara.*   Severe sandstorm.

Irigwe *West Africa.*   Niger-Kordofanian langauge.

irmandades *Brazil.*   Roman Catholic lay societies and brotherhoods. In Colonial era, voluntary associations, religious groups and professional guilds.

Iroo *Sierra Leone.*   Natives of the coast of Cape Palmas.

irq *Saudi Arabia.*   Long line of sand.

Isaaq *Somalia.*   One of four SAMAAL clan-families.

Isala *Burkina Faso.*   GOUROUNSI peoples along the Ghana border.

Isamal *Philippines.*   Minor Christian ethnic group on Samal Island.

Isan *Thailand.*   Inhabitant of northeast region.

Isanzu *Tanzania.*   1. Ethnic group. 2. Niger-Kordofanian language.

Isekiri *Nigeria.*   Niger-Kordofanian language.

ishamvu *Burundi.* All the lands owned by an individual.

Ishan *Nigeria.* Ethnic group in Bendel State.

ishe *Southern Africa.* Hereditary chief of a kingdom among the SHONA Karanga.

ishindi *Zambia.* LUNDA chief.

ishtaraki *Arab countries.* Socialist.

isibongo *Southern Africa.* Patrilineal clan among the NGUNI.

isibongo *Zimbabwe.* NDEBELE term for family surname or clan name.

isidlodlo (plural: izidlodlo) *Zimbabwe.* Hair woven into light rings on the heads of NDEBELE and NGUNI men.

isigodlo (plural: izigodlo) *Zimbabwe.* SINDEBELE term for the quarter inhabited by the king's wives.

Isinay *Philippines.* Minor ethnic group in the Luzon.

isla *Paraguay.* Small clusters of trees in the prairie.

Islam *Islamic countries.* Literally submission. Religion founded in the seventh century by Prophet Muhammad and based on the Koran.

Ismaili *Islamic countries.* Heretical Shia sect in Islam who regard Ismail as the seventh IMAM. Known also as the seveners; orthodox Shiites, known as the Twelvers, believe in 12 IMAMS.

Ismailiyyah *Sudan.* SUFI order in Kordofan Province.

Isnag *Philippines.* Austronesian language.

Isoko *West Africa.* Niger-Kordofanian language.

Issa *Horn of Africa.* Clan of the DIR clan-family found primarily in Djibouti.

issadiya *Mauritania.* Offerings and tithes paid to a SHAYKH or head of an Islamic brotherhood.

istiqlal *Arab countries.* Day fixed for visiting friends and relatives.

istunka *Somalia.* Stick fight or mock battle held annually at Afgoy on the Shebelle River.

Isuwu *West Africa. See* BIMBIA.

Itatin *Bolivia.* Amazon Indian group speaking a GUARANI language in Santa Cruz department.

Itawit *Philippines.* Austronesian language.

Ite *Bolivia.* Amazon Indian group speaking a CHAPACURAN language in central Beni department.

itegeko *Rwanda and Burundi.* Labor or produce owed to chief as tribute or tax payment.

Iteso *Kenya.* 1. Nilotic speaking ethnic group.

Ithas *Burma.* Shan ethnic group.

Itonama *Bolivia.* Amazon Indian group in east Beni department.

Itongo *Rwanda and Burundi.* Produce of the field.

Itoreauhip *Bolivia.* Amazon Indian group speaking a CHAPACURAN language in central Beni department.

Itsekiri *Niberia.* Ethnic group in Bendel State.

Ivatan *Philippines.*   1. Christian ethnic group of Batanes and Babuyan islands. 2. Austronesian language.

Ivbie *Nigeria.*   Niger-Kordofanian language.

Iwa *Southern Africa.*   Ethnic group.

iwei *Angola.*   Coin, ¹⁄₁₀₀ths of a KWANZA.

Ixiama *Bolivia.*   Amazon Indian group speaking a TACANAN language in north La Paz department.

Ixil *Central America.*   1. Maya tribe. 2. Mamean linguistic group.

ixim *Central America.*   Maize.

iyaite *Nepal.*   Secular marriage.

iylaq *Afghanistan.*   Pasturelands in high altitudes used by nomads for grazing.

iyluw *Burma.*   Hereditary priesthood of the KAYAH.

Izere *Nigeria.*   Niger-Kordofanian language.

Izarguien *Western Sahara.*   Large nomadic TEKNA tribe.

izibongo *Zimbabwe.*   NDEBELE term for praises.

Izi-Ezaa-Ikwo-Mogo *Nigeria.*   Niger-Kordofanian language.

izzat *India.*   Honor as the menstruum of social relationships.

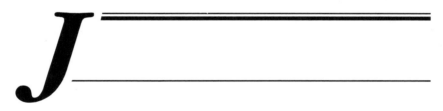

Jaaliyin *Sudan.*   One of the two large groups of Arab tribes.

jabal *Arab countries.*   Mountain.

Jabar Khayal *Afghanistan.*   GHILAZAI tribe.

jacal *Mexico.*   Primitive hut made of mud and brush or cornstalk.

Jacaltec *Central America.*   Maya tribe.

Jacalteco *Guatemala.*   Mayan language.

Jacaria *Bolivia.*   Amazon Indian group in east Beni and Santa Cruz departments.

Jack-Jack *West Africa.*   Variant of ALLADIAN.

jaggery *South Asia.*   Sugar confection made from palm sap.

jagir *India and Pakistan.*   Large estates granted as a royal favor.

jagirdar *India and Pakistan.*   Holder of JAGIRS.

jaguay *Ecuador.*   Popular song form set to the strokes of scythes at harvest time.

Jahadilah, al *Saudi Arabia.*   Tribe.

jahaliyah *Arab countries.*   Ignorance, especially in religious matters.

jai alai *Mexico.* Properly, *juego de pelota.* Game like handball played on a walled court with a hard ball caught and thrown with a wicker basket attached to the arm.

Jai Hind *India.* Literally, victory to India, or Hindustan. National slogan, especially during the struggle for independence.

Jain *India.* Practitioner of JAINISM.

Jainism *India.* Non-BRAHMINistic religion established by Mahavira around 500 B.C. It shares similarities with both Hinduism and Buddhism, particularly with the former regarding transmigration of souls and with the latter regarding asceticism and nonviolence.

jaisi *Nepal.* BRAHMIN among the PAHARI.

jaiwa *Burma.* Literally, saga teller. KACHIN priest.

Jaji *Afghanistan.* GHILAZAI tribe.

jajmani *India.* System of reciprocity built into social relationships.

jakat *Bangladesh.* Variant of ZAKAT. Almsgiving.

Jakun *Malaysia.* 1. Major ethnic cluster divided into Land Jakun and Sea Jakun and including: Somalais, Semok Beris, Mah Meris, Orang Selitas, Orang Kualas, Orang Bukat, Temuan, Belands, Mantera, Biduanda, Orang Ulu, Orang Kanaq, Udai, and Orang Laut. 2. Archaic form of Malay.

jalabiya *Arab countries.* Long-sleeved, flowing loose robe.

jalapena *Mexico.* Type of spicy cheese with peppers.

Jallaba *Sudan.* Small merchants and traders.

jalle *Somalia.* Comrade; since 1971 title of all members of Supreme Revolutionary Council.

jam *India.* Title borne by certain native princes of Kathiawar.

jam *Senegal.* Slaves among the WOLOF.

jamaha (plural: jamahayo) *Somalia.* Agricultural community established by an Islamic brotherhood.

jamahiriya *Arab countries.* 1. Republic (variant spellings). 2. In Libya, used as a synonym for people's power.

Jama Mapun *Philippines.* MORO group on Cagayan islands.

jambiya *Arab countries.* Short dagger with curved blade, worn at the waist.

jambur *Senegal.* WOLOF term for freeborn persons.

Jamden *Indonesia.* Austronesian language.

jampan *India.* Sedan chair with two poles borne on the shoulders of four men.

Jamshidi *Afghanistan.* See CHAHAR AIMAK.

Jamshidi *Iran.* Indo-Iranian ethnic group in Khorasan.

Janabah (singular: Junaybi) *Oman.* Nomadic tribe.

janai purni *Nepal.* Festival of changing the sacred thread worn by BRAHMINS across their chests, celebrated on the day of the full moon in the month of Shrawan.

janaka *India.* A type of RASA.

jandarma *Turkey.* Gendarmerie.

jangada *Brazil.* Balsa wood raft with canvas sail; thus, *jangadeiros.*

janggano *Zimbabwe.* Reciprocal work.

janpan *India.* Type of sedan or portable chair carried by two pairs of men in hill stations.

japti *India.* Sequestration of land for nonpayment of rent or taxes.

Jara *West Africa.* Afro-Asiatic language.

jarabe tapatio *Mexico.* National folk dance in which a man in a CHARRO or cowboy suit and a woman in a CHINA POBLANA circle a large SOMBRERO.

jaraf *Senegal.* Title of a provincial chief.

Jarai *Indochina.* 1. Subgroup of KHMER LOEU. 2. Austronesian language.

jarana *Mexico.* 1. Small guitar. 2. Staccato dance of Yucatan.

Jarawa *West Africa.* Niger-Kordofanian language.

jardin infantile *Colombia.* Kindergarten.

jarib *Afghanistan.* Unit of area equal to 0.5 acres.

jaspe *Central America.* Method of dyeing thread.

jat *Guyana.* Any ethnic group or community.

Jat *India and Pakistan.* Martial group in northern India, including both Hindus and SIKHS.

Jatakas *India.* One of the sacred books of Buddhism.

Jatapu *India.* DRAVIDIAN language.

jati *India.* Tribe in the Hindu social organization.

jatiya *Nepal.* Modified form of the caste system.

Jatiya Sangsad *Bangladesh.* National legislature.

jatra *India and Bangladesh.* Plays performed outdoors.

Jatt *Pakistan.* Baluchi ethnic group.

Jaunsari *India.* Indo-European language.

Javanese *Indonesia.* Austronesian language.

jawan *India.* Common soldier.

Jawi *Malaysia.* Arabic script in which BAHASA MALAYSIA is sometimes written.

jaxanke *Senegal.* Ethnic group of MALINKE origin, noted as fanatic Islamic proselytizers.

jaysh *Morocco.* Tribe, especially Hilalian Arab tribe, exempted from land taxes in return for military service.

Jazairiyah *Algeria.* Official Arabic name for Algeria.

jebala *Morocco.* Tribal group in the Rif region.

jecas *Brazil.* Lower class rural people in Sao Paulo.

jeepney *Philippines.* Colorfully decorated and painted taxi holding up to 10 passengers.

jefatura *Central America.* Residence of the JEFE, or chief.

jefe *Spanish America.* Civil or military chief.

jefe maximo *Spanish America*   Supreme chief.

jefe politico *Spanish America*   Political chief of a canton.

jefe supremo *Panama*   Supreme chief of the National Guard.

Jeh *Vietnam*   Austro-Asiatic language.

jeito *Brazil*   Way of getting around regulations or systems.

jeitoso *Brazil*   Wheeler-dealer.

jellaba *Chad*   Sudanese Nilotic traders.

jemaa *Morocco*   BERBER tribal council.

jemadar *India* and *Pakistan*   Title of second rank of native officers in a company of sepoys.

Jemala *Sudan*   Camel nomads of the GUHAYNA tribe.

jemba *Malaysia*   Unit of length equal to 144 ft.

jemma *Morocco*   Annually selected council of local tribal leaders.

jengkal *Malaysia*   Unit of length equal to nine inches.

Jera *West Africa*   Niger-Kordofanian language.

Jere *Tanzania*   Subgroup of NGONI.

jeri *Senegal*   Pular term for land watered only by rainfall.

jerib *Afghanistan*   Unit of area equal to half an acre.

jeshn *Afghanistan*   Celebration of Afghan independence.

jey khampa *Bhutan*   Title of the head of the DRUK KARGUE monastic order.

jezzail *Afghanistan*   Rifle fired from a forked rest.

Jha *Nepal*   BRAHMIN caste of NEWARis.

Jhangar Kumkale *Nepal*   Minor ethnic group.

Jharra *Nepal*   Pure-blooded CHETRI caste.

jheel *India*   Marsh or shallow lake.

jhum *South Asia*   Fields cultivated by swidden, or slash-and-burn farming techniques, especially among the Nagas.

jibbah *India*   Long cotton shirt, usually worn outside.

Jibu *West Africa*   Niger-Kordofanian language.

Jie *Uganda*   Eastern Nilotic ethnic group.

Jicaque *Central America*   Indian tribe.

Jicara *Central America*   Calabash cup decorated with simple carvings made from the fruit of the jicara tree.

jiffo-paying group *Somalia*   Kin responsible for paying or receiving blood money in case of a homicide.

jiifto *Somalia*   Classical form of poetry with short lines broken in the middle by a pause.

jihad *Islamic countries*   Holy war against infidels.

jihaz *Arab countries*   Bridal gifts.

Jiji *Tanzania*   Ethnic group.

jilacata *Bolivia*   Chief of an AYMARA Indian community.

jilal *Somalia*   Hot, dry, dusty season of the northeast monsoon, from December to March or April.

jilla or **zilla** *India and Nepal.* Subdivision of an ILAKA, or district.

jina *India.* In JAINISM, victor or savior, especially, *Jina,* name applied to Mahavira Vardhamana, founder of JAINISM.

Jinga *Angola.* MBUNDU subgroup.

jingal *India.* Small portable piece of ordnance mounted on a swivel.

Jinghpaw *South Asia.* Tibeto-Burmese ethnic group.

Jingpo *Burma.* Sino-Tibetan language.

Jinja *Tanzania.* Niger-Kordofanian language.

jinocuao *Nicaragua.* NAHUATL term for a sacred tree.

jipijapa *Panama.* Panama hat, made from the fine, white fiber of the jipijapa palm.

Jirel *Nepal.* Minor ethnic group.

jirgah *Afghanistan and Pakistan.* Tribal council or assembly among the PUSHTUNS or PATHANS.

jirib *Afghanistan.* Unit of area equal to half an acre.

Jita *Tanzania.* 1. Ethnic group. 2. Niger-Kordofanian language.

Jivaro *Ecuador.* Primitive Indian tribe of the ORIENTE.

jiziya *Islamic countries.* Poll tax levied on non-Muslims by Muslim rulers.

Jju *West Africa.* Niger-Kordofanian language.

jnana *India.* Knowledge, especially esoteric knowledge gained through the Tantras and Scriptures. See TANTRISM.

jnana marga *India.* Metaphysical path of salvation through the acquisition of knowledge.

joala *Lesotho.* Strong beer made from sorghum.

jobs *Congo.* Native dance.

jocha *Spanish America.* Tax or levy for holding a FIESTA.

jodhpurs *India.* Riding breeches of heavy cloth fitting closely at knees and ankles.

jogo de bicho *Brazil.* Lottery in which animals serve as symbols in place of numbers.

Jola *Gambia.* Ethnic group related to the SERER.

Jola *Senegal.* Ethnic group in area around the Casamance River.

Joluo *Sudan.* Nilotic ethnic group.

jongo *Gambia.* Slaves among the Mandingo.

Jongor *Chad.* Afro-Asiatic language.

joola or **jhula** *India.* Rude form of suspension bridge.

jora *Ecuador.* Sprouted corn used as chief ingredient in the preparation of CHICHA.

jornalero *Spanish America.* Day laborer in rural areas or farms.

joropera *Venezuela.* Full skirt of brightly colored cotton or other material.

joroporo *Venezuela.* National ballroom dance.

joshi *India.* Astrologer.

jothishyam *India.*   Casting of horoscopes; by extension, astrology.

jour ouvert *Trinidad and Tobago.*   Pre-carnival festivity with crowds shuffling in time to music.

jowar *South Asia.*   Sorghum or millet.

Juang *India.*   Austro-Asiatic language.

Jucumani *Bolivia.*   Indian group in Potosi department.

jueces *Spanish America.*   Judges.

juez de canton *Central America.*   Chief of a CANTON.

juez de instruccion *Paraguay.*   Judge who investigates a case and obtains evidence preliminary to a trial.

juez de mesta *Central America.*   Chief of a COMARCA.

juiz de paz *Brazil.*   Justice of the peace.

jugujugu *Honduras.*   BLACK CARIB celebration with dancing.

Juhayna *Sudan.*   One of the two large groupings of Arab tribes in the Sudan based on traditional genealogies.

juhhal *Syria.*   Ignorant mass of DRUZE, as distinguished from the elect.

juis *Afghanistan.*   Open water ditch for irrigation, drinking, cooking and washing clothes.

juiz *Malawi.*   Chief, judge or leader.

Jukun *West Africa.*   Niger-Kordofanian language.

Jukun Wukari *West Africa.*   Niger-Kordofanian language.

Jula *West Africa.*   Niger-Kordofanian language.

Julaha *Pakistan.*   Low caste of weavers.

juma *Afghanistan.*   Friday, the Muslim sabbath.

jumaah menteri *Malaysia.*   Cabinet.

Jumba *Gabon.*   Ethnic group along the Ogooue River.

jumbe *East Africa.*   Literally, lord. Title of head of Arab slave-trading principality.

jumma *India.*   Total assessment of land revenue from an estate.

jumma bundee *India.*   Determination of the amount of land revenue due for a year.

Junam *Uganda.*   Western Nilotic ethnic group.

jundi *Saudi Arabia.*   Private in the Saudi army. Also, *jundi jadid.*

jungpen *Bhutan.*   Governor or chief of a DZONG.

junjun *Gambia.*   Small drum used by the WOLOF to announce the arrival of a chief.

junta municipal *Paraguay.*   Municipal board.

juntes receptores *El Salvador.*   Supervisory council in a polling place.

Jur Modo *Sudan.*   Nilo-Saharan language.

jusi *Philippines.*   Textile made of banana plant fibers.

jutka *India.*   Literally but ironically, quick. Horse-drawn cab in Tamil Nadu resembling a box with open ends.

juzgado *Spanish America.*   Court.

juzgado de distrito *Central America.*   District council.

juzgado de partido *Spanish America.* Territorial court of first in-stance.

juzgado letrado *Spanish America.* Single-judge court in rural areas.

jyaaBe (singular: jyaado) *Senegal.* Lower stratum of slaves among the TOUCOLEURS.

Jyapu *Nepal.* Agricultural rural caste of SUDRAS.

Kaa *Botswana.* Ethnic group.

kaabah *Islamic countries.* Most sacred place of Islam in Mecca, a small structure containing a black meteorite in the Great Mosque.

Kaba *West Africa.* Nilo-Saharan language.

Kababish *Sudan.* Camel-herding Arab tribe of the JUHAYNA group in the Kordofan.

kabaka *Uganda.* Title of the ruler of Buganda.

kabari *Nigeria.* Brass trumpet.

kabaro *Ethiopia.* Drum made from a wood bowl with skin stretched over one of the ends.

Ka'b, Bani (singular: Ka'bi) *Oman.* Tribe.

Kabenda *Zambia.* Congolese LUNDA tribe in the Luapula Valley.

Kabile *Turkey.* Tribe.

Kabinah *Jordan.* Subgroup of the BEDOUIN tribe Beni Sakhr.

kabir, al *Senegal.* Pilgrimage to Mecca; HAJ.

Kabiya *West Africa.* Niger-Kordofanian language.

kabja *India.* Blouse.

Kabole *Somalia.* Non-Somali group along the Shabelle River.

Kabre *West Africa.* Ethnic cluster comprising Kabre, *Losso, Lamba, Tamberma, Mossi* and *Logba.*

kabujang *South Korea.* Heads of households.

kabupaten *Indonesia.* Former administrative division.

Kabyle *Algeria.* 1. Major BERBER tribe in the Kabylie Mountains. 2. Afro-Asiatic language.

kacccherie *South Asia.* Government office.

Kachchi *India.* Indo-European language.

Kachhwaha *India.* RAJPUT tribe of Jaipur and Amber.

kachim bet *Chad.* Lineage group among Arabs.

Kachin *Burma.* Mongoloid, mostly animist people. Also *Jinghpaw.*

kadah *Egypt.* Unit of weight equal to 1.7 litres.

kadala *Chad.* Titles of the chiefs of Doza clans of the TOUBOU.

Kadara *West Africa.* Niger-Kordofanian language.

Kadavu *Fiji.* Austronesian language.

kadayan *Sabah.* *See* BRUNEI.

Kadazan *Malaysia.* 1. Ethnic group in Sabah. 2. Austronesian language.

kading *Philippines.* Brass mouth harp among the IBOLO.

kadjidi *Chad.* Small ethnic group of former slaves.

kadkudah *Iran.* Village headman or tribal leader.

kadmul *Chad.* Green turban, symbol of authority among the TOUBOU and TOMAGHERA clans in northern region.

Kado *Mali.* Ethnic group.

Kadu *Burma.* Eastern upland Tibeto-Burman ethnolinguistic group of wet-rice cultivators.

Kadugli *Sudan.* Niger-Kordofanian language.

kafaa *Yemens.* Equality.

Kaffir *Southern Africa.* Term applied to Bantu speakers, especially the southern NGUNI.

kaffis (singular: kfiz) *Tunisia.* Volume equal to 5.6 hectoliters.

kaffiyah *Arab countries.* White or checkered cotton cloth, about four-feet square, folded into a triangle and worn with two points falling over the shoulders and a third hanging down the back. Also, *shutra.*

Kafima *Angola.* OVAMBO subgroup.

kagana *Chad.* Formerly, the royal counselors.

Kagayanen *Philippines.* Austronesian language.

kagisano *Botswana.* Traditional TSWANA notion of peace, harmony and unity.

Kagula *Tanzania.* Niger-Kordofanian language.

Kaguru *Tanzania.* Ethnic group in Kilosa and Mpwapwa.

Kagyutpa *Bhutan.* One of the Red Hat orders of Tibetan Buddhism.

Kahe *Tanzania.* Ethnic group.

kahinat *Ethiopia.* Clergy in the Ethiopian Orthodox Church, including priests, deacons and some monks.

Kahluri *India.* Indo-European language.

kahtein *Burma.* Large-scale gifts to the Buddhist SANGHA.

kaigama *Chad.* Title of commander in chief in the army of Karnem-Bornu empire.

Kaikadi *India.* DRAVIDIAN language.

Kaili *Indonesia.* Austronesian language.

kaimakan *Turkey.* Administrator of a county.

kaimal *India.* Title of a NAIR chief in Kerala.

kain *Indonesia.* BATIK sarong.

kaing *Burma.* System of cultivation along rivers and streams.

kaingin *Philippines.* Swidden, or slash-and-burn cultivation.

Kajang *Malaysia.* Ethnic group in Sarawak.

kajawah *India.* Litter or pannier used in pairs on camels.

kaka *Central African Republic.* BAYA ethnic group in Upper Sangha.

kakanin *Philippines.* Dessert made with rice dough.

kaki *Malaysia.* Unit of length equal to one foot.

Kakism *Congo.* Cult founded by Simon M'Padi who claimed to be Kimbangoui's heir, so called because of the khaki uniforms worn by its adherents. Also, *N'Gounzism.*

Kako *West Africa.* Niger-Kordofanian language.

Kakwa *Central Africa.* 1. Eastern Nilotic ethnic group. 2. Nilo-Saharan language.

kala *Burma.* Foreigner, as a term of reproach.

Kala *Zaire.* Ethnic group.

Kalabit *Sarawak.* Austronesian language.

kalabule *Ghana.* General term for corruption and antisocial activities including graft, smuggling, hoarding, embezzlement and black marketeering.

Kalagan *Philippines.* Austronesian language.

kalak *Central African Republic.* Title of kings of WADAI.

Kalaka *Botswana.* Ethnic subgroup.

kalaleng or **tongali** *Philippines.* Nose flute in northern Luzon.

Kalam *Papua New Guinea.* Papuan language.

kalambaan *Senegal.* Political chief of a caste of woodworkers among the TOUCOLEURS.

Kalamian *Philippines.* Christian ethnic group of Calamian Islands.

Kalanga *Southern Africa.* 1. SHONA-speaking ethnic group. 2. Niger-Kordofanian language.

Kalanga *Zimbabwe.* One of the six main clusters of the SHONA language; also known as Western Shona.

kalantar *Iran.* Leader of a subtribe.

kal baisakhi *Bangladesh.* Literally, the calamities of Baisakh. The month of April characterized by storms and hurricanes.

Kalbiyah *Syria.* ALAWITE confederation.

kalenda *Trinidad and Tobago.* Dance of African origin.

Kalenjin *East Africa.* 1. Ethnic cluster of seven subgroups: *Kipsigis, Nnandi* (including *Terik*), *Tugen Elgeyo, Pokot, Marakwet* and *Sabaot* (including *Kony* and *Pok*). 2. Nilo-Saharan language.

kalesa *Philippines.* Horse-drawn buggy of Luzon.

kalibit *Philippines.* KALINGA harp of bamboo.

kalifa *Turkey.* Variant of CALIPH.

Kaliko *Zaire.* Nilo-Saharan language.

kalima *Islamic countries.* Muslim creed.

Kalinga *Philippines.* 1. Pagan IGOROT group. 2. Austronesian language.

kalinga *Rwanda and Burundi.* Royal drum, the symbol of TUTSI authority.

Kali Yuga *India.* Era dated from 3102 B.C. Also YUDDHISTHIRA ERA.

Kalki *India and Nepal.* Incarnation of VISHNU as destroyer of the world.

kal kidan *Ethiopia.* Civil marriage.

Kallahan *Philippines.* Austronesian language.

kalok hoe *Burma.* Literally, family spirit. Among MONS, a kin group of all male members of a given lineage.

kalolak *Senegal.* Village quarter inhabited by the DIOLA.

kalpa *India.* Cosmic period in Hinduism consisting of one cycle of creation and destruction of the world, equal to 8.64 billion years.

kalpul *Guatemala.* QUICHE public magistrates.

Kalundwe *Zaire.* Ethnic group.

Kama *India.* God of love in Hinduism.

Kamadia *Chad.* Subgroup of the TOUBOU.

kamango *Malawi.* Goblet-shaped drum.

Kamano *Papua New Guinea.* Papuan language.

Kamar *India.* DRAVIDIAN language.

Kamba *Congo.* Subgroup of KONGO.

Kamba *Kenya.* 1. Central Bantu group in Eastern Province. 2. Niger-Kordofanian language.

Kambari *West Africa.* Niger-Kordofanian language.

Kambatong *Philippines.* Coconut shell guitar among the IBALOI.

Kambera *Indonesia.* Austronesian language.

Kami *Nepal.* Metalworking class among the untouchables.

Kami *Tanzania.* Niger-Kordofanian language.

kamis *Ethiopia.* Full-length, wide-sleeved cotton gown, sometimes embroidered on the front and back and tied around the waist with a string.

kamitua *Indonesia.* Head of a hamlet.

kammis *Pakistan.* Class of craftsmen.

kamnan *Thailand.* Headman of a commune or TAMBON.

kampung *Indonesia.* Urban quarter or neighborhood.

Kam Tai *Thailand.* Name by which the Lu are known.

Kamuku *West Africa.* Niger-Kordofanian language.

kamveu *Cameroon.* Hereditary council of notables that advised the FONS or BAMILEKE chiefs.

Kamwe *West Africa.* Afro-Asiatic language.

kan *South Korea.* Standard unit of measure equal to 64 to 81 sq ft.

kan *Burma.* Composite of destiny, fate and luck determining the moral balance sheet of Buddhists.

Kana *West Africa.* Niger-Kordofanian language.

Kanauji *India.*   Indo-European language.

Kanauri *India.*   Sino-Tibetan language.

Kanbu (plural: kanbu dul) *North Korea.*   Party cadre.

kanda *Congo.*   Clan.

Kanda *Congo.*   Ethnic group.

kandingan *Philippines.*   Muslim wedding dance in which the knees are bent outward and the fingers held stiffly together.

Kanembu *Chad.*   Literally, people of the south. Group in northeast, also found in Nigeria and Niger.

kang *Burma.*   Among Chinese SHANS, villages grouped as administrative units.

kangal *Senegal.*   WOLOF term for the nobility.

Kangwane *Swaziland.*   Native name for Swaziland.

Kangyaga *West Africa.*   See BUILSA.

Kanhobal *Central America.*   MAYA tribe.

kani *Congo.*   Headman in MBOSHI ethnic group.

kanimba or **kayumba** *Sierra Leone.*   God, among the VAI.

Kaniok *Zaire.*   Ethnic group.

Kanjari *India.*   Indo-European language.

kanji *India.*   Water in which rice has been boiled.

Kanjobal *Central America.*   MAYAN language.

Kankanaey *Philippines.*   Austronesian language.

Kankanai *Philippines.*   Pagan IGOROT group.

Kannada *India.*   DRAVIDIAN language, official language of Karnataka State.

Kano *Guinea.*   MANDE-speaking ethnic group.

kanongesha *Zambia.*   Title of LUNDA chief.

kansuksa chansung *Thailand.*   Higher education.

kantar *Arab countries.*   Unit of weight varying from 346.5 lb to 99 lb, according to the produce.

kantiba *Ethiopia.*   Mayor.

kanu *Sierra Leone.*   God, among the LIMBA.

kanungo *India.*   Register of a TAHSIL.

Kanuri *West Africa.*   1. Ethnic group, descendants of the MAGUMI clan of KANEMBU and ZAGHAWA intermixed with Sao. Also, *Bornuane.* 2. Nilo-Saharan language.

kanwa *India.*   Hindu sage.

kanwatphon kansuksa *Thailand.*   School examination.

Kanyok *Zaire.*   Niger-Kordofanian language.

kanzo *Haiti.*   Ordeal by fire as a VOODOO rite.

kanzu *East Africa.*   Loose shirt of Arab origin that extends almost to the ground.

Kaonde *Southern Africa and Zaire.*   1. Congolese ethnic group. 2. Niger-Kordofanian language.

Kaone *Zaire.*   Ethnic group of southern savanna.

kapente *Zambia.* Painted women.

kaperraj *Central America.* Cloth covering used to cover foodstuffs, or as a scarf. Also, *perrajes.*

kapikulular (singular: kapikulu) *Turkey.* Literally, slaves of the state. Ottoman military corps. Christian boys collected as tribute in the Balkans, converted to Islam and trained by the army.

kapitan *Malaysia.* Headman of a Chinese enclave.

kapok *Ghana.* Silk cotton tree.

kapr *Sierra Leone.* Magistrate among the TEMNE.

Kapsiki *Cameroon.* 1. Northern ethnic group. 2. Afro-Asiatic language.

Kapuibo *Bolivia.* Amazon Indian group of PANOAN language in north Beni department.

kapuva or **kapurala** *Sri Lanka.* Priests serving lesser gods in Buddhism.

Kara *Central African Republic.* Ethnic group in Upper Kotto and Birao.

Kara *Tanzania.* Ethnic group in the Lake Victoria region.

Karaboro *Burkina Faso.* 1. Ethnic group along Ivory Coast border; branch of the SENUFO. 2. Niger-Kordofanian language.

karachakan *Thailand.* Civil servant.

karamat *Morocco.* Miracles attributed to the MARABOUTS.

karamokho *Senegal.* Spiritual leader among the MANDING and SARAKOLE.

Karang *West Africa.* Niger-Kordofanian language.

Karanga *Southern Africa.* SHONA-speaking ethnic group.

Karanga *Zimbabwe.* Dialect of SHONA; also Southern Shona.

Karangaa *West Africa.* Nilo-Saharan language.

karani *Burundi.* System of training young royal attendants.

Karava *Sri Lanka.* Fisherman caste, largely Christian.

karazana *Madagascar.* Extended family.

Kardecism *Brazil.* Spiritist cult founded by Alain Kardec.

Karekare *West Africa.* Afro-Asiatic language.

Karen *Burma.* Large, partly Christian, ethnic group of the SHAN States and the dominant group in Karenni State and in the coastal plains of lower Burma and Tennasserim. The two largest Karen subgroups are *Sgaw* and *Pwa.*

Karen *Southeast Asia.* Sino-Tibetan language.

karez *Pakistan and Afghanistan.* Tunnel connecting a series of shafts sunk into a mountainside and leading to the valley bottom.

Kari *West Africa.* Niger-Kordofanian language.

karigo *Malawi.* One-string lute played with a bow.

Karinya *Venezuela.* Indian tribe.

karma *India.* Mechanism that regulates the functioning of the chain of life, specifically, a blind force, like the law of gravity, that determines one's position in life and also the tendency of that life to good or evil.

Karmali *India.* Austro-Asiatic language.

Karnataka *India.* One of the two major forms of Indian music—the other being Hindustani. It is dominant in the south.

Karomjong *Uganda.* 1. Eastern Nilotic ethnic group. 2. Nilo-Saharan language.

kaross *Zimbabwe.* Blanket made of animal skins.

Karya *India.* Conduct of life, as part of TANTRA.

karyenda *Burundi.* Sacred drum.

kasaba *Turkey.* Town.

Kasai *Zaire.* Ethnic group.

kasar *Malaysia.* Literally, rough or crude. Abrasive or uncultured behavior as opposed to HALUS.

Kasem *West Africa.* Niger-Kordofanian language.

Kasena *Ghana.* GRUSI group in the Upper Region.

Kasena *West Africa.* Ethnic group of GOUROUNSI cluster.

kasettrakam *Thailand.* Agriculture.

Kashmiri *India.* Indo-European language.

Kasiguranin *Philippines.* Austronesian language.

kasma *Algeria.* Party council.

Kasma (plural: kasmaat) *Algeria.* Governing body of FLN (National Liberation Front) composed of elected committees from all party cells.

kason nyaung ye *Burma.* Festival held early May on the full moon day of Kason marking the birthday, enlightenment and nirvana of the Buddha.

kassabah *Egypt.* Unit of length equal to 12.6 meters.

Kasseng *Laos.* Austro-Asiatic language.

Kassonke *Mali.* Niger-Kordofanian language.

kat *Arab countries and Somalia.* Mild narcotic, derived from the leaves of the kat, or QAT, plant, universally chewed.

Katab *West Africa.* Niger-Kordofanian language.

Katanga *Zaire.* Ethnic group in Katanga Province.

katar *India.* Short dagger.

katcha *India.* Raw or unfinished, as opposed to pukka.

katcheri *India.* Court.

katchi-katchi *Congo.* Native dance.

kateeb *Maldives.* Village headman.

katha *India.* Type of entertainment in Maharashtra consisting of a narrative recitation interspersed with music and singing.

kathak *India.* Popular semiclassical story-dance of north India consisting of five elements: *angika* or posture, *mudra* or hand movement, *abhinaya* or mime, *gati* or gliding movement, and *tatkar* or foot movement.

kathakali *India.* All-male folk pantomime and dance played al fresco, often extending from sunset to dawn. The stylized postures and gestures of the actors are accentuated by grotesque masks.

kath al kitab *Iraq.* Signing of the marriage contract.

kathen *Cambodia.* Festival during which gifts are presented to the Buddhist monks.

Kathir, al (singular: Kathiri) *Oman.* Large tribe of eastern Arabia.

kathowbow *Burma.* Sacred poles of the KAYAH peoples, made of straight trimmed teak, often 40 feet high, and a foot or so in diameter.

kati *Malaysia.* Unit of weight equal to 21 oz.

katiba *Western Sahara.* Unit of the Sahrawi Popular Liberation Army, the military wing of the Polisario Front.

katiba *Yemens.* Battalion.

katikiro *Uganda.* Title of the prime minister of Buganda.

katipulle *Sri Lanka.* Sinhalese high caste.

Katla *Sudan.* Niger-Kordofanian language.

Katu *Indochina.* Austro-Asiatic language.

Katu *Vietnam.* Highland ethnic group along the Laos border.

kaubure *Kiribati.* Magistrate.

Kaugel *Papua New Guinea.* Papuan language.

Kaum *Afghanistan.* Major tribe.

kauman *Indonesia.* SANTRI, or orthodox Muslim, quarter in town.

kauoman ni beretitenti *Kiribati.* Vice president.

kaupule *Vanuatu.* Magistrate.

kava *Polynesia.* Drink made from the root of an arrowroot plant.

kavir *Iran.* Salt crest in the Central Plateau.

kaviraj *India.* AYURVEDIC physician.

Kawari *India.* Indo-European language.

Kawi or **Ekaws** *Burma.* Ethnic group.

Kawi *Indonesia.* Old Javanese language written in PALI alphabet but with SANSKRIT admixture. Classical poetical and prose works were written in this language between 11th and 14th centuries.

kaya *Malaysia.* The wealthy class.

Kayah *Burma.* Ethnic group, formerly, Red Karens or Karennis.

kayaing *Burma.* Territorial unit, as a district or division.

Kayan *Brunei.* Austronesian language.

Kayan *Malaysia.* Ethnic group, part of Bahan in Sarawak.

kayasth *India.* Important Hindu subcaste in north India.

Kayla *Ethiopia.* See FALASHA.

kayon *Indonesia.* Leaf-shaped, intricately carved leather symbol of a supernatural being in a WAJANG.

kazaler (singular: kaza) *Turkey.* Counties as unit of local administration.

kazembe *Zambia.* Royal titles for persons who helped the LUNDA gain control over the salt deposits of the upper Lualaba.

kazhakam *India.* In south India, a political party.

kazi *Sikkim.* 1. Hereditary nobility. 2. *Islamic countries.* Judge and registrar.

ke *Cameroon.* Special dance among the BAMILEKE marking transition to adulthood.

keba *Burma.* Village reserved for outcastes and beggars.

kebaja *Indonesia.* Tight, lowcut, long-sleeved blouse.

kebaro *Ethiopia.* Two-headed tympani.

kebe *Mauritania.* MARABOUT of the first rank.

kebele *Ethiopia.* Urban neighborhood association.

Kebumtamp *Bhutan.* Sino-Tibetan language.

kebyar *Indonesia.* New style of dance made popular by Mario in the 1920s.

keddah *India.* Enclosure constructed to entrap elephants.

kedest *Ethiopia.* Second circle in an Orthodox church for communicants.

Kefa *Ethiopia.* Afro-Asiatic language.

kefetegna *Ethiopia.* Urban group or association. See KEBELE.

keftanya *Ethiopia.* Group of six to 12 KEBELES.

Kekchi *Central America.* One of the MAYAN dialects making up the KEKCHIAN language group.

Kekchian *Central America.* Linguistic group of the Proto-Guatemala-Yucatan language family of the MAYAN cluster.

Kela *Zaire.* Niger-Kordofanian language.

Kelabit *Malaysia.* Ethnic group in Sarawak.

Kelabitic Muruts *Indonesia.* Ethnic group of Kalimantan.

kelay *Afghanistan.* Small village.

Kele *Zaire.* Niger-Kordofanian language.

kella *Egypt.* Unit of measure equal to 3.63 gallons.

keluarga *Malaysia.* Group of close kin to whom one is obliged for social benefits.

kelurahan *Indonesia.* Administrative village.

Kemak *Indonesia.* Austronesian language.

kemanjah *Morocco.* Stringed instrument.

Kembat *Ethiopia.* 1. East Cushitic peoples. 2. Afro-Asiatic language.

ken or **khen** *Burma.* Mouth organ among the LAHU.

Kendari *Indonesia.* Austronesian language.

Kenga *Chad.* 1. Subgroup of the HADJERAYS. 2. Nilo-Saharan language.

kente *Ghana.* Cloth woven in long bands about four inches wide and sewn together to form a toga with colorful patterns and designs.

kentiba *Ethiopia.* Office of mayor.

Kenuzi-Dongola *Sudan and Egypt.* Nilo-Saharan language.
Kenyah *Malaysia.* 1. Ethnic group, part of Bahan in Sarawak. 2. Austronesian language.
Kenyang *Cameroon.* Niger-Kordofanian language.
Kenyi *Uganda.* Eastern BANTU ethnic group.
Keopara *Papua New Guinea.* Austronesian language.
kepala *Indonesia.* Head or leader.
kepaladaerah *Indonesia.* Local executive chief.
ker *Senegal.* WOLOF term for house or compound; by extension, a family.
Kera *West Africa.* Afro-Asiatic language.
kerar *Ethiopia.* Lyre with six to 10 strings.
kerdja bakti *Indonesia.* Community service.
Kereba *Tanzania.* 1. Ethnic group. 2. Niger-Kordofanian language.
Kerere *Tanzania.* Tribe in Lake Victoria region.
ketjamatan *Indonesia.* Subprovince.
Kerinchi *Indonesia.* Austronesian language.
Kete *Zaire.* Ethnic group.
ketjapi *Indonesia.* Boat-shaped plucked zither.
ketu *Brazil.* Ceremonial official who circumcises children in African rites.
ketua kampong *Malaysia.* Village headman.
Kewa *Papua New Guinea.* Papuan language.
Keyo *Kenya.* KALENJIN ethnic group on the western bank of the Kerio River.
Kgatla *Botswana.* Early offshoot of HURUTSHE. Also BAKGATLA.
kgotla *Botswana.* Enclosure in a village that serves as courthouse, town hall and forum. It is usually under the control of the tribal chief.
kha *Laos.* Slave.
khadder *India.* Handspun cotton that symbolized, during the struggle for independence, economic self-sufficiency. Also, *khadi.*
khaen *Thailand.* Musical instrument in the northeast made of several bamboo pipes.
khaima *Western Sahara.* Tent made of goat or camel hair.
khaiyatin *Syria.* An Alawite confederation.
Khajon *Bangladesh.* Tribal group.
Khalaj *Iran.* Ural-Altaic language.
khalasi *India.* General outdoor servant; also, artilleryman.
khalat *Afghanistan.* Great coat with long sleeves, usually embroidered.
khalifa *West Africa.* Head or ruler. Also *alifa.*
khalom *Senegal.* Type of lute with resonator made of a gourd.
Khalsa *India.* Brotherhood of militant SIKHS into which members are initiated through the ceremony of PAHUL, or baptism, which consists

of eating sweet buttered flour. All members of the Khalsa bear the name of Singh.

khalwa *Sudan.* Village Koranic school.

Kham *Nepal.* Sino-Tibetan language.

Khambu *Nepal.* Division of RAI.

khammis *Algeria.* Sharecropping arrangement in farms owned by absentee landlords.

khamsah *Arab countries.* Lineage composed of all patrilineal kinsmen within five generations.

khamsin *Arab countries.* Hot wind blowing north from the Sahara during fall and winter. Shortened form of rih al khamsin, wind of 50 days.

Khamti Shan *Burma.* Shans living in Khamti, an extensive rice plain.

khamu *Nepal.* Means of transportation consisting of two baskets suspended from ropes from either end of a yoke and carried over the shoulder.

khan *South and Central Asia.* Literally, lord or prince. Title of Muslim rulers; by extension a title of respect.

khana kromakan changwat *Thailand.* Provincial advisory board.

khanarathamontri *Thailand.* Cabinet or council of ministers.

khanate *South and Central Asia.* Principality of a Khan.

Khandesi *India.* Indo-European language.

khaniqat *Iran.* Tomb of a dead SUFI saint.

khanjar *Oman.* Large covered dagger.

khanum *South and Central Asia.* Wife of a KHAN.

khanum *Turkey.* Lady of rank, especially, the chief lady of a harem.

khao *Thailand.* Food crop, usually meaning rice.

khao phansa *Thailand.* Rainy season from July to October.

khaophot *Thailand.* Maize.

khao vong *Vietnam.* Celebration other than religious or traditional festivities.

Kha Punoi *Laos.* Austro-Asiatic language.

Kharadjite *Islamic countries.* Literally, to go out. The first dissident sect to split from the main body of Islam over the claims of Ali. They were persecuted by both Shiites and Sunnis.

kharaj *Arab countries and India.* Tax or tribute levied on non-Muslims by Muslim rulers.

kharaj *Arab countries.* Houses and fields.

Kharia *India.* Austro-Asiatic language.

kharif *India.* Crop sown at the beginning of the rainy season. Compare *rabi.*

Kharoti *Afghanistan.* GHILAZAI tribe.

Kharus, Bani (singular: harusi) *Oman.* Small tribe of western Hajur.

kharwar *Afghanistan.* Unit of weight equal to 1,180 lb.

Khashm bet *Sudan.* Literally, threshold of a house or tent. Subclan of Omadiyyah tribe.

Khasi *India.* 1. Aboriginal tribe. 2. Austro-Asiatic language.

khasiya *Nepal.* BRAHMIN group among the PAHARI.

Khassonke *Mali.* Ethnic group.

khatib *Malaysia.* Reader in a mosque.

Khatmiyyah *Sudan.* SUFI order founded by M. Uthman al Mirghani in early 19th century.

Katri *Nepal.* Kshatriyya caste among the PAHARI.

Khatri *India.* Subcaste of the Kayasthas in Rajasthan, Punjab and Uttar Pradesh.

Khaybar *Saudi Arabia.* Tribe in the Hejaz.

khayl *Afghanistan.* Lineage.

khazana *India.* Public treasury in the charge of a KHAZANCHI.

khazanchi *India.* Official in charge of the state treasury.

khbar *Western Sahara.* A kind of oral news bulletin.

kheda or **keddah** *India.* Enclosure for entrapping elephants.

khedive *Egypt.* Former title of a Turkish ruler or viceroy.

khel *India and Burma.* Among the Nagas, division of a village.

khene *Laos.* Seven-tone wind instrument made from bamboo.

kherif *Chad.* Season of heavy rains from mid-July to mid-September.

khet *Cambodia.* Province.

khidmutgar *India.* Male waiter.

khilat *India.* Dress of honor presented by a superior on ceremonial occasions.

khir *Pakistan.* Sweetened boiled milk.

Khirwar *India.* DRAVIDIAN language.

Khmer *Cambodia.* 1. Native people of Cambodia, variously described as Caucasoid, DRAVIDIAN or Mongoloid. 2. Austro-Asiatic language of Mon-Khmer stock, the national language of Cambodia.

Khmer Krom *Cambodia.* Ethnic Khmer.

Khmer Loeu *Cambodia.* Upland group of the KHMER.

Khmu *Thailand and Laos.* 1. Mon-Khmer highland group. 2. Austro-Asiatic language.

khoa-Cu *Vietnam.* Triennial civil service examinations.

khoi *Zimbabwe.* Hottentot.

Khoisan *Southern Africa.* Group of African languages, including Bushman languages and Hottentot, characterized by the use of click sounds.

khoja *Iran and South Asia.* Title of Iranian Shiite Muslim noble.

Khojah *Iran and South Asia.* ISMAILI group that follows the Aga Khan.

khom *Vietnam.* Subdivision of a hamlet.

khon *Thailand.* Masked classical form of Thai dance drama.

Khona *India.* Kolarian aboriginal tribe in central India. See also KOL.

khong vong *Laos.* Sixteen cymbals arranged on a semicircular frame of wood or cane.

Khorasani *Iran.* Ural-Altaic language.

Khorat Thai *Thailand.* Descendants of Khmer women and Thai soldiers.

Khos *Pakistan.* Mountain group in Chitral district in North West Frontier Province.

khotla *Lesotho.* Village meeting place where the chief hears disputes and renders judgments.

khoueng *Laos.* District or province under the jurisdiction of a chao khoueng.

Khouloughlis *Libya.* Literally, sons of servants or slaves. Caste of mixed Turkish and Arab parentage in Tripolitania.

khoum *Mauritania.* Coin, ¹⁄₁₀₀ths of an OUGUIYA.

Khowar *Pakistan.* Indo-European language.

khru *Thailand.* Teacher.

Khua *Vietnam.* See CUA.

Khugiani *Afghanistan.* GHILAZAI tribe.

khukri *Nepal.* Broad, curved knife or short sword carried around around by the GURKHAS.

khulafa (singular: khalifa) *Morocco.* Overseers of wards in a town.

khum *Cambodia.* Commune.

khun *Thailand.* Polite form of address, such as Mr. or Mrs.

khunto *Malawi.* Cylindrical drum.

khurd *Afghanistan.* Unit of weight equal to 0.25 lb.

khuskhus *India.* East Indian grass used for making mats and screens.

khutbah *Arab countries.* Engagement.

khutbah *Islamic countries.* Friday sermon in a mosque.

khuwe *Mauritania.* Female initiate in an Islamic brotherhood.

khuwwah *Arab countries.* Protection money paid by the weaker tribe to the stronger.

khuy *Laos.* Flute.

khwan *Thailand.* Soul or spirit as distinguished from the body.

khyal *India.* Form of love song devised by Sultan Hassan Shah Sharqui of Jaunpur.

khyrat *Afghanistan.* Large amount of food given to the poor during festivals.

kia *Zimbabwe.* One-room hut for African servants behind European houses.

kibbe *Saudi Arabia.* Diced meat.

Kibet *Chad.* Nilo-Saharan language.

kiblah *Islamic countries.* Direction toward the KAABAH at Mecca toward which Muslims turn when praying .

Kibse *West Africa.* Ethnic group of NINISI cluster.

kich or **kich noi** *Vietnam.*   Play or drama.

kifle hagers *Ethiopia.*   Administrative region.

Kiga *Uganda.*   Western BANTU ethnic group.

kigabuo *Burundi.*   Circle of ritual trees to mark royal graves.

Kikongo *Angola.*   Language of the KONGO tribe.

Kikuyu *Kenya.*   1. BANTU-speaking ethnic group of central Kenya with many independent subgroups ruled by local elders. 2. Niger-Kordofanian language.

kila *India.*   Fortress.

kiladar *India.*   Commander of a fortress.

kilang *Philippines.*   Alcoholic drink made from sugarcane in Bisayan.

Kilba *West Africa.*   Afro-Asiatic language.

kili *Sri Lanka.*   Ritual impurity attributed to women in the time of menses, childbirth or puberty.

Kilwa *Tanzania.*   Dominant tribe until the 15th century.

kimbanda *Angola.*   Diviner or herbalist who can communicate with spirits.

Kimbanguism *Southern Africa.*   Quasi-Christian black messianic cult founded by Simon Kimbangu in 1921.

Kimbu *Tanzania.*   1. Ethnic group. 2. Niger-Kordofanian language.

Kimbundu *Angola.*   Language of the Mbundi.

kimchi *Korea.*   National dish, a highly seasoned mixture of pickled cabbage, onions and other vegetables.

Kim Il Sung chuui *North Korea.*   Kim Il Sungism, or Communist philosophy of production associated with Kim Il Sung. Also, *hyong myong sasang.*

Kim Il Sungism *North Korea.*   See CHUCH'E SASANG.

kimpolo *Burma.*   Literally, tiger skin. Article of clothing worn by chief dignitaries in winter as a mark of honor in north Burma.

kin *Burma.*   Village guard.

kina *Papua New Guinea.*   Monetary unit.

Kinaray-A *Philippines.*   Austronesian language.

Kindiga *Tanzania.*   Ethnic group.

Kinga *Chad.*   Collective name for a number of ethnic groups near Mongo and Melfi.

Kinga *Tanzania.*   1. Ethnic group. 2. Niger-Kordofanian language.

king amphoe *Thailand.*   Subdistrict, unit of AMPHOE.

kip *Laos.*   Monetary unit.

kipande *Kenya.*   Personal registration of Africans introduced after World War I.

Kipat *Nepal.*   Ethnic group.

kipat *Nepal.*   Untaxed land owned in common among the Tamang.

Kipirse *Burkina Faso.*   Ethnic group of the NINISI cluster.

Kipsigis *Kenya.*   Largest KALENJIN ethnic group.

kiranga *Burundi.* Ancestral heroes of a clan who serve as spirit mediators.

Kirantis *Nepal.* Collective name for the RAIS and LIMBUS.

Kirdi *Cameroon.* Pagan ethnic group speaking a FULFULDE language.

Kirghiz *Afghanistan.* Turkic Mongolian people, a majority of whom live in the Soviet Union in the Kirghiz Republic.

Kiribati *Kiribati.* Austronesian language.

Kirifi *West Africa.* Afro-Asiatic language.

kiri-kiri *Congo.* Native dance.

Kiriwina *Papua New Guinea.* Austronesian language.

kirtan *India.* Devotional song in Bengal.

Kirundi *Burundi.* Language of Burundi, related to Kinyarwanda, part of the BANTU subgroup of the central branch of the Niger-Congo family.

kisaeng *Korea.* Geisha.

Kisama *Angola.* MBUNDU subgroup.

kisan *India.* Farmer.

Kishanganjia *India.* Indo-European language.

kishka *Ecuador.* QUECHUA interpreter in legal and other matters.

Kishtwari *India.* Indo-European language.

Kisii or **Gusii** *Kenya.* BANTU-speaking ethnic group.

kissaniaat *Morocco.* Separate markets within Muslim quarters, usually enclosed by gates.

Kissi *Liberia.* Ethnic group in the upper Lofa County.

Kissi *West Africa.* Sudanic-speaking people, principally in Sierra Leone. Also, *Gissi.*

kist *India.* Any of the installments in which land revenue is payable to the state treasury.

kiswah *Saudi Arabia.* Ornate, gold embroidered black damask cover of the KAABAH.

kitab *South Asia.* Book.

kitchen kaffir *Zambia.* Pidgin used by Europeans and Asians in communicating with Africans.

Kitemoka *Bolivia.* Amazon Indian group of CHAPACURAN language stock in central Beni department.

kitman *Arab countries.* Among KHARADJITES, dissimulation or concealment in times of persecution and danger.

kitmatgar *India.* Servant who serves meals and waits at tables.

Kituba *Zaire.* Niger-Kordofanian language.

kiya *Islamic countries.* Analogical reasoning used to interpret the Koran or *Hadith* (the sayings of Muhammad).

Kizilbash *Afghanistan.* Tribe.

kkoktuk-Gaksi *North Korea.* Puppet play.

Klaoh *West Africa.* Niger-Kordofanian language.

klong *Thailand.*   Any of the latticework of canals in central Thailand.

klongthad *Thailand.*   Thick, large drum.

klui *Thailand.*   Bamboo flute.

kmungo *North Korea.*   Harp.

knobkerrie *Zimbabwe.*   Stick with a heavy knob at one end.

ko *Burma.*   Literally, brother. Form of address between equals; *koko,* if intimate.

Koalib *Sudan.*   Niger-Kordofanian language.

kobi raj *Bangladesh.*   Village physician. Compare KAVIRAJ.

kobo *Nigeria.*   Coin, ¹⁄₁₀₀ths of a naira.

koch *India and Bangladesh.*   Sino-Tibetan language.

Koda *India.*   Austro-Asiatic language.

Kodaga *India.*   KSHATRIYA subcaste in Coorg.

Kodagu *India.*   DRAVIDIAN language.

Kodi *Indonesia.*   Austronesian language.

Kodoy *Chad.*   Branch of the Meba clans north of Abeche in Ouadai.

kofia *Kenya.*   Small embroidered hat.

Kofyar *West Africa.*   Afro-Asiatic language.

Koho *Vietnam.*   1. Ethnic group in Ho Chi Minh and Khanh-Hoa. 2. Austro-Asiatic language.

Kohumono *West Africa.*   Niger-Kordofanian language.

koji *South Korea.*   Labor in repayment of loans of money or food.

Kokomba *Ghana.*   GURMA group in the northeast.

Kol *India.*   1. Kolarian aboriginal tribe of Chota Nagpur. 2. Unclassified language.

Kolami *India.*   DRAVIDIAN language.

kolan *Sri Lanka.*   Folk drama.

Kolana-Wrsin *Indonesia.*   Papuan language.

Kolarian *India.*   KOL language.

kolas *Philippines.*   Type of music made by striking together two pieces of iron, among the IBALOI.

Koli *India.*   1. Tribe in central India. 2. Indo-European language.

kolla *Bolivia.*   1. Highland Indian. 2. Relating to the highlands. Compare CAMBA.

kolla *Ethiopia.*   Hot zone consisting of the Danakil depression, lowlands of Eritrea, eastern Ogaden and the tropical valleys of the Blue Nile and the Tekezi River.

Kom *Cameroon.*   Ethnic subgroup of the TIKAR people.

Koma *Sudan.*   Ethnic group in Darfung.

Koma *Sudan and Ethiopia.*   Nilo-Saharan language.

Komba *Papua New Guinea.*   Papuan language.

Komo *Zaire.*   1. Ethnic group. 2. Niger-Kordofanian language.

Komono *Burkina Faso.*   Ethnic group of the SENUFO cluster.

kompang *Philippines.*   Work gang or community.

komveu *Cameroon.* Advisory council among the BAMILEKE.

Kon *Cameroon.* Niger-Kordofanian language.

Konagi *Senegal.* Ethnic group related to the BASARI.

Konda *Zaire.* Ethnic group.

Konda-Dora *India.* DRAVIDIAN language.

kondoism *Kenya.* Armed robbery by organized gangs.

Kongo *Southern Africa.* 1. BANTU-speaking people dominant in Angola, Zaire and western parts of southern Africa. Also, *Bakongo.* 2. Niger-Kordofanian language, spoken by the Kongo. Also, *Kikongo.*

kongsan tachak *North Korea.* Communist party colleges.

kongsen *Indonesia.* Corporate land ownership by a village.

kongsi *Malaysia.* Chinese organization or society in which all members work together dividing living costs and sharing profits.

kongthom *Cambodia.* Set of tuned bronze bowls arranged in a semicircular frame.

Konianke *Guinea.* Forest ethnic group in Beyla region.

konifa *Saudi Arabia.* Highly sweetened pastry.

Konjo *Indonesia.* Austronesian language.

Konjo *Uganda.* 1. Western BANTU ethnic group. 2. Niger-Kordofanian language.

Konkani *India.* Indo-European language, related to KANNADA.

Konkomba *West Africa.* 1. Ethnic group of the MOSSI cluster along the Oti River. Also, *Kpunkpamba.* 2. Niger-Kordofanian language.

Kono *Sierra Leone.* 1. Ethnic group in Kono district. 2. Niger-Kordofanian language.

Konongo *Tanzania.* 1. Ethnic group. 2. Niger-Kordofanian language.

konor *Ghana.* Paramount chief of the KROBO.

Konso *East Africa.* Afro-Asiatic language.

koochi *Afghanistan.* Nomad, used pejoratively.

Koozime *Central Africa.* Niger-Kordofanian language.

kopje *Zimbabwe.* Small hill or granite outcropping.

Kor *Vietnam.* See CUA.

kora *Guinea.* Lute-harp consisting of a large calabash and long wooden pole with three to six metal or fiber strings, played by GRIOTS.

korale *Sri Lanka.* District.

Koran *Islamic countries.* Literally, recitation. Muslim scripture with 114 chapters.

Koranko *Sierra Leone.* Ethnic group.

korao *Madagascar.* Literally, young men. Migrant workers.

korbaj *Egypt.* Labor levy.

Korean *Koreas.* Ural-Altaic language written in a 15th-century phonetic script.

Korekore *Zimbabwe.* SHONA-speaking ethnic group.

Koro *Nigeria.* Niger-Kordofanian language.

Korop *West Africa.*   Niger-Kordofanian language.

Korwa *India.*   Austro-Asiatic language.

kos *India.*   Measure of distance equal to two miles.

kot *Nepal.*   Royal court or assembly.

kota *Indonesia.*   Municipality.

Kota *Central Africa.*   Niger-Kordofanian language.

Kota *Gabon.*   Ethnic group in the northeast.

Kote *Zaire.*   Ethnic group.

kotoko *Ghana.*   Privy council of the ASANTE.

Kotoko *West Africa.*   Ethnic group.

Kotokoli *Togo.*   Ethnic cluster comprising Kotokoli, *Bassari* and *Tchamba.*

Kotoko-Logone *West Africa.*   Afro-Asiatic language.

Kotoku Akyem *Ghana.*   One of the branches of the AKYEM in the eastern region.

kotwal *India.*   Former title of a superintendent of a police station.

Kougni *Congo.*   Subgroup of the Kongo.

Kouka *Chad.*   Ethnic group in Batha Prefecture, subgroup of the LISI.

Koulango *Ivory Coast.*   Ethnic subgroup of the Voltaic people.

Kouranko *Guinea.*   Forest ethnic group of Kissidougou region.

kourdiala *Senegal.*   Patrilineage among the SERER.

Kouri *Chad.*   Sahelian ethnic group.

Kovareka *Bolivia.*   Amazon Indian group in central Beni department.

koy *Chad.*   The uninitiated among the Sara.

koy *Turkey.*   Village as a unit of local administration.

Koya *India.*   DRAVIDIAN language.

koya *Malawi.*   Unit of weight equal to 2,419 kg.

koyin *Burma.*   Novices in a monastery.

kpe *Cameroon.*   Coastal ethnic group.

Kpelle *Liberia.*   1. MANDE-speaking peoples in Bong county. Also, *Kessi, Kpwesi.* 2. Niger-Kordofanian language.

Kpesi *Ghana.*   GUAN people along the coast in the Tema area.

kra *Ghana.*   Spark of life that comes from Onyame, the AKAN supreme god.

kraal *Southern Africa.*   Group of houses surrounding an enclosure for livestock.

Krachi *West Africa.*   Niger-Kordofanian language.

Krahn *Liberia.*   1. Kru branch of the KWA-speaking peoples. 2. Niger-Kordofanian language.

Krakye *Ghana.*   Guan ethnic group. Also KRACHI.

krasung *Thailand.*   Ministry of the central government.

kraton *Indonesia.*   Royal courts of central Java.

kraw *Burma.*   Headman of a WA village.

Kreda *Chad.*   Subgroup of *Daza.*

kremt *Ethiopia.* Rainy season.

Krepi *Ghana.* EWE group in the Volta region.

Kresh *Sudan.* Nilo-Saharan language.

Krim *Sierra Leone.* 1. Ethnic group, a branch of SHERBRO. 2. Niger-Kordofanian language.

Krio *Sierra Leone.* Creole language.

kris *Malaysia.* Knife of Indonesian origin with a decorated hilt.

kriya *India.* Ritual as part of TANTRA.

Krobo *Ghana.* ADANGBE group along the right bank of the Volta.

krom *Thailand.* Government department or agency.

Krongo *Sudan.* Niger-Kordofanian language.

krontihene *Ghana.* Commander of an AKAN military force.

kroo *Sierra Leone.* Small dugout canoe.

Krou *West Africa.* Ethnic cluster including *Bakoue, Triboue, Tahou, Ourouboue, Touyo, Tabou, Bapo Tepo, Trepo* and *Oubi.*

Kru *Liberia.* KRUMEN-speaking people in Sinoe county.

kru *Sierra Leone.* God, among the TEMNE.

Kru *West Africa.* Sudanic speaking people noted as sailors and stevedores.

Krumen *West Africa.* Niger-Kordofanian language.

krut *Thailand.* State emblem, featuring a mythological bird.

kruu *Cambodia.* Spirit practitioner.

ksar *Morocco.* Fortified BERBER mountain or oasis village.

kshatriya *India.* Warrior caste, second in the hierarchical caste system.

Ksunda *Nepal.* Minor ethnic group.

k'thi thra *Burma.* Medical practitioner, usually a herbalist, among the KAREN.

ku *South Korea.* Ward, as a unit of local administration.

Kuba *Zaire.* Ethnic group of southern savanna.

Kubo *Botswana.* Ethnic group.

Kubu *Indonesia.* Ethnic group of Sumatra.

kuchong jang *South Korea.* Heads of wards.

Kudiana *Sri Lanka.* Upper Hindu caste.

kudumbam *Sri Lanka.* Family.

kuduo *Ghana.* Brass ceremonial vessels.

kudyapi *Philippines.* Six-string lute.

kugerera *Burundi.* To receive uncultivated land, the grant varying according to the person's social standing.

kuhhan *Saudi Arabia.* Oracles and soothsayers.

Kui *India.* DRAVIDIAN language.

Kui *Southeast Asia.* MON-KHMER highland group. Also, *Soai.*

kujitegemea *Tanzania.* Self-reliance and local initiative, in contrast to reliance on foreign aid and government programs.

kujur *Sudan.*   Religious figure possessed by a tutelary spirit or demon.
Kuka *Chad.*   Nilo-Saharan language.
Kukele *West Africa.*   Niger-Kordofanian language.
Kukhoe *South Korea.*   National Assembly.
kukhonta *Swaziland.*   Voluntary bond of homage and allegiance offered to a superior.
Kuki Chin *Burma and India.*   Tibeto-Burman speaking tribe in East Assam (Naga Hills, Manipur, and Lushai Hills) and north Burma.
kukmin chonghwa *South Korea.*   National solidarity.
Kukna *India.*   Indo-European language.
Kuku *Sudan.*   Ethnic group.
kukura *Burundi.*   Rite of puberty.
Kulango *West Africa.*   Niger-Kordofanian language.
Kulangu *West Africa.*   Ethnic group of LOBI cluster.
kulba *Afghanistan.*   Unit of area equal to 20 acres.
Kulere *West Africa.*   Niger-Kordofanian language.
kulinism *India.*   System of Hindu elitism to perpetuate BRAHMIN exclusiveness and genetic purity.
kulintangan *Philippines.*   MORO xylophone of wood or brass. Also, *gabbang.*
kulkarni *India.*   Accountant in central and west India.
Kullo *Ethiopia.*   Afro-Asiatic language.
kullo tanche *North Korea.*   Mass organization.
Kului *India.*   Indo-European language.
Kulung *West Africa*   Niger-Kordofanian language.
kumai *Nepal.*   BRAHMIN caste among the PAHARI.
Kuman *Uganda.*   Nilo-Saharan language.
Kuman *Uganda.*   Western Nilotic ethnic group.
Kumana *Bolivia.*   Amazon Indian group of CHAPACURAN language stock in east Beni department.
kumari *Nepal.*   Vestal virgin of the Shakya caste, chosen as the "living goddess" for a year.
Kumauni *Nepal and India.*   Indo-European language.
Kumba *Nepal.*   Minor ethnic group.
kumbh mela *India.*   Literally, pot festival. Largest of Hindu religious festivals held periodically in north India, every three years at Hardwar, Nasik and Ujjain and every 12 years at Allahabad.
kumbi *India.*   KSHATRIYA subcaste.
kumintang *Philippines.*   TAGALOG folk dance.
kumrabai *Sierra Leone.*   Principal adviser to the BAI, or TEMNE chief.
kumsan *Morocco.*   Long cotton shirt reaching to the ankles and gathered at the waist with a wide sash.
kun *Cambodia.*   Diocese or territorial division of the Buddhist SANGHA.
kun *Korea.*   County.

Kuna *Panama.* Macro-CHIBCHAN language.

Kunama *East Africa.* Nilo-Saharan language.

kun chip *South Korea.* Literally, big house. Elder in a kinship organization.

Kunda *Southern Africa.* 1. Congolese LUBA group. 2. Niger-Kordofanian language.

kundaehwa *South Korea.* Modernization.

kundiman *Philippines.* Popular sentimental music.

Kunema *Ethiopia.* Northern peoples.

Kunfel *Ethiopia.* AGEW-speaking people.

kungdawn ga *Burma.* Dowry of a girl with no brothers.

kungdo *South Korea.* Archery.

kunko *Gambia.* Short adze-shaped tool used by peanut farmers.

kunsu *South Korea.* County chief.

kuntow *Malaysia.* Chinese art of self-defense.

Kupsabing *Uganda.* Nilo-Saharan language.

Kurama *West Africa.* Niger-Kordofanian language.

Kuranko *Gambia.* 1. MANDING ethnic group. 2. Niger-Kordofanian language.

Kurave *Bolivia.* Amazon Indian group in central Beni department.

Kurd *West Asia.* Ethnic group, found chiefly in Iran, Iraq, and Turkey, believed to be descendants of the ancient Medes.

Kurdish *West Asia.* Indo-European language of the KURDS.

Kuria *East Africa.* 1. Ethnic group. Also, *Tendo.* 2. Niger-Kordofanian language.

Kurku *India.* Austro-Asiatic language.

Kurmanji *West Africa.* Indo-European language.

kurongora *Rwanda and Burundi.* Ceremony following wedding in which the bride is blessed and crowned with flowers and sent to her new home.

kurta *India.* Long, loose-fitting collarless shirt.

kuru *Turkey.* Coin, 1/100ths of a Turkish lira.

Kurumba *West Africa.* 1. Ethnic group of the NINISI cluster. 2. Niger-Kordofanian language.

Kurux *India and Nepal.* DRAVIDIAN language.

Kusaal *West Africa.* Niger-Kordofanian language.

Kusasi *Ghana.* MOLE DAGBANI group in the Upper Region.

Kusasi *West Africa.* Ethnic group of the MOSSI cluster. See MOLE-DAGBANE.

kushti *India.* Form of wrestling.

Kusu *Zaire.* Niger-Kordofanian language.

kusule *Nepal.* Class of untouchables comprising public sweepers and musicians.

kuta *Ethiopia.* Double layered shawl worn by men.

kutcha *South Asia.* Literally, raw or rough. House made of bamboo, straw or reed walls and roof over a mud floor.

Kuteb *West Africa.* Niger-Kordofanian language.

kutho *Burma.* In Buddhism, merit obtained by adhering to moral precepts and doing good deeds.

kuti *Thailand.* Living quarters in the wat compound.

kuttab *Islamic countries.* Muslim religious school.

Kutu *Tanzania.* 1. Ethnic group. 2. Niger-Kordofanian language.

Kuvi *India.* DRAVIDIAN language.

Kuwaa *Liberia.* KRUAN speaking people in Lofa county.

Kuwahla *Sudan.* Arab tribe.

kuwui (plural: kuwesia) *Sierra Leone.* Extended family occupying the same locality among the MENDE.

Kuy *Southeast Asia.* Austro-Asiatic language.

kuyok *North Korea.* Urban district.

Kuyonon *Philippines.* Minor ethnic group in Calimianes.

Kwa *Ghana.* Subgroup of BANTU-speaking Ibibio people comprising AKAN, NZEMA, TWI-FANTE, EWE and GUAN.

kwacha *Zambia, Malawi.* Monetary unit.

Kwadi *Angola.* Khoisan language.

Kwahu *Ghana.* AKAN group.

Kwaio *Solomon Islands.* Austronesian language.

Kwakwa *West Africa.* Sudanese-speaking people include the *Abe, Ajukru, Alagya, Ari, Ati, Avikam, Gwa, Kyama,* and *Mekyibo.*

Kwaluthi *Southern Africa.* MBO subgroup.

Kwamato *Angola.* OVAMBU subgroup.

Kwambi *Namibia.* 1. MBO subgroup. 2. Niger-Kordofanian language.

Kwangali *Angola.* 1. Ethnic group. 2. Niger-Kordofanian language.

Kwanyama *Angola and Namibia.* 1. Kongo subgroup. 2. Niger-Kordofanian language.

kwanza *Angola.* Monetary unit.

Kwara'ae *Solomon Islands.* Austronesian language.

kwa ti kodra *Central African Republic.* Village renovation work initiated under David Dacko.

kwatura *Rwanda.* Initiate in BABANDWA, a politico-religious fraternity.

Kwavi *Tanzania.* Ethnic group.

Kwawu *Ghana.* TWI ethnic group.

Kwaya *Tanzania.* Ethnic group.

Kwena *Botswana.* Main body of HURUTSHE from whom the Batswana trace their descent.

Kwere *Tanzania.* Ethnic group on the coast or eastern Morogoro.

Kwese *Zaire.* Niger-Kordofanian language.

kwian *Thailand.* Unit of measurement, equal to 50 baskets of rice.

kwin *Burma.* Literally, circle. Unit of revenue administration introduced by the British.

kwipeu *Cameroon.* Descendants of the founder among the BAMILEKE.

kwi shongora *Burundi.* Long, lyrical rhythmical song.

Kyaka *Papua New Guinea.* Papuan language.

Kyamba *Ghana.* GURMA group sometimes called Basara who speak Tobote.

kyat *Burma.* Monetary unit.

kyaung *Burma.* Term denoting both monastery and school.

kyaungtaik *Burma.* Cluster of Buddhist monasteries.

kye *South Korea.* Mutual assistance society or credit union.

Kyerepong *Ghana.* GUAN group in the eastern region.

Kyerpon *Ghana.* GUAN ethnic group. Also, *Cherepong.*

Kyibaku *West Africa.* Afro-Asiatic language.

kyi waing *Burma.* Musical instrument consisting of a series of bell metals or gongs.

ky muc *Vietnam.* Village council of notables.

kyokosi *Ghana.* ANYI-BAWLE ethnic group.

Laamang *Cameroon.* Afro-Asiatic language.

laamBe or **lawakooBe** *Senegal.* Rulers among the TOUCOLEURS.

laban *Arab countries.* Yogurt.

laban *Burma.* Sacrificial posts erected outside the sacred groves of the KACHINS.

labbai *India.* Corruption of *Arab.* TAMIL-speaking Muslim.

labwor *Uganda.* Ethnic group related to Tepeth.

Lacandon *Mexico.* Isolated Indian tribe speaking a MAYA dialect.

lacro *Paraguay.* Hominy.

Ladakhi *India.* Sino-Tibetan language.

ladang *India.* Permanent dry land.

ladino *South America.* Term applied to all individuals who have adopted the dominant Hispanic cultural and social traits.

lady elephant *Swaziland.* Title of the queen mother.

lagoe *Brazil.* Moist land on the edge of a reservoir or lake.

Lagoon Cluster *West Africa.* Family of ethnic groups.
Lahu *Southeast Asia.* 1. Tibeto-Burman ethnic group. 2. Sino-Tibetan language.
Lahuli *India.* Sino-Tibetan language.
Laiaicha *Western Sahara.* One of the subtribes of the REGUIBAT ECH CHARG.
laibon *East Africa.* Ritual expert among the MASAI.
laichu *Ecuador.* An Indian who has attained the same social status as a white.
laiharbo *India.* Folk dance. See MANIPURI.
Laime *Bolivia.* Indian group in south Potosi department.
Laipisi *Bolivia.* Indian group of Zamucoan languages in CHACO.
Laka *Central African Republic.* Ethnic group related to the SARA.
Laka *West Africa.* 1. Ethnic group. 2. Nilo-Saharan language.
lakh *India.* One hundred thousand, ¹⁄₁₀₀th of a CRORE. Properly, *laksham.*
lakon *Thailand.* Dance drama with pantomime in which the players neither wear masks nor sing.
Lakshmi *India.* Hindu goddess of prosperity.
Lala *Southern Africa.* Congolese LUNDA tribe in Luopula Valley.
Lala-Bisa *Zambia.* Niger-Kordofanian language.
Lali *Congo.* Subgroup of the KONGO.
Lalia *Zaire and Congo.* Niger-Kordofanian language.
lalla *Morocco.* Title of respect for females of high rank.
lalmee *Afghanistan.* Nonirrigated dry farming and farmland.
Lalung *India.* Sino-Tibetan language.
lalwadi *Haiti.* Dance leader in a carnival.
lam *Senegal.* WOLOF and PULAR titles for a provincial chief.
Lamani *India.* Indo-European language.
lamba *Madagascar.* Shawl worn by men and women or a burial shroud.
Lamba *Central and West Africa.* 1. Niger-Kordofanian language. 2. Ethnic group of the KABRE cluster.
lamba chauki *India.* Long easy chair with extended arms that serve as foot rests.
lambanog *Philippines.* Alcoholic liquor made from coconut and sugarcane.
lambi *Haiti.* Musical instrument made from a conch.
Lambia *Tanzania.* 1. Ethnic group. 2. Niger-Kordofanian language.
Lame *West Africa.* Afro-Asiatic language.
lamidate *Cameroon.* FULANI chiefdom.
lamide (plural: lamiba) *Cameroon.* FULANI politico-religious leader.
lamido (plural: lamibe) *Senegal.* Title of FULBE chiefs.
Lampung-Komering *Indonesia.* Austronesian language.
lam ray *Vietnam.* Swidden, or slash-and-burn cultivation.

lamthong *Laos.*   Folk dance accompanied by the KHENE.

lamvong *Cambodia.*   Popular dance.

lana *Morocco.*   Secular music.

lancados *Guinea-Bissau.*   Portuguese settlers and half-caste traders with African wives.

Land Dayak *Malaysia.*   Ethnic group in Sarawak.

Landouma *Guinea.*   Ethnic group related to the BAGA.

landy *Afghanistan.*   Dried meat, part of the winter diet.

lang *Vietnam.*   Village.

Langa *Zaire.*   Ethnic group.

langage *Haiti.*   Language spoken by VOODOO priests during rituals.

Langi *Tanzania.*   Niger-Kordofanian language.

Lango *Uganda.*   1. Western Nilotic ethnic group. 2. Nilo-Saharan language.

Lanza *Honduras.*   Dance based on the lancer quadrille.

Lanzin *Burma.*   Burma Socialist Program Party, ruling party since 1974.

Lao *Laos.*   Principal ethnic group along the banks of the Mekong River. In Thailand, known as *Valley Thai.*

laobe *Senegal.*   Woodworkers among the WOLOF.

Lao Sung *Laos.*   Mountaintop Laotian.

Lao Tai *Laos and Thailand.*   Ethnic group, mostly non-Buddhist, including BLACK TAI, RED TAI, Tai Nue, LU and Phumi.

Laotian *Laos.*   Southeastern Thai dialect of the Thai group of the Indo-Chinese family.

lappa *Liberia and Sierra Leone.*   Piece of cotton cloth about a yard wide and several yards long, wrapped around the body at the waist.

laptot *Senegal.*   Boatman on the Senegal River.

Lara *Indonesia.*   Austronesian language.

Larecaja *Bolivia.*   Dialect of AYMARA language.

larigo *Mexico.*   Ring at the end of a cinch in a Mexican saddle.

largo *Brazil.*   Wide section of a street.

Larte *Ghana.*   GUAN ethnic group.

Larteh-Cherepon-Anum-Boso *West Africa.*   Niger-Kordofanian language.

las *Somalia.*   Cistern dug for collecting and conserving rainwater.

lascar *India.*   Sailor or common foot soldier in the Indian defense forces.

lascoreen *Maldives.*   Militia composed of LASCARS.

Lashari *Iran.*   BALUCHI tribe.

lassi *South Asia.*   Milk from which butter fat and curds have been removed and drunk, usually iced, during summer.

Lassis *Pakistan.*   Ethnic group in Baluchistan.

lastro *Brazil.*   Plot of land set aside exclusively for one crop.

Lat *Vietnam.*   Highland ethnic group, a subgroup of the KOHO.

lathi *India.*   Police stick made of bamboo carried around by unarmed policemen.

latifundio *Spanish America.* Large estate. Also, *latifundium.*

latifundismo *Spanish America.* Semifeudal system of large landholdings, going back to colonial times.

latifundista *Spanish America.* Holder of a LATIFUNDIO.

latigo *Mexico.* Strong strap fastened to the saddletree of a Mexican saddle.

Lan *Solomon Islands.* Austronesian language.

Lauan *Fiji.* Austronesian language.

laudo *Uruguay.* Wage-rate award.

lava lava *Oceania.* Draped cloth, knotted at the waist on one side and hanging just above or below the knees, usually worn by men.

La Violencia *Colombia.* Period of near anarchy and chronic violence from the late 1940s through the mid-1960s.

lavoura branca *Brazil.* Cash crops other than coffee and other export crops.

lavrador *Brazil.* Small farmer.

Lawa *Thailand.* Austro-Asiatic language.

lawan *Chad.* Among Arabs, scion of the oldest lineage group.

lawBe (singular: labbe) *Senegal.* Woodworkers among the TOUCOLEURS.

layiklik *Turkey.* Secularism as one of the six "arrows" of Ataturkism.

Laz *Turkey.* Caucasian ethnic group.

lazimah *Iraq.* Land to which a revokable title has been granted by the state for a specified period.

le *Burma.* Paddy field. Also, system of cultivation in the river valleys.

le *Vietnam.* Festival, celebration or ritual.

lebaran *Indonesia.* Holiday celebrating the end of Ramadan.

lebe *Indonesia.* Influential men in a village.

Lebou or **Lebu** *Senegal.* Ethnic group of the Cape Vert Peninsula.

Lebouihat *Western Sahara.* One of the largest subtribes of the REGUIBAT ECH-CHARG.

Lebu *Senegal.* See LEBOU.

lechon *Philippines.* National FIESTA dish, a pig stuffed with banana and tamarind leaves and boiled rice and roasted whole on a bamboo spit over charcoal.

Leco *Bolivia.* Amazon Indian group in La Paz department.

Ledo *Indonesia.* Austronesian language.

le dong tho *Vietnam.* The ritual of the first-ground stirring, one of the most important traditional ceremonies, held during the first week of New Year.

leff (plural: ifuf) *Morocco.* A loose form of tribal confederation among the BERBERS.

Lega *Zaire.* 1. Ethnic group of the Central Rain Forest. 2. Niger-Kordofanian language.

legadero *Mexico.* Stirrup strap in a Mexican saddle.

Legbo *West Africa.*   Niger-Kordofanian language.

legso *Ethiopia.*   Song sung by women in honor of a deceased person.

legua *Paraguay.*   Measure of distance equal to 5 km.

le ho dien *Vietnam.*   Annual rice-transplanting ceremony.

le hon Nhan *Vietnam.*   Wedding ceremony.

le khai tam *Vietnam.*   Ceremony of the "opening of the heart and mind," on the first day of formal learning.

Lela *West Africa.*   Niger-Kordofanian language.

Lele *Zaire.*   1. Ethnic group. 2. Afro-Asiatic language.

Lelemi *West Africa.*   Niger-Kordofanian language.

lem *Laos.*   Wealthy person.

lema *Uruguay.*   Title or label adopted by a national political party composed of several SUB-LEMAS, or groups, which, in turn, are composed of tendencias or factions.

Lemba *Zambia.*   Congolese LUNDA tribe in the Luapula Valley.

Lemba *Zimbabwe.*   Small ethnic group related to the VENDA speaking a dialect of SHONA.

Lembe *Zaire.*   Ethnic group of the southern savanna.

lempira *Honduras.*   Monetary unit.

Lemtouna *Western Sahara.*   A BERBER SANHAJA people.

Lencas *Nicaragua.*   Subtribe of the CHONTALES.

Lendo *Zaire.*   Ethnic group.

Lendu *Zaire.*   Ethnic group.

lengha *India.*   Narrow-legged trousers.

Lengolo *Zaire.*   Ethnic group of the Central Rain Forest.

Lengua *Paraguay.*   Indian language.

leniol (plural: leggi) *Senegal.*   Among the TOUCOLEURS, patrilineage.

Lenje *Zambia.*   1. BANTU tribe in south central region. 2. Niger-Kordofanian language.

leone *Sierra Leone.*   Monetary unit.

leopards *Haiti.*   Elite unit of the Haitian army under Francois Duvalier.

lepacho *Paraguay.*   National hardwood tree.

Lepcha *Bhutan and Sikkim.*   1. Ethnic group. 2. Sino-Tibetan language.

leqamemheren *Ethiopia.*   Chief of learned men in the Orthodox Church.

Lese *Central Africa.*   Nilo-Saharan language.

le tao quan *Vietnam.*   Feast of the household gods.

le thanh minh *Vietnam.*   Literally, feast of the pure light. Festival on April 5, 15 days after the vernal equinox.

le that tich *Vietnam.*   The double-seven festival on the seventh day of the seventh lunar month celebrating the love affair of the daughter of the Jade Emperor.

le thuong dien *Vietnam.*   Annual festival when the rice plants are in bloom.

le thuong tan *Vietnam.*   Festival during which the first fruits of the harvest are sampled.

le tich dien *Vietnam.*   Plowing ceremony.

leting *Lesotho.*   Light beer made from sorghum.

letpet *Burma.*   Pickled tea of the SHANS.

le trang nguyen *Vietnam.*   Festival of learning.

letsema (plural: matsema) *Lesotho.*   Obligatory feudal labor performed by men for the tribal chief, abolished in the 1940s.

levante *Morocco.*   Wind blowing from the northeast in the summer.

Leya *Zambia.*   BANTU tribe.

Lhomi *Nepal.*   Sino-Tibetan language.

Lia *Zaire.*   Ethnic group.

libandla *Swaziland.*   Royal advisory council; properly, *libandla lake ngwana.*

liboko *Lesotho.*   Tribal totems.

Libolo *Angola.*   MBUNDU subgroup.

libra *Central America.*   Unit of weight equal to 1 lb.

libutfo (plural: emabutfo) *Swaziland.*   Class of royal warriors.

lice *Turkey.*   Lycee.

licenciado *Spanish America.*   Degree awarded on completion of undergraduate university studies.

lider *Philippines.*   Political power broker.

lidloti *Swaziland.*   Ancestral spirits.

lifafa tsidiq *Ethiopia.*   Scroll inscribed with a magical inscription in Ge'ez and worn for protection.

li-goi *Burma.*   Village headman or chief among the LAHU.

ligubu *Swaziland.*   Musical instrument, a string wooden bow with inverted calabashes as resonators.

Lihoja *Lesotho.*   Ethnic group akin to the BATAUNG.

lij *Ethiopia.*   Lord, title of nobles.

likay *Thailand.*   Dance drama based on historical or current themes.

Liko *Zaire.*   Niger-Kordofanian language.

Likoula *Congo.*   Subgroup of MBOSHI.

Likpe *Ghana.*   Small CENTRAL TOGO group in the Volta Region.

likudu *Zaire.*   Lineage.

lilangeni (plural: emalangeni) *Swaziland.*   Monetary unit.

lilawu *Swaziland.*   Bachelor's quarters or barracks.

Lilse *Burkina Faso.*   Ethnic group of NINISI cluster.

Limba *Sierra Leone.*   1. Ethnic group. 2. Niger-Kordofanian language.

limbo *Zimbabwe.*   A kind of coarse calico.

Limbu *Nepal.* 1. Ethnic group occupying the most easterly section of the Himalayas between Arun River and the Sikkim border. Also, *Yakthumba, Subbha.* 2. Sino-Tibetan language.

Limbum *West Africa.* Niger-Kordofanian language.

limitada *Spanish America.* Collective partnership with limited liability.

limosna *Spanish America.* Small monetary offering to the statue of a saint.

limpieza de sangre *Spanish America.* Purity of blood as a determinant of social status.

Lingala *Zaire.* Niger-Kordofanian language.

Lingayat *India.* Hindu sect worshipping the lingam, or phallus, of Siva.

linger *Senegal.* Queen mother.

lingua geral *Brazil.* Modified form of the Tupi Guarani language spoken in Brazil before the introduction of Portuguese.

Lio *Indonesia.* Austronesian language.

Lipe *Bolivia.* Indian group of Atacaman language stock in Potosi department.

lipenga *Malawi.* Singing horn.

Liptako *West Africa.* Ethnic group.

liqoqo *Swaziland.* National council of advisers.

liquid ambar *Honduras.* Sweet gum tree, generally 100 feet or more tall and up to five feet in diameter.

liquiliqui *Venezuela.* Suit of white cloth consisting of trousers and a large shirt fastened with gold or leather buttons, sometimes worn with a sash.

lisenti *Lesotho.* Coin, 1/100ths of a LOTI.

Lisi *Chad.* SAHELian ethnic group.

lisokancanti *Swaziland.* The first circumcised son of the first royal consort.

Lisu *Burma and Thailand.* Ethnic group, speaking a Sino-Tibetan language.

literatura do cordel *Brazil.* Pamphlet literature sold at fairs.

lithoko *Lesotho.* BASOTHO praise poems.

litunga *Zambia.* Paramount chief of the Lozi.

liwa *Arab countries.* Province.

liwa *Saudi Arabia.* Major general in the Saudi army.

liwali *Tanzania.* Arab herdsman.

Liwatiyah (singular: lutiyah) *Oman.* KHOJA or ISMAILI sect of Shias.

Liyuwa *Angola.* Unclassified language.

lkhaon bassak *Cambodia.* Dance drama.

lkhaon khaol *Cambodia.* Nonclassical play.

Lla *Zambia.* BANTU ethnic group.

llacta *Ecuador.* Backwoods country.

llaneros *Venezuela.*   People of the LLANOS, or plains.

llanos *Spanish America.*   Plains, especially flat prairies.

llicallas *Peru.*   Woman's shawl.

lluchu *Bolivia.*   Knitted tuque with earflaps worn by highland Indians.

lo *Vietnam.*   Province.

lo *Ivory Coast.*   Secret age-graded society among the SENOUFO. Also, PORO.

loa (plural: loa) *Haiti.*   Anthropomorphic spirit or god in VOODOO.

Lobala *Zaire.*   Ethnic group.

Lobi *Burkina Faso.*   Ethnic group in Gaoua and Diebougou regions.

Lobi *Ghana.*   MOLE DAGBANE group in the northwest.

Lobi *West Africa.*   Niger-Kordofanian language.

lobo *Honduras.*   Offspring of a Negro father and an Indian mother.

loboella *Lesotho.*   Area where thatching grass is grown and grazing is allowed only at certain times.

lobola *Southern Africa.*   Payment of dowry, usually in cattle, from the bridegroom to the father of the bride.

localismo *Nicaragua.*   Provincialism or parochialism.

localites *Zaire.*   Locality, as a unit of local administration.

locro *Paraguay.*   Soup made of white corn and meat.

lodha *India.*   KSHATRIYA subcaste of Uttar Pradesh and Rajasthan.

Lodhi *India.*   Indo-European language.

loe jirgah *Afghanistan.*   National Council of Notables composed, from 1964, of both houses of Parliament and chairmen of the provincial JIRGAHS.

loe woleswal *Afghanistan.*   Administrator of a LOE WOLESWALI.

loe woleswali *Afghanistan.*   Subdivision of a province, composed of many districts.

Logba *West Africa.*   CENTRAL TOGO group of the KABRE cluster.

Logo *Zaire.*   1. Ethnic group. 2. Nilo-Saharan language.

Logooli *Kenya.*   Niger-Kordofanian language.

lohar *India and Pakistan.*   Member of a Hindu subcaste employed as craftsmen in wood or metal.

loi cadre *Francophone Africa.*   French enabling act establishing universal suffrage.

Loinang *Indonesia.*   Ethnic group of Sulawesi.

loing *Lesotho.*   Mountain country.

Lokele *Zaire.*   Ethnic group.

lok kho *Burma.*   Sacred gates among the AKHA marking entrance to their villages.

Loko *Sierra Leone.*   Ethnic group in Bombali district.

Loko *Sierra Leone and Nigeria.*   Niger-Kordofanian language.

Lok Sabha *India.*   Lower house of Parliament.

Lolaki *Indonesia.*   Austronesian language.

Lo-lo *Vietnam.*   Tibeto-Burmese speaking highland ethnic group along the Laos and Thai borders.

Lolo *Mozambique.*   Ethnic group of the Makua-Lomue cluster. Also, *Kokola, Alola.*

Lolobi *Ghana.*   CENTRAL TOGO ethnic group in the Volta region.

Loloda *Indonesia.*   Papuan language.

Loma *Liberia.*   MANDE-speaking people in upper Lofa county. Also, *Lorma, Buzi.*

Loma *West Africa.*   Niger-Kordofanian language.

Lombi *Zaire.*   Ethnic group.

Lombo *Zaire.*   Niger-Kordofanian language.

Lomotwa *Zaire.*   Ethnic group.

Lomue *Southern Africa.*   Ethnic group of Makua-Lomwe cluster. Also, *Lomwe.*

long *Vietnam.*   Dragon, one of the four sacred animals. Also, *Rong.*

longhouse *Malaysia.*   In Sarawak and Sabah, a tribal house built of wood on stilts on river banks, consisting of a number of independent family apartments joined longitudinally under a common roof.

longo *Ecuador.*   Minor Indian not old enough to hold public office.

Longuda *West Africa.*   Niger-Kordofanian language.

longyi *Burma.*   Wraparound skirt worn by both men and women.

loshar *Nepal.*   Tibetan new year's day festival celebrated with songs and dance.

Losso *Togo.*   Ethnic group of KABRE cluster.

lota *India.*   Small round vessel of brass or copper.

loteria *Nicaragua.*   Raffle.

loti (plural: maloti) *Lesotho.*   Monetary unit.

Lotuko *Sudan.*   1. Nilotic Negro ethnic group in Equatoria Province. 2. Nilo-Saharan language.

loy kratong *Thailand.*   Festival of lights on the night of the full moon in November.

Loze *Zambia.*   1. Congolese ethnic group speaking a Berotse language. 2. Niger-Kordofanian language.

Lozi *Zimbabwe.*   BANTU-speaking ethnic group in Barotseland.

Lu *Southeast Asia.*   1. Group of LAO TAI, known in Thailand as *Kam Tai.* 2. Sino-Tibetan language.

Lua *Thailand.*   MON-KHMER highland ethnic group.

luang *Thailand.*   Title of distinction for a person in royal service.

Luano *Zambia.*   Congolese LUNDA tribe in Luapula Valley.

Luba *Zaire.*   Ethnic group of southern savanna.

Luba-Kasai or **Luba Shaba** *Zaire.*   Niger-Kordofanian language.

Lubu *Indonesia.*   Austronesian language.

lubyo *Burma.*   Literally, group of bachelors. Unmarried men, 15 and older, who conduct village festivals.

luc doc *Vietnam.* The six cardinal virtues: *tri* or wisdom; *nhan* or benevolence; *jin* or sincerity; *nghia* or righteousness; *trung* or moderation; and *hoa* or harmony.

Luchazi *Zambia and Angola.* 1. Congolese ethnic group. 2. Niger-Kordofanian language.

ludruk *Indonesia.* Nontraditional form of drama.

Lue *Thailand.* Ethnic group.

Luena *Angola.* NGANGUELA subgroup.

Luganda *Uganda.* Niger-Kordofanian language.

Lugbara *Central Africa.* 1. Central Sudanic ethnic group. 2. Nilo-Saharan language.

Luguru *Tanzania.* Ethnic group of Uluguru mountains.

Luimbi *Angola.* Niger-Kordofanian language.

lukhmat al khanuq *Yemens.* Ordeal by poison.

lukiko *Uganda.* State council of Buganda.

lukindi *Malawi.* Form of land tenure among NGONDE and Nyakyusa tribes.

Luko *West Africa.* Niger-Kordofanian language.

luksit wat *Thailand.* Temple boys doing odd jobs in WATS.

Lulua *Zaire.* Ethnic group.

luluai *Papua New Guinea.* Representative of the central government at the local level.

Lumbu *Central Africa.* Niger-Kordofanian language.

Luna *Zaire.* Niger-Kordofanian language.

Lunda *Southern Africa and Zaire.* 1. Ethnic group of southern savanna. 2. Niger-Kordofanian language.

Lunda-Chokwe *Angola.* Ethnic group, a branch of the LUNDA.

Lundayeh *Sabah.* Austronesian language.

lundu *Brazil.* Afro-Brazilian dance using umbigadas or navel to navel bump.

lunfardo *Argentina.* Italianized Spanish dialect.

lungi *India.* Cloth wrapped around the body once or twice at the waist and tucked in at the upper edge. Also, *dhoti.*

Lungu *Zambia.* Tanzanian ethnic group.

Luntu *Zaire.* Ethnic group.

Lunya *Kenya.* Collective name for 16 subgroups: *Bakusu, Kabras, Kakalelelwa, Kakamega, Khayo, Kiso, Marach, Maragoli, Marama, Nyala, Nyole, Samia, Tachoni, Tiriki, Tsotso* and *Wanga.*

Luo *East Africa.* 1. Nilotic ethnic group divided into some 30 subgroups, including *Karacuonyo, Kano, Alego, Gem, Samia* and *Ungeya.* 2. Nilo-Saharan language.

Lao Theung *Laos.* Mon-Khmer-speaking hill tribe.

Lupaca *Bolvia.* AYMARA dialect in La Paz department.

lurah *Indonesia.*   Headman of a KELURAHAN, or village, or KAMPUNG, or urban neighborhood.

Luri *Iran.*   Indo-European language.

Lurs *Iran.*   Ethnic group related to the KURDS.

lusendvo *Swaziland.*   Family or kniship council consisting of all males.

Lusengo *Zaire.*   Niger-Kordofanian language.

Lushai *India.*   Sino-Tibetan language.

Luvale *Zambia.*   1. Congolese ethnic group. 2. Niger-Kordofanian language.

luveve *Swaziland.*   Traditional Swazi hunting horn.

Luwo *Sudan.*   Nilo-Saharan language.

Luwu *Indonesia.*   Austronesian language.

Luyana *Zambia.*   Niger-Kordofanian language.

Luyia *Kenya.*   Niger-Kordofanian language.

luzum *Jordan.*   Close consultative group.

lwei *Angola.*   Coin, ¹/₁₀₀ths of a KWANZA.

Lwena *Angola.*   Ethnic group.

ly *Vietnam.*   Unicorn, one of the sacred animals.

lycee *Francophone Africa.*   Secondary school on the French model.

Lyele *West Africa.*   Niger-Kordofanian language.

Lyembe *Zaire.*   Ethnic group.

ly truong *Laos.*   Chief of a commune.

Ma *Liberia.*   Ethnic group in Limba County.

Maa *Vietnam.*   Highland ethnic group, subgroup of the KOHO.

maabuBe (singular: maabe) *Senegal.*   Weaver class among the TOU-COLEURS.

maakida (singular: akida) *Tanzania.*   Political agents.

maalemin (singular: maalem) *Western Sahara.*   Artisans and craftsmen.

Maanyan *Indonesia.*   Austronesian language.

Maba *Chad.*   1. Collective name for a group of mountain tribes in Ouadai and Biltine. 2. Nilo-Saharan language.

Mabaan-Jumjum *Sudan.*   Nilo-Saharan language.

ma-baap *India.*   Literally, father and mother. Nickname applied to British civil servants in colonial times.

Maca *Mozambique.*   Ethnic group on the coast.

macaiad *Somalia.*   Teahouse where men gather to drink *cha,* or tea.

macambo *Brazil.*   Shantytown in Recife.

macana *Guatemala.*   Pointed planting stick used in farming.

macana *Peru.*   Woman's shawl.

machetismo *Spanish America.*   Political violence or terrorism through indiscriminate massacres.

Machinga *Tanzania.*   Ethnic group.

machisi *Zimbabwe.*   Litter or palanquin slung below one or two poles and carried by porters.

machismo *Spanish America.*   Literally, maleness. Complex of beliefs and attitudes stressing the superior role of the male in society and defining the concept of masculinity in terms of that role.

Maconde *Mozambique.*   Ethnic group.

maconha *Brazil.*   Marijuana.

Mada *West Africa.*   Niger-Kordofanian language.

madal *India and Nepal.*   Narrow barreled drum.

madam *Afghanistan.*   String instrument, like a ukulele.

mada sara *Haiti.*   Female itinerant traders.

maddalam *India.*   Cylindrical drum in Kerala.

madhab *Egypt.*   Muslim code of jurisprudence.

Madi *Central Africa.*   1. Sudanic ethnic group. 2. Nilo-Saharan language.

madina *Arab countries.*   City quarter inhabited by a particular ethnic group.

madjelis permusjawaratan rakjat *Indonesia.*   People's Consultative Assembly.

Madjingaye *Chad.*   SARA subgroup in Moyen-Chari.

madrasah *Islamic countries.*   Muslim school or college.

madrina *Spanish America.*   Godmother.

madu *Burma.*   Among KACHINS, sovereignty or ownership, as the prerogative of a ruler or head of family.

maduka (singular: duka). *India.*   Small retail stores.

Madurese *Indonesia.*   1. Ethnic group of Java. 2. Austronesian language.

mae chi *Thailand.*   Buddhist nuns.

mafisa *Lesotho.*   Custom by which a chief placed his cattle in the care of his followers.

mafuto *Brazil.*   Rural peasant or rustic.

Magadhi *India.*   Indo-European language.

Magagula *Swaziland.*   SOTHO clan.

magal *Senegal.*   Annual pilgrimage to Touba, seat of the MURIDIYA Islamic Brotherhood.

magani *Philippines.*   Custom of obtaining leadership and status and the right to wear red clothes through killing a certain number of people, among pagans in Mindanao.

Maganja *Mozambique.*   See CHUABO.

Magar *Nepal.*   1. Tibet-Nepalese ethnic group. Also, *Mangar Tshong.* 2. Sino-Tibetan language.

maghi *Bangladesh.*   Tribal group. See MARMA.

Maghrib *North Africa.*   The western Islamic world, including Libya, Tunisia, Algeria and Morocco. Distinguished from MASHRIQ, eastern Islamic countries.

Maghrib al-Aqsa *Morocco.*   Literally farthest west. Morocco.

maghzan *Algeria.*   Tribes allied to the ruler.

maghzanis *Morocco.*   Militia men under arms in rural areas.

Magindanaon *Philippines.*   Austronesian language.

Magindanao *Philippines.*   Moro group in Mindanao.

magistrados *Spanish America.*   Justice.

maglalatik *Philippines.*   Folk dance in which male dancers clap together coconut shells.

magonia *Ethiopia.*   Prayer stick or crutch used to mark time in meditation.

Magumi *Chad.*   Major clan of the ZAGHAWA.

Maha *Sudan.*   Sudanic-speaking subgroup. See NUBI.

maha *Sri Lanka.*   Main growing season in rain-fed cultivation system, with the sowing from August to October and harvesting from February to March.

maha amat *Laos.*   Superior grade of civil service.

Mahabharata *India.*   One of the two great Hindu epics composed between 200 B.C. and 200 A.D. consisting mostly of legends, religious lore and cosmogony.

mahadun wun *Burma.*   Ecclesiastical censor who prepares a list of all ordained monks.

Mahafaly *Madagascar.*   Southern ethnic group.

mahal *India.*   A palace or edifice, as Taj Mahal.

Mahali *India.*   Austro-Asiatic language.

mahalla *Islamic countries.*   Alley in urban area devoted to a particular business or crafts.

mahalla *Morocco.*   Government military expedition into dissident territory.

mahanayoyok *Thailand.*   Lay leader of the congregation in the Buddhist merit-making ceremony.

Mahanikaya *Thailand.*   One sect of the Buddhist SANGHA.

mahant *India.*   Abbot of a Hindu temple.

mahar *Sri Lanka.* Dowry.

maharaja *India* and *Nepal.* Title of native ruler.

maharani *India.* Queen of a native state.

maharishi or **maharshi** *India.* Hindu sage or abbot of a monastery, usually leader of a cult or sect.

mahathera *Burma.* Great elder monk.

Mahathera Samahom *Thailand.* Supreme Council of the Buddhist SANGHA.

mahatma *India.* Literally, great soul. Title applied to Mohandas Karamchand Gandhi (1869–1948).

Mahayana *Buddhist countries.* Literally, the great vehicle. One of two major Buddhist sects, dominant in Nepal, China, Tibet, Mongolia, Korea and Japan, and therefore known also as Northern Buddhism. Its scriptures are written in Sanskrit. Mahayana regards Buddha as only one of an infinite number of Buddhas who would be adored and to whom offerings and prayers should be made. The goal of Mahayana is not merely the individual nirvana but the good of the human community.

mahdi *Islamic countries.* Messianic concept of a once and future Islamic leader who will "fill the world with justice," and exterminate all infidels.

maheber *Ethiopia.* Voluntary association of men or women holding periodical feasts.

mahelata kene *Ethiopia.* Outer court of an Orthodox Church.

Mahi *Benin.* Ethnic group.

mahila mandal *India.* Women's organization.

Mahinde *Mozambique.* See CHUABO.

mahiya (plural: emahiya) *Swaziland.* Loincloth worn by Swazi men.

mahkamat al Sharia al kubra *Arab countries.* High court of Sharia law.

mahkamat al umur al mustajalah *Saudi Arabia.* Court of first instance.

Mahl *Benin.* Ethnic group of the EWE family.

Mahongive *Gabon.* BAKOTA linguistic group.

mahori *Thailand.* Traditional orchestra of central Thailand.

mahout *India.* Elephant driver.

mahr *Islamic countries.* Bride money. In Iran, marriage contract.

mahra (singular: mahri) *Oman.* Non-Arab people of southern Arabia of Himyarite stock.

Mahratta *India.* Hindu people of western India. Also, *Maratha.*

Mahri *Oman.* Afro-Asiatic language.

Mahsud *Afghanistan and Pakistan.* Warlike tribe in North-West Frontier.

mahsuh *Lebanon.* Follower of a ZAIM, or political boss.

mai *Chad.* Former title of king.

maidan *India.* Open space or commons used as an esplanade or parade ground.

mailo *Uganda.* Unit of area equal to 1 sq mi.

Mainty *Madagascar.* Black MERINAS.

maistry *India.* Overseer of a hired gang of coolies.

Maithili *India.* Indo-European language.

majalla *Tunisia.* Code of personal status.

Majdhubiyyah *Sudan.* Localized Islamic brotherhood, or *tariqah,* associated with the Majdhub family.

majhab *Bangladesh.* Islamic fellowship group.

Majhi *Nepal.* Minor ethnic group.

Majhwar *India.* Unclassified language.

Maji *Ethiopia.* Afro-Asiatic language.

Majing-Ngama *West Africa.* Nilo-Saharan language.

majlis (plural: majalis) *Islamic countries.* Council or assembly, generally applied to national legislatures.

majlis al aala *Morocco.* Supreme court.

Majlis al Ayyan *Jordan.* Council of Notables, the upper house of Parliament.

Majlis al Nuwab *Morocco and Jordan.* House of Representatives.

Majlis al Shaab *Egypt.* People's Assembly.

Majlis al Ummah *Jordan.* National legislature.

Majlis esh Shura *Qatar.* Advisory council of the EMIR, without legislative powers.

majlis raja raja *Malaysia.* Conference of rulers.

majumbe (singular: jumbe) *Tanzania.* Village headmen.

majumdar *India.* Revenue accountant in charge of revenue accounts, or *jama.*

Makanne *Somalia.* Non-Somali group along Shabelle River.

Makasai *Indonesia.* Papuan language.

Makasarese *Indonesia.* Ethnic group of Sulawesi

Makassar *Indonesia.* Austronesian language.

makdas *Ethiopia.* Sanctuary in an Orthodox Church.

Makere *Zaire.* Ethnic group.

makhzan *Algeria.* Provileged tribes with the right to collect taxes.

makhzar *Morocco.* Central government.

Makikite *Afghanistan.* Islamic school.

Makil *Western Sahara.* Arab BEDOUIN people of Yemeni origin.

Makiritare *Venezuela.* Indian tribe.

makk *Sudan.* Title of a tribal and local chief.

Makka *Paraguay.* Indian ethnic group in CHACO.

Makoa *Madagascar.* Western ethnic group.

Makolo *Zambia.* Social unit of the LOZI.

makomiya *Ethiopia.*   Tall crutch used by all monks.

Makonde *Southern Africa.*   1. Ethnic group. 2. Niger-Kordofanian language.

Makran *Indonesia.*   Austronesian language.

Makran *Pakistan.*   Ethnic group in Baluchistan including Darzada, Nakib and Lori.

maktab *Islamic countries and India.*   Primary school attached to a mosque.

Makua *Southern Africa.*   1. Ethnic group of Makua-Lonue cluster. 2. Niger-Kordofanian language.

makuannet *Ethiopia.*   Local gentry and lower-level civil servants, collectively.

Makusi *Guyana.*   Carib-speaking Amerindian tribe.

makuta (singular: likuta) *Zaire.*   Coin, $\frac{1}{100}$ths of a ZAIRE.

malabar *Madagascar.*   Long shirt that reaches down to the knees.

mal adda *Nepal.*   District officer for the collection of land taxes.

Malagasy *Madagascar.*   Austronesian language.

malak *Ethiopia.*   War chief among the Somali.

malakat *Ethiopia.*   Trumpet.

Malakote *Kenya.*   Niger-Kordofanian language.

Malangeni *Swaziland.*   Collective name for the royal princes.

Malay *Malaysia and Indonesia.*   Austronesian language, properly, BAHASA MALASIA. Also *Baba Malay, Bazar Malay.*

MALAYALAM *INDIA.*   DRAVIDIAN language with heavy SANSKRIT intermixture.

malazzim awwal *Saudi Arabia.*   First lieutenant in Saudi army.

Malele *Zaire.*   Ethnic group.

Male *Ethiopia.*   Afro-Asiatic language.

Malgbe *West Africa.*   Afro-Asiatic language.

malguzar *India.*   Revenue tax collector.

malhafa *Western Sahara.*   Flowing robes worn by women.

malik *Afghanistan.*   Elected head of a village.

malik *Arab countries.*   Ruler.

Malikiyya *West Africa.*   Brand of Islamic brotherhood. See TIDJANIYA.

Malila *Tanzania.*   1. Ethnic group. 2. Niger-Kordofanian language.

Malinke *West Africa.*   1. Large ethnic cluster who gave their name to Mali. Their empire was the largest in Africa in the 13th and 14th centuries. Also, *Mandingo.* 2. Niger-Kordofanian language.

malipenge *Malawi.*   Dance with gourd trumpets.

malka *Ethiopia.*   Literally, likeness. Form of religious poetry.

Malla *Nepal.*   NEWARI KSHATRIYA caste.

mallah or **mellah** *Morocco.*   Traditional Jewish quarters in a town.

mallam *West Africa.*   Koranic scholars and teachers.

mallot *Bangladesh.*   Islamic fellowship group.

maloca *Brazil.*   Shantytown in Porto Alegre and Belo Horizonte; slum dwelling in the south.

malong *Philippines.*   Long, oblong cloth wrapped around the body by Maianao Muslims.

Malto *India.*   DRAVIDIAN language.

malu *Malaysia.*   Social handicap resulting from shyness, shame or embarrassment.

malungo *Brazil.*   Term for comrade among people of African origin.

Malvi *India.*   Indo-European language.

Mam *Central America.*   1. MAYA tribe. 2. Language group of the MAMEAN linguistic stock.

Mama *West Africa.*   Niger-Kordofanian language.

Mamasa *Indonesia.*   Austronesian language.

Mambai *Indonesia.*   Austronesian language.

mambi *Cuba.*   Guerrilla fighters.

Mambila *West Africa.*   Niger-Kordofanian language.

mambo *Haiti.*   VOODOO priestess.

mambo *Mozambique.*   Chief among the TONGA.

mambo (plural: vamambo or vadzi mambo) *Zimbabwe.*   King or paramount chief.

Mambwe *Tanzania.*   Ethnic group.

Mambwe-Lungu *Southeastern Africa.*   Niger-Kordofanian language.

Mamean *Central America.*   One of the major linguistic divisions of the MAYA family of languages.

mameluco *Brazil.*   MESTIZO.

mamlakah *Islamic countries.*   Kingdom, used in official names of countries.

mammy *Ghana.*   Female entrepreneur providing marketing services and capital for small fishermen.

Mampella *Ghana.*   Language of the MAMPRUSI.

Mamprusi *Ghana.*   MOLE-DAGBANE ethnic group.

Mamuju *Indonesia.*   Austronesian language.

Mamvu *Zaire.*   Ethnic group of northern savanna.

Mamvu *Zaire and Central Africa.*   Nilo-Saharan language.

man *Iran.*   Unit of weight equal to 300 kg.

Man *Vietnam.*   Highland ethnic group. Also, *Dao, Yao, Zao.*

mana *Polynesia.*   Spiritual charisma attributed to holy people.

mana *Zimbabwe.*   SHONA household.

Managuenses *Nicaragua.*   Inhabitants of Managua.

manaca *Honduras.*   Corozo palm, also called cahoon palm, fronds of which are used for thatching.

Manasi *Bolivia.*   Indian dialect of Chiquitoan in eastern Beni and northern Santa Cruz departments.

Manasir (singular: Mansuri) *Oman.*   Tribe of eastern Arabia.

manau *Burma.* Sacrifices among the KACHIN to Madai, or sky spirits.

Mancagne *Senegal.* Ethnic group.

Man Cao Lan *Vietnam.* Variant of Kam Tai.

manche *Ghana.* Paramount chief of the GA and ADANGBE.

Manda *Tanzania.* Niger-Kordofanian language.

mandala *India and Nepal.* Formalized design in TANTRIC Buddhism showing five Buddhas.

mandamiento *Spanish America.* System of work regulation for extracting labor from Indians after abolition of the ENCOMIENDA system in 1720.

mandao *Brazil.* Rural boss or CORONEL.

mandapam *India.* Platform, usually in front of a Hindu temple.

Mandar *Indonesia.* Austronesian language.

Mandara *Cameroon.* Ethnic group around the southern border of Lake Chad.

Mandara *West Africa.* Afro-Asiatic language.

Mandari *Sudan.* Ethnic group.

Mandaya *Philippines.* Ethnic group in Surigao Province.

Mande *West Africa.* Subgroup of Sudanic language family comprising Mande-Tan or northern Mande and Mande-Fu or southern Mande. The former is spoken by Bambara, Diula, Fulanke, Kagoro, Kason, Kono, Karanko, Malinke Sarakole, Vai, Wasulu and Yarse and the latter of Dan, Dialonke, Gagu, Gbande, Gbunde, Guro, Kpelle, Loko, Lomo, Mano, Mande, Samo and Susu. Also, Mandingo.

Mandeali *India.* Indo-European language.

Mandija *Central African Republic.* BAYA subgroup.

Manding *West Africa.* 1. Variant of MALINKE. 2. Niger-Kordofanian language.

Mandingo *West Africa.* See MANDE.

Mandinka *West Africa.* Niger-Kordofanian language.

Mandjaque *Senegal.* Ethnic group.

Mandjon *Cameroon.* Tribal association of the BAMILEKE.

mandub *Morocco.* Representative of the sultan.

Mandyak *West Africa.* Niger-Kordofanian language.

maneaba *Polynesia.* Council hall.

maneaba ni maungatabu *Kiribati.* House of Assembly.

Manerero *Botswana.* Ethnic subgroup.

Manesono *Bolivia.* Indian group in south Beni department.

Mangal *Afghanistan.* GHILAZAI tribe.

Manganja *Malawi.* LUNDA group in the Mwanza tributary area of the Shire Valley.

mangas *Brazil.* Farm land or plot used for pasturage.

Mangbetu *Zaire.* Nilo-Saharan language.

manger *Haiti.* Feast or sacrifice.

manger-yam *Haiti.* Two-day VOODOO harvest festival in November.

Manggarai *Indonesia.* Austronesian language.

mang ay yang *Philippines.* Sacred songs of the IBALOI.

Mangbetu *Zaire.* Ethnic group of northern savanna.

Mangisa *West Africa.* Niger-Kordofanian language.

Mangutu *Zaire.* Ethnic group of northern savanna.

Mangyan *Philippines.* Non-Christian ethnic group on Mindoro Island.

Manikongo *Angola.* Title of kings of the Kongo.

Maninka *West Africa.* Variant of MALINKE or MANDING.

Maninkakan *Guinea.* Language of MANINKA.

manipeba *Brazil.* The best variety of manioc.

manioc *West Africa.* Cassava.

Manipuri *India.* 1. Folk dance originating in Manipur. It is danced by both men and women, either accompanied by a chorus of singers or providing their own vocal accompaniment. One form, known as LAI-HARBO, or the merrymaking of the gods, is especially popular. 2. Sino-Tibetan language. Also, *Meithei.*

Manja *West Africa.* Niger-Kordofanian language.

Manjako or **Mandyako** *Guinea-Bissau.* Senegambian ethnic group.

Mankanya *West Africa.* Niger-Kordofanian language.

Mano *Liberia.* 1. Eastern branch of the MANDE. Also, *Ma, Mah.* 2. Niger-Kordofanian language.

Manobos *Philippines.* 1. Pagan mountain group in Mindanao. 2. Austronesian language.

manohra *Thailand.* Popular dance in the south.

manqad *Yemens.* Legal system prevalent in the eastern Yemens and in the Hadhramaut.

manqad al manqid *Yemens.* Judge of the MANQID group.

Manqid *Yemens.* Itinerant Arab caste.

mansa *Guinea.* Traditional MANDE title for village chief.

mansa *Senegal.* MALINKE title for king.

mansab *Yemens.* SAYYID with temporal power.

mansabdar *India.* Quasi-feudal official in Mughal times who was assigned lands on the condition that he supplies a certain number of horses and troops to the army when called upon to do so.

Mansaka *Philippines.* Austronesian language.

man sampalang *Thailand.* Cassava.

manso *Somalia.* Poetic form, generally light love songs, containing two to eight lines.

Manta *Cameroon.* Niger-Kordofanian language.

mantika (plural: manatik) *Arab countries.* Administrative district, subdivision of a province.

Mantion *Indonesia.* Papuan language.

mantra *India.*   Text of the VEDAS or a secret magical formula, chanted by the Hindus for invoking occult powers.

mantri *India.*   Minister. Through Portuguese, this term became mandarin.

mantri sabha *India.*   Cabinet or council of ministers.

Manya *West Africa.*   Niger-Kordofanian language.

Manya Krobo *Ghana.*   ADANGBE branch of eastern KROBO on the Volta Plains.

Man-Yao *Laos.*   Ethnic group.

Manyika *Southern Africa.*   1. SHONA-speaking ethnic group. 2. Niger-Kordofanian language.

Manyika *Zimbabwe.*   One of the main SHONA clusters.

manzana *Central America.*   Unit of area equal to two acres.

ma ohis *Tahiti.*   Traditional Polynesians.

Maori *Polynesia.*   1. Aboriginal inhabitants of New Zealand. 2. Austronesian language.

mapakat *Indonesia.*   Consensus; agreement.

mapales *Colombia.*   Music of African origin.

Mapes *Venezuela.*   Indian tribe.

Maphetla *Lesomo.*   *See* BAPHEILA.

maphrao *Thailand.*   Coconut.

Mapuche *Chile.*   Literally, people of the land. Araucanian tribe.

Mapudungu *Southern America.*   Indian language.

maqam *Arab countries.*   Shrine of a local holy man.

maquisard *Algeria.*   Guerrilla fighter during the war of independence.

Mar *Burma.*   Northern CHINS.

marabout (plural: maraboutim) *Islamic countries.*   Muslim ascetic or holy man.

marabountimn *Libya.*   Men of the soil. See RYAL AL BILAD.

maracuja *Brazil.*   Passion flower fruit.

marae *Polynesia.*   Temple altar or sacred enclosure.

marafo *Brazil.*   Crude rum or CACHACA.

Marakwet *Kenya.*   KALENJIN group in the Rift Valley.

maramat *India.*   Public works.

Maranao *Philippines.*   MORO group in Mindanao.

Maranao *Philippines.*   1. Ethnic group in Mindanao. 2. Austronesian language.

Maranse *Burkina Faso.*   Ethnic group of SONGHAI origin.

maratabat *Philippines.*   Face or honor among the MORO.

Mararit *Central Africa.*   1. SAHELian ethnic group. 2. Nilo-Saharan language.

Maratha *India.*   Properly, Maharatta. Marathi-speaking Hindu group who carved out an empire in western India in the 18th century.

Marathi *India.*　Indo-European language.

Maravi *Southern Africa.*　Cluster of BANTU speaking people in Mozambique and Malawi.

Marba *Chad.*　Afro-Asiatic language.

marchas *Paraguay.*　Marches, or a series of movements by settlers to new colonies.

marchinha *Brazil.*　Dance rhythm related to the samba.

mare *Burma.*　KACHIN village cluster. Also, *mareng.*

Marghi *West Africa.*　Afro-Asiatic language.

margmados *Paraguay.*　The poor.

maria *Honduras.*　Striped, open-grained tropical hardwood.

Maria *India.*　DRAVIDIAN language.

mariachi *Mexico.*　Band of strolling musicians.

marigots *Mauritania.*　Branching channels of the Senegal River that are dry in summer.

marimba *Spanish America.*　Musical instrument similar to the xylophone. Wooden boxes of irregular shapes and sizes hang beneath the keys made of hormigo wood and serve as resonators.

marimberos *Spanish America.*　MARIMBA musician.

maringa *Cameroon.*　Dance from Ghana.

marinyet *Ethiopia.*　Friendship group among the HARARI.

Marivio *Nicaragua.*　Nahua dialect of Mexican origin.

Marka *Mali.*　Ethnic group descended from the Sarakole.

Marka *Mali and Burkina Faso.*　Niger-Kordofanian language.

markaz (plural: marakiz) *Arab countries.*　Administrative district, subdivision of a province.

marmite *Haiti.*　Cooking pot.

maro *West Africa.*　Urban quarters inhabited by foreigners. Also, *Wangara, Zongo.*

maromba *Brazil.*　Floating raft or corral for cattle in the Amazon region.

Maropa *Bolivia.*　Amazon Indian group of TACANIAN language stock in Beni department.

marran *Philippines.*　Hot, spicy food made from banana.

marre *Haiti.*　Literally, tied. Tamed VOODOO spirit.

marsum jamhouri *Lebanon.*　Presidential order.

marta *Libya.*　Unit of weight equal to 16 kg.

maru mahan *Sri Lanka and South India.*　Son-in-law.

Marwari *India.*　1. Caste of moneylenders, mostly JAIN by religion. 2. Indo-European language.

masa *Nicaragua.*　Corn paste.

Masa *West Africa.*　Afro-Asiatic language.

Masaba *Central and East Africa.*　Niger-Kordofanian language.

Masaco *Bolivia.*　Pastry mixture of ground yucca and lard.

masafent *Ethiopia.* Formerly, princes of the royal family.

Masai *East Africa.* Nilo-Hamitic tribe, originally nomadic pastoralists.

Masakin *Sudan.* Niger-Kordofanian language.

masala *India.* Ingredients of a curry.

Masalit *Chad.* 1. Ethnic group in Ouadai along the Sudan border. 2. Nilo-Saharan language.

masanko *Ethiopia.* Single-string violin or fiddle. Also, *tacha wota.*

masawe *Malawi.* Native dance. See VIMBUZA.

Masbateno *Philippines.* Austronesian language.

mascates *Brazil.* Literally, peddlers. Term applied to Portuguese merchants.

masco vada *Brazil.* Brown sugar.

Maseko *Tanzania.* Subgroup of the Ngoni.

masenko *Ethiopia.* One-string instrument plucked or played with a horse hair bow.

Masenrempulu *Indonesia.* Austronesian language.

Mashaikh (singular: shaikh) *Arab countries.* Religious scholars of Qahtani ancestry.

Mashi *Southern Africa.* Niger-Kordofanian language.

Mashriq *Arab countries.* Eastern Arab world, as distinguished from MAGHREB.

masion *Central America.* Lodging house for transient Indians near market areas.

masir *Senegal.* Joking relationship among the SERER.

masjid *Islamic countries.* Mosque.

masmudi *Egypt.* Rhythmic music reflecting Western influences.

masnavi *India.* In Urdu and Persian, a long poem based on historical events.

Massa *West Africa.* Ethnic group in the Logone River Valley. Also, *Banana.*

Massalat *West Africa.* 1. SAHELian ethnic group. 2. Nilo-Saharan language.

Massango *Gabon.* Ethnic group related to the ESHIRA.

Massape *Brazil.* Rich fertile black alluvial soil in the northeast zona da mata.

massina *Sri Lanka.* Permissible marriage partner among the SINHALESE.

Massoufa *Western Sahara.* One of the nomadic SANHAJA tribes.

mastaba *Egypt.* Bench made of mud brick.

mastate *Central America.* Bark cloth.

Matabele *Southern Africa.* Any of two offshoots of the NGUNI, one found in Transvaal and the other in Zambia and Zimbabwe. Also, NDEBELE.

Mataco *Argentina.* Macro-Guaicuruan language.

Matagalpas *Central America*   Indians of the central highlands.

matai *Samoa*   Titled village family head.

Matakam *West Africa*   1. Ethnic group. 2. Afro-Asiatic language.

Matal *Cameroon*   Afro-Asiatic language.

Matambe *Tanzania*   Ethnic group.

mataqalis *Fiji*   Village group forming an extended social unit.

matate *Central America*   Small net bag made of rush pith with two short handles, usually carried by men. Also, *chim, redes, morral, bolsas* or *guonn gochos.*

matatu *Kenya*   Van that plies as a taxi.

Matawirah *Syria*   An ALAWITE confederation.

mate *Paraguay*   *See* YERBA MATE.

mate amargo *Paraguay*   Bitter MATE, drunk hot or cold.

Matengo *East Africa*   1. Ethnic group. 2. Niger-Kordofanian language.

math *India*   Hindu monastery.

matho yekchin *Burma*   Ceremonial weaving of five yards of orange cloth for a monk's robe between dusk and dawn.

mati *Guyana*   Bond between persons associated in the same work.

matona *Lesotho*   Informal group of counselors and advisers of a chief.

matrukah *Iraq*   Land reserved for public purposes.

Matsebula *Swaziland*   One of the most important Swazi clans, one called "true Swazi," or *bemdzabuko.* The first royal consort must always be chosen from this clan.

matshube *Cameroon*   FULANI retainers in the court of the LAMIDO.

Matsouanism *Congo*   Syncretic and politico-messianic movement founded in 1927 by Andre Matsou as Amicalism.

matthayom su *Thailand*   Secondary education.

Matumbi *Tanzania*   1. Ethnic group. 2. Niger-Kordofanian language.

mace *Vietnam*   Unit of area equal to 2.47 acres.

Mau *West Africa*   Niger-Kordofanian language.

mau a pule *Western Samoa*   Political movement advocating restoration of monarchical rule.

maulana *Islamic countries*   Authority on Muslim law and theology.

maulvi *Islamic countries*   Itinerant preacher.

maund *India*   Unit of weight varying from two lb to 160 lb, according to the nature of the produce.

maung *Burma*   Title of address toward a male of lesser status than the speaker.

Maure *Mauritania*   Arabized variant of MOOR, from which the name of the country is derived.

mausa *Gambia*   MANDINGO title for king.

Maviha *Southern and Eastern Africa*   Niger-Kordofanian language.

Maues *South America*   Indians of the lower Tapajoz and Amazon region speaking a Tupi-Guarani language.

Mau-Mau *Kenya.*   Secret society among the KIKUYU formerly active in armed struggle against colonial rule.

Mawali *India.*   Hill tribe of the Western Ghats.

Mawchi *India.*   Indo-European language.

mawdo *Senegal.*   Master of an extended family among the TOUCOLEURS. Also, *dyomgalle.*

mawe (plural: mawesia) *Sierra Leone.*   Extended family among the MENDE.

Mawia *Tanzania.*   Ethnic group.

mawkun *Burma.*   Epic poetry.

mawpa *Burma.*   Seer and shaman among the LAHU.

mawpi *Burma.*   LISU sorcerer and spirit doctor.

Mawu *Ghana.*   Supreme EWE deity.

Maxi-Gbe *West Africa.*   Niger-Kordofanian language.

maya *India.*   Phenomena as illusions.

Maya *Central America.*   Collective term for one of the most important ethnic clusters of Indians, famed for their calendar, architecture and textiles. The major periods of their history are the Old Empire from 317 to 987 and the New Empire from 987 to 1697. Among the more important Maya tribes are *Campeche, Chiapol, Chol, Chontol, Lacandon, Kekchi, Quintana Roo, Tzeltal, Tojolebal* and *Tzotzil.*

manjil *Sudan.*   Title of chief under the Funj sultanate.

Mayan *Central America.*   Member of the MAYA ethnic group.

Mayo *Guinea.*   Subgroup of the TENDA.

Mayo *Mexico.*   Azteco-Tanoan language.

Mayogo *Zaire.*   Niger-Kordofanian language.

mayorazgo *Bolivia.*   Primogeniture.

mayordomos *Central America.*   Persons conducting a FIESTA.

mayu-dama *Burma.*   Among the KACHINS, affinal relationships established by marriage.

Mayuriana *Bolivia.*   Amazon Indian group in central Beni department.

mayrmana *Afghanistan.*   In PASHTO, honorific of married women. Compare *begum.*

Mazahua *Central America.*   1. Subgroup of the PIPIL Indians. 2. Oto-Manguean language.

mazamorra *Paraguay.*   Dessert prepared from corn cooked with coal ash and served with milk.

Mazandrani *Iran.*   1. Ethnic group along the Caspian coast, related to the Iranians but speaking a different language. 2. Indo-European language.

Mazatec *Mexico.*   Ethnic group.

Mazateco *Mexico.*   Oto-Manguean language.

Mazhabi *India.*   Low-caste SIKHS.

mazombismo *Brazil.* Tendency among upper classes to deprecate things Brazillian and to idealize foreign cultures.

mazombos *Brazil.* White person born in the New World, as opposed to REINOIS.

mazon *Haiti.* Dance of African origin.

mazouk *Haiti.* Lively dance resembling the polka.

Mba *Zaire.* 1. Ethnic group of Central Rain Forest. 2. Niger-Kordofanian language.

Mbai or **Mbaye** *Chad.* SARA subgroup in the southern region.

Mbai *West Africa.* Nilo-Saharan language.

mbai-be *Chad.* Village chief among the SARA.

Mbaka *Central African Republic.* Group of clans of BANTU origin.

Mbala *Zaire.* 1. Ethnic group of southern savanna. 2. Niger-Kordofanian language.

Mbama *Congo and Gabon.* Niger-Kordofanian language.

Mbang *Central African Republic and Chad.* Title of the hereditary kings of the BAGUIRMI kingdom.

Mbanja *Zaire.* Ethnic group.

Mbanza *Congo and Zaire.* Niger-Kordofanian language.

mbari *Kenya.* Lineage unit among the KIKUYU.

Mbati *West Africa.* Niger-Kordofanian language.

Mbato *Ivory Coast.* 1. Ethnic group, one of the LAGOON CLUSTER. 2. Niger-Kordofanian language.

Mbaya *Paraguay.* Indian ethnic group, branch of Guaycurti.

Mbe *West Africa.* Niger-Kordofanian language.

Mbede *Gabon.* Ethnic group.

Mbelime *Benin.* Niger-Kordofanian language.

Mbembe *West Africa.* Niger-Kordofanian language.

Mbere *Congo and Gabon.* Niger-Kordofanian language.

Mbere *East Africa.* Ethnic group.

Mbesa *Zaire.* Ethnic group.

Mbete *Gabon.* Ethnic group.

Mbimou *Central African Republic.* BANTU-speaking group in Upper Sangha.

Mbimu *West Africa.* Niger-Kordofanian language.

mbira *Zimbabwe.* SHONA musical instrument with 25 to 30 iron rods fixed to resonant wooden bases of various shapes.

Mbo *Southern Africa.* Bantu-speaking people, related to NYANJA.

mbocaya *Paraguay.* Common native palm.

Mbole *Zaire.* 1. Niger-Kordofanian language. 2. Ethnic group.

M'Bona *Malawi.* Territorial cult of the MANGANJA people in Lower Shire Valley.

Mbondo *Angola.* MBUNDU subgroup.

mbondvo *Swaziland.* Hardy shrub used in rituals.

Mboo *West Africa.*   Niger-Kordofanian language.

Mboshi *Congo.*   Boubangui ethnic group.

Mbosi *Congo.*   Niger-Kordofanian language.

M'boum *West Africa.*   Southern ethnic group.

Mbuela *Angola.*   NGANGUELA subgroup.

Mbugu *Tanzania.*   Non-BANTU ethnic group.

Mbugwe *Tanzania.*   Ethnic group around Lake Manyara.

Mbuja *Zaire.*   Ethnic group.

Mbukushu *Angola.*   Ethnic group.

Mbukushu *Southern Africa.*   Niger-Kordofanian language.

Mbum *West Africa.*   Niger-Kordofanian language.

mbumba *Southern Africa.*   Lineage of matrilineal descent.

Mbun *Zaire.*   Ethnic group.

Mbunda *Angola.*   NGANGUELA subgroup.

Mbunda *Southern Africa.*   Niger-Kordofanian language.

Mbundu *Angola.*   1. Ethnic group. 2. Niger-Kordofanian language.

Mbunga *Tanzania.*   1. Ethnic group of ZULU-NGONI origin. 2. Niger-Kordofanian language.

m'chiikumbi (plural: achikumbi) *Malawi.*   Progressive farmer.

Mdluli *Swaziland.*   One of the "true Swazi" clans.

mecanicos *Brazil.*   Artisans.

mecapal *Central America.*   Broad leather strap for the forehead with attached ropes for carrying bags or goods on the back.

mecate *Central America.*   Maguey cord of 65 feet for measuring land.

mecate *Mexico.*   Unit of area equal to $\frac{1}{10}$th of an acre.

mechero *Bolivia.*   Lamp made by inserting a wick into a can or bowl of kerosene.

Mechi *Nepal.*   THARU ethnic group.

mechouar *Morocco.*   Government building.

mechta *Algeria.*   Village.

medialunas *Uruguay.*   Long bamboo spears capped with crescents of steel used by GAUCHOS to hamstring cattle.

mediana *Spanish America.*   Medium-sized landholding.

mediana propriedad *Central America.*   Class of FINCAS, or farms between 88 and 350 acres in size.

medianero *Uruguay.*   Tenant farmer.

medieria *Central America.*   Mixed land-tenancy system in which the owner provides the land, seed, implements and cash advances in return for 50 percent of the crop.

medina *Islamic countries.*   City, especially the native quarters.

medio *Honduras.*   Measure of volume for grains equal to 46 liters.

medio acomodados, los *Spanish America.*   The middle class.

Medlpa *Papua New Guinea.*   Papuan language.

Medogo *Chad.*   Subgroup of the LISI.

Medumba *West Africa.*   Niger-Kordofanian language.

medyata *Egypt.*   Guest house.

M'een *Ethiopia and Sudan.*   Nilo-Saharan language.

me'etu'apaki *Tonga.*   Traditional Tongan dance involving the carrying of flat wooden figures resembling canoe paddles.

Mehape *Malawi.*   Witchcraft eradication movement, begin in 1933.

mehari *Morocco.*   Riding camel.

mehr *Bangladesh.*   Dowry.

mehtar *India.*   Literally, prince. Euphemistic name for sweepers and scavengers.

meiacao *Brazil.*   Sharecropping system in Minas State; thus *meiros,* sharecroppers.

Meithei *India.*   Sino-Tibetan language.

mejat *Western Sahara.*   Small tribe along the northern coast.

mejbur *Mauritania.*   Plundering raid employing less than 40 camels. Compare GAZI.

mejorana *Panama.*   Five-string native guitar.

mekhum *Cambodia.*   Head of a KHUM.

mekwamiya *Ethiopia.*   Prayer stick.

Mekyibo *Ivory Coast.*   Any of the LAGOON ethnic cluster. Also, *Vetere, Eotile, Ewotre, Byetri, Papaire.*

mela *India.*   Religious fair.

Melabuganon *Philippines.*   MORO group in Palawan.

Melanau *Sarawak.*   Austronesian language of the Melanau people.

meleka *Sierra Leone.*   God, among the KISSI.

mellah *Morocco.*   Jewish quarter of a town.

mellia *Tunisia.*   Woman's loose drape, like a SARI.

melmastia *Afghanistan.*   Obligation under the PUSHTUNWALI to provide hospitality and afford protection to strangers.

melqagna *Ethiopia.*   District governor's deputy.

memher *Ethiopia.*   Head abbot of an Orthodox monastery.

men *Senegal.*   Literally, breast milk. Matrilineage among the WOLOF.

menasir *Western Sahara.*   Ethnic group formerly large and numerous.

Mende *West Africa.*   1. Ethnic group divided into numerous independent subgroups. 2. Niger-Kordofanian language.

mendoub *Morocco.*   Title of the sultan's representative.

mengala *Central America.*   LADINOS who have learned Indian dialect and adopted Indian customs.

mengkyaw *Burma.*   Strict ascetic order of SHAN Buddhist monks.

meniha *Western Sahara.*   Lending of livestock by wealthy herd owners to less fortunate nomads.

Menka *West Africa.*   Niger-Kordofanian language.

mensu *Paraguay.*   Plantation worker receiving less than minimum wages and working in poor living conditions.

mentalidad Altoperuana *Bolivia.* Literally, upper Peruvian mentality. Provincialism as a national characteristic.

Mentaweians *Indonesia.* Ethnic group of Sumatra.

Mentawi *Indonesia.* Austronesian language.

menteri basar *Malaysia.* Chief minister of a state.

Menya *Papua New Guinea.* Papuan language.

Meo *Southeast Asia.* Ethnic group, also found in south China, living in the highlands. Also, *Miao.*

Mepa *Tanzania.* Ethnic group.

meqda *Ethiopia.* Innermost circle of a church.

merantau *Indonesia.* Custom of the males going on extended trips away from home.

merdeka *Indonesia.* Freedom.

merengue *Spanish America.* Popular dance form consisting of an eight-measure slow melody followed by a fast one. Its principal feature is a limping sidestep.

Meri *West Africa.* Afro-Asiatic language.

merienda *Mexico.* Snack.

Merina *Madagascar.* Largest national ethnic group, in the central highlands.

meringue *Haiti.* Variant of the merengue.

merrise *Chad.* Alcoholic liquor distilled from dates.

Meru *East Africa.* 1. Ethnic group. 2. Niger-Kordofanian language.

mesa *Spanish America.* Polling place.

Mesaka *West Africa.* Niger-Kordofanian language.

mesas de dinero *Venezuela.* Literally, money desk. Financial practice facilitating the movement of short-term securities.

Mesengo *Ethiopia.* Nilo-Saharan language.

Mesmedje *Chad.* Afro-Asiatic language.

Meshrano Jirgeh *Afghanistan.* House of Elders, the upper house of the national legislature.

meson *El Salvador.* Large building.

Mesqel *Ethiopia.* Festival on September 27/28 celebrating the Discovery of the True Cross.

mestico *Brazil.* Variant of MESTIZO.

mestiza *Philippines.* National woman's costume with a low square neckline and butterfly sleeves. Also, *terna, Mariaclara.*

mestizaje *Spanish America.* Fusion of Indian and white population resulting in a large MESTIZO population.

mestizo *Spanish America.* Person of mixed, generally Indian and white, descent.

mestizoization *Spanish America.* See MESTIZAJE.

metate *Spanish America.* Stone on which corn is ground.

metis *Senegal.* Person of mixed French-African descent.

metizeje *Venezuela.* Genetic mixture of Indian, white and Negro races.

Metoku *Zaire.* Ethnic group.

meyen *Nepal.* SHERPA temporary herdsmen's settlement in the high mountains.

mezcal *Mexico.* Strong alcoholic drink.

mezzeh *Lebanon.* Appetizers.

mfantsipim *Ghana.* Language of the FANTE-AKAN spoken in central and western coastal areas.

Mfecane *Lesotho.* Literally, crushing. Period of disastrous inter-clan warfare during the building up of the ZULU kingdom.

mfengu *Zimbabwe.* NGUNI-speaking people.

mfukwane *Swaziland.* Sacred herd of the Swazi king, never used in ploughing.

Mfumte *West Africa.* Niger-Kordofanian language.

mfumu *Malawi.* Chief of a Chewa family.

mfundisi (plural: abafundisi) *Zimbabwe.* SINDEBELE term for teacher.

Mfunu *Zaire.* Ethnic group.

mganga *Tanzania.* Physician.

mhondoro *Zimbabwe.* CHISHONA word for tutelary spirits known as lion spirits that communicate through living mediums.

Midgan *Somalia.* Ethnic subgroup, descended from pre-Islamic hunting people.

Midob *Sudan.* Ethnic group.

Mien *Southeast Asia.* Sino-Tibetan language.

mieu *Vietnam.* Small shrine or altar for the worship of spirits.

Migili *West Africa.* Niger-Kordofanian language.

mi gyaun *Burma.* Crocodile zither of the MONS with three strings and seven to nine frets. The sound box is carved in the form of a crocodile.

mihrab *Islamic countries.* Niche or alcove in a mosque indicating the direction toward Mecca.

Mijikenda *Kenya.* Literally, nine tribes. Ethnic cluster comprising *Giriyama, Duruma, Digo, Chunyi, Rabai, Ribe, Kambe, Jibana* and *Kauma.*

Mikhifore *Guinea.* MANDE-speaking ethnic group.

Mikir *India.* Sino-Tibetan language.

mikitil woreda *Ethiopia.* Subdistrict.

milad sharif *Islamic countries.* The Koran chanted or recited.

miliciano *Cuba.* Militia policeman who performs guard duty.

milk *Morocco.* Private freehold land.

milla *Turkey.* People.

millet *Turkey.* Religious community under the Ottomans.

Millet Meclisi *Turkey.* National Assembly.

millieme *Egypt.* Coin, 1/1000ths of an Egyptian pound.

milpa *Central America.* Small plot of cornfield interplanted with other crops.

Mimamsa *India.* One of the six orthodox systems of Hindu philosophy founded by Jaimini dealing with VEDIC rituals and ceremonies.

Mimi *Chad.* SAHELian ethnic group.

Min *Burkina Faso.* Ethnic group of the SENUFO cluster.

Min *Burma.* Prince or subordinate ruler.

Mina *Togo.* Collective term for GA and ANE ethnic groups.

Mina *India.* Indo-European language.

mina *Arab countries.* Port.

Minahasa *Indonesia.* Ethnic group of Sulawesi.

Minangkabau *Indonesia.* Ethnic group of Sumatra.

Minangkabau *Indonesia and Malaysia.* Austronesian language.

minbar *Islamic countries.* Raised lectern or pulpit in a mosque.

minca *Bolivia.* Voluntary collective work on public lands.

mindihay *Somalia.* Literally, knife bearers. Putative descendants of the original treaty-makers among the SAAB.

mindul *Somalia.* One-room hut with cylindrical walls and a round or conical roof.

mineiro *Brazil.* Literally, miner. Native of state of Minas Gerais.

mineros *Paraguay.* Indian laborers working as virtual slaves in YERBA MATE plantations.

minga *Ecuador.* Form of cooperative labor. See MINCA.

mingaco *Chile.* Cooperative labor among the Mapuche.

Minianke *Mali.* Ethnic group related to the SENUFO.

minifundio *Spanish America.* Small landholdings.

minifundismo *Spanish America.* Excessive fragmentation of landholdings.

minifundista *Spanish America.* Small independent landholders with 12 acres or less.

ministeriales *Colombia.* Pro-administration supporters during the Herran presidency.

ministerio *Spanish America.* Ministry.

minjok *South Korea.* Nation.

minjokchok minjujuui *South Korea.* National democracy.

mintadi *Congo.* Figures placed in the homes of absent chiefs to protect their families and property.

mintaka *Algeria.* Subdivision of a WILAYA.

miombo *Tanzania.* Savanna woodland.

mir *India.* In Mughal times, head of a department.

mir ab *Afghanistan.* Official in charge of allocation of water and repair of ditches and QANATS.

miri *Arab countries.* Government land.

Mirifle Confederacy *Somalia.*   A clan family. See Rohenweyn.

miri tapu *Arab countries.*   Government land under permanent private occupation.

mirza *Iran.*   Title of ISMAILI or KHOJA official or notable.

misafir odasi *Turkey.*   Guest house.

misambwa *Uganda.*   Spirits among the GANDA.

Misari *Middle East.*   Branch of the ISMAILI sect.

mishara *Iraq.*   Unit of area equal to 0.25 hectares.

Misirie *Chad.*   Nomadic DJOHEINA Arab group found in Ouadai prefecture.

Miskito *Central America.*   1. Indian tribe of the Atlantic coast mixed with Negro groups. Also, *Mosquito.* 2. Unaffiliated language.

Misr *Egypt.*   Ancient name for Egypt.

misside *Guinea.*   Village or cluster of villages with a mosque.

mistela *Guatemala.*   Drink made of wine, cinnamon and sugar.

mita *Spanish America.*   Formerly, conscript labor system under which all able-bodied Indian men had to present themselves periodically for short periods of work in the mines.

mitayo *Spanish America.*   Variant of mita.

Mithaq al Watani *Lebanon.*   National covenant of 1943 under which all political positions are shared by members of religious denominations on the basis of their percentage of the population at the time of the 1932 census.

mitimae *Bolivia.*   Forced colonization.

mitote *Nicaragua.*   Dance among the Chorutegnans of Tezoatega at the time of cacao harvest.

Mitsoga *Gabon.*   OKANDE linguistic groups.

Mixe *Mexico.*   1. Indian tribe in the southeast. 2. Mazatlan language.

Mixtec *Mexico.*   Ethnic group in southern highlands.

Mixteco *Mexico.*   Oto-Manguean language.

miyombo *Mozambique.*   Deciduous open woodland.

mizimu *Malawi.*   Ancestral spirits.

Mizque *Bolivia.*   Andean Indian group in Cochabamba department.

Mkatshwa *Swaziland.*   NGUNI clan.

mlechcha *India.*   Literally barbarian. Persons or groups outside the caste system, considered ritually unclean. Also, taboos and degree of pollution associated with such groups.

Mlimo *Zimbabwe.*   SINDEBELE term for god.

Mmani (singular: Manil) *Guinea.*   Ethnic group.

M'nong *Vietnam.*   1. Highland ethnic group in central highlands speaking a Mon-Khmer language. 2. Austro-Asiatic language.

Mo *Ghana.*   GRUSI tribe.

Moba *Togo.*   1. Ethnic cluster comprising Moba and KONKOMBA. 2. Niger-Kordofanian language.

Mober *West Africa.*   Afro-Asiatic language.
Mocha *Ethiopia.*   Afro-Asiatic language.
moda *Brazil.*   Ballad.
moderados *Mexico.*   Moderates.
modi *Guinea.*   Term of address among the PEUL equal to Mr.
modibo *Guinea.*   Term of address among the PEUL equal to sir.
Mofu *West Africa.*   Afro-Asiatic language.
mofussil *India.*   Provincial town.
Mofou *Cameroon.*   Northern ethnic group.
Moghamo-Menemo *Cameroon.*   Niger-Kordofanian language.
mogya *Ghana.*   AKAN term for blood, or the physical and maternal side of the family.
mohafazat *Arab countries.*   Province.
mohafez *Arab countries.*   Governor.
mohlam *Laos.*   Folk theater.
Mohmands *Pakistan and Afghanistan.*   Warlike tribe in Northwest Frontier Province.
Mohorais *Comoros.*   Inhabitants of the island of Mayotte.
mohur *India.*   Former gold coin.
Mojo *Bolivia.*   Arawakan language of Beni department.
Mojoan *Bolivia.*   Ethnolinguistic Indian group.
moka *Papua New Guinea.*   Traditional exchange of pigs as gifts between allies in the highlands of New Guinea.
mokata *Saudi Arabia.*   Province.
Mokole *West Africa.*   Niger-Kordofanian language.
mokru *Guyana.*   Jungle reed.
moksha *India.*   Eternal bliss, equivalent to heaven, through extinction or release from the cycle of life.
mola *Panama.*   Part of the blouse of CUNA Indian women, consisting of a decorative cloth over which brightly colored fabrics are sewn together in geometric patterns.
molam *Thailand.*   Popular entertainment consisting of a declamation sung to the accompaniment of a seven-tone panpipe.
Mole-Dagbane *West Africa.*   Group of culturally and linguistically related peoples in Ghana and Ivory Coast, including the *Birifo, Builsa, Dagari, Dagomba, Gurma, Konkomba, Kusasi, Mamprusi, Mossi, Nabdan, Nankansi, Nanumba, Tallensi, Walla* and *Yansi.*
molendero *Honduras.*   Mill used with METATES to prepare corn for tortillas.
molo *West Africa.*   18-string musical instrument.
moloj *Central America.*   Nightly rounds made by members of the COFRADIAS just before the Holy Week for collecting money. Also *zarabanda.*
molongo *Cameroon.*   Supreme council of the BAKWERI clan chiefs.

molote *Guatemala.* Spool of wool yarn.

Moma *Zaire.* Ethnic group.

Momand *Afghanistan.* GHILAZAI tribe.

Mombwe *Zambia.* Tanzanian ethnic group in the northeast.

momo *Nepal.* SHERPA food of chopped goat or mutton wrapped in a spiced dough.

Mon *Burma and Thailand.* Mon-Khmer-speaking people, whose ancestors ruled an empire in Burma with the capital at Pegu until 1757. Also, *Talaing.*

Mon *Southeast Asia.* Austro-Asiatic language.

mondop *Thailand.* Square cubicle structure, either plain or with pillars around it, with a pyramidal superstructure formed by many dome-shaped roofs topped by a slender pinnacle.

mong *Burma.* SHAN term for town or township.

Mongo *Zaire.* Ethnic group of the Central Rain Forest.

Mongondow *Indonesia.* Austronesian language.

Mongo-Nkundu *Zaire.* Niger-Kordofanian language.

monhinga *Burma.* Thin rice noodle with fish curry.

Moni *Indonesia.* Papuan language.

Monimbo *Nicaragua.* Indian ethnic group.

monipuri *Bangladesh.* Elaborately costumed communal celebration at full moonlight after the harvest.

moniteur *Rwanda and Burundi.* Elementary school teacher.

Monjombo *Central Africa.* Niger-Kordofanian language.

Mon-Khmer *Southeast Asia.* 1. Linguistic stock represented by Khasi in Assam, Mon, Palaung and Wa in Burma, Cambodian in Cambodia, Semang and Saka in Malaysia and dialects in the Nicobar Islands. 2. Ethnic groups speaking these languages.

Mono *Zaire.* Niger-Kordofanian language.

Monom *Vietnam.* Highland ethnic group northeast of Kontum.

monsoon *South Asia.* Seasonal wind bringing heavy rains blowing from the southwest from April to October and from the northeast from October to December.

Montagnard *Vietnam.* Collective name for highland ethnic groups.

monte *Honduras.* Uncultivated land assigned to each Indian village.

monte *Paraguay.* Forest areas or highlands.

montepio *Uruguay.* Contributors to a retirement fund or pension.

montera *Bolivia.* Hard leather hat worn by QUECHUA men and women near Sucre.

Montol *West Africa.* Afro-Asiatic language.

montuno *Panama.* Male cotton shirt and trousers adorned with picturesque embroidery called *pintas.*

montura *Honduras.* Saddle resembling Western saddle, but with a saddle horn.

montuvio *Ecuador.*   Plantation worker. Also, acculturated Indian of the COSTA.

Moore *West Africa.*   Niger-Kordofanian language.

mophato *Lesotho.*   Circumcision school.

moplah *India.*   Malayalam-speaking Muslim.

Moporoubocono *Bolivia.*   Amazon Indian group in Beni department.

moqadem *Western Sahara.*   President of AIR ARBAIN or war council.

moqueca de peixe *Brazil.*   Ragout of fish and shellfish cooked in oil and pepper and wrapped in banana leaves.

moradores *Brazil.*   Sharecroppers in the northeast.

moranca *Guinea-Bissau.*   Extended family groups within villages, especially among the BALANTAS.

morcha *India.*   Strike leading to disruption of public life.

mordida *Spanish America.*   Bribe, but without any negative connotations.

More *Burkina Faso and Ghana.*   Language of the MOSSI.

morenada *Bolivia.*   Highland Indian dance imitating Negro dress and music.

Moreno *Central America.*   BLACK CARIB or persons with dark skins, not necessarily Negroid.

moreno *Latin America.*   Pure-blooded Negro.

morgan *Swaziland.*   Unit of area equal to 2.11 acres.

morgado *Brazil.*   Inheritance law based on primogeniture, abolished in 1835.

Mori *Indonesia.*   Austronesian language.

mori *Liberia.*   Learned Muslim who inscribes amulets.

morisco *Honduras.*   Offspring of a Spanish father and a MULATA mother.

Morisco *West Africa.*   MOOR or Moorish.

Morlaca *Ecuador.*   The CHOLO of Cuenca.

Morma *Bangladesh.*   Tribal group in the Chittagong tract. Also, MAGHI.

Moro *Bolivia.*   Indian group of ZAMUCOAN linguistic stock in CHACO.

Moro *Sudan.*   Niger-Kordofanian language.

Moro *Philippines.*   Muslim ethnic group in Mindanao, Palawan and Sulu Archipelago.

moro-moro *Philippines.*   Informal drama reenacting the struggle of Spanish Christians and their ultimate victory over the Moors.

moros, los *Guatemala.*   Literally, dance of the Moors. Long dance drama with no dialogue, depicting the Spanish Christian struggle against the Moors.

Moru *Sudan.*   1. Sudanic ethnic group in Equatoria. 2. Nilo-Saharan language.

morubixada *Brazil.*   Military chieftains of TUPI tribes.

morung *India and Burma.*   Communal house for boys in NAGA villages.

Moscoes *Honduras.*   Caribbean coastal tribe.

Mosi *Chad.*   Afro-Asiatic language.

mosquetas *Panama.*   Pendant or hoop earrings with circles of pearls.

Mossi *West Africa.*   1. Sudanic-speaking ethnic group of KABRE cluster. 2. Niger-Kordofanian language.

Motilones *Colombia.*   Indian ethnic group.

motlotiehl *Lesotho.*   Chief of state, with the title of king.

Motozintlic *Central America.*   MAYA tribe.

Motsa *Swaziland.*   SOTHO clan.

Motu *Papua New Guinea.*   Austronesian language.

mou *Chad.*   Among the SARA, councilors.

Moubi *Chad.*   Ethnic group in Oum Hadjer district.

moudiria *Comoros.*   Subdivision of a region.

Moubi *Chad.*   SAHELian ethnic group.

Moundang *Chad.*   Ethnic group in southwest Chad related to SARA.

Mousgoum *Cameroon.*   Northern ethnic group.

moutia *Seychelles.*   Dance similar to the SEGA of Mauritius.

Movima *Bolivia.*   Amazon Indian group in Beni department.

moya *Ecuador.*   Low-level meadow or orchard in the coastal region.

mozo *Nicaragua.*   Temporary migrant harvesters.

Mpama *Zaire.*   Ethnic group.

Mpepo *Tanzania.*   Ethnic group.

mpfumu mpu *Congo.*   Crowned chief of the KONGO.

mpifakatiavana *Madagascar.*   Quasi kinsman through social ties.

mpompo *Cameroon.*   Niger-Kordofanian language.

Mpondo *Zimbabwe.*   1. Bantu-speaking people of the southern Nguni group. 2. Their language.

Mpongwe *Gabon.*   MYENE-speaking ethnic group.

Mpoto *Southern Africa.*   Niger-Kordofanian language.

Mpukusha *Botswana.*   Ethnic subgroup.

Mput *Zaire.*   Ethnic group.

mridangam *India.*   In south India, a large drum.

Mros or **Moorangs** *Bangladesh.*   Tribal group in Chittagong tract.

Mru *Burma, Bangladesh and India.*   Sino-Tibetan language.

mtfanenkosi (plural: bant fapenkosi) *Swaziland.*   Prince who is not an heir to the throne.

muallamin *Mauritania.*   Craftsman caste.

muang *Thailand.*   Autonomous commune composed of extended families.

muban *Thailand.*   Village.

Mubi *Chad.*   Afro-Asiatic language.

mucama *Brazil.*   Favorite slave or black maid.

mucambo *Brazil.*   Slum in the north.

mudali *Sri Lanka.*   Sinhalese high caste.

mudaliar *India.* Non-BRAHMIN TAMIL caste in south India.

mudaliar *Sri Lanka.* Chief local official under Dutch rule.

mudang *South Korea.* Sorceresses practicing folk medicine.

mudas *Brazil.* Coffee seedlings sold by itinerant muleteers.

Mudejar *Morocco.* Morisco.

mudejar *Paraguay.* Spanish-Moorish style.

mudhif *Iraq.* Tribal guest house, coffeehouse and meeting place.

mudir *Arab countries.* Local official, especially head of a district or subdistrict.

mudir *Egypt.* Rector of a university.

mudiiyaat (singular: mudiriyat) *Arab countries.* Subdistricts.

mudra *India.* Literally, gesture. Position of hands and fingers used in dancing and rituals to convey symbolic meaning.

mudzimu *Zimbabwe.* SHONA term for ancestor spirit.

muene *Mozambique.* Hereditary chief among the MAKUA Lomue.

muezzin *Arab countries.* Person who calls the Muslim faithful to prayer from the minaret of a mosque.

muffrage *Yemens.* Family room or room for socialization in a home.

mufti *Afghanistan.* Prosecuting attorney.

mufti *India.* Plain clothes worn by an official on duty as opposed to uniform.

mufti *Islamic countries.* 1. Expounder of Muslim law. 2. Local Islamic head.

Mugabe *Uganda.* Title of ruler of Anakole.

Mughal *India.* Imperial Muslim dynasty which ruled India between 1526 and 1857. Among its important rulers were Akbar and Shah Jehan.

muhaafaza (plural: muhaafazat) *Arab countries.* Province.

muhaafazaat (singular: muhafazat) *Libya.* Governorate.

muhaafiz *Arab countries.* Governor.

muhajirun *Saudi Arabia.* Emigrants.

Muhammadijah *Indonesia.* Orthodox Muslim reform movement launched in 1912.

Muharram *Islamic countries.* 1. The first month of the Muslim year. 2. Shiite festival held during this month commemorating the death of Ali, son-in-law of the prophet, at the Battle of Karbela.

muhtar *Turkey.* Local headman.

muhtarafa *India.* Under British rule, variety of imposts and taxes other than land revenue.

muhtasib *Morocco.* Overseer of a craft guild.

mujahidin *Algeria.* Guerrilla fighter during the struggle for independence.

mujahir *Pakistan.* Refugees.

mujtahid *Bangladesh.* Freedom fighter.

mujtahid *Iran.* Religious scholars.

muka kiranga *Burundi.* Chief organizer of a umaganuro festival.

mukaddam *India.* Headman of a village or a group of workers.

mukama *Uganda.* Title of the rulers of Bunyoro and Toro.

mukhiya *Nepal.* Village headman.

mukhya mantri *India.* Chief minister of a state.

mukim *Malaysia.* Smallest administrative division comprising several villages.

mukiwa (plural: vakiwa) *Zimbabwe.* CHISHONA term for European.

muktar (plural: mukhtaara) *Arab countries.* Headman of a village.

muktiar *India.* Power of attorney.

mukube *Zimbabwe.* Single-stringed musical instrument.

Mukulu *Zambia.* Congolese LUNDA tribe in Luapula Valley.

mul *Cambodia.* Angular script used in modern KHMER.

mulata *Brazil.* Mulatto woman.

mulamin *Morocco.* Veils worn by men of the SANHAJA tribe.

mulato *Spanish America.* Offspring of a Negro father and Spanish mother.

mulay *Morocco.* Literally, lord. Praenominal title for a descendant of a prophet in the male line.

mulazzim awwal *Saudi Arabia.* First lieutenant in the Saudi army.

mulazzim thani *Saudi Arabia.* Second lieutenant.

mulk *Iraq.* Land under full private ownership.

mulki *India.* Native of the former state of Hyderabad.

Mulki Ain *Nepal.* Legal code.

mullah *Islamic countries.* Muslim religious leader and preceptor.

mulmi *Nepal.* Headman of the TAMANG.

Mulondo *Angola.* NKHUMBI subgroup.

Mumbaka *West Africa.* Niger-Kordofanian language.

mumbo-jumbo *Gambia.* Formerly, in Mandingo society, village judge dressed in leaves and speaking a secret cant.

mumin *Arab countries.* Person trained in a religious school.

Mumye *West Africa.* Niger-Kordofanian language.

mutah *Iran.* Temporary marriage permitted under Shiite law for men away from home or on travel.

Muna *Indonesia.* Austronesian language.

Muna-Butung *Indonesia.* Ethnic group of Sulawesi.

Munda *India.* KOLARIAN aboriginal tribe of Central India.

Mundang *West Africa.* Niger-Kordofanian language.

Mundani *West Africa.* Niger-Kordofanian language.

Mundari *India and Nepal.* Austro-Asiatic language.

mundu *India.* Long cloth made of thin cotton worn as a skirt, especially by men.

Mundu *Sudan.* Sudanic people related to the AZANDE. 2. Niger-Kordofanian language.

mung *Burma.* Principality of a KACHIN chief.

mung dawa *Burma.* KACHIN chief.

Mungaka *West Africa.* Niger-Kordofanian language.

munguza *Brazil.* Porridge prepared from corn and coconut milk.

muni *India.* Hindu or JAIN anchorite who has taken a vow of silence.

municipalidad *Spanish America.* Municipal council.

municipio *Spanish America.* Local administrative unit consisting of a CABACERA and one or more ALDEAS, or rural settlements.

Munji-Yidgha *Afghanistan.* Indo-European language.

munshi *India.* Teacher or composer of documents.

munsif *India.* Judge.

muong *Laos.* District.

Muong *Southeast Asia.* Austro-Asiatic language.

Muong *Vietnam.* Ethnic group related to the Vietnamese living in Thanh-Hoa, Sari-La, Ha-Tay, Nghia-Lo and Hoa-Binh.

muqaddam *Islamic countries.* Chief of a TARIQA, or Islamic brotherhood.

muqaddam *Morocco.* Variant of MUKADDAM.

muqaddam *Saudi Arabia.* Lieutenant colonel in the Saudi army.

murabit *Mauritania.* Intercessor with miraculous powers in an Islamic brotherhood.

murali *India.* See BANSRI.

Mure *Bolivia.* Amazon Indian group of CHAPACURAN linguistic stock in Pando department.

murenge (plural: mirenga) *Zimbabwe.* CHISHONA term for warlike spirit or rebellion.

murhi *Nepal.* Unit of dry measure equal to 160 lbs.

Muria *India.* DRAVIDIAN language.

murid *Islamic countries.* Disciple of a SUFI order; also, discipline in a Sufi setting.

Muridiya *Senegal.* Islamic brotherhood founded by Amadou Bamba.

Murle *Sudan.* 1. Nilotic ethnic group. 2. Nilo-Saharan language.

muroyi *Zimbabwe.* Sorcerer or witch.

Murra *Saudi Arabia.* One of the larger tribes in east central region.

murshid *Islamic countries.* Spiritual guide or religious teacher.

murshid *Turkey.* Variant of MURID.

muruah *Saudi Arabia.* Manliness.

murumbi (plural: varumbi) *Zimbabwe.* CHISHONA term for European. See also MUKIWA, MURUNGU.

murumbo *Malawi.* Bowl-shaped drum.

murungu (plural: varungu) *Zimbabwe.* CHISHONA term for European.

Murut *Malaysia.* Ethnic group in Sarawak.

Musallis *India and Pakistan.* Low caste of sweepers and scavengers.

musem *Morocco.* Celebration honoring the birthday of a local marabout.

Musey *Chad.* Southern ethnic group in the Chari River Valley, related to the MASSA.

Musgu *West Africa.* Afro-Asiatic language.

musha (plural: misha) *Southern Africa.* Among the SHONA-Karanga, a settlement or KRAAL composed of several households under the authority of a SAMUSHA.

mushaa *Arab countries.* Communal ownership of land.

mushaira *India.* Literary or musical salon.

Mushikongo *Angola.* Subgroup of KONGO.

mushir *Saudi Arabia.* General in the Saudi army.

mushrikun *Saudi Arabia.* Polytheists.

musho *Ethiopia.* Song sung by women in honor of a deceased person. Compare LEGSO.

musikong bambong *Philippines.* Bamboo band consisting of string, wind, and percussion instruments.

musjawarat *Indonesia.* Discussion leading to consensus through synthesis of opposing views.

musnud *India.* Cushion used by native princes in place of a throne.

musseque *Angola.* Slum in Luanda and other cities. Also, *muceque.*

mussola *India.* Surf boat on the Coromandel coast.

Mustafians *West Asia.* Branch of the ISMAILIS.

mustawfis *Iran.* Accountant.

Musuraqui *Bolivia.* Indian group of the ZAMUCOAN language in CHACO and Santa Cruz departments.

mutasarifiyyah *West Asia.* Governorate.

mutasarrifiyyat (singular: mutssarifiyyat) *Libya.* Districts.

mutassarif *West Asia.* Under the Ottomans, governor.

mutawwt (plural: mutawiah) *Arab countries.* Religious leader or ULEMA of the IBADI sect.

mutawwiuun *Arab countries.* Religious police charged with the enforcement of Islamic laws and rendering of assistance to pilgrims.

Mutayr *Saudi Arabia.* Ethnic group.

mutirao *Brazil.* Communal help for an individual in building a house, etc.

mutoni *Burundi.* Courtier.

mutorwa (plural: vatorwa) *Zimbabwe.* CHISHONA term for stranger.

mutualista *Spanish America.* Mutual aid society.

mutunci *Nigeria.* Manhood or self-respect.

mutupo *Southern Africa.* SHONA lineage name.

mutupo (plural: mitupo) *Zimbabwe.* CHISHONA term for clan name.

muudul *Somalia.*   One-room house in which a cylindrical framework of slender posts and vines is plastered with mud, ashes and dung and a nine-foot high center pole supports a conical thatched roof.

Muwahhidun (singular: muwahhid) *Oman.*   Islamic unitarians following a form of WAHHABISM.

Muyong *West Africa.*   Afro-Asiatic language.

muzdoor *India.*   Industrial worker, distinguished from a KISAN, or farmer.

muzukuru *Zimbabwe.*   SHONA chief-maker and expert in genealogy.

Mvae *Cameroon.*   Southern forest subgroup of the Fang.

mvena *Malawi.*   CHEWA drum.

Mveni *Mozambique.*   Muslim coastal ethnic group.

mvet *Gabon.*   Calabash with strings.

mvila *Congo.*   Clan leaders among the KONGO.

mwabi *Malawi.*   Ordeal by drinking poison to prove innocence.

Mwaghavul *West Africa.*   Afro-Asiatic language.

mwalimu *Tanzania.*   Literally, teacher. Title of former president, Julius Nyerere.

mwami (plural: bwami) *Rwanda and Burundi.*   Title of TUTSI monarchs.

Mwanga *East and Southern Africa.*   Niger-Kordofanian language.

mwant yaav *Zaire and Southern Africa.*   Literally, king of vipers. Title of LUNDA kings.

Mwari *Zimbabwe.*   CHISHONA for high god.

Mwela *Angola.*   Niger-Kordofanian language.

mwembu *Burkina Faso.*   Holder of the office of Muslim IMAM in Ouagadougou.

Mwera *Tanzania.*   1. Ethnic group. 2. Niger-Kordofanian language.

mwezi *Burundi.*   1. One of the two royal spears used on ritual occasions. 2. Literally, handsome as moonlight. Title of the kings of Burundi.

Mwimbi *Kenya.*   Niger-Kordofanian language.

mwini dziko *Mozambique.*   Tribal chief among the CHEWA.

mwini mbumba *Malawi.*   Chief of a lineage group who has authority over brothers and sisters.

mwini mzinda *Malawi.*   Literally, owner of the secret place. Leading personage in a tribe.

mwo lam *Laos.*   Priest among the tribal TAI.

Myanma *Burma.*   In Burmese, Burma. Also, *Myanma Pyi,* Land of the Burmans.

Myene *Central Africa.*   Niger-Kordofanian language.

myo *Burma.*   Town or township. Thus, *myo-wun,* mayor; *myo-ok,* township office; *myo-thugyi,* headman.

myon *South Korea.*   Rural township, subdivision of a county.

myon jang *South Korea.*   Head of township.

myosa *Burma.* Chief of the Northern SHANS.

Mzab *Algeria.* Afro-Asiatic language.

M'zabite *Algeria.* BERBER group in M'zab region in central Sahara.

mzee *Kenya.* Old man or elder.

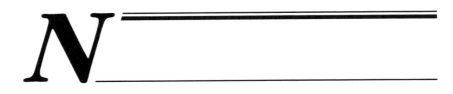

na or **naba** (plural: nabdema or nanamse) *Ghana.* Title of MOLE-DAG-BANE ruler or chief.

na *Thailand.* Rice farm.

naama *Western Sahara.* Slaves born under the tent of the owner and often treated as members of the family.

naba (plural: nanamse) *Burkina Faso.* MOSSI ruler.

nabaddon *Somalia.* Peacekeeper, new title of an elder after the 1969 coup.

Nabahinah (singular: Nabhani) *Oman.* Section of the Beni Riyam tribe.

Nabak *Papua New Guinea.* Papuan language.

Nabo *Sierra Leone.* Secret society among the LIMBA.

nabomnt fwanza *Swaziland.* Queen regent.

Nabte *Ghana.* Language of NAMNAM.

nacatamale *Nicaragua.* Large TAMALE with cornmeal dough exterior and an interior made of spice, meat, raisins, etc.

nadagama *Sri Lanka.* Folk opera.

nadante *Senegal.* Permanent reciprocal work group among the WOLOF.

Nadar *India.* Low caste of toddy makers.

nadhir *Morocco.* Administrator of a habous or religious trust.

nadhr *Iran.* Fulfillment of a vow for a special favor of Allah.

nae *Thailand.* A form of oboe.

naegak *North Korea.* Cabinet.

Nafaanra *Ghana.* Niger-Kordofanian language.

Nafana *Burkina Faso.* Ethnic group of SENUFO cluster.

Naga *India.* 1. Hill tribe of Mongoloid origin, formerly headhunters but now almost entirely Christian, including *Angami, Ao, Sema, Konyak, Chakhesang, Lotha, Phom, Khiemnungam, Chang, Yimchunger, Rengma, Zeliang-Kuki* and *Sangtan.* 2. Sino-Tibetan language.

nagana *Central Africa.* Cattle disease, related to sleeping sickness, which also attacks humans.

nagar *India.*   Town.

nagarit *Ethiopia.*   Drum, three to five feet in length, with skins stretched over the two ends.

nageswara *India.*   Literally, snake-note. The south Indian fife.

Nago *Togo.*   Ethnic group of the YORUBA cluster.

nahia (plural: nawahi) *Arab countries.*   Locality or subdivision of a district.

Nahua *Central America.*   Ethnic group of southern highlands.

nahual *Guatemala.*   Person's guardian animal.

nahyah *Yemens.*   Small towns.

Nahuatl *Mexico.*   Azteco-Tanoan language.

nai *Thailand.*   Literally, master. Lowest rank of the traditional nobility.

nai amphoe *Thailand.*   District officer.

naib *Saudi Arabia.*   Sergeant in the Saudi army.

naib *Malaysia.*   Assistant of a PENGHULU.

naib arif *Saudi Arabia.*   Lance corporal in the Saudi army.

naibon *Laos.*   Village headman.

naik *India.*   Leader, chief, or general. Also, corporal in the army.

nai kong *Laos.*   Civil servant assigned to tribal areas.

al na'im (singular: na'imi or nu'aymi) *Oman.*   Tribe.

naingandaio adipati *Burma.*   Head of state, title of Dr. Ba Maw, 1941–45.

Nair *India.*   Non-BRAHMIN caste in Kerala.

naira *Nigeria.*   Monetary unit.

nai tesseng *Laos.*   Chief of a canton.

naiza bazi *Afghanistan.*   Tent-pegging sport.

najd (plural: nijad) *Oman.*   Highland or plateau.

najwa *Botswana.*   Ethnic subgroup.

Nakanai *Papua New Guinea.*   Austronesian language.

Nakhuda *Oman.*   In Persian, captain of a DHOW or boat.

nakomse (singular: nakombga) *Burkina Faso.*   MOSSI nobility.

nak tham *Thailand.*   Novice or monk who has completed an elementary course in Buddhist dharma.

Nalou *Guinea.*   1. Ethnic group on the lower Rio Nunez and Kogan rivers. 2. Niger-Kordofanian language.

Nalus *Guinea-Bissau.*   Senegambian people related to BISSAGOS.

nam *Vietnam.*   Baron, a rank of the nobility.

nama *Namibia.*   KHOISAN language.

namadi *Mauritania.*   Nomadic hunters in el-Djouf desert.

namaj *Bangladesh and Islamic countries.*   Daily Muslim prayers. Also *namaz.*

Nambali *Ghana.*   Small EWE group in Volta Region.

namboodiri *India.*   Malayalam-speaking high-caste BRAHMIN.

Nambya *Zimbabwe.*   Niger-Kordofanian language.

Namnam *Ghana.* MOLE-DAGBANE ethnic group in the Upper East Region.

nampla *Thailand.* Fish sauce, staple feature of Thai cuisine.

Nampruli *West Africa.* Niger-Kordofanian language.

Nam-Tong or **Treu-Thua** *Vietnam.* THERAVADA, or lesser wheel, in Buddhism.

Namwanga *Zambia.* Tanzanian ethnic group in the northeast.

nan *India and Afghanistan.* Unleavened bread.

Nanaicas *Nicaragua.* Subtribal group of the CHONTALES.

Nanakpanthi *India.* Nonmilitant SIKH seeking peaceful resolution of sectarian conflicts.

nanavati *Afghanistan.* Right of asylum and obligation to accept truce offer, under the PUSHTUNWALI code.

Nancere *West Africa.* Afro-Asiatic language.

Nande *Zaire.* Ethnic group.

Nandi *Kenya.* Second largest KALENJIN group.

Nandi *Zaire.* Niger-Kordofanian language.

nanduti *Paraguay.* Literally, spider web. Lace made to resemble spider web.

Nanerge *Burkina Faso.* Ethnic group of SENUFO cluster.

naneria *Ecuador.* Brotherhood.

nang *Thailand.* Shadow play.

nang-hau *Vietnam.* Concubine.

nangnat *Laos.* A form of xylophone.

Nango *Tanzania.* Ethnic group.

Nang Xu Tham *Laos.* Liturgical language of Buddhist clergy, derived from PALI and SANSKRIT.

Nankansi-Gurense *Ghana.* MOLE-DAGBANE ethnic group in the Upper East Region.

Nanumba *Ghana* MOLE-DAGBANE ethnic group in the Northern Region.

Nanzwa *Zimbabwe.* Cluster of people in Wanke district.

Nape *Bolivia.* Amazon Indian group of CHAPACURAN linguistic stock in Beni department.

Napore-Nyangea *Uganda.* Eastern Nilotic ethnic group.

naqib *Saudi Arabia.* First sergeant in Saudi army.

nar *Western Sahara.* Tribal brand used to identify livestock.

Nara *Ethiopia.* Nilo-Saharan language.

narasinghe *Nepal.* Serpent-shaped copper trumpet.

nargileh *Arab countries.* Water pipe.

narigba *Ivory Coast.* Lineage of the SENUFO.

Narikana *Burkina Faso.* Ethnic group of the MOSSI cluster.

Nasiol *Papua New Guinea* Papuan language.

Nasir *Afghanistan.* GHILAZAI tribe.

nasrani *Arab countries.* Term applied to Christians by Muslims.

Nateni *West Africa.* Niger-Kordofanian language.

National Panchayat *Nepal.* Parliament.

nattukutta *Sri Lanka.* TAMIL folk play.

natural *Guatemala.* Indian, in the sense of aboriginal.

naturales *Philippines.* Native Filipinos.

natwin *Burma.* Ear-piercing rite for girls.

Nauri *Iran.* BALUCHI ethnic group.

Nauru *Nauru.* Austronesian language.

nautch *India.* Kind of ballet danced by DEVADASIS, or temple-prostitutes.

navetan *Senegal.* WOLOF term for migrant farmer.

Navruz *Iran.* New year.

nawab *India.* In Mughal times, deputy ruler or governor of a province.

nawahin *Jordan.* Subdistrict.

nawaratri *Nepal.* See GHATASTHAPANA.

Nawom *Togo.* Niger-Kordofanian language.

Naxalite *India.* Maoist guerrillas and terrorists formerly active in West Bengal.

nayandi ves sellama *Sri Lanka.* Kandyan dance.

nayiri *Ghana.* Paramount chief of the MAMPRUSI.

nayok rathomantri *Thailand.* Prime minister.

nazar *India.* Literally a vow or votive offering. Ceremonial gift from an inferior to a superior.

Nazim *India.* Variant of NIZAM.

nazir *Islamic countries.* Inspector; official of a civil court; warden of a mosque.

nazir *Sudan.* Head of a tribe.

Nazkara *Zaire.* Ethnic group of northern savanna.

Nbukushu *Namibia.* Niger-Kordofanian language.

nda bot *Cameroon.* Extended family among the PAHOUIN.

ndaka *Zaire.* Ethnic group.

ndali *Tanzania.* Ethnic group.

Ndali *Tanzania.* Niger-Kordofanian language.

Ndamba *Tanzania.* 1. Ethnic group. 2. Niger-Kordofanian language.

n'dana *Congo.* Hardy tsetse-resistant breed of cattle.

ndaro *Rwanda and Burundi.* Small hut outside the KRAAL where round stones are placed as a ritual.

Ndau *Mozambique.* 1. Ethnic group of the SHONA-Karanga cluster. Also, *Vandau, Buzi, Mossrize.* 2. Niger-Kordofanian language.

Ndau *Zimbabwe.* One of the main SHONA clusters.

Ndebele *Southern Africa.* 1. Ethnic group, offshoot of the NGUNI, also, MATABELE. 2. Niger-Kordofanian language.

Ndembu *Angola.*   MBUNDU subgroup.

Ndembu *Zambia.*   Congolese ethnic group.

Ndembu *Zaire.*   Ethnic group.

Ndendeuli *Tanzania.*   Ethnic group.

Ndengereko *Tanzania.*   1. Ethnic group. 2. Niger-Kordofanian language.

Ndengese *Zaire.*   Ethnic group.

Nde-Nsele-Nta *West Africa.*   Niger-Kordofanian language.

Nderobo *Kenya.*   Ethnic group.

Ndiwa *Gabon.*   Ethnic group.

ndlovukazi *Swaziland.*   Literally, lady elephant. Title of queen mother.

Ndo *Central Africa.*   Nilo-Saharan language.

Ndogo *Central Africa.*   1. Sudanic ethnic group. 2. Niger-Kordofanian language.

ndoki *Congo.*   Witches, among the KONGO.

Ndombe *Tanzania.*   Niger-Kordofanian language.

Ndonga *Namibia.*   Niger-Kordofanian language.

Ndongo *Angola.*   Division of the Western MBUNDU.

Ndoro *West Africa.*   Niger-Kordofanian language.

Ndoumou *Gabon.*   MBEDE-speaking people along the M'passa River.

Nduga *Indonesia.*   Papuan language.

ndugu *Tanzania.*   Comrade, as a title.

Ndunga *Zaire.*   Ethnic group of the Central Rain Forest.

Ndwandwe *Swaziland.*   Tribe of the BEMBO-NGUNI clan.

neburaed *Ethiopia.*   Chief monk of Axum and Addis Ababa monasteries.

nech lebasha *Ethiopia.*   Auxiliary police force.

nechombo *Zimbabwe.*   Acolyte who assists in a spirit-medium ritual.

neftenya *Ethiopia.*   Soldiers granted land for meritorious service.

neggadras *Ethiopia.*   Chief officer of a market.

negrismo *Cuba.*   Literary genre focusing on black culture and life-styles.

negritude *Senegal, Haiti.*   Spirit of black cultural experience synthesizing Negro culture and traditions in the Old and New Worlds.

negro de ganho *Brazil.*   Slave who worked at a trade and whose wages were turned over to his master.

negros bocais *Brazil.*   Literally, raw blacks. The lowest stratum of negroes.

negusa negast *Ethiopia.*   Literally, king of kings. Title of former Ethiopian emperor.

Nehru jacket *India.*   Long, narrow jacket or coat that buttons up front with a high collar, popularized by Jawaharlal Nehru.

nem *Burkina Faso.*   Political authority among the MOSSI.

nem *Vietnam.*   Sausage-type pork dish.

nen *Thailand.*   Novice or junior member of the SANGHA.

neno *Senegal.*   WOLOF term for caste.

Nenyo *Gambia.*   Caste of artisans among the WOLOF.

Nepali *Nepal.*   Indo-European language.

nerebgye *Nicaragua.*   Popular dance rhythm.

Neto *Mozambique.*   Ethnic group of the MAKUA Lomwe cluster.

newala *Swaziland.*   Annual ceremony in December, marking the first fruits of the coming new year.

Newar *Nepal.*   Ethnic group, partly Hindu and partly Buddhist.

Newari *Nepal.*   1. Sino-Tibetan language. 2. Of the NEWAR ethnic group.

new riel *Cambodia.*   Monetary unit.

nga *Burma.*   Cattle as ritual property, among the KACHINS.

Ngada *Indonesia.*   Austronesian language.

Ngaju *Indonesia.*   Austronesian language.

Ngalik *Indonesia.*   Papuan language.

Ngalum *Indonesia and Papua New Guinea.*   Papuan language.

Ngambwe *Angola.*   NYANEKE subgroup.

Ngame *West Africa.*   Afro-Asiatic language.

Ngando *Zaire.*   Niger-Kordofanian language.

Ngandu *Zaire.*   Ethnic group.

nganga *Congo.*   Diviners and medicine men, among the KONGO.

nganga *Zimbabwe.*   SHONA medicine men.

Nganguela *Angola.*   Ethnic group comprising *Lwena, Luvale, Mbunda* and *Luchazi,* from which the name of the country is derived.

nganzo *Burundi.*   Royal tombs.

ngapi *Burma.*   Salted paste of fish or shrimp, staple of Burmese diet.

ngay gio *Vietnam.*   Death anniversary as part of ancestor worship. Also, *ngay ky nhat.*

ngay gio ho *Vietnam.*   Celebration of the anniversary of the founder of an extended family or clan.

ngay gio lang *Vietnam.*   Anniversary of the death of the patron saint of a village. Also, *ngay than ky.*

Ngbaga *Zaire.*   Ethnic group.

Ngbaka *Central Africa.*   Niger-Kordofanian language.

Ngbaka *Zaire.*   Ethnic group.

Ngbandi *Zaire.*   1. Ethnic group. 2. Niger-Kordofanian language.

Ngbee *Zaire.*   Ethnic group.

Ngemba *West Africa.*   Niger-Kordofanian language.

Nge-Nge *Zaire.*   Ethnic group.

Ngengele *Zaire.*   Ethnic group.

Ngenyo *Senegal.*   Artisans among the WOLOF.

nge-ra-kol-be *Chad.*   Literally, he who nourishes the village. Chief of the soil.

Ngere *Guinea.*   *See* GUERZE.

ngewo *Sierra Leone.*   God among the MENDE.

nghe-su *Vietnam.*   Patron saint of a trade or profession.

ngi *West Africa.*   Niger-Kordofanian language.

Ngindo *Tanzania.*   1. Ethnic group. 2. Niger-Kordofanian language.

Ngio *Thailand.*   SHAN ethnic group, also known as *Thai Yai, Thai Long* or *Great Thai.*

Ngizim *West Africa.*   Afro-Asiatic language.

Ngoma *Zaire.*   Ethnic group of southern savanna.

ngoma *Zimbabwe.*   Drum.

Ngomba *West Africa.*   Niger-Kordofanian language.

Ngomba *Zaire.*   Ethnic group.

Ngombale *West Africa.*   Niger-Kordofanian language.

Ngombe-Doko *Zaire.*   Ethnic group of the Central Rain Forest.

Ngombi *Zaire.*   Niger-Kordofanian language.

Ngombo *Zambia.*   Congolese LUNDA tribe in Luapula Valley.

Ngonde *Malawi.*   Ethnic group.

Ngondo *Cameroon.*   DOUALA Council of Notables.

Ngoni *Southern Africa.*   1. Ethnic group, offshoot of the ZULUS. 2. Niger-Kordofanian language.

Ngoni *Zimbabwe.*   Variant of NGUNI, applied to migrant bands of the MFECANE era.

Ngowe *Gabon.*   Branch of the ESHIRA.

Ngozi *Zimbabwe.*   Class of malevolent SHONA ancestor spirits.

Ngqika *Southern Africa.*   Subgroup of the XHOSA.

ngultram *Bhutan.*   Monetary unit.

Nguerze *Guinea.*   *See* GUERZE.

Ngulu *Southern Africa.*   1. Ethnic group. 2. Niger-Kordofanian language.

Ngumba *Central Africa.*   Unaffiliated language.

ngundu (plural: jingundu) *Angola.*   Matrilineage.

Nguni *Southern Africa.*   Major ethnic group comprising five subgroups: refugees from the wars of the Zulu king Chaka who have regrouped into the *Fingo, Bhaca, Nhlangwini* and *Xesibe;* the southern Nguni including the *Xhosa, Mpondo, Mpondomise, Nquabe, Qwathi, Bomvana* and *Thembu;* the northern Nguni, or *Zulu;* the *Swazi;* and more recent offshoots such as *Ngoni, Shangana* and *Ndebele.*

Nguni *Zimbabwe.*   Cluster of BANTU languages divided into southern (MPONDO, THEMBU and XHOSA) and northern (Swazi and Zulu).

ngunzism *Zaire.*   Indigenous prophetic movements, as KIMBANGUISM, which combine Christian and pagan elements, usually around a black prophet. From *ngunza,* prophet.

Nguru *Southern Africa.*   BANTU-speaking people.

Nguruimi *Tanzania.*   Ethnic group.

Ngruimi *Tanzania.*   Niger-Kordofanian language.

ngultram *Bhutan.*   Monetary unit.

Nguu *Tanzania.*   Niger-Kordofanian language.

Ngwaketse *Southern Africa.*   Subgroup of the Tswana or west Sotho.

Ngwana *Mozambique.*   Ethnic group of the NGUNI cluster.

ngwane wonke *Swaziland.*   Swazi Supreme Council, which meets only in times of impending wars.

Ngwato *Southern Africa.*   Subgroup of the TSWANA or west Sotho.

ngwazi *Malawi.*   Literally, chief or provider. Title of President Hastings Banda.

ngwee *Zambia.*   Coin, 1/100ths of a KWACHA.

ngwenyama *Swaziland.*   Literally, lion. Title of Swazi king.

Ngwo-oshi *West Africa.*   Niger-Kordofanian language.

Ngyemboon *West Africa.*   Niger-Kordofanian language.

Nhang *Vietnam.*   1. Highland ethnic group speaking a Sino-Thai language. 2. Joss sticks.

nhimbe *Zimbabwe.*   Mutual-help parties.

nhlambelo *Swaziland.*   Sacred enclosure or sanctuary at the upper end of the cattle shed in the royal village used for a variety of ritual purposes.

Nho-Giao or **khong-Giao** *Vietnam.*   Confucianism.

nhowe *Zimbabwe.*   A branch of the ZEZURU cluster of SHONA speakers.

nhtu *Burma.*   KACHIN swords as ritual objects.

nhucuana *Mozambique.*   Village chief among the NGUNI.

Nhungwe *Mozambique.*   Ethnic group of the lower Zambesi cluster. Also, *Nyunwe, Nhungue.*

nhuom rang *Vietnam.*   Blackening of teeth as a cosmetic practice.

Nias *Indonesia.*   Austronesian language.

Niasans *Indonesia.*   Ethnic group of Sumatra.

nibia *Guyana.*   Slender bush rope.

Nicaros *Nicaragua.*   Language family. See UTAZTECAN.

Nicobarese *India.*   Austro-Asiatic language of Nicobar islands.

Niellim *Chad.*   SARA clan on both sides of the Chari River.

nielloware *Thailand.*   Black metalware engraved with designs filled with an alloy consisting of sulfur combined with silver, copper or lead.

Nienige *Burkina Faso.*   Ethnic group of the HABE cluster.

Nihang *India.*   See AKALI.

nihimo (plural: mahimo) *Mozambique.*   Group of matrilineally related kin among the Makira-Lomue.

Nikaya *Sri Lanka.*   Buddhist sect.

Nilamba *Tanzania.*   Niger-Kordofanian language.

Nimadi *India.*   Indo-European language.

nimaz *Afghanistan.*   In DARI, prayer or prayer time.

ninera *Honduras.*   Teenage girl trained in child care and employed in day nurseries.

ningas-cogen *Philippines.* Sudden spurt of enthusiasm followed by a slowing down and an eventual slipping back into old habits.

Ninisi *Burkina Faso.* Ethnic cluster. Also, *Tinguimbissi.*

Ninzam *West Africa.* Niger-Kordofanian language.

Nioniosse *Burkina Faso.* Ethnic group of the NINISI cluster.

nirvana *Buddhist countries.* Literally, blown out like a candle. State of complete oblivion or annihilation of the self, considered the goal of Buddhist dharma.

Nissan *Papua New Guinea.* Austronesian language.

nitalinda *Rwanda and Burundi.* Huntsmen and couriers.

nitimwana *Rwanda and Burundi.* Female attendants of a king.

nixtamal *Guatemala.* Softened grains of corn for making tortillas.

nizam *India.* Former ruler of the native state of Hyderabad.

nizam *Saudi Arabia.* Administrative regulation.

nizam *Turkey.* Professional army.

njanja *Zimbabwe.* A branch of the ZEZURU cluster of SHONA speakers.

Njanyi *West Africa.* Afro-Asiatic language.

njayei *Sierra Leone.* Secret society among the MENDE for dealing with fertility and mental illness.

Njebi *Central Africa.* Niger-Kordofanian language.

njelelo *Malawi.* Female dance among the CHEWA.

Njemps *Kenya.* Maa-speaking people south and east of Lake Baringo.

Nkambule *Swaziland.* Clan of "latecomers" of Sotho origin.

nkap *Cameroon.* Marriage among the BAMILEKE in which no payments are made.

nkazi *Congo.* Lineage head.

Nkem-Nkum *West Africa.* Niger-Kordofanian language.

nkhombo *Malawi.* Singing horn.

nkhoswe wamkulu *Malawi.* Chief of the lineage group who is guardian of his brothers and sisters and their children.

Nkhumbi *Angola.* Ethnic group related to the NYANEKE.

nkisi *Congo.* Nature spirits and their material representations.

nkobi alubaku *Congo.* Sacred baskets containing relics among the eastern KONGO.

Nkole *Uganda.* Western BANTU ethnic group.

Nkomi *Gabon.* MYENE-speaking ethnic group.

Nkonya *Ghana.* GUAN ethnic group in the Voltaic Region.

Nkonya *West Africa.* Niger-Kordofanian language.

nkosi or **imkosi** *Swaziland.* Ruler, king or chief.

Nkoswe *Mozambique.* Head of the oldest and most prestigious lineage among the CHEWA.

Nkoya *Zambia.* Niger-Kordofanian language.

Nku *Zaire.* Ethnic group.

nkulumba *Malawi.*   Leader of an INGULILE, or village age group.

Nkulunkulu *Zimbabwe.*   NGUNI name for high god.

nkundla (plural: tinkundla) *Swaziland.*   Rural district council, each consisting of local chiefs.

Nkutshu *Zaire.*   Ethnic group.

Nkutu *Zaire.*   Niger-Kordofanian language.

Nkwenda *Malawi.*   Mourning dance for men and women.

nkwendo *Malawi.*   Percussion instrument consisting of a notched section of a bamboo upon which a smaller stick is rubbed producing a rasping sound.

nodong chokwidae *North Korea.*   Workers' and peasants' Red Guard.

nodongjaku *North Korea.*   Workers' district, as a unit of local administration.

nom *Vietnam.*   Writing system based on Chinese characters. Also, *chu nam.*

nomi *Malawi.*   Among the SENA, a young people's group.

nomoli *Sierra Leone.*   Small stone figures carved in soapstone or other soft stone.

Non *Senegal.*   Niger-Kordofanian language.

non *Vietnam.*   Conical hat made of latania leaves.

nong trai *Vietnam.*   Agricultural settlement.

Nonualco *El Salvador.*   Indian ethnic group in La Paz.

nordestino *Brazil.*   Northeasterner.

normalistas *Brazil and Spanish America.*   Teachers, graduates of a normal school.

no rooz *Afghanistan.*   Literally, new day. First day of the Afghan solar calendar.

nor sor *Thailand.*   Right to cultivate.

Nouni *West Africa.*   Niger-Kordofanian language.

Nounouma *Burkina Faso.*   Ethnic group of the GOUROUNSI cluster.

nritta natya *India and Bangladesh.*   Ballet, especially based on the works of Rabindranath Tagore.

Nsaw *Cameroon.*   Tribal unit of the TIKAR peoples.

Nsenga *Southern Africa.*   Niger-Kordofanian language.

Nsenga *Zambia.*   Congolese LUBA group in the southeast.

nsima *Malawi.*   Warm maize porridge.

Nso *West Africa.*   Niger-Kordofanian language.

Nsongo *Angola.*   Niger-Kordofanian language.

nta *Burma.*   Household, among the KACHINS.

ntare *Burundi.*   One of the two royal spears, used for ritual purposes.

Ntcham *West Africa.*   Niger-Kordofanian language.

ntemi *Tanzania.*   Title of chief.

nthiki or **nthikura** *Malawi.*   Barrel-shaped drum.

Ntomba *Zaire.* Ethnic group.

ntore *Rwanda and Burundi.* Formerly, vassal or military aide in the court of the MWAMI.

Ntruber *Ghana.* CENTRAL TOGO ethnic group.

Ntrubu *Ghana.* Small TOGO group in the Volta Region.

Ntum *Cameroon.* Southern forest subgroup of FANG.

Ntumba *Zaire.* Niger-Kordofanian language.

Ntwumuru or **Nchumuro** *Ghana.* Guan ethnic group allied to KRAKYE.

Nuba *Sudan.* Sudanic speaking people in Kordofan.

Nubi or **Nubian** *Sudan.* Sudanic-speaking people divided into four principal subgroups: *Dangala, Feyadicha, Kenuzi* and Maha.

nucleo escolar *Bolivia.* Rural school offering all six grades of primary education.

Nuer *Sudan and Ethiopia.* 1. Nilo-Saharan people divided into *Gaajak, Gaajok, Luo, Lak, Gawaar, Bul, Dok, Leek, Thiang, Nyuong, Gaagwang, Aak, Dor, Bor, Wot* and *Lang.* 2. Nilo-Saharan language.

nulla *Somalia.* Dry watercourse turning into a stream during rains.

Numana-Nunku-Gwantu *West Africa.* Niger-Kordofanian language.

numdah *India.* Felt pad or coarse woolen covering used as a saddle.

numshang *Burma.* Sacred grove at the entrance to KACHIN villages.

Nung *Vietnam.* 1. Highland ethnic group speaking a Thai language of the Kadai family. 2. Sino-Tibetan language.

Nungu *West Africa.* Niger-Kordofanian language.

Nunuma *Ghana.* Small GRUSI group.

nuoc mam *Vietnam.* Fermented fish sauce, staple of Vietnamese diet.

Nupe *Nigeria.* Ethnic group including subgroups as Batau, Beni, Kye-Dye, Eghagi, Ebe, and Benu.

Nupe *West Africa.* 1. Ethnic group. 2. Niger-Kordofanian language.

Nuristan *Afghanistan.* Mountainous region, northeast of Kabul, south of the Hindu Kush.

Nuristani *Afghanistan.* Tribe, formerly called Kafirs or infidels, speaking a Dardic language.

nurtiya *Sri Lanka.* Musical play of Indian origin.

Nusayris *Syria.* Variant name for ALAWITE.

nu'u *Western Samoa.* Village.

Nwenshi *Zaire.* Ethnic group.

NyaBwa *West Africa.* Niger-Kordofanian language.

Nyai (plural: Banyai) *Zimbabwe.* SHONA.

nyaka gon chaukpa *Burma.* Leadership qualities.

Nyakyusa *Tanzania* and *Malawi.* Ethnic group.

Nyakusa-Ngonde *Tanzania.* Niger-Kordofanian language.

Nyakwai *Uganda.* Eastern Nilotic ethnic group.

Nyali *Zaire.* Niger-Kordofanian language.

nyama *Guinea.* Spirit or soul, among the MALINKE.

nyamalo *Gambia.* MANDINGO equivalent of a GEWEL.

nyamuraza *Rwanda.* Promiscuous women.

Nyamwanga *Tanzania.* Ethnic group.

Nyamwezi *Tanzania.* 1. Ethnic group. 2. Niger-Kordofanian language.

Nyaneke *Angola.* 1. Ethnic group of Bantu-speaking people related to the Mbo. 2. Niger-Kordofanian language.

Nyang *Zaire.* Niger-Kordofanian language.

Nyanga *Zaire.* Ethnic group of the eastern highlands.

Nyangea *Uganda.* Ethnic group.

Nyangbo *Ghana.* CENTRAL TOGO ethnic group.

Nyanja *Southern Africa.* 1. Ethnic group of the MARAVI cluster. 2. Niger-Kordofanian language.

Nyanji *Malawi.* Ethnic group related to the CHEWA.

Nyankole *Uganda.* Niger-Kordofanian language.

Nyari *Zaire.* Ethnic group of the Central Rain Forest.

Nyasa *Tanzania.* Ethnic group.

Nyaturu *Tanzania.* Niger-Kordofanian language.

Nyau *Malawi.* Cult or secret society characterized by masked dances by men.

Nyaw *Thailand.* KAM TAI ethnic group.

nyawa *Malaysia.* Life soul.

Nyaya *India.* One of the six orthodox systems of Hindu philosophy codified by Gautama in *Nyayasutra,* dealing with epistemology and the laws of analysis, reasoning and discussion.

Nyangbara *Sudan.* Ethnic group.

nyeenyBe (singular: nyeeno) *Senegal.* Middle caste of artisans among the TOUCOLEURS.

Nyemba *Angola.* Niger-Kordofanian language.

nyerchen *Bhutan.* Tax collector in a district.

nyere *Zimbabwe.* Panpipe.

Nyiha *Tanzania.* Ethnic group.

Nyiha *Tanzania.* Niger-Kordofanian language.

Nyika *Tanzania.* Ethnic cluster of eight groups: *Digo, Duruma, Rabai, Ribe, Chonyi, Kambe, Kauma* and *Jihana.*

nyika *Kenya.* Wilderness.

nyika *Zimbabwe.* CHISHONA term for the territory of a chiefdom.

nyika *Zimbabwe.* SHONA chiefdom.

Nyintu *Zaire.* Ethnic group of Central Rain Forest.

nyora *Zimbabwe.* Cicatrization marks or tattoo.

Nyore *Central and East Africa.* 1. BANTU subgroup of the Kavirondo. 2. Niger-Kordofanian language.

Nyoro *Central Africa.* Western Nilotic ethnic group. Also, *Bakitara.*

Nyuli *Uganda.* 1. Eastern BANTU ethnic group. 2. Niger-Kordofanian language.

Nyungwe *Mozambique.*   Niger-Kordofanian language.
Nzabi *Gabon.*   Ethnic group.
nzambi *Congo.*   Supreme creator among the KONGO.
Nzema *Ghana.*   Niger-Kordofanian language.
Nzema *Ghana and Ivory Coast.*   AKAN ethnic group.

oba *Nigeria.*   Chief among the YORUBA, Edo and Itsekiri.
Obamba *Gabon.*   MBEDE-speaking people.
Obanliku *West Africa.*   Niger-Kordofanian language.
obeah *Guyana.*   Magic and witchcraft of West African origin; by extension, witch doctor.
obi *Nigeria.*   Chief of Onitsha.
obolo *West Africa.*   Niger-Kordofanian language.
oboma *Sierra Leone.*   Deputy chief of the TEMNE.
obrajes *Peru.*   Work center in Andean villages where Indians are hired to weave wool into clothes.
obrero *Spanish America.*   Blue-collar worker, as distinguished from EMPLEADO and CAMPESINO.
obrigado *Brazil.*   Sharecropper living on ENGENHO land
oca *Brazil.*   Indian dwelling made of bamboo.
ocarina *Guatemala.*   Flute made of reeds, cane or bone.
ochenio *Peru.*   The eight-year dictatorship of Manuel Odria, 1948–56.
ocote *Guatemala.*   Pitch pine splints from okote pine for starting fires.
ocupante de hecho *Paraguay.*   Squatter.
ocupante gratuito *Costa Rica.*   Squatter.
ocupantes *Brazil.*   Squatter on public or absentee-owned land.
oday *Somalia.*   Elder.
odehye *Ghana.*   Member of royal blood of the reigning stool in an AKAN state.
odekuro (plural: adekurofo) *Ghana.*   Headman of a village.
odhani *India.*   Smaller SARI.
Odual *West Africa.*   Niger-Kordofanian language.
odwira *Ghana.*   National purification festival of the AKAN, the most important day in the Akan calendar.
ody *Madagascar.*   Talisman.
oficina *Chile.*   Nitrate factory.
oga *Gabon.*   Title of the king of MPONGWE.

Ogbah *West Africa.*   Niger-Kordofanian language.
Ogbia *West Africa.*   Niger-Kordofanian language.
ogun *Haiti.*   VOODOO god of war.
ohene (plural: ahene) *Ghana.*   AKAN chief, king or ruler.
ojo *Guatemala.*   Evil eye.
ojotas *Peru.*   Sandals made from worn tires.
Okande *Equatorial Guinea.*   Ethnic group along the Ogooue River, east of Okano River junction.
Okande *Gabon.*   Ethnic group.
oke *Egypt.*   Unit of weight equal to 1.24 kg.
Okebo *Zaire.*   Ethnic group.
Okiek *Kenya.*   1. Kalinjin group of hunters. 2. Nilo-Saharan language.
Okobo *Nigeria.*   Niger-Kordofanian language.
okoume *Congo.*   Brown African mahogany.
Okpamheri *West Africa.*   Niger-Kordofanian language.
ok phansa *Thailand.*   End of the rainy season.
Okrika *West Africa.*   Niger-Kordofanian language.
okyeame *Ghana.*   Spokesman of the ASANTEHENE.
ola *India.*   Palm leaf written over with a stylus and bound together to form a book.
olaria *Brazil.*   Kiln.
oligarchia *Spanish America.*   Oligarchy; landed aristocracy.
omadiya *Sudan.*   Subgroup of a tribe
oman (plural: aman) *Ghana.*   Community or district.
omanahene *Ghana.*   Chief of the Ashanti (ASANTE).
Omariyya *West Africa.*   Branch of Islamic brotherhood. See TIDJANIYA.
ombiasi *Madagascar.*   Healer-diviners among the ANTAIMORO.
omda *Sudan.*   Head of an OMADIYA.
omdeh *Egypt.*   Unpaid village official.
Omotik *Kenya.*   Ethnic group in the Rift Valley.
oncenio *Peru.*   The 11-year rule of President Auguste B. Leguia (1919–30).
ondol *South Korea.*   System of heating by running flues through a stone floor.
Ondulacoes *Brazil.*   Literally, waves. Brazilian revolutionary movements of the 19th century.
Ongamo *Tanzania.*   Ethnic group.
ong do *Vietnam.*   Private teacher or tutor with no official status who holds classes in his own home.
oni *Nigeria.*   Priest king of Ife.
Ooli *Zaire.*   Ethnic group.
oopla *India.*   Cow dung patted into cakes and dried for use as fuel.
oracione *Haiti.*   Incantation associated with VOODOO.
orang bedikir *Malaysia.*   Religious singing.
orang besar *Malaysia.*   Wealthy and influential people.

orang kamping biasa *Malaysia.*   Ordinary village people.

orang kebanyakan *Malaysia.*   Common people.

Oraon *India.*   KOLARIAN aboriginal tribe in Chota Nagpur.

orde baru *Indonesia.*   Literally, new order. The post-Sukarno era that began in 1966.

orde lama *Indonesia.*   Literally, old order. The Sukarno era that ended in 1966.

ordenancas *Brazil.*   Colonial militia troops.

Orientales *Uruguay.*   Uruguayans.

originaire *Francophone Africa.*   Assimilated French African who possessed the legal rights of a French citizen but was allowed to retain customary law in certain categories, as inheritance, marriage and divorce.

originario *Bolivia.*   Member of COMUNIDAD with ancestral rights.

Oring *West Africa.*   Niger-Kordofanian language.

orisha *Brazil.*   Pantheon of deities of African origin.

Oriya *India.*   Indo-European language.

orkoiyot (plural: orkoik) *Kenya.*   Ritual leader of the KIPSIGIS and NANDE.

Orma *Kenya.*   Ethnic group.

ornato *Guatemala.*   Head tax paid to the MUNICIPALIDAD.

Orokaiva *Papua New Guinea.*   Papuan language.

Orokolo *Papua New Guinea.*   Papuan language.

Oromo *Ethiopia* and *Kenya.*   Afro-Asiatic language.

Oromo *Ethiopia.*   Variant name for GALLA.

Oron *West Africa.*   Niger-Kordofanian language.

orornismos asesores *Nicaragua.*   Advisory institutions of the Council of Ministers.

Ortue *Bolivia.*   Amazon Indian group of Beni department.

Orue *Turkey.*   Ritual fasting. See SAUM.

Orungu *Gabon.*   MYENE-speaking ethnic group in Ogooue Delta.

osagyefo *Ghana.*   Literally, redeemer. Self-assumed title of Kwame Nkrumah, president of Ghana, 1956–66.

Oso *Cameroon.*   Niger-Kordofanian language.

ossobuco *Argentina.*   Stew made of beef shank.

ostan *Iran.*   Province.

ostandar *Iran.*   Governor general of a province.

Otavalos *Ecuador.*   Ethnic group in Imbabura Province.

Ot Danum *Indonesia.*   Austronesian language.

oto *Panama.*   Plant whose roots are used in cooking.

Oto-Manguean *Central America.*   Of or relating to Oto, a North American Indian tribe, and Mangues, a Meso-American Indian tribe of Nicaragua.

Otomi *Mexico.*   1. Indian tribe of the states of Mexico and Hidalgo, known for their red woolen garments and fancy baskets. 2. Oto-Manguean language.

Otore *Sudan.*   Niger-Kordofanian language.

Otuque *Bolivia.*   Indian group of BOROROAN languages in Santa Cruz department.

Ouagadougou *Burkina Faso.*   Ethnic group of the MOSSI cluster.

oualo *Senegal.*   River-flooded land suitable for rice cultivation.

ouapi *Haiti.*   Dice game.

ouankoulou *Cameroon and Chad.*   Paramount chief of the TOUBARI.

Ouassoulounke *Guinea.*   Ethnic group in west Kankan.

ouatchi *Togo.*   Ethnic group in Anecho and Tabligbu.

oud *Egypt.*   Mandolin-like musical instrument with seven pairs of strings.

oued *Morocco.*   Variant of WADI.

ouguiya *Mauritania.*   Monetary unit.

Oujda Group *Algeria*   Former president Houari Boumedienne's closest supporters during the Algerian war of independence. From Oujda, a town in Morocco, where the group was formed.

Oule *Burkina Faso.*   Ethnic group of the HABE cluster.

Ouled Sliman *Chad.*   Arab tribe.

ouvidor general *Brazil.*   Colonial chief justice.

Ovambo *Angola.*   Ethnic group, also known as MBO, divided into 13 independent subgroups of which the KWANYAMA and NDONGA are the most important.

Ovimbundu *Angola.*   Ethnic group, also known as MBUNDU, divided into 13 independent kingdoms: *Chingolo, Chitata, Chivula, Chiyaka, Ekekete, Kakonda, Kalukembe, Mbailundu, Ngalangi, Ndulu, Sambu, Viye,* and *Wambu*

oware *Ghana.*   Akan game for two players who use a board with two parallel rows of six holes, pebbles being moved between the holes.

oxota *Peru.*   Indian sandal with a sole made of twisted vegetable cord and a rope thong.

Oyoko *Ghana.*   One of the principal AKAN clans.

ozi *Burma.*   Song, music and dance in ceremony for Buddhist initiates.

ozlah *Yemens.*   Groups of villages.

pa *South Korea.*   Segment of a lineage.

paanga *Tonga.*   Monetary unit.

pabasa ng pasiyon *Philippines.*   Chanting of Christ's Passion in rhymed verse.

Pacaguara *Bolivia.* Amazon Indian group of PANOAN language stock in Beni department.

Pacoh *Southeast Asia.* Austro-Asiatic language.

Pacoh *Vietnam.* Highland ethnic group in central region speaking a Mon-Khmer language.

pada *India.* Devotional song called also ABANGA in Maharashtra.

Padaung *Burma.* Ethnic group related to the KARENS.

Padhola *Uganda.* Western Nilotic ethnic group.

padrino *Spanish America.* Ceremonial kinship name given to grandparents by their grandchildren.

padroado *Brazil.* Spiritual jurisdiction of the state.

padshah *India.* Emperor, title especially applied to MUGHAL rulers.

paengman *Thailand.* Tapioca.

Paez *Colombia.* Macro-Chibchan language.

Pagabete *Zaire.* Niger-Kordofanian language.

page *Brazil.* Native healer.

Pagelanca *Brazil.* Syncretist cult fusing African and Amerindian spiritism.

pagri *India.* Turban.

pagne *West Africa.* Rectangular cloth wrapped around the body from the breast to the ankles.

paharen *India.* Upper garment, like a long shirt.

pahari *India.* Hillmen.

Pahari *Nepal.* Indo-Nepali ethnic group also called *kha, Khasiya, Khosh, Parbate* and *Parbatiya.*

Paharia *India and Bhutan.* Ethnic group.

Pahouin *Cameroon.* Southern forest ethnic group. Also, PANGWE.

pahul *India.* Among the SIKHS, ceremony of initiation into the KHALSA, in which sweet buttered flour is used.

pai *Burma.* Series of life-cycle ceremonies among Chinese SHANS.

pai bintha bat *Thailand.* Daily rounds for alms by Buddhist monks.

Pai Cone *Bolivia.* Amazon Indian group of Arawakan linguistic stock in Santa Cruz and Beni.

paik *India.* Inferior civil servant, as messenger or courier.

paisa (singular: paise) *India.* Coin, $\frac{1}{100}$ths of a RUPEE.

paja *Ecuador.* Straw used in making Panama hats.

paja brava *Ecuador.* Coarse grass grown in the Andean Plateau, used for thatch and fuel.

Pajadincas *Guinea-Bissau.* Senegambian people.

pajak *Malaysia.* System of tenancy in which the tenant pays the landlord several years' rent in advance at a reduced rate.

paje *Brazil.* Tribal medicineman.

pakhwaj *India.* Drum resembling MRIDANGAM.

pakikisama *Philippines.* Art of getting along with people or peers.

palacetes *Brazil.* Palatial homes built in the 19th century.

Palanan *Philippines.* Isolated ethnic group in Isabela Province.

palang *India.* Bed or bedstead as distinguished from a charpoy.

palankin *India.* Box litter for traveling in former times, with two poles projecting before and behind, and borne on the shoulders of four to six men.

Palau *Palau.* Austronesian language.

Palaung *Burma.* Mon-Khmer-speaking highland ethnic group.

palaver house *Liberia.* Town hall and community center.

Palavi *Iran.* Indo-Iranian ethnic group in Mazandaran.

Palawan *Philippines.* Pagan and Muslim ethnic group.

Palawano *Philippines.* Austronesian language.

Palembeng *Indonesia.* Austronesian language.

palenque *Colombia.* Wooden stockade.

palenque *Costa Rica.* Building with a thatched roof built of wood or concrete, used as a restaurant or dance hall.

Pali *India.* Indo-European language, one of the PRAKRIT or Aryan vernaculars. It is the sacred language in which most Buddhist scriptures are written.

palmatoria *Brazil.* Punishment for unruly soliders in which the victim was lashed to stakes on the ground and beaten on hands and feet.

palo volador *Guatemala.* Flying pole dance, of Aztec origin performed to give thanks for a good corn crop.

Paluo *Uganda.* Western Nilotic ethnic group.

Pama *Bolivia.* Amazon Indian group of TACANAN linguistic stock in Beni department.

pamai *Thailand.* Forest.

Pambia *Central Africa.* Niger-Kordofanian language.

Pamona *Indonesia.* Austronesian language.

pamong pradja *Indonesia.* Regional administration appointed by the central government.

Pampangan *Philippines.* 1. Lowland ethnic group. 2. Austronesian language.

pampas *South America.* Vast grassy plains without trees.

pampero *Uruguay.* Chilly wind blowing from the south in winter.

Pana *Burkina Faso.* Ethnic group along Mali border.

Pana *Central Africa.* Niger-Kordofanian language.

panadero *Honduras.* Village baker

pana pana *Honduras.* Exchange of labor similar to barn raising in early rural United States.

papagallos *Honduras.* Very cold northerly wind.

Panameno *Panama.* Native of Panama.

pancha *Nepal.* Member of a PANCHAYAT.

panchama *India.* Inferior groups of people who fall outside the Hindu caste system, such as *Ullala, Vellala, Pulaya, Paraya* and *Ezhava.* Also, UNTOUCHABLE, SCHEDULED CASTE, HARIJAN, ADIVASI or *avarna.*

panchangam *India.* Native almanac on the basis of which horoscopes are cast by astrologers.

panchayat *India and Nepal.* Council of local self-government, with the village as the basic unit of administration.

panchayat raj *India and Nepal.* System of village self-government.

Panch Shila *India.* Literally, five principles. Guiding principles of Indian foreign policy, including nonalignment.

panda *India.* Hindu priest.

pandal *India.* Temporary roofed-over area for special outdoor functions.

pandango sa ilau *Philippines.* Candle dance.

pandaram *India.* Hindu ascetic or mendicant in south India.

panela *Spanish America.* Crude brown sugar.

panelinha *Brazil.* Literally, little pot. Informal mutual help network helping to promote the upper mobility of the middle class.

panga or **bongo** *Nicaragua.* Dugout boat cut from large logs of royal cedar, mahogany, guanacaste or similar wood.

Panga *Zaire.* Ethnic group.

pangasi *Philippines.* Alcoholic drink made from rice in Bisayan.

Pangasinan *Philippines.* 1. Lowland ethnic group. 2. Austronesian language.

pangkat *Malaysia.* Rank.

pangulu *Indonesia.* Headman in a MINANGKABAU village.

Pangwa *Tanzania.* 1. Ethnic group. 2. Niger Kordofanian language.

Pangwe *Cameroon.* Ethnic group. See PAHOUIN.

panikkar *India.* Caste of astrologers in Kerala.

Panjapaos *Afghanistan.* PUSHTUN subgroup comprising *Nurzais, Alizais* and *Ighaqzais.*

panminjok hoengwi *South Korea.* National unification.

pano *Cape Verde.* Distinctive shawl or sash made of six strips worn by women.

Panoan *Bolivia.* Group of related Indian languages in Pando and Beni departments.

panolon *Colombia.* Traditional woman's cotton shawl.

pansala *Sri Lanka.* Buddhist elementary school.

pansori *South Korea.* Form of operetta that evolved from rituals related to omen-telling.

pan supari *India.* Areca nut, betel and lime chewed together as an exhilarant.

Panthay *Burma.* Sino-Tibetan ethnolinguistic group, mainly Muslim.

pantheru *Sri Lanka.* Kandyan dance.

Pantja Sila *Indonesia.* Literally, five principles. Guiding principles of the Indonesian Constitution: Belief in one supreme god; just and civilized humanity; nationalism; democracy; social justice. Compare PANCH SHILA.

pantun *Malaysia and Indonesia.* Simple, four-line verse.

pao *Afghanistan.* Unit of weight equal to 1 lb.

Pao *India.* Sino-Tibetan language.

papagayo *Nicaragua.* Literally, parrot storms. See PAPAGALLO.

papaloi *Haiti.* Popular name for HOUNGAN or VOODOO priest.

papa zaca *Haiti.* VOODOO god of agriculture.

papel *West Africa.* Niger-Kordofanian language.

Papiamentu *Netherlands Antilles.* Unaffiliated language.

Papuan *Oceania.* Tentative name of family of languages spoken in Papua New Guinea and the Pacific Islands.

paqo *Bolivia.* AYMARA shaman practicing white magic.

para *Bangladesh.* Neighborhood.

Para *Tanzania.* Niger-Kordofanian language.

para (plural: paralav) *Turkey.* Coin, ¼₀₀₀ths of a Turkish LIRA.

parabaik *Burma.* Old manuscript on soft bamboo rubbed with a mixture of charcoal and rice water.

paracaidistas *Mexico.* Literally, parachutists. Squatters.

paramahamsa *India.* Literally, supreme swan. Ascetic who has attained the highest level of renunciation of the world and union with the infinite.

paramo *Ecuador.* High, windswept, treeless plains of the Andean region.

Paranan *Philippines.* Austronesian language.

parang *Trinidad and Tobago.* House-to-house Christmas caroling to the accompaniment of guitar.

parasitos *Costa Rica.* Literally, parasites. Squatters.

Paravate *Nepal.* Collective name for BRAHMIN CHETRI, DAMAIS, KAMIS, and SARKHI castes.

parcela *Spanish America.* Small plot or subsistence farm.

parceloro *Colombia.* Needy farmer.

Pardhi *India.* Indo-European language.

pardo *Brazil.* Literally brown. Mulatto racial color, intermediate between white and black.

Pare *Tanzania.* Ethnic group.

parentela *Brazil.* Network of kinspeople or extended family.

parentesco *Ecuador.* Kinship.

pariah *India.* Low Hindu caste of drummers.

Parian *Philippines.* Chinese community in Manila.

paribar *Bangladesh.* Patrilineally extended household.

Parihar *India.* See AGNIKULA.

parillada *Argentina.*   Mixed grill.

parish *Jamaica.*   Principal administrative subdivision.

parishad *Bangladesh.*   Village as a unit of local administration.

parishad *India.*   Coordinating body, as a ZILLA *parishad.*

Parji *India.*   Indo-European language.

parrilla *Uruguay.*   Neighborhood grill where broiled and roasted meat is sold.

parroquia *Ecuador.*   Parish, the smallest of the territorial units.

Parsi *India and Iran.*   Ethnic group of Persian origin, most of whom are Zoroastrians by religion.

particular *Colombia.*   Evangelical Protestant.

partidario *Ecuador.*   Sponsor or guarantor of sharecroppers.

partido *Paraguay.*   Rural district.

pasacalle *Ecuador.*   Dance that evolved from the Spanish pasodoble.

Pasajeono *Bolivia.*   Amazon Indian group of TACANAN linguistic group in Beni department.

pasalar (singular: pasa or pasha) *Turkey.*   Holders of top rank in civil or military establishments.

pasar *Indonesia.*   Variant of bazaar.

pasco *Costa Rica.*   Formal walk in the town square.

Pasemah *Indonesia.*   Austronesian language.

pasha *Morocco.*   Mayor.

pasha *Arab countries.*   Title, originally given to provincial governors under Ottoman rule.

Pashayi *Afghanistan.*   Indo-European language.

pashminer *Nepal.*   Soft woolen scarves.

Pashto *Afghanistan.*   Indo-European language. Also, *Pushtu.*

pasillo *Colombia.*   Dance in a minor key.

pasisir *Indonesia.*   Coastal; of or relating to coastal people.

pasoh *Burma.*   LONGYI with extra yardage, worn by men on ceremonial occasions.,

pasos *Philippines.*   Procession of floats during Passion Week depicting scenes of Christ's suffering.

passing *Mexico.*   Assimilation of Indians into the MESTIZO community through the adoption of Spanish manners and dress.

Patamona *Guyana.*   Carib-speaking Amerindians.

patangok *Philippines.*   Musical instrument with 30 bamboo tubes played like the Javanese ANGKLUNG.

pataxte *Guatemala.*   Tree, closely related to the cacao, the fruit of which is used as a substitute for cacao in beverages.

patel *India.*   Headman of village in Marathi and Gujerati areas.

patente *Venezuela.*   Business license fee or tax.

Pathan *Afghanistan and Pakistan.*   PUSHTU speaking tribe in eastern Afghanistan and North West Frontier Province in Pakistan.

patimokkha *Thailand.* Section of the Buddhist canon comprising rules of conduct for monks.

patis *Philippines.* Fish sauce.

patni *India.* Type of land tenure in Bengal under which a *patni* or subdivision of a ZAMINDARI was held by a *patnidar* with right of inheritance or sale.

pato *Argentina.* Mixture of basketball and polo in which an inflated leather bag (originally a pato or duck) is the object of the contest.

patra *India.* Astrological almanac.

patrao *Brazil.* Literally, patron. Boss, sponsor or father figure.

patria chica *Mexico.* Literally, small fatherland. Parochialism.

patron (plural: patrones) *Spanish America.* Literally, patron, Paternalistic relationship between two persons of unequal status.

patronato *Spanish America.* Special privileges granted by the state in Spanish times to the military and the church.

patronismo *Spanish America.* System of social and political patronage.

patron-mozo *Spanish America.* Master-servant in a *patronato* relationship.

pattadi *India.* District.

Pattae *Indonesia.* Austronesian language.

pattalar *Burma.* Xylophone with 24 graduated bamboo slats mounted on a decorated black-and-gold semicircular sound box.

patti *Sri Lanka.* SINHALESE high caste.

Pattinjoe *Indonesia.* Austronesian language.

pattu *Sri Lanka.* Group of villages.

patus *Niue.* Heads of families.

patut *Malaysia.* Proper or seemly.

patwari *India and Nepal.* Village headman.

pau de Arara *Brazil.* Literally, parrot perch. Truck for migrants.

paulista *Brazil.* Native of Sao Paulo.

Pauna *Bolivia.* Amazon Indian group of Arawakan linguistic stock in Santa Cruz department.

paung pyi *Burma.* Turban worn by chiefs or aristocrats in Haka Chin area.

pauro *Bolivia.* In the Oriente, a well or basin holding water through the dry season.

Pauserna *Bolivia.* Amazon Indian group of TUPIAN linguistic stock in Beni and Santa Cruz departments.

Pawar *India.* See AGNIKULA.

Pawi *Burma.* Southern CHINS.

pawku *Burma.* Priest or shaman among the LAHU.

Paxaxon *Laos.* Republic, as part of the official name of the country.

paya *Burma.* Title of respect.

Paya *Honduras.*   Indian ethnic group in the northeast.

payador *Uruguay.*   Broncobuster.

Payagua *Paraguay.*   Indian ethnic group of the GUARANI family.

payghla *Afghanistan.*   Term of address to a woman, equal to miss.

paysannat *Francophone Africa.*   Planned agricultural settlement.

Pear *Cambodia.*   Subgroup of the KHMER LOEU.

pe-de-moleque *Brazil.*   Cake made of fermented manioc meal.

Pedi *Botswana.*   Ethnic subgroup.

pe-duro *Brazil.*   Native breed of Amazon cattle.

pegasse *Guyana.*   A variety of tropical peat.

pekarangan *Indonesia.*   Small home gardens.

pelegos *Brazil.*   1. Trade union leaders as government puppets. 2. Sheepskin horse blanket.

pelle (singular: fedde) *Senegal.*   Age group or cohort among the TOU-COLEURS.

pelog *Indonesia.*   Seven-tone tuning system for the GAMELAN.

pelota de guante *Spanish America.*   Game played by teams wearing gloves attached to disk-shaped wooden paddles, used to propel a heavy ball of hard rubber.

pelucones *Chile.*   Literally, bigwigs. Conservatives.

Pemba *Tanzania.*   Ethnic group in Zanzibar.

pena *Argentina.*   Group of friends in a club.

Penan *Malaysia.*   Nomadic ethnic group in Sarawak.

Pende *Zaire.*   Ethnic group of southern savanna.

pengadilan negeri *Indonesia.*   District court.

pengadilan tinggi *Indonesia.*   High courts.

penggawa *Malaysia.*   1. District official. 2. Ruler of a MUKIM in Kelantan.

penghulu *Malaysia.*   District official below a PENGGAWA.

peninsulares *Spanish America.*   Historically, a person born in Spain, and thus a pure Spaniard.

penjuru *Malaysia.*   Unit of area equal to 14,400 sq ft.

penlop *Bhutan.*   Formerly, a provincial chief who enjoyed broad autonomous powers.

Penoqui *Bolivia.*   Amazon Indian group of CHIQUITOAN linguistic stock in Santa Cruz.

peoes *Brazil.*   Ranch hands.

peon *Spanish America.*   Common laborer.

peones *Spanish America.*   Followers of a CAUDILLO.

peonia *Guatemala.*   Unit of area equal to 82 acres.

pepa de oro *Ecuador.*   Cacao bean.

pepenadores *Mexico.*   Persons scavenging trash heaps for a living.

pequena propriedad *Central America.*   Landholding between 35 to 88 acres.

perahera *Sri Lanka.* Annual pageant at Kandy when a relic of the Buddha is carried in torchlight procession.

peranakan *Indonesia.* Indonesianized Chinese.

peranakan tionghoa *Indonesia.* Chinese of Indonesian origin.

perbekel *Indonesia.* Head of a DESA. Also, *bendesa.*

perceria *Cape Verde.* Sharecropper system.

perch *Malaysia.* Unit of length equal to five meters.

percha *Guatemala.* Teasel for raising nap on woolen cloth.

perdana menteri *Malaysia.* Prime minister.

Pere *Zaire.* Ethnic group.

Pere *Central Africa.* Niger-Kordofanian language.

pereza criolla, la *Uruguay.* Violence as a national characteristic.

pergana *India.* Subdivision of a district in Bengal.

peribahasa *Indonesia.* Short proverbs.

pericon *Uruguay.* National dance in triple time, like the French minuet.

peristyle *Haiti.* Roofed open-sided area of a VOODOO temple for dancing and ceremonies.

Pero *West Africa.* Afro-Asiatic language

Perovosan *Bolivia.* Amazon Indian group in Beni department.

personalismo *Spanish America.* Complex of beliefs and behavior stressing personality, prestige, character and appearance of individuals rather than ideology.

pertengahan *Malaysia.* Middle class. Compare ADAHERTA.

pesero *Mexico.* Taxi that plies between regular points like a bus.

pesewa *Ghana.* Coin, $\frac{1}{100}$ths of a CEDI.

pesh-kesh *India.* Literally, first fruits. Gift or offering to a superior on ceremonial occasions.

peshwa *India.* Formerly, prime minister in Maratha principalities.

petaca *Honduras.* CARIB basket or hamper.

petate *Nicaragua.* Grass mats used on beds.

petats *Papua New Guinea.* Austronesian language.

petit blanc *Haiti.* White person of minor status.

petro *Haiti.* One of two principal groups of VOODOO deities.

pettah *India.* Suburb of a fort or town attached to and adjacent to a fort.

Peul *West Africa.* Variant of FULANI. Large Poular-speaking Muslim ethnic cluster.

peyon *Guatemala.* Shaggy wool rug.

phak kanmuang *Thailand.* Political parties that become active only during or prior to elections.

Phaleng *Botswana.* Ethnic subgroup.

phansa *Thailand.* Buddhist lent.

phaw khun *Thailand.* Thai king as the father of the people.

Phende *Zaire.* Niger-Kordofanian language.

phi *Thailand and Laos.* Variety of spirits having power over human beings.

Phi ban *Laos.* Tutelary spirit of the Lao.

phikhok *Cambodia.* Fully ordained monk.

phisak bauchia *Cambodia.* Festival commemorating the enlightenment and death of Buddha.

pho *Vietnam.* Consomme-type soup with beef and noodles popular in the north.

pho bon *Laos.* Village headman in the south.

phra *Thailand.* Prefix or title indicating princely status. Also, honorific for Buddhisit monks.

phrai *Thailand.* Generic term for commoners.

phra phum *Thailand.* Guardian spirit of a house.

phra sangharaja *Laos.* Religious head of the Buddhist SANGHA.

phraya *Thailand.* Princely title conferred on holders of second highest rank in civil government, as viceroys.

phu *Vietnam.* 1. Form of poetic essay used to describe nature, traditions or human emotions. 2. Protection.

phuak wat *Thailand.* Buddhist laity affiliated to a particular WAT, or temple.

Phuan *Thailand.* Thai-speaking ethnic group.

phumi *Cambodia.* Village.

phungu *Malawi.* Elderly woman who is the chief of a CIMBA.

phu noi *Thailand.* Inferior person of low status.

phuong *Vietnam.* 1. Phoenix, one of the four sacred animals. 2. Village association of merchants and craftsmen.

phus *Nepal.* Temporary SHERPA herdsmen's settlement in the alpine pastures.

Phu-Thai *Thailand.* KAM-TAI or LU.

phuwarachaken *Thailand.* Governor of a province.

phu yai *Thailand.* Superior or a person of high status.

phuyaiban *Thailand.* Elder of a village.

pialeras *Honduras.* Rawhide lasso.

piamuene *Mozambique.* Tribal official with authority to decide important ritual and spiritual matters among the MAKUA-LOMUE.

Piaroa *Venezuela.* 1. Indian tribe. 2. Indian language.

piastre *Lebanon.* Coin, $\frac{1}{100}$ths of a Lebanese pound.

picadillo *Honduras.* Vegetable dish with chopped avocado or potato.

picar *India.* Retail dealer, intermediary or broker.

Pinchinglis *Equatorial Guinea.* Pidgin English dialect in which trade is conducted.

picota *India.* Additional allowance added to goods.

picottah *India.*   Sway pole, an ancient instrument for raising water consisting of a long lever pivoted on an upright post weighted on the short arm and bearing a line and bucket on the long arm.

pidgin *Papua New Guinea.*   English Creole.

pifano *South America.*   Wooden fife carved from reed with six finger holes.

pijevalle *Honduras.*   Palm nuts similar in taste to chestnuts.

pik *Tunisia.*   Unit of length equal to 50 to 65 centimeters.

pikul *Malaysia.*   Unit of weight equal to 131 lb.

pila *Guatemala.*   Stone or cement trough into which water flows from a pipe or stream.

Pila *West Africa.*   Niger-Kordofanian language.

pilada *Ecuador.*   Threshing and polishing of rice.

Pilapila *Ghana.*   GURMA group in Eastern and ASANTE regions.

pillai *India.*   Title of a class of superior SUDRAS in south India.

pilon *Nicaragua.*   Wooden mortar.

Piman *Mexico.*   Ethnic group in the northwest.

Pimbe *Mozambique.*   Ethnic group of the MARAVI cluster.

Pimbwe *Tanzania.*   1. Ethnic group. 2. Niger-Kordofanian language.

pina *Philippines.*   Textile woven of pineapple fiber.

pinai *Thailand.*   Oboe-like musical instrument with a conical reed bore having six holes.

pinati *Indonesia.*   Shaman in Makaserese villages.

Pindari *India.*   Formerly, a member of a band of plunderers in western and central India under MAHRATTA rule.

pingo *Uruguay.*   Saddle pony of the GAUCHO.

pinjrapole *India.*   Veterinary hospital in Gujerat.

Pinoco *Bolivia.*   Amazon Indian group of CHIQUITOAN linguistic stock in Santa Cruz department.

pinole *Guatemala.*   Sweet drink made of dry-toasted maize, flavored and seasoned with cacao, panela, aniseed, ginger, cinnamon and other condiments.

pinolillo *Nicaragua.*   Drink made from toasted corn and cocoa.

Pinyin *West Africa.*   Niger-Kordofanian language.

pipal *India.*   One of the great fig trees.

pipante *Nicaragua.*   Narrow, flat-bottomed, shallow dugout canoe made of royal cedar.

piphat *Thailand.*   Percussion orchestra consisting of three groups of instruments. Also, *wong piphat, gong teng ting.*

Pipikoro *Indonesia.*   Austronesian language.

Pipil *Guatemala.*   Non-Mayan Indian tribe in the southern highlands.

pipiolo *Chile.*   Literally, novice. Early 19th-century liberal.

piquet *Haiti.*   Professional mercenary who lent his services to politicians aspiring to the presidency.

pir *South Asia.*   Muslim holy man who serves as a spiritual guide to his followers.

pirata *Colombia.*   Urban or suburban settlement in which householders hold title to the land but have not complied with zoning laws and municipal regulations.

pirca *Ecuador.*   Wall or fence in a rural area.

pirit *Sri Lanka.*   Protective chants.

pirivenas *Sri Lanka.*   Buddhist schools.

pisco *Chile.*   Mild domestic liquor distilled from grape juice.

pistolao *Brazil.*   Person of a higher class acting as protector and benefactor of a person of a lower class.

pita *Honduras.*   Form of agave whose fiber is used in the manufacture of thread, hammocks and paper.

pitafloja *Guatemala.*   Fine durable grass fiber used to make rain capes, nets and cords.

pite *Colombia.*   Game of pitching pennies.

pithitham bun *Thailand.*   Buddhist merit-making ceremony.

pitji *Indonesia.*   Black velvet cap worn by Muslims.

pito *El Salvador.*   Whistle, six to 12 inches long, with six finger holes to vary the tone.

pitonu'u *Samoa.*   Subdivision or sector of a village.

pitso *Lesotho.*   Gathering or assembly for approving laws.

Pitu Vluna Salu. *Indonesia.*   Austronesian language.

placage *Haiti.*   Cohabitation without formal marriage.

place, la *Haiti.*   Chief assistant of a VOODOO priest.

placee *Haiti.*   Person of the opposite sex sharing living quarters.

plan basico *Central America.*   Academic program offered in secondary schools.

pla tu *Thailand.*   Little mackerel, important part of Thai diet.

playas *Paraguay.*   Low-lying forest or open grassland in the floodplains of streams and channels.

plegado *Guatemala.*   Pleated woman's skirt.

Pnar *India.*   Austro-Asiatic language.

poblacion *Philippines.*   Official seat of a municipality.

poblacionista *Mexico.*   Policy or program favoring population growth.

Pocomam *Guatemala.*   MAYAN language.

Pocomchi *Guatemala.*   MAYAN language.

poddar *India.*   Assayer.

poderes *Uruguay.*   Any of the three branches of government.

poder popular *Cuba.*   People's power.

Podoko *West Africa.*   Afro-Asiatic language.

Podzo *Mozambique.*   1. Ethnic group of the lower ZAMBEZI CLUSTER. Also, *Morromeu, Chipango.* 2. Niger-Kordofanian language.

poeng mang *Thailand.*   Drum, used to accompany songs.

Pogolo *Tanzania.* Niger-Kordofanian language.

Pogoro *Tanzania.* Ethnic group of Ulanga district.

poi *Western Samoa.* Starchy paste made from boiled taro roots softened by pounding in a stone mortar.

Poi *Zaire.* Ethnic group.

poikyaung *Burma.* Liberal SHAN Buddhist sect wearing modern garb.

Pointsettism *Mexico.* U. S. interference in Latin American affairs, after Joel R. Poinsett, 1779–1851, first U.S. ambassador to Mexico.

poisha *Bangladesh.* Coin, ¹⁄₁₀₀th of a TAKA.

Pojulu *Sudan.* Ethnic group.

Poke *Zaire.* Niger-Kordofanian language.

Pokomam *Central America.* One of the three MAYAN linguistic stocks making up the KEKCHIAN family.

Pokomam *El Salvador.* MAYAN Indians west and south of Lempa River.

Pokomo *Kenya.* 1. Ethnic group on the banks of the Tana River. 2. Niger-Kordofanian language.

Pokonchi *Central America.* One of the three linguistic stocks making up the KEKCHIAN family.

Pokonchi *Honduras.* MAYA tribe.

Pokoot *Central Africa.* Nilo-Saharan family.

Pokot *Kenya.* Most northerly KALENJIN group.

Polane *Lesotho.* Former name of northern NGUNI people, now called BAPHETLA.

poligar *India.* Subordinate feudal chief.

poligono das secas *Brazil.* Literally, drought polygon. The eight northeast and northern states subject to drought: Maranhao, Piaui, Ceara, Pernambuco, Rio Grande do Norte, Sergipe, Alagoas, and Bahia.

pollera *Panama.* Female garment, the national costume of the country. It is a two-piece outfit consisting of a blouse or *comisa* and a skirt or *polleron,* with elaborate lace-fringed petticoats worn beneath the skirt. The blouse has two ruffles, the shorter one overlapping the sleeve. The ankle-length *polleron* is bell-shaped gradually tapering outward from the waist to the lace-trimmed hemline several yards in width.

polowidjo *Indonesia.* Nonstaple food crops.

pombe *Kenya.* Beer. Also, *tembo.*

pombeiro *Brazil.* Owner of fishing rafts who rents them out in return for a portion of the catch and first option to purchase the remainder at a lower price.

pombeiro *Central African Republic.* Congolese METIS who in the 19th century served as intermediaries for the Portuguese slave traders.

pomdan (plural: pomdo) *Guinea.* Statuette of human figures from four to six inches in height carved from soft materials such as steatite and schist.

Pomo *Central Africa.*   Niger-Kordofanian language.

pon *Burma.*   Spiritual power inherent in all matter, of which the main elements are *gon* (virtue) and *awza* (authority).

pon *North Korea.*   Literally, root or source. Lineages.

Ponape *Micronesia.*   Austronesian language.

poncho *Spanish American.*   Cloak, often waterproof, with a slit in the middle for the head to go through.

poderosos do sertao *Brazil.*   Literally, lords of the backlands. Ranchers and landlords of the interior in colonial times.

pondok *Indonesia.*   Rural Islamic school often founded by a HAJI who uses the students as an inexpensive labor pool.

pongal *India.*   South Indian harvest festival in TAMIL Nadu.

Pongo *West Africa.*   Coastal ethnic group.

pongyi *Burma.*   Ordained Buddhist monk.

ponna *Burma.*   BRAHMIN adviser to a king, usually an astrologer.

pon pong *Thailand.*   Drum.

pooye (singular: foyre) *Senegal.*   Nuclear family among the TOU-COLEURS.

Popoloca *Mexico.*   Oto-Manguean language.

Popolocan *Mexico.*   Ethnic group in southern highlands.

populacho, el *Guatemala.*   The common people.

Porfiriato *Mexico.*   The administration of Porfirio Diaz, 1877–80, 1884–1911.

porknockers *Guyana.*   Free-lance prospectors for gold and diamonds.

poro *West Africa.*   Male secret society that initiates young men in bush schools.

porococa *Brazil.*   Tidal phenomenon in the Amazon River.

poroes *Brazil.*   Basement housing units in multiple dwellings.

Porohanon *Philippines.*   Austronesian language.

porork *Thailand.*   Lay sponsor of a novice or monk.

porongo *Paraguay.*   Small, gourdlike vessel used for drinking mate.

porros *Colombia.*   Music of African origin.

porte *Turkey.*   Literally, high gate. Formerly, the Ottoman sultan. Also, SUBLIME PORTE.

portenos *Argentina.*   Literally, people of the port. Residents of Buenos Aires.

portero *Guatemala.*   Cattle grazing ground.

portete *Ecuador.*   Minor mountain pass.

portugan *Yemens.*   Mixture of spices, chalk and crushed stone, for smoking.

Porturero *Bolivia.*   Indian ethnic group of ZAMUCOAN linguistic stock in Santa Cruz department.

posho *Kenya.*   Ration of food given to laborers.

posole *Guatemala.* Cold drink made from ground boiled corn mixed with water and seasoned.

posseiro *Brazil.* Peasant farmer-owner of a MINIFUNDIO.

posteencha *Afghanistan.* Sheepskin or fox fur waist-length coat with intricate embroidery.

postes administratives *Francophone Africa.* Administrative posts.

posto *Lusophone Africa.* Rural subdivision of a CIRCUNSCRIOES CIVIS.

Potosino *Central America.* MAYA tribe.

potreros *Paraguay.* Large, fenced pasture.

potyguar *Brazil.* Inhabitant of the state of Rio Grande do Norte.

Pougouli *Brukina Faso.* Ethnic group related to DYAN and DAGARI.

pouin *Haiti.* Powerful VOODOO charm.

Poul *West Africa.* Variant of PEUL.

pouvoir en cassation *Morocco.* Legal power of abrogation exercised by a superior court over the judgments of a lower court.

pove or **pubi** *Gabon.* OKANDE linguistic group.

powindah *Afghanistan.* Nomadic caravan traders.

poya days *Sri Lanka.* Movable sabbath days, according to the Buddhist lunar calendar.

Poya *Honduras.* Indian tribal group of the northeast.

prabhu *India.* Clerical caste in western India

prachathipatai *Thailand.* Democracy.

prachum *Cambodia.* Festival honoring the dead in September.

Pradhan *Nepal.* NEWARI KSHATRIYA caste.

pradhana mantri *India.* Prime minister.

pradhan nyayalya *Nepal.* Supreme court.

pradhan pancha *Nepal.* Chief of PANCHAYAT.

Prakrit *India.* Demotic form of SANSKRIT and the spoken vernacular in pre-Christian times.

prang *Thailand.* Tower ending in a pinnacle.

prathet *Thailand.* Kingdom, as used in the official name of the country.

prathom suksia *Thailand.* Elementary education.

prazero *Mozambique.* Recipient of a land lease or *prazo.*

precoristas *Costa Rica.* Squatters.

prefectura *Chile.* First-class police station.

prefeito *Brazil.* Mayor.

prehatin *Indonesia.* Awareness on the part of member of a family of the range of possible conflicts and an appropriate adaptation of individual behavior to that awareness.

premier president *Senegal.* Chief justice.

president de section *Senegal.* Presiding justice of a section of the Supreme Court.

presidio *Portuguese Africa.* Interior fort as the center of an administrative or military district.

prestation *Cameroon.* Formerly, a form of conpulsory labor introduced by the French under which all unassimilated blacks had to furnish the government with 10 days of free labor a year.

preto *Brazil.* Black person.

pret savan *Haiti.* Learned priest of any sect.

priere guinee *Haiti.* VOODOO prayer.

prijaji *India.* Upper crust of society, including the intelligentsia and the bureaucracy.

primicia *Spanish America.* First fruits collected as an offering by the church.

primera, de *Spanish America.* Upper crust of society.

principal *Guatemala.* Prominent Indian leader.

principales *Guatemala.* Elders or leading members of an Indian community.

principismo *Uruguay.* Political principles.

prinyatri *Thailand.* Bachelor's degree.

prioste *Ecuador.* Highland Indian official charged with the supervision of a FIESTA.

prix-des-yeux *Haiti.* Literally, prize of the eyes. Highest degree of VOODOO initiates.

procuradores judiciales *Nicaragua.* State attorney with limited functions.

procureur general *Senegal.* Attorney general.

profesional *Argentina.* Vocational education at the secondary level.

profesores taximetros *Colombia.* Literally, taxicab professors. Part-time professors holding a number of teaching positions at various institutions from and to which they rush by taxi.

projatantri *Bangladesh.* Republic, as used in the official name of the country.

proletario *Nicaragua.* Lower class.

pronunciamento *Spanish America.* Manifesto or public declaration defining the policy and program of an institution or group.

propinsi *Indonesia.* Provinces.

proposition de loi *Ivory Coast.* Bill sponsored by a private member of the National Assembly.

proprietario *Philippines.* Middle-class landowner.

proselitismo *Venezuela.* Political propaganda.

Proto-Chiapas *Mexico.* Ethno-linguistic group in Chiapas State.

provedor-mor *Brazil.* Chief financial adviser to the colonial government.

provincia *Ecuador.* Province.

provisorios *Brazil.* Provisional troops maintained by local bosses to wage political battles.

ptso *Sikkim.* Patrilineal class among the LEPCHA.

pu *North Korea.* Ministry.

publique *Haiti.* Public bus with fixed routes but no fixed schedules.

puchero *Paraguay.* Boiled meat and vegetables, similar to Irish stew.

pueblo *Spanish America.* Common people.

pueblo de ratas *Uruguay.* Literally, rat towns. Rural slums.

pueblos jovenas *Peru.* New towns, usually of jerry-built houses.

puestero *Uruguay.* Ranger in charge of sheep or cattle.

puggree *India.* Turban.

puita *Brazil.* Afro-Brazilian cult drum.

puja *India.* Hindu worship.

pujari *India.* Hindu priest.

pukka *India.* Ripe, mature, substantial or permanent, as opposed to KATCHA.

Puku-Geeri-Keri-Wipsi *West Africa.* Niger-Kordofanian language.

pul *Afghanistan.* Coin, 1/100ths of an AFGHANI.

pula *Botswana.* Monetary unit.

pulayan *India.* Member of an untouchable class in south India.

Puleanga Fakatui'o *Tonga.* Kingdom of [Tonga].

pulperia *Uruguay.* Club, barroom and general store of the PAMPAS.

pulperio *Uruguay.* Owner of a PULPERIA.

pulque *Mexico.* Cactus beer.

pulwar *Bangladesh.* Sampan-like boat.

pulwar *India.* Keelless riverboat.

pum *Burma.* Class of MON historical writings on the exploits of the great kings.

Punan *Malaysia.* Nomadic ethnic group in Sarawak.

pundit (female: pundita) *India.* Learned man, especially in the VEDAS. Often used as an honorific or title.

pundok *Malaysia.* Islamic school.

Punjabi *India.* Indo-European language.

punkah *India.* Large, fixed but swinging fan suspended from the ceiling, formed of cloth stretched on a rectangular frame and pulled to and fro by a rope to agitate the air in hot weather.

punto *Cuba.* Music.

Punu *Central Africa.* Niger-Kordofanian language.

pupu *Polynesia.* Subdivision of a parish for Bible study.

Puquina *Bolivia.* Indian linguistic stock comprising URU and CHIPAYA.

Puquinan *Bolivia.* Member of the PUQUINA linguistic group.

purak *South Korea.* Hamlet.

Puranas *India.* Collective name for a class of Hindu BRAHMINIC writings, 18 in number, containing cosmogony interwoven with legends and genealogies of kings.

purdah *Islamic countries.* Seclusion of women both within the home and in public. Also, the long, loose shroud-like garment and veil worn by women in public for this purpose.

puri *India.* Puffed pancake.

Purik *Pakistan* and *India.* Sino-Tibetan language.

puro *Honduras.* Native cigar.

purohit *India.* Hindu priest.

purva mimamsa *India.* One of the six orthodox schools of Hindu philosophy founded by Jaimini, emphasizing the ethical rather than the speculative side of the VEDAS.

pusat *Indonesia.* Jakarta, the capital, as the center of the nation.

pushtin *Afghanistan.* Heavy embroidered sheepskin coat.

Pushtun *Afghanistan.* Principal ethnic group. Also, *Pashtun, Pathan.*

Pushtunwali *Afghanistan.* Traditional code of conduct of the PUSHTUNS governing social obligations and defining crime and punishment.

putelees *Bangladesh.* Single-sail boats capable of carrying up to 35 tons.

putra *India.* Type of RAGA.

pwe *Burma.* Theatrical performance or musical opera with dancing that often lasts for a whole night, or at least eight hours.

pya *Burma.* Coin, 1/100ths of a KYAT.

pyazat *Burma.* Musical comedy.

pygmy *Zaire.* Ethnic group of the Central Rain Forest.

pyidawtha *Burma.* Literally, happy land. Welfare state under a socialist regime.

Pyithu Hluttaw *Burma.* People's Assembly, the Burmese parliament.

qabba *Sudan.* Muslim shrine.

qabila *Islamic countries.* BERBER or Arab Bedouin tribe.

qabilah *Arab countries.* Tribe, with a common ancestor.

qada (plural: aqdiyat) *Arab countries.* District.

qadi (plural: qudah) *Arab countries.* Islamic judge or magistrate dispensing justice according to the SHARIA.

Qadi Kolahi *Iran.* Indo-Iranian ethnic group in Khorasan.

qadi madhab *Arab countries.* DRUZE judge who settles disputes on personal status.

Qadiriya *North Africa.* Islamic brotherhood founded by Sidi M. Abd al Kader al Djilani in the 12th century.

Qahtani *Yemens.* Southern Arab.

Qahtari *Saudi Arabia.* Ethnic group.

qaid *Morroco. See* CAID.

qaim maqam *Arab countries.* Governor of a district.

qaim maqmiyyah (plural: maqamiyyatan) *Arab countries.* District.

Qajar *Iran.* Ethnic group to which the former royal family belonged.

Qamri *Afghanistan.* Lunar calendar.

qanat *Arab countries.* Underground water channels.

qanum *Arab countries.* Harp, a trapezoidal box with 78 strings, played with wooden mallets.

Qara *Oman.* Aboriginal tribe.

Qaramitah (singular: Qarmati) *Oman.* Fundamentalist Islamic sect that rose in Iraq in the 9th century.

Qarepakh *Iran.* Nomadic tribal group in Khorasan.

qarya *Arab countries.* Precinct of a village or town.

qasabah *Jordan.* Short reed or flute.

Qashqai *Iran.* Ural-Altaic language.

Qashqai *Iran.* Large Turkic group.

qasidah *Arab countries.* Particular form of ode containing 15 to 120 couplets, all with the same rhythm and meter and intended to be sung. Each line consists of the same or very similar sequence of vowels.

qat *Arab countries.* Shrub resembling tea plant, whose leaves when chewed impart a mildly narcotic effect.

qaum *Afghanistan.* Clan or ethnic lineages.

qawali *South Asia.* Muslim devotional song.

Qawasim (singular: Qasimi) *Oman.* Tribe.

qawm *Morocco.* Group of people with a common ancestor; also, a corps of native auxiliary troops.

qaws *Arab countries.* Dry southwest wind.

qayls *Yemens.* Chieftains.

qaymaq *Afghanistan.* Lumps of milk curds with a distinctively salty flavor, generally eaten at breakfast.

qaysarya *Morocco.* Covered SUK devoted to textiles and jewelry.

qazi *Islamic countries.* Variant of QADI.

qene *Ethiopia.* A form of poetry consisting of two to 11 verses.

qene mahlet *Ethiopia.* Outer court of an Orthodox church.

qerar *Ethiopia.* Lyre with five or six strings.

qhobosheane *Lesotho.* Flat-topped steep-sided mountain used as a fortress.

qibla *Saudi Arabia.* Variant of KIBLAH.

Qimant *Ethiopia and Sudan.* Afro-Asiatic language.

Qimant *Ethiopia.* AGEW-speaking peoples.

qirsh *Saudi Arabia.* ¹/₂₀th of a riyal.

qishlaq *Afghanistan.* Winter headquarters of most nomadic and semi-nomadic groups.

Qitab, Bani (singular: Qitbi) *Oman.* Tribe.

qiya *Arab countries..* Analogy for elaborating and extrapolating the intent of the Sharia.

qodat *Western Sahara.* Court.

qorma or **kurma** *South Asia.* Meat dish.

qoz *Sudan.* Region of elongated sandy dunes and hills.

qrut *Afghanistan.* Dried cheese eaten as sour cream.

quada *Yemens.* Major cities or urban settlements.

quad-i-azam *Pakistan.* Literally, great leader. Title of Mohammed Ali Jinnah, founder of Pakistan.

Quaiti *Yemens.* Ethnic group.

quami *Afghanistan.* Former military conscription system based on age groups.

quan *Vietnam.* 1. Mandarins or civil servants. 2. District as a unit of provincial administration.

quartillo *Costa Rica.* Unit of weight equal to 71 lb.

quebracho *Paraguay.* Hard wood from which tannin is extracted.

Quechua *Spanish America.* 1. Literally, deep valley. Extensive tribal cluster spread over the highland areas of Peru, Bolivia, Ecuador, north Chile and northwest Argentina. 2. Language of the Quechua, which became the lingua franca of Indians after the Spanish conquest.

quena *Peru.* Wooden flute of the AYMARA and QUECHUA Indians.

quequisque *Honduras.* Purple root plant.

quermada *Brazil.* Burning land for cultivation under the slash and burn system.

quetzal *Guatemala.* 1. National bird. 2. Monetary unit.

quetzal *Mexico.* Indian folk dance in which dancers wear headdress depicting the QUETZAL bird.

quetzalcoatl *Central America.* Literally, bird-snake. Mythical creature worshipped by the Aztecs as a god-hero.

Quiche *Central America.* MAYAN language.

Quiche *Honduras.* MAYA tribe.

quijongo *El Salvador.* Bow similar to the CARAMBA, with a jar at the end.

quilca *Ecuador.* Minor functionary.

quilombos *Brazil.*   Former fugitive slave settlements.
quina *Ecuador.*   Native flute.
quincha *Ecuador.*   Mixture of mud and straw used in wattle construction.
Quintana Roo *Mexico.*   MAYAN ethnic group.
Quiriquire *Venezuela.*   Indian tribe east of Lake Maracaibo.
Quoc Hai *Vietnam.*   National Assembly.
Quoc-Ngu *Vietnam.*   Romanized writing script of Vietnamese language devised by Roman Catholic missionaries.
Qara (singular: Qarawi) *Oman.*   Non-Arab people in Dhofar.
qurban *Ethiopia.*   Church sacrament, as the liturgical celebration of the Eucharist.
qurush *Saudi Arabia.*   Coin, ¹⁄₂₀th of a RIYAL.
quy *Vietnam.*   Tortoise, one of the four sacred animals.

rab *Mauritania.*   Arabized upper class of warriors.
raba *Senegal.*   Caste of drummers and weavers among the WOLOF.
rababah *Arab countries.*   BEDOUIN one-stringed violin with a narrow body and a straight neck.
Rabha *India.*   Sino-Tibetan language.
rabi *India.*   Crops sown after the rains in autumn and harvested in spring.
Rabinal *Central America.*   Language group, member of QUIICHEAN linguistic family.
Rabinal *Honduras.*   MAYAN tribe.
rabula *Brazil.*   One who practices law without a formal degree.
rachasp *Thailand.*   Gradation of vocabulary and terms of address in communicating with superiors or inferiors.
rada *Haiti.*   One of the two principal groups of VOODOO deities.
Rada *Vietnam.*   Austronesian language.
radala *Sri Lanka.*   SINHALESE high caste.
rafiq (plural: rufaqa) *Oman.*   Companion or escort across tribal territory.
raga *India.*   Traditional Hindu melodic form consisting of certain prescribed combinations of notes, designed to create certain emotional

moods, each with its own characteristic signature. The principal ragas are six in number and are called JANAKAS, or father raga. Each janaka raga has five wives called RAGINIS. Each RAGINI has six sons called PUTRAS. The family of ragas thus consists of 216 members. Each raga has a particular season and a particular time of night or day associated with it and some are ascribed magical powers.

ragbenle *Sierra Leone.* Secret society among the TEMNE.

ragini *India.* See RAGA.

ragmala *India.* Literally, garland of RAGAS. Miniature paintings of RAGAS and RAGINIS depicting the mood assigned to each.

rago *Burundi.* Fence around each family property.

Rahanweyn *Somalia.* One of the five clan families descended from the SAAB. They are sometimes called the MIRIFLE CONFEDERACY.

rahab *Arab countries.* Musical instrument with one string, similar to a violin.

rai *Nepal.* Tibeto-Nepalese ethnic group. Also, *Jimdar, Kiranti, Kirat,* and *Kirata.*

Rai *Nepal.* Sino-Tibetan language.

raikar *Nepal.* System of land tenure.

raiamandreny *Madagascar.* Literally, father and mother. Term applied to elders in an extended family.

raini *Zimbabwe.* SHONA village composed of houses built in a straight line.

rais *Egypt.* President.

rais *Saudi Arabia.* Captain.

rais al baladiyah *Iraq.* Mayor.

raiyatan *Nepal.* State land assigned to peasants.

raiyyah *Arab countries.* Partly sedentary Arabs who are nomadic only in the winter.

raj *India.* Sovereignty; system or pattern of government.

raja *India.* Ruler of a minor principality.

Rajawan *Burma.* Class of MON historical writings dealing with genealogies.

Rajbandari *Nepal.* NEWARI KSHATRIYA caste.

Rajbangsi *India and Nepal.* Indo-European language.

Rajbhansi *Sikkim and Nepal.* Ethnic group.

Raji *Nepal.* Minor ethnic group.

rajkaria *Sri Lanka.* Traditional obligation to serve in the army.

rajpramukh *India.* The principal RAJA in a confederation of RAJAS.

Rajput *India.* Warlike people inhabiting Rajasthan (formerly Rajputana) believed to have descended from foreign invaders such as the Huns, Gujars and Sakas, and later admitted to the KSHATRIYA caste. They are divided into 36 clans of whom the most prominent are *Gurjara Pratoharas, Chauhans, Chalukyas, Chandellas, Tomaras, Kalachuris* and *Rashtrakutas.*

rajya *Nepal.* Former system of land tenure in small principalities under which hereditary rulers held royal charters permitting them to collect taxes.

Rajya Sabha *India.* Council of State, the upper house of Indian Parliament.

raki *Turkey.* National drink distilled from fermented raisins and flavored with anise.

rakshi *Nepal.* Alcoholic beverage distilled from rice and millet.

Ralte *Burma.* Sino-Tibetan language.

Ramadan *Islamic countries.* 1. The ninth month of the Muslim year. 2. Fast prescribed by the Koran and observed during this month when orthodox Muslims do not take food or water from sunrise to sunset.

Ramang *Burma.* Chief of a confederation of WA villages.

Ramayana *India.* One of the two great Hindu epics ascribed to the poet Valmiki in the second century B.C., consisting of 24,000 couplets divided into seven books dealing with the exploits of Ramachandra, an incarnation of Vishnu.

ramlah (plural: rimal) *Oman.* Sandy region.

Ram Rajya *India.* Literally, kingdom of Rama. Ideal Indian polity based on ancient VEDIC ideals of the age of RAMAYANA.

ramwong *Indonesia.* Social dance.

rana *India.* Ruling RAJPUT prince.

rana *Nepal.* Former prime ministers who were effectively rulers from mid-19th century to 1957.

Rana *Nicaragua.* Indians of the Atlantic coast.

ranad ok *Thailand.* Treble xylophone with 21 seasoned wooden bars.

ranad thum *Thailand.* Alto xylophone with 17 wooden resonance bars.

rancheria *Bolivia.* Hamlet in a region of dispersed hamlets.

ranchero *Uruguay.* Rural slum.

ranchito *Guatemala.* Small rural hut.

ranchos *Spanish America.* One-room house with combined cooking, living and sleeping quarters.

range *Guyana.* Barrack-like tenement.

Rangi *Tanzania.* Ethnic group.

rani *India.* Queen, wife of a RAJA.

ranopango *Madagascar.* Rice water, the national beverage.

rao *India.* Title of prince or chief under the MAHRATTAS.

rapadou *Haiti.* Syrup produced while refining sugar.

rapadura *Brazil.* Crude brown sugar sold in kilo blocks.

rara *Haiti.* Band of torchbearers and religious worshippers during Holy Week.

Rarotongan *Cook Islands.* Austronesian language.

ras *Arab countries.* Cape or peninsula.

ras *Ethiopia.* Prince or duke.

rasa *Indonesia.* The evocative mood in a dramatic performance.

Rashidiyyah *Sudan.* Islamic brotherhood founded by Ibrahim Rashid al Diwayhi.

rashtrapati *India.* Title of president of the republic.

Rastafarian *West Indies.* Member of a black religious cult, RASTAFARI-ANISM.

Rastafarianism *Jamaica.* African religious cult that rejects European elements in Christianity and reveres former emperor of Ethiopia, Haile Selassie.

rasul *Arab countries.* Prophet.

Ratahan *Indonesia.* Austronesian language.

Rataning *Chad.* Nilo-Saharan language.

ratha *India.* Chariot.

rathabanklang *Thailand.* Central government including the executive, legislature and judiciary.

rathamontri *Thailand.* Cabinet minister.

ratiwisahakit *Thailand.* State-owned enterprises.

ravane *Mauritius.* Musical instrument, a drum made of goatskin, used in SEGA music.

Rawang *Burma.* Sino-Tibetan language.

rawda *Iran.* Religious session usually held in a garden in which the rawda khwan sings and speaks.

ray *Cambodia.* Slash-and-burn or swidden cultivation practiced by KHMER LOEU.

raya *Turkey.* Literally, herd. Common people.

ray amen'dreny *Madagascar.* Literally, father and mother. President of the republic.

rayah *Algeria.* Tribes belonging to the MAKHZAN.

rayet *Iran.* Serf clan among the KURDS.

rayo *Philippines.* Two-wheeled cart hauling produce and people in rural Visaya.

raywoon *Burma.* Officer in charge of a port or river.

razana *Madagascar.* Relating to ancestors.

razzia *Algeria.* Plundering expedition or foray.

rebab *Islamic countries.* See RABABAH.

rebana *Indonesia.* Arabic drum.

rebozo *Spanish America.* Graceful scarf or stole made of silk or cotton, which covers the head and shoulders.

recado *Uruguay.* Traditional GAUCHO saddle, consisting of *sudaderas,* sweat cloth, *mandiles,* wool layer, *carona,* leather topping, *cojinillo,* sheepskin, and *sob repuesto,* final leather covering.

reclusao *Brazil.* Prisoners.

reclusion *Panama.* Imprisonment.

redes *Guatemala.* Large bag or net made of thin rope, usually open mesh.

Red Hat Order *Nepal and Bhutan.* Tantric sect of Buddhism of Tibetan origin.

Redjang *Indonesia.* Austronesian language.

Redjan-Lamping *Indonesia.* Ethnic group of Sumatra.

Red Thai *Vietnam.* Ethnic group in Thanh-Hoa.

reduccion *Spanish America.* Under Spanish rule, forcible relocation of dispersed highland Indians to compact and planned settlements.

reducciones *Paraguay.* Jesuit mission stations in colonial times.

reducoes *Brazil.* Former agricultural colonies and settlements of converted Indians.

refajos *Guatemala.* Skirts worn by Indian women.

refalosa *Chile.* Scarf dance.

reg *Mauritania.* Flat, clayey or stony place.

regentes *Brazil.* Provisional teachers who have not completed their certification program.

reggae *Jamaica.* Popular music and dance with African elements.

regidor *Bolivia.* Councilman, member of a town CABILDO.

regidor *Spanish America.* Indian official in highland areas assisting religious authorities.

regidoria *Angola.* Village as the basic unit of local government.

Reguibat or **Erguibat** (singular: Reguibi) *Western Sahara.* Largest tribe.

regulo *Guinea-Bissau.* Paramount African chief.

regulos *Mozambique.* Chiefs.

reinois *Brazil.* Brazilian white born in Portugal. Compare PENINSULARES.

reis al foriq *Sudan.* Head of the camp.

reise *Turkey.* Mayor.

religioso *Colombia.* Roman Catholic private school.

relong *Malaysia.* Unit of area equal to 576 sq ft.

remocao *Brazil.* Transfer of judicial officers for political reasons.

Rendille *Kenya.* 1. Eastern Cushitic speakers related to the SOMALI. 2. Afro-Asiatic language.

Rengao *Vietnam.* Central highland ethnic group of MON-KHMER stock speaking a BAHNARIC language.

Rengao *Vietnam.* Austro-Asiatic language.

Renois *Brazil.* Portuguese immigrants who returned to Portugal after acquiring wealth.

repartimiento *Spanish America.* In Spanish times, a distribution or assignment of Indian laborers and forced sale of goods to Indians.

Repelita *Indonesia.* Acronym for Rantjana Pembangunen Lima Tahun, Five Year Development Plan.

republica *Brazil.* Boarding house for secondary and university students.

rer *Ethiopia.* Lineage group.

rer *Somalia.* Nomadic hamlet.

rer *Somalia.* Prefix meaning descendant of.

Rer Issa *Somalia.* Non-Somali group along the Shabelle River.

rescatador *Bolivia.* Middle man in farm marketing.

rescates *Brazil.* Officially sanctioned slave-hunting expeditions into the interior.

resguardo *Colombia.* Reservation for Indians.

Reshe *West Africa.* Niger-Congo language.

residencia *Spanish America.* In colonial times, investigation of official acts at the end of the term in office of a high official.

residency *Malaysia.* District in Sabah.

restingas *Brazil.* Hummocks of land on the Amazonian flood plain.

resto del pais *Panama.* Literally, the rest of the country, i.e., all parts of the country excluding Panama City.

reth *Sudan.* King of the SHILLUKS.

retirantes *Brazil.* Refugees from northeast drought regions.

revendeuses *Togo.* Retail merchants.

reyais *Bangladesh.* Lineage with an outer fringe of other members.

Rhade *Vietnam* and *Cambodia.* Subgroup of the KHMER LOEU.

ri *North Korea.* Village.

riachiakenak *Cambodia.* Head of the Buddhist clergy.

rial *Iran.* Monetary unit.

Riang *India.* Sino-Tibetan language.

Riang Lang *Burma.* Austro-Asiatic language.

ribat *Morocco.* Military fortress; also, place of spiritual retreat.

ricos *Nicaragua.* Rich.

rickshaw *India.* Small, two-wheeled carriage with a folding top, pulled by one man.

ridda *Islamic countries.* Apostasy.

Rifaiya *Somalia.* One of the SUFI orders.

Riff *Maghreb.* Afro-Asiatic language.

Riffian *Maghreb.* See BERBER.

ri jang *South Korea.* Village head.

rimBe (singular: dimo) *Senegal.* Upper stratum of free people among the TOUCOLEURS.

ringgit *Malaysia.* Monetary unit.

Riograndense *Brazil.* Inhabitant of Rio Grande do Sul.

Rioplatenses *Uruguay.* Of or relating to the Rio de la Plata.

riqq *Jordan.* Circular tambourine. See DAFF.

risaldar *India.* Commander of a cavalry regiment.

rishi *India.* In VEDIC times sage, patriarch or magus possessing extraordinary spiritual powers and wisdom. There are six orders of rishis: *devarishi* or one ranked with the gods; *brahmarishi,* or founder of a BRAHMIN gotra or gens; *saptarishi,* one identified with the Seven Stars; *srutarishi,* one able to hear and communicate divine wisdom; *rajarishi,* one who is a philosopher-king; and *maharishi,* or great RISHI.

rist *Ethiopia.*   Principle of land tenure among the AMHARA by virtue of descent from the original holder, so long as the claim was recognized by the cognatic descent group.

riyal *Saudi Arabia.*   Monetary unit.

Riyam, Bani (singular: Riyami) *Oman.*   Tribe.

roaya *Iran.*   Traditional peasant farmer.

rob *Egypt.*   Unit of weight equal to 1.8 gallons.

robab *Afghanistan.*   Variant of *rebab.* Stringed instrument with six catgut strings.

Robo *West Africa.*   Niger-Kordofanian language.

roca *Brazil.*   Cultivated clearing in a forest.

roca *Sao Tome and Principe.*   Cocoa or coffee plantation.

rocambor *Bolivia.*   Form of whist with an ancient Spanish deck of 48 cards.

roceiros *Brazil.*   Small farmers.

roceiros *Sao Tome and Principe.*   Plantation owners or managers.

Rocorona *Bolivia.*   Amazon Indian group of CHAPACURAN linguistic stock in Pardo department.

rodillera *Guatemala.*   Woolen knee-length skirts worn by Indian men.

rodiya *Sri Lanka.*   The lowest SINHALESE caste.

rogaciones *Spanish America.*   Public prayers for specific acts on the part of god. Also *rogativas.*

roghhan zard *Afghanistan.*   Clarified butter. Also, *ghwari.*

Roglai *Vietnam.*   Highland ethnic group speaking an Austronesian language.

roh *Malaysia.*   Intellect.

Rohanweyn *Somalia.*   One of the two SAAB clan-families, also called the Mirifle Confederacy.

roja *Bangladesh.*   Fasting.

Rolong *Botswana.*   Earliest TSWANA immigrants.

Romany *Iran.*   Indo-European language.

romeria *Guatemala.*   Pilgrimage.

romuzava *Madagascar.*   National dish, consisting of boiled rice with or without greens and with a little meat or fish.

romwong *Thailand.*   Folk dance.

rondador *Ecuador.*   Panpipe made from bamboo reed.

rondalla *Philippines.*   String-music ensemble made up of mandolins and guitars.

Ronga *Mozambique.*   1. Ethnic group of the TSONGA cluster. 2. Niger-Kordofanian language.

Rongkong *Indonesia.*   Austronesian language.

rongrien rat *Thailand.*   Private schools.

rongsie khao *Thailand.*   Rice mill.

roniat *Cambodia.*   Wooden xylophone.

roobdoon *Somalia.*   Rainmaking ceremony among the SAAB.

roora *Zimbabwe.*   Bride wealth.

ropani *Nepal.*   Unit of area equal to ⅛th of an acre.

rosario *Spanish America.*   Religious procession.

rosca *Bolivia.*   Literally, the screw. National elite class whose power base was destroyed in the 1952 revolution.

rosca, la *Costa Rica.*   Literally, a twisted pastry. Informal decision-making elite groups.

rosquillas *Nicaragua.*   Dish prepared from corn and cheese.

rossio *Brazil.*   Urbanized piece of communal land on the outskirts of a city.

rotl *Egypt.*   Unit of weight equal to 0.45 kg.

roto *Chile.*   Literally, torn or broken. The urban poor.

Rotse *Botswana.*   Ethnic subgroup.

Rotti *Indonesia.*   Austronesian language.

Rounga *Chad.*   Southern ethnic group.

roza *Guatemala.*   Process of clearing a field for cultivation.

Rozui *Zimbabwe.*   A SHONA cluster.

r'tal *Tunisia.*   Unit of weight equal to 500 to 1,300 grams.

ruana *Colombia.*   Cloak similar to a PONCHO.

ruband *Afghanistan.*   Little veil for covering the nose and mouth, while in the presence of a sovereign or reading the Scriptures.

rubicha *Paraguay.*   Title of a GUARANI tribal chief.

rudzi *Mozambique.*   Patrilineage among the SHONA.

Rufiji *Tanzania.*   Ethnic group.

rugo *Burundi.*   Traditional KRAAL or homestead.

ruhaniyyat *Shiite countries.*   Revered Shiite clergy or mullahs who claim responsibility for leading Shiites pending the anticipated return of the 12th imam.

ruhhal *Arab countries.*   Nomadic BEDOUINS.

Ruihi *Tanzania.*   Niger-Kordofanian language.

Rukuba *West Africa.*   Niger-Kordofanian language.

rukinzo *Burundi.*   Royal drum.

Rukunegara *Malaysia.*   Literally, principles of the nation. National Ideology.

rukun tetangge *Indonesia.*   Group of 40 to 50 households.

Rukurato *Uganda.*   State council of Bunyoro.

Rumai *Burma.*   Austro-Asiatic language.

rumi *Malaysia.*   Roman script in which BAHASA MALAYSIA is sometimes written.

rumal *India.*   Handkerchief or head covering.

Rundi *Central Africa.*   Niger-Kordofanian language.

Rundi *Zaire and East Africa.*   Ethnic group.

Runga *Central Africa.*   Nilo-Saharan language.

Rungi *Tanzania.*   Niger-Kordofanian language.

Rungwa *Tanzania.*   Ethnic group.
Rungu *Tanzania.*   Ethnic group.
Rungus *Sabah.*   Austronesian language.
runn *India.*   Sand flat and salt wasteland, often covered by high tides.
ruoth *Kenya.*   Clan chief among the LUO.
rupee *India.*   Monetary unit.
rupiah *Indonesia.*   Monetary unit.
rurales *Mexico.*   Rural policeman during the PORFIRIATO.
ruralistas *Uruguay.*   Rural voters.
ruropolis *Brazil.*   Group of AGROPOLISes.
Rusha *Tanzania.*   Niger-Kordofanian language.
Ruund *Southern Africa.*   Niger-Kordofanian language.
Ruwahah, Bani (singular: Ruwahi) *Oman.*   Tribe.
Ruwala *Saudi Arabia.*   Northern tribe.
ruza *Afghanistan.*   Fasting during the RAMADAN.
Rwala *Jordan.*   Camel-breeding BEDOUIN group.
Rwanda *Rwanda and Uganda.*   Niger-Kordofanian language.
ryal al bilad *Libya.*   The MARABOUTIM, or men of the soil.
ryot *India.*   Peasant.
ryotwari *India.*   Land tenure in which the farmer pays his taxes directly to the government.

Saab *Somalia.*   Sedentary agricultural tribe living between the Juba and the Shabelle rivers and comprising the DIGIL and RAHANWEYN clan-families.
Saamia *East Africa.*   Niger-Kordofanian language.
Sab *Horn of Africa.*   Literally, low. Clans of low status.
Sabaeans *Iraq.*   Urban group. Also, *Mandaeans.*
Sabaot *Kenya.*   1. Collective name for four groups of KALENJIN people: Kony, Spaei, Pok and Bungomek. 2. Nilo-Saharan language.
sabha *India and Nepal.*   Assembly.
sabkhah (plural: sibakh) *Oman.*   Salt marsh.
sabon gari *Nigeria.*   New towns.
sabuku *Zimbabwe.*   SHONA tax register.
Sacapulteco *Guatemala.*   MAYAN language.

sacatinta *Guatemala.*   Plant, the fresh leaves of which are used to make a bluing dye.

Sack *Thailand.*   Thai-speaking ethnic group.

Sacosi *Bolivia.*   Amazon Indian group in Beni department.

Sa'd, Yal (singular: Yal Sa'di) *Oman.*   Tribe along the Batinah coast.

sadad *Morocco.*   Peace courts.

Sadaejuii *North Korea.*   Literally, flunkyism. Servility in politics.

Sadama *Ethiopia.*   East Cushitic people.

Sadani *India.*   Indo-European language.

sadaqat *Arab countries.*   Freewill gifts.

sadar jangi kotwali *Nepal.*   Military courts.

sadhu *India.*   Mendicant.

sadone *Burma.*   Traditional female hairstyle, a coil of hair built up into a cylinder around a framework of combs and pins.

Sadozai *Iran.*   BALUCHI tribe.

sadr *India.*   Chief judge.

sadza *Zimbabwe.*   Thick millet porridge.

safari *India and Africa.*   Big game hunting.

Safen *Senegal.*   Niger-Kordofanian language.

Safi *Afghanistan.*   GHILAZAI tribe.

Safwa *Tanzania.*   1. Ethnic group. 2. Niger-Kordofanian language.

Sagala *Tanzania.*   Niger-Kordofanian language.

Sagara *Tanzania.*   Ethnic group.

sagmin *North Korea.*   Commoners.

sahah *Jordan.*   Open space or commons in a village.

sahakom *Thailand.*   Cooperative society.

Saharia *India.*   Indo-European language.

sahib *India and Pakistan.*   Sir or master. Term of address to a superior.

Sahel *West Africa.*   Group of countries immediately below the Sahara Desert including Chad, Gambia, Mali, Mauritania, Senegal, Burkina Faso and Niger.

Sahelian *West Africa.*   Of or belonging to the SAHEL group.

sahijahari *India.*   Liberal SIKH, especially in religious practice.

Saho *Ethiopia.*   Muslim group speaking an Eastern Cushitic language.

Sahrawi *Western Sahara.*   Native of the Sahara, especially Western Sahara.

Sahwi *Ghana.*   ANYI-BAWLE ethnic group.

saidas *Brazil.*   Short wraps of toweling.

saifi *Iraq.*   Summer crop.

Sai'id Al bu (singular: Al bu Sa'idi) *Oman.*   Tribe.

saing waing ah pwe *Burma.*   Percussion orchestra.

saivism *India.*   Hindu sect dedicated to the worship of Siva, the creator.

Saka *Zaire.*   Ethnic group.

Saka era *India.*   Hindu era established by King Kanishka in 78 AD.

sakala   sanghaparinayaka   somdech   phra   sangharaja *Thailand.*   Buddhist patriarch and head of the SANGHA.

Sakalava *Madagascar.*   Western ethnic group.

Sakata *Zaire.*   1. Ethnic group. 2. Niger-Kordofanian language.

sakdi na *Thailand.*   System of social ranking based on royal allocation of rice lands.

sakieh *Egypt.*   Waterwheel with buckets attached to its rims, used in irrigation.

SakkesBe (singular: sakke) *Senegal.*   TOUCOLEUR caste.

sakti *India.*   Personified creative energy in each of the female Hindu gods.

saktism *India.*   Hindu sect devoted to the worship of Sakti, the female aspect of the BRAHMA.

Sakuye *Kenya.*   Galla-speaking tribe related to the GABBRA.

sala *Spanish America.*   Section or chamber of the supreme court.

Sala *Zambia.*   1. BANTU tribe in south central region. 2. Niger-Kordofanian language.

salaa *Cambodia.*   Open hall in a WAT.

sala dambaung *Cambodia.*   One-man provincial tribunal.

saladeros *Uruguay.*   Place where jerked beef is salted and prepared for the market.

Salafism *North Africa.*   Revival of Islamic orthodoxy through reforms advocated by Jamaluddin al-Afghani, Mohammad Abduh and Rashid Rida.

salah al salih *Arab countries.*   Ways of pious ancestors in WAHHABISM.

salah lahouk *Cambodia.*   Justice of the peace.

salaka *Madagascar.*   Dress consisting of a band of soft cloth passed through the legs and then wound three times around the waist with the ends hanging down the front and back.

salam aleikum *Arab countries.*   Literally, peace be unto you. Standard greeting.

Salampusu *Zaire.*   1. Ethnic group. 2. Niger-Kordofanian language.

salang *Burma.*   Title of elders or leaders among the KACHIN.

salanga *Chad.*   Dried fish.

sala okret *Cambodia.*   Three-man criminal court.

sala outor *Cambodia.*   Court of appeal.

Salasca *Ecuador.*   Indian group in Tungurahua Province.

salat *Islamic countries.*   Ritual prayer made five times daily.

salaw *Thailand.*   Spike fiddle.

Salihiya *Somalia.*   SUFI order founded by Muhammad ibn Salih.

salita *Nicaragua.*   Living room in a ranch-style house.

saltena *Bolivia.*   Pastry of meat, vegetables and spices, popular as a snack.

Saluan *Indonesia.*   Austronesian language.

Sama *Sabah and Philippines.*   Austronesian language. Also, *Balanging.*

sama *Morocco.*   Religious music.

Samaal *Somalia.*   Pastoral nomads of four clan-families: *Darod, Dir, Isaq* and *Hawiya.*

samadh *India.*   Place of immolation or burial, especially the tomb of a Hindu yogi supposed to be lying in a state of trance.

samadhi *India.*   Among the Hindus, state of mystical contemplation in which the distinction between the self and the outer world disappears.

samaj *South Asia.*   Group or fellowship, usually of a religious nature.

Samal *Philippines.*   MORO group in Sulu and Zambango.

Samassa *Mauritania.*   MARABOUTS from Kingul.

samba *Brazil.*   African dance adapted as a ballroom dance in syncopated duple time.

Sambaa or **Shambala** *Tanzania.*   Ethnic group.

sambal *Malaya and Indonesia.*   Condiment made of peppers, fruits and fish, usually eaten with curry.

Sambal *Philippines.*   1. Minor ethnic group in Luzon. 2. Austronesian language.

sambandam *India.*   Marriage, among the TAMILS.

sambidhan *Nepal.*   Constitution.

Sambo *Central America.*   Offspring of a Negro and an Indian or mulatto.

Sambo-Miskite *Honduras.*   Mixed ethnic group of Miskito coast, blending white, Negro and Sumu Indian strains.

Sambu *Angola.*   OVIMBUNDU subgroup.

sambuk *Oman.*   Large DHOW or boat.

Samburu *Kenya.*   1. Northern MAA-speaking group in Samburu district. 2. Nilo-Saharan language.

sameney *Cambodia.*   Buddhist monk or novice.

Samia *Uganda.*   Eastern BANTU ethnic group.

samiel *North Africa.*   Hot, dry, sand-laden desert wind; SIMOOM.

samiti *India.*   Council, as in PANCHAYAT samiti.

Samkhya *India.*   One of the six orthodox systems of Hindu philosophy founded by Sage Kapila in sixth century B.C. based on dualism of spirit and matter. Also, *Sankhya.*

Sammaniyyah *Sudan.*   Islamic brotherhood founded by Muhammad al Samman.

Samo *Burkina Faso.*   Ethnic group of MANDE cluster.

Samo *West Africa.*   Niger-Kordofanian language.

Samoan *Samoa.*   Austronesian language.

Samogho *Burkina Faso.*   Ethnic group of the MANDE cluster.

samohong noyon *Philippines.*   Agricultural cooperative at the barrio level.

samon *Ethiopia.* Right to tribute in perpetuity granted formerly to the Orthodox Church.

sampho *Cambodia.* Horizontal drum tapped at both ends with the fingers.

sampot *Cambodia.* KHMER national costume consisting of cotton or silk up to 10 feet long and a yard wide wrapped around the waist, fastened in front. The top is twisted, passed between the legs and tucked into the waistband at the back to give the appearance of loose trousers.

samsara *India.* In Hinduism, the endless cycle of births, deaths and rebirths to which man is subject.

samskara *India.* Life-cycle ceremonies.

Samu *Nicaragua.* Indians of the Atlantic region.

samuragwe *Burundi.* Chief of a family.

samusha *Southern Africa.* Head of a KRAAL among the SHONA-Karange.

san *Dominican Republic.* Revolving credit association providing low-interest credit.

San *Zimbabwe.* Bushmen.

sanad *India.* Certificate, patent or deed of grant by the government conferring certain privileges and rights.

sanad *Islamic countries.* Chain of authorities authenticating a *hadith* or saying of Muhammad, the process being *isnad,* or going back.

Sanaga *West Africa.* Niger-Kordofanian language.

sanatan *India.* Modified Arya Samaj marriage ceremony.

Sanchi *Vietnam.* Highland ethnic group in the north speaking a Sino-Tibetan language.

sancocho *Panama.* Stew or soup made with chicken breast, yucca, yam and plantains.

sandali *Afghanistan.* Wooden table placed over a charcoal brazier with a blanket spread over it extending to the floor.

sandara *Malaysia.* All persons related by blood or marriage within a kinship group.

Sandawe *Tanzania.* 1. Pre-BANTU ethnic group. 2. KHOISAN language.

sande *West Africa.* Secret society for women with political, juridical, religious and educational functions. Its "bush schools" initiate women into the lore and traditions of the community. Compare PORO.

sandinganbayan *Philippines.* Court with special jurisdiction over civil and criminal cases involving graft and corruption.

Sandinista *Nicaragua.* Followers of Agusto Cesar Sandinista, 1895–1933, celebrated Nicaraguan revolutionary killed by U.S. supporters.

sandunga *Mexico.* Kind of waltz from Tehuantepec.

Sanga *West Africa.* Niger-Kordofanian language.

Sangam *India.* School of TAMIL literature of the third and fourth centuries.

sangguniang bayan *Philippines.*   Municipal or provincial council.

Sangha *Buddhist countries.*   Buddhists religious establishment comprising all orders of monks.

Sangha *Zaire and Congo.*   Ethnic group.

Sangihe *Philippines.*   Austronesian language.

Sangil *Philippines.*   Muslim ethnic group in Mindanao.

Sangir *Philippines.*   MORO group in Mindanao.

Sangire *Indonesia.*   Austronesian language.

sangley *Philippines.*   Foreigners resident in the country.

sangmin *South Korea.*   Commoners.

Sango *Central African Republic.*   Official language and lingua franca; also, the UBANGUIAN people who speak it.

Sangu *Tanzania.*   1. Ethnic group. 2. Niger-Kordofanian language.

Sanhaja *Western Sahara.*   One of the main ancestors from whom the SAHRAWIS, MOORS, TUAREG, KABYLES, RIFFIANS and BERBERS are descended; also the Berber tribal confederation including Lemtuna, Hahwara and Massufa.

sanjak *Turkey.*   Former administrative district, subdivision of a VILAYET.

sankh or **chaukh** *India.*   Shell used in Hindu temples.

sanjuanito, el *El Salvador.*   National dance.

sanoj *India.*   Exogamous subdivision of a JATI or caste.

sansa or **zanza** *North Africa.*   Musical instrument consisting of a wooden box with tongues of bamboo or iron at the top.

San Simoniano *Bolivia.*   Amazon Indian group of CHAPACURAN linguistic stock in Beni department.

Sanskrit *India.*   Sacred and literary Indo-European language in which Hindu Scriptures are written.

santaane *Senegal.*   Work group formed to assist a member among the WOLOF.

Santa Fe *Paraguay.*   Folk dance.

Santali *India.*   Austro-Asiatic language.

Santals *India.*   KOLARIAN. Ethnic group.

santana dharma *India.*   In Hinduism, complex of obligations and duties.

Santeria *Caribbean countries.*   African religion transplaced to the Caribbean.

santero *Cuba.*   Leader of an Afro-Cuban cult.

santigis *Sierra Leone.*   Among the TEMNE, leading men who serve in various capacities as constables and judges.

santiguar *Central America.*   Making the sign of the cross.

santiyo-Tiyo *Guinea.*   Village chief among the MANINKA.

santon *North Africa.*   Muslim holy man, or MARABOUT.

santri *Indonesia.*   Orthodox Muslims, as distinguished from the ABANGAN.

Santrokofi *Ghana.*   CENTRAL TOGO ethnic cluster.

santur *Afghanistan.*   Zither-like musical instrument with a harmonium keyboard.

sanuk *Thailand.*   Value system emphasizing fun and pleasure.

sanyasi *India.*   Ascetic or holy man who lives from alms.

Sanye *Kenya.*   Hunters and gatherers in the southern Taru district.

sanzi *North Africa.*   Variant of SANSA.

Sanziu *Vietnam.*   Highland ethnic group in the north.

Sao *Central Africa.*   Ethnic group from which the KOTOKO and KANURI are descended.

sao *Burma.*   SHAN title of respect.

Saoch *Cambodia.*   Subgroup of the KHMER LOEU.

saopha or **sawbwa** *Burma.*   Hereditary prince among the SHANS.

Saokkyi *Burma.*   Literally, the big book. Manual of village administration in Upper Burma.

sapa changwad *Thailand.*   Provincial council.

sapa tanbon *Thailand.*   Communal council.

sapat *India.*   Sandal.

sapha *Thailand.*   Council.

saphaphutan *Thailand.*   Lower house of parliament.

Sapiboca *Bolivia.*   Amazon Indian group of TACANAN linguistic stock in Beni department.

sapo *Bolivia.*   Literally, frog. Popular game in which disks or coins are tossed at a target surmounted by the image of an openmouthed frog.

Sapo *Liberia.*   Niger-Kordofanian language.

saquiyah *North Africa.*   Animal-driven waterwheel, used in irrigation.

Sara *Chad.*   Mostly pagan southern ethnic group.

Saraguros *Ecuador.*   Ethnic group of Loja.

Sarahuli *Gambia.*   Ethnic group.

Sarak *Afghanistan.*   Subgroup of the Turkmans.

Sarakole *West Africa.*   MANDE-speaking Muslim people whose ancestors ruled a vast and wealthy empire in Ghana from the 9th to the 11th century. Also, *Gadjaga, Marka, Serewoulle, Soninke.*

Saramaccan *Suriname.*   English-based creole.

saran *Afghanistan.*   Stringed musical instrument with a flat semispherical sound box and a small bow. Also, *saranda.*

sarangi *India.*   Nonfretted musical instrument.

sarani *Afghanistan.*   NURISTANI chordophone.

sarapes *Mexico.*   Blanket-like outer garment.

saravan *Iran.*   BALUCHI ethnic group.

Sarave *Bolivia.*   Amazon Indian group of Arawakan linguistic stock in Santa Cruz and Beni departments.

sardar *South Asia.*   1. In Bangladesh, leader of a lineage group; or REYAIS. 2. Military chief. 3. Village headman or chief. 4. Valet or servant. 5. Honorific applied to SIKHS.

sardauna *Nigeria.* Spiritual head of the HAUSA.

sare *Cameroon.* Group of houses.

sari *Ghana.* Chief of a ZONGO or strangers' quarters in a town.

sari *India.* National women's dress consisting of a long piece of cotton or silk wrapped around the body with one end falling nearly to the feet and the other end thrown over the head or shoulder.

sarifah *Iraq.* Reed and mud huts along the Euphrates.

sarigan *Bangladesh.* Boatman's song.

sarinda *India.* Stringed musical instrument played with a bow.

sari sari *Philippines* General store run by the Chinese.

sarkar *India.* Government.

sarkhi *Nepal.* Leather-working class of untouchables.

sarn dika *Thailand.* Supreme court; *sarn uthorn* court of appeal.

sarod *India.* Stringed musical instrument of Persian origin with 25 strings.

sarong *Indonesia.* Brightly colored printed cloth worn as a skirt by men and women.

sarouel *Western Sahara.* Floppy cotton trousers worn beneath the DRAA.

sarpech *India.* Ornament of gold, silver or jewels worn in front of a royal turban.

sarraf *Iraq.* Traditional moneylenders. Variant of SHROFF.

Sarwa *Botswana.* Bushmen.

Sarwa *Zimbabwe.* Bantu name for SAN people.

Sasak *Indonesia.* 1. Ethnic group of Lumbok. 2. Austronesian language.

Sasani *Iran.* Indo-Iranian ethnic group in Gilan.

sastra *India.* Any Hindu sacred book containing legal principles.

satang *Thailand.* Coin, 1/100th of a BAHT.

Satar *Nepal.* Minor ethnic group.

sati *India.* Former Hindu custom of the immolation of the widow on the husband's funeral pyre.

satigi *Senegal.* Title of the kings of Futa Toro.

satiyo-tiyo *Gambia.* Village chief.

satyagraha *India.* Literally, desire of truth. Program of nonviolent civil disobedience, including public fasting and defiance of regulations, in order to compel the authorities to desist from a course of action.

satyagrahi *India.* Person engaged in SATYAGRAHA.

saum *Turkey.* Ritual fasting as an Islamic obligation. Also, ORUE.

saung kauk *Burma.* Harp with 14 strings attached to a pole that arches out of a resonator box.

savoka *Madagascar.* Secondary vegetation in a fallow field.

saw *Thailand.* Traditional form of singing in the north.

sawah *Indonesia.* Irrigated rice field or method of cultivating rice on irrigated land.

sawba *Burma.* Title of hereditary SHAN chief.

saweisia *Sierra Leone.* Concoction made of herbs, soil and water, usually for ritual cleansing of crimes or social offenses.

sawm *Islamic countries.* Fasting during the months of RAMADAN, as one of the five pillars of Islam.

sawti *Burma.* Minor sect of SHAN monks.

say *Saudi Arabia.* Running between the hills of Safa and Marwa during the HAJ pilgrimage commemorating the travails of Hagar, the mother of Ishmael, and concubine of Abraham.

saya *Burma.* Wise man, as a titular prefix.

Saya *West Africa.* Afro-Asiatic language.

sayadaw *Burma.* Learned and respected monk presiding over a monastery.

sayana *Bolivia.* Plot of land in which a COLONATO enjoys usufruct privileges in return for unpaid labor.

sayer *India.* Variable and arbitrary imposts, including tolls and duties.

sayyid *Islamic countries* Title of a descendant of Prophet Muhammad.

saz *Turkey.* Stringed instrument.

saza *Uganda.* County.

scheduled caste *India.* Inferior caste outside the caste system afforded special protection under a schedule of the Constitution.

scheduled tribe *India.* Aboriginal tribe afforded special protection under a schedule of the Constitution.

scuffling *Jamaica.* Marginal economic activities of the urban poor.

Sea Gypsies *Philippines.* *See* BADJAO.

seba *Zaire.* Ethnic group of southern savanna.

seBBe (singular: ceDDo) *Senegal.* Warrior caste among the TOUCOLEURS.

Sebei *Uganda.* Eastern Nilotic ethnic group.

sebkha *Western Sahara.* Salt pan.

seccion *Bolivia.* Unit of local government corresponding to a municipality.

seconde *Haiti* Middle-sized drum in the trio of VOODOO drums.

Secoya *Ecuador.* Indian tribe in the Oriente Province.

Sedang *Vietnam.* 1. Highland ethnic group in Kontum. 2. Austro-Asiatic language.

seer *South Asia.* Unit of weight equal to 15.6 lb.

sef *Chad.* The hot dry season from mid-March to mid-May.

sefuwa *Chad.* Lineage of the MAGUMI clan that founded Kanem Kingdom in the ninth century.

sefwi *Ghana.* ANYI-BAWLE AKAN group between Wiawso and Bibiani and between Tano and Ankobra Rivers.

sega *Mauritius.* Type of music characterized by a rhythmic beat and regular hip movements introduced by African slaves.

sega *Reunion.* National dance, usually boisterous.

Segeju *Tanzania.* Ethnic group.

segundos *Nicaragua.* Middle class. Also, *los medios acomodades.*

seguro del salud *Uruguay.* Health insurance.

sehadet *Turkey.* Variant of SHAHADA.

sehir *Turkey.* City.

Seibani *Yemens.* Ethnic group.

Seke *Gabon.* Ethnic group comprising BENGA and BAKOUELE.

Sekpele *Ghana.* Niger-Kordofanian language.

sekretaris negara *Indonesia.* State secretary.

sekrete *Haiti.* Person who handles the financial matters of another.

Selayar *Indonesia.* Austronesian language.

Sele *Angola.* OVIMBUNDU subgroup.

Seleka *Botswana.* Ethnic subgroup.

seluka *Sudan.* Alluvial land that forms part of the Nile Channel but is exposed during the low-water season.

selva *Peru.* Geographic region including the eastern slopes of the Andes and Amazon lowlands.

Semai *Malaysia.* Austro-Asiatic language.

Semang *Malaysia.* MON-Khmer-speaking Negrito tribe.

Semangat *Malaysia.* Life-activating force in living things.

semanya *Ethiopia.* Marriage under a civil contract.

sembrando el petroleo *Venezuela.* Literally, sowing the petroleum. Official policy of recycling oil revenues into economic development projects.

semiinternado *Cuba.* Semiboarding schools.

semn *Sudan.* Clarified butter.

sen *Cambodia.* Coin, 1/100ths of a NEW RIEL.

sen *Indonesia.* Coin, 1/100ths of a RUPIAH.

sena *Southern Africa.* 1. Ethnic group of the lower Zambezi cluster. Also, *Sena Chueza, Sena Podzo.* 2. Niger-Kordofanian language.

sene *West Samoa.* Coin, 1/100ths of a TALA.

Senegalization *Senegal.* Program of removing vestiges of colonial rule and introducing authentic indigenous institutions to replace them.

Senga *Southern Africa.* Ethnic group of the MARAVI cluster.

Sengele *Zaire.* Ethnic group.

sengi *Zaire.* Coin, 1/100ths of a MAKUTA and 1/10,000th of a ZAIRE.

senitis *Tonga.* Coin, 1/100ths of PAANGA.

Senoi *Malaysia.* Negrito tribe.

Senoufo *West Africa.* Niger-Kordofanian language.

Sentani *Indonesia.*   Papuan language.

Senufo *West Africa.*   Large ethnic group including *Minanka, Sinerbe, Tagba, Folo, Mbuin, Niara, Gimini* and *Kapalara.*

Senussiyyah *Sudan.*   SUFI order that spread to Libya.

Senya *Ghana.*   GUAN group on the coast.

senzala *Brazil.*   Slave quarters in a plantation.

sepak raga *Malaysia.*   Kind of soccer played with a light ball made of plaited rattan.

sepoy *Indian.*   Private in the Indian army.

se pyan *Burma.*   Main meat dish.

ser *India.*   Unit of weight varying with the produce and the region.

Serahuli *Gambia.*   Ethnic group.

serai *Islamic countries.*   Short form of caravanserai, a resthouse.

Serawi *Indonesia.*   Unclassified language.

sere *Afghanistan.*   Unit of weight equal to 16 lb.

Sere *Sudan.*   Sudanic people related to the AZANDA.

SeremBe *Senegal.*   Religious leader among the TOUCOLEURS.

serenata *Mexico.*   Promenade.

Serer *Senegal.*   Sudanic-speaking non-Muslim people divided into Serer None and Serer Sino.

Serere-Sine *Senegal and Gambia.*   Niger-Kordofanian language.

seriat *Turkey.*   Islamic law.

serigne *Senegal.*   Title of any MARABOUT of the MURIDIYYA brotherhood.

serimpi *Indonesia.*   Classical dance.

serin *Senegal.*   WOLOF term for Islamic teachers and leaders.

seringal *Brazil.*   Rubber plantation.

serrania *Bolivia.*   Mountain area lower than the altiplano.

serrano *Ecuador.*   People of the Sierra.

sertanejo *Brazil.*   Person from the SERTAO, or the northwest.

sertanista *Brazil.*   Backlands explorer.

sertao *Brazil.*   Hinterland or interior backlands.

service civique *Ivory Coast.*   Use of military conscripts in civilian projects.

servilleta *Guatemala.*   White cloth used to cover or wrap food.

sesaya *Burma.*   Traditional medical practitioner.

sett or **chetty** *India.*   Merchant, broker or chief of a private corporation.

seyfu *Gambia.*   Title granted to protectorate chiefs.

seyh *Turkey.*   Literally, chief. Honorific for the master of a TARIQAH.

seyhul *Turkey.*   The grand MUFTI as the leader of the Islamic community.

seypis *Pakistan.*   Artisan families.

sgaw *Burma.*   Subgroup of the KARENS.

shabak *Iraq.*   KURDish-speaking SHIITE group.

shabbaz *Afghanistan.*   Bow for the ROBAB.

Shabelle *Somalia.*   Non-Somali group along the Shabelle River.

Shadhiliyyah *Sudan.*   TARIQAH founded by Abu al Hasan Ali al Shah-dili.

shaduf *Sudan.*   Counterweighted pole and bucket used in irrigation.

Shafi *Yemens.*   Yemeni SUNNI who follows the Shafi School of Islamic law.

Shagawu *Nigeria.*   Afro-Asiatic language.

shaghalay *Afghanistan.*   Title of address equivalent to sir.

shah *Iran.*   Title of emperor.

Shahada *Islamic countries.*   Creed of Islam recited as a pillar of the faith.

shahbanou *Iran.*   Formerly, the empress.

shahrestan *Iran.*   District.

Shahsavan *Iran.*   Ethnic group in Azerbaijan.

Shai Adangbe *Ghana.*   Ethnic group related to the ADA and KROBO.

shair *Malaysia.*   Long narrative poem composed of quatrains with a moral or didactic message.

Shaixu *Senegal.*   Wise old religious leader, usually a MARABOUT.

Shake *Gabon.*   BAKOTA linguistic group.

shalwar kameez *India, Pakistan and Bangladesh.*   Female dress consisting of a long shirt and matching trousers.

shamal *Saudi Arabia.*   Strong northeast wind.

Shamba *East Africa.*   Small agricultural plot or smallholding.

Shambaa *Tanzania.*   Ethnic group.

Shambala *Tanzania.*   Niger-Kordofanian language.

shamiana *India.*   Awning or flat tent roof, usually without sides.

Shamis, Al Bu (singular: Shamsi) *Oman.*   Buraymi Oasis tribe.

shamma *Ethiopia.*   Shawl draped around the shoulder and arms and, sometimes, the head.

Shamman *Saudi Arabia.*   Tribe in Jabal Shammar.

Shamsi *Afghanistan.*   Solar calendar.

Shan *Burma.*   Thai-speaking Hinayana Buddhist lowland and valley people. Also, *Tai.*

Shanga *Nigeria.*   Niger-Kordofanian language.

Shangaan *Swaziland.*   Ethnic group.

Shangana *Mozambique.*   Ethnic group of the TSONGA cluster.

Shango *Trinidad and Tobago.*   Cult of African origin.

Shangwe *Zimbabwe.*   Small SHONA community speaking a subdialect of Korekore.

Shankelle *Ethiopia.*   Negroid ethnic group on the western border.

shar or **char** *Western Sahara.*   Secular war as distinguished from JIHAD.

sharaf *Lebanon.*   Family honor.

Sharchagpakha *Bhutan.*   Sino-Tibetan language.

Sharia *Islamic countries.* Islamic law based on the Koran and the Sunna.

sharif *Morocco.* Title of descendants of the Prophet Muhammad through his daughter Fatima.

sharqi *Middle East.* Humid southeastern wind along the Trucial coast.

Sharqiyyin, al (singular: Sharqi) *Oman.* Tribe of Fujayrah.

shastri *India.* Man versed in Hindu law or SASTRA.

Shavasha *Zimbabwe.* Branch of ZEZURU cluster of SHONA speakers.

shave *Zimbabwe.* Spirits of strangers who die without proper burial, in Shona tradition.

shawish *Saudi Arabia.* Sergeant.

Shawiya *Algeria.* Afro-Asiatic language.

Shawiyah (singular: Shawawi) *Oman.* Mountain nomads, generally goatherds.

shaykh or **sheikh** *Arab countries.* Tribal chieftain.

shaykh al mashaykh *Jordan.* Paramount SHAYKH.

Shayqiyyah *Sudan.* Arab tribe of JAALIYYIN group.

shaysh *Western Sahara.* Turban worn by men, a black cloth about two meters long, wrapped around the head leaving only the eyes open. Also, *litham.*

shebuja *Rwanda and Burundi.* Lord or patron in a UBUHAKE relationship.

sheegat *Somalia.* Client in a patron-client relationship.

shehu *Chad.* Variant of SHAYKH. Royal title adopted by the Al-Kanemi dynasty.

Sheikat *Tunisia.* Principality under a shaykh.

sheikh al nashayikh *Saudi Arabia.* King, as the SHAYKH of shaykhs.

Sheko *Ethiopia.* Afro-Asiatic language.

Shenafir *Yemens.* Ethnic group.

Sherarat *Saudi Arabia.* Tribe.

Sherbro *Sierra Leone.* 1. Ethnic group in Bonthe and Moyambe districts. 2. Niger-Kordofanian language.

Sherpa *Nepal.* 1. BHOTE group including the GURKHAS, famous as Himalayan mountain guides. 2. Sino-Tibetan language.

Shi *Zaire.* 1. Ethnic group of the Eastern highlands. 2. Niger-Kordofanian language.

Shia *Islamic countries.* Major heretical sect in Islam, which regards Ali, the son-in-law of Prophet Muhammad, as his true successor and rejects the first three caliphs.

shiat *Arab countries.* Party, group or faction.

Shidle *Somalia.* Non-Somali group, branch of the Mobiler.

shifta *East Africa.* Armed bandit.

Shihuh (singular: Shihuhi or Shihi) *Oman.* Mountain tribe.

Shiite *Islamic countries.* Followers of the Shia sect.

shikari *India.* Sportsman or game hunter.

shikko *Burma.* Act of prostration before a king, an image of the Buddha or a PONGYI.

Shila *Zambia.* Congolese LUNDA tribe in Luapula Valley.

shilela *Ethiopia.* Boasting songs of warriors.

Shilha *Maghreb.* Afro-Asiatic language.

Shilluk *Sudan.* Nilotic ethnic group along the White Nile.

shin *Burma.* Term of address for a Buddhist monk in Upper Burma.

Shin *Ethiopia.* Lineage council.

Shina *Pakistan.* Indo-European language.

shinbyu *Burma.* Ritual by which each male Buddhist becomes a monk for a short time in his early years.

Shinlaung *Burma.* Boy novice initiated in a Buddhist SHINBYU ceremony.

shintiyan *Islamic countries.* Loose trousers worn by women.

Shinwari *Afghanistan.* GHILAZAI tribe on the north slope of Safed Koh.

Shipibo-Conibo *Peru.* Indian language.

shir *Horn of Africa.* Council of elders in a clan or lineage.

shirara *Somalia.* Six-string lute decorated at the top with ostrich plumes.

shirastadar *India.* Head ministerial officer of a court who receives complaints and properly certifies them.

Shirazi *Tanzania.* Mixed Negro-Persian ethnic group in Pemba and Zanzibar.

shiribaha *Iran.* Form of bride wealth or marriage payment.

shirk *Saudi Arabia.* Worship of anything but God, among the WAHHABIS.

shirkat *Afghanistan.* Joint stock company owned by public or private interests.

Shishans *Jordan.* See CHECHENS.

shitwi *Iraq.* Winter crop.

Shluh *Morocco.* Large tribal confederation in the south and southwest.

shma *Saudi Arabia.* Among orthodox Muslims, head covering of a square white silk.

Shona *Southern Africa.* 1. Ethnic cluster divided into numerous independent groups, including *Bargwe, Buja, Chikunda, Duma, Karanga, Korokore, Manyika, Mari, Ndau, Rozwi, Tawara, Teve, Tonga* and *Zezuru.* Also, *Chona, Xona.* 2. Niger-Kordofanian language.

Shoshangane *Mozambique.* Ethnic group of the NGUNI cluster.

shouters *Trinidad and Tobago.* Fundamentalist Christian sect among the blacks.

shroff *India.* Money changer.

shromby *Afghanistan.* Watered yogurt with pieces of mint and cucumber. See DOGH.

Shuar *Ecuador.*   Indian language.
shum *Ethiopia.*   Title of chief.
shura *Afghanistan.*   Parliament.
shura *Arab countries.*   Islamic tradition of consultation among equals.
shurfa *Maghreb.*   Descendants of the prophet.
Shurkriyyah *Sudan.*   Ethnic group of southern Kassala Province, subgroup of Jamala or Guhayna clan.
shurtah *Libya.*   National police.
Shwe *Burma.*   Austro-Asiatic language.
shwe pyidaw *Burma.*   Literally, golden land. Burmese name for Burma.
si *North Korea.*   City.
Sia *Burkina Faso.*   Ethnic group of the MANDE cluster.
Siane *Papua New Guinea.*   Papuan language.
siba *Afghanistan.*   Tradition of resistance to central political authority.
siba *Morocco.*   Dissidence; unrest; insurrection against central government.
sibaca *Swaziland.*   Swazi dance.
sibaya *Swaziland.*   Enclosure for cattle in a Swazi homestead.
sibongo *Swaziland.*   Patrilineal clan.
Sidamo *Ethiopia.*   Afro-Asiatic language.
sidang *Malaysia.*   Assistant to a PENGHULU.
Sidau *Burundi.*   Courtly dance.
sidi *Algeria.*   Honorary title used by a MARABOUT.
sidwaba *Swaziland.*   Women's shirt.
sidziya *Swaziland.*   Skin apron worn over the shirt by men.
sienu (singular: sie) *Sierra Leone.*   Patpilineal clans.
sierra *Spanish America.*   Highlands.
sifsari *Tunisia.*   Woman's white cloak or wraparound shawl.
signare *Senegal.*   Wealthy women traders.
Sigua *Tanzania.*   Ethnic group.
Siguas *Nicaragua.*   Language family. See UTAZTECAN.
Sihanaka *Madagascar.*   Ethnic group of the central highlands.
sijang *South Korea.*   Mayor.
sijo *North Korea.*   Poem composed of three couplets.
sika diwa *Ghana.*   GOLDEN STOOL.
Sikh *India.*   Members of a monotheistic politico-religious community founded around 1500.
sikhara *Burma.*   Spire of a Buddhist pagoda.
Sikhism *India.*   Monotheistic religion founded by Guru Nanak, consisting of both Hindu and Muslim elements. Its principal Scripture, the *Adi Granth,* is kept at the Golden Temple at Amritsar under the control of the *Gurmata,* the council of the guru.
Sikhule *Indonesia.*   Austronesian language.
sikidi *Madagascar.*   Mode of divination of Arab origin.

Sikka *Indonesia.*   Austronesian language.

Sikkimese *Sikkim.*   Sino-Tibetan language.

siksa *Honduras.*   MISKITO word for banana.

sikulu (plural: tikulu) *Swaziland.*   Hereditary chief of a principality.

Silam *Burkina Faso.*   MOSSI ethnic group.

silbay *Philippines.*   Six-hole end-blown double-reed flute of the ILO-CANO.

silsilad al baraka *Somalia.*   Literally, chains of blessing. Heads of SUFI orders.

sima *Sri Lanka.*   Territorial and temporal jurisdiction of lesser gods.

Simaa *Zambia.*   Niger-Kordofanian language.

simidor *Haiti.*   Song leader at a COMBITE.

simoom *North Africa.*   Desert wind. See SAMIEL.

simpatia *Guatemala.*   Complex of emotions characterized by congeniality and empathy.

simsar *Morocco.*   Muslim rental agent for Europeans.

Sinabo *Bolivia.*   Amazon Indian group of PANOAN linguistic stock in Pando department.

Sinagoro *Papua New Guinea.*   Austronesian language.

sinakulo *Philippines.*   Religious drama or passion play.

sinarquismo *Mexico.*   Promoting public order, as opposed to anarchy and lawlessness.

Sinasina *Papua New Guinea.*   Papuan language.

Sindebele *Zimbabwe.*   Language of the NDEBELE, related to ZULU.

Sindhi *Pakistan.*   Indo-European language.

sindicato *Spanish America.*   Smallest unit of a labor organization.

sindicato campesino *Bolivia.*   Peasant syndicate or league.

sindico *Spanish America.*   Lower-level public prosecutor and legal representative of the mayor.

sindur *Bangladesh.*   Red caste mark on female foreheads.

singarga *Malawi.*   Diviner.

Sinhalese *Sri Lanka.*   1. Dominant ethnic group, mostly Buddhist. 2. Indo-European language.

sinig *Senegal.*   Cultivators among the SERER.

sinigang *Philippines.*   Popular meat or fish preparation boiled with spices.

sinokoti *Swaziland.*   Cloak made of antelope skin or cattle horn used by men and women to cover the upper part of their bodies.

sipahi *Turkey.*   Cavalry.

Sira *West Africa.*   Niger-Kordofanian language.

Siracua *Bolivia.*   Indian group of ZAMUCOAN linguistic stock in Santa Cruz department.

Siraiki *India and Pakistan.*   Indo-European language.

sircar *India.*   Variant of SARKAR.

sirdar *India.*   Variant of SARDAR.

sirf *Iraq.*   Land owned and occupied by the state.

Sirhan *Jordan.*   BEDOUIN tribe.

Sirikwa *Kenya.*   MAA-speaking people, originally in Uasin Gishu Plateau.

Siriono *Bolivia.*   Indian group of TUPIAN linguistic stock in Beni and Santa Cruz departments.

sirkal *Iraq.*   Clan leader serving the SHAYKH as foreman.

Sisala *Ghana.*   GRUSI group in upper west region.

Sissala *Burkina Faso.*   GOUROUNSI ethnic group.

Sissala *West Africa.*   Niger-Kordofanian language.

SiSwati *Swaziland.*   BANTU language of the SWAZIS.

sitar *India.*   Nonfretted musical instrument with three or more strings, invented by Amir Khusru.

Sitges Agreement *Colombia.*   Agreement of 1957 between the leaders of the Liberal and Conservative parties that created the National Front.

sitio *Philippines.*   Cluster of scattered dwellings.

sitoa *Oceania.*   Small trading ship the decks of which are set up as stores.

situpa *Zimbabwe.*   Registration certificate.

Siva *India.*   The middle god of the Hindu trinity considered as the sustainer of the universe, as distinguished from BRAHMA, the creator and VISHNU the destroyer.

sive *Swaziland.*   Lowest unit of tribal territorial organization.

sitwundan *Burma.*   Territorial army during British rule and the early years of the Union.

Siwol Yusin *South Korea.*   Revitalizing Constitution of 1972.

siya *Sierra Leone.*   Patrilineal clan among the SUSU and YALUNKA.

sjambok *Zimbabwe.*   Whip about two meters long made of animal hide and used for driving livestock.

skerm *Zimbabwe.*   Temporary fence of thorn trees to protect travelers at night.

skoi thom *Cambodia.*   Large tripod drum struck with a padded stick.

skokiaan *Zimbabwe.*   Alcoholic beverage made from fermented cereals spiked with toxic ingredients.

slamet *Indonesia.*   1. State of peaceful and harmonious existence free of strife and disruptive influences. 2. Javanese ritual meal characterized by slamet.

slendro *Indonesia.*   Five-tone tuning system for the GAMELAN.

smala *Algeria.*   Camp of an important tribe with families and servants.

smartars *India.*   BRAHMINS of central and south India who follow traditional legal institutions rather than written Scriptures.

smriti *India.*   Traditions handed down from ancient sages in Hinduism.

so *Laos.*   Two-stringed violin.

So *Southeast Asia.* Austro-Asiatic language.

So *Zaire.* Ethnic group.

Soa *Indonesia.* Ethnic group in the Moluccas (Maluku).

Soai *Thailand.* Ethnic group on the Cambodian border.

soba *Angola.* Local African chiefs recognized by the Portuguese in return for collaboration.

sobador *Nicaragua.* Folk medicine man.

soban *South Korea.* Literally, western group. Officials and scholars as a group of YANGBAN.

socialist emulation *Cuba.* Socialist competition in which one worker sets the standard and others try to reach it.

sociedad anonima *Spanish America.* Limited corporation.

sociedad colectiva *Spanish America.* General partnership.

sociedad de responsabilidades limitada *Spanish America.* Limited liability company, usually abbreviated as SRL.

sociedad en comandita *Spanish America.* Limited partnership.

sociedad, la *Honduras.* Literally, the society. Upper social crust.

Soga *Uganda.* 1. Eastern BANTU ethnic group. 2. Niger-Kordofanian language.

sohak *South Korea.* Literally, Western learning. Name given to Christianity in the 18th and 19th centuries.

sokari *Sri Lanka.* Mime drama.

sol (plural: soles) *Peru.* Monetary unit.

Solanki *India.* *See* AGNIKULA.

soldaan *Somalia.* Variant of sultan. Head of a clan.

soldaderas *Mexico.* Indian women who accompanied their men to battle.

Solhajet *Nepal.* Group of GURUNG.

Soli *Zambia.* 1. BANTU ethnic group in the southwest. 2. Niger-Kordofanian language.

Solomec *Central America.* Language group, of MAMEAN linguistic stock.

Solomec *Honduras.* MAYA tribe.

Solor *Indonesia.* Austronesian language.

Solubah *Jordan.* Group of despised BEDOUINS, supposedly descended from crusaders, mostly tinkers and smiths.

somaj *Bangladesh.* Small worship group.

Somali *Somalia.* Afro-Asiatic language.

somalo *Somalia.* Monetary unit, also known as Somali shilling.

Somba *Benin.* Ethnic group of the Voltaic cluster.

Somono *Mali.* Fisherman caste of the BAMBARA.

Somrai *West Africa.* Afro-Asiatic language.

son *Guatemala.* Folk dance.

sonam *Nepal.* Religious merit or brownie points on the accumulation of which nirvana depends for a Buddhist.

sonda *Sri Lanka.*   Permissible marriage partner among TAMILS.

Sondwari *India.*   Indo-European language.

song *Vietnam.*   River.

Songe *Zaire.*   Niger-Kordofanian language.

Songhai *West Africa.*   1. Sudanic-speaking people who founded a great empire in the 15th and 16th centuries that was destroyed by the Moors in 1591. 2. Nilo-Saharan language.

Songhay *Niger.*   See SONGHAI.

songkran *Thailand.*   Festival marking the end of the dry season.

song na *Thailand.*   Long thin drum.

Songo *Angola.*   MBUNDU subgroup.

Songomeno *Zaire.*   Niger-Kordofanian language.

Songye *Zaire.*   Ethnic group of southern savanna.

Soninke *Mauritania.*   Variant name of SARAKOLE.

Soninke *West Africa.*   Niger-Kordofanian language

Sonjo *Tanzania.*   BANTU ethnic group.

Sonongo *Angola.*   Subgroup of the KONGO.

soottiBe *Senegal.*   Ex-slaves among the TOUCOLEURS.

sopa paraguaya *Paraguay.*   Heavy cake made of ground corn, cheese, onions and milk.

Sora *India.*   Austro-Asiatic language.

sorabe *Madagascar.*   Sacred manuscripts.

sorba *Western Sahara.*   Ambassador charged with negotiation of tribal treaties.

sorliya *Ghana.*   Original NA or the paramount chief of WA.

Soropalca *Bolivia.*   AYMARA dialect in Potosi department.

Sorsogon *Philippines*   Austronesian language.

sortijas *Paraguay.*   Equestrian events.

Sosso *Angola.*   Subgroup of the KONGO.

Sotho *Lesotho.*   1. Collective name for the Tswana, or western Sotho, the Pedi, Lobedu and other eastern Sotho, and the Suto, or southern Sotho. 2. Niger-Kordofanian language.

soudure *Sahel.*   Famine or scarcity of food just before the harvest.

souk *Arab countries.*   Traditional bazaar.

soukhouan *Laos.*   Wedding feast.

soukous *Congo.*   Dance

sous prefecture *Francophone countries.*   Sub-prefecture.

Soussis *Maghreb.*   See BERBER.

Soussou or **Sosso** or **Susu** *Guinea.*   Ethnic group.

Southern Mande *Ghana.*   MANDE ethnic group.

sowar *India.*   Cavalryman.

sowcar *India.*   Native broker or banker.

sowei *Sierra Leone.*   Wooden helmet worn by officials of the SANDE secret society.

spahi *West Asia.*   Provincial cavalry unit under the Ottomans.

sralay *Cambodia.*   Double-reed oboe.

Sranan *Suriname.*   English-based Creole.

Sre *Vietnam.*   Highland ethnic group, a subgroup of the KOHO.

sreshta *Nepal.*   KSHATRIYA caste among the NEWARIS. Also, *Sheshyo.*

srok *Cambodia.*   District.

sruti *India.*   VEDIC texts based on divinely inspired knowledge or revelation.

ssirum *South Korea.*   Wrestling.

sso ou syo *Burma.*   LU woman's short jacket, usually sky blue or black worn over a red blouse with a skirt and petticoat.

staten *Suriname.*   National legislature.

sthanakvasis *India.*   Sect of JAINS that rose in the 19th century as a protest against idolatry and temple worship.

Stieng *Vietnam.*   1. Highland ethnic group along the Cambodian border. 2. Austro-Asiatic language.

stool *Ghana.*   Symbol of a chief's authority and legitimacy. Thus, *destool, enstool.*

stridana *India.*   Literally, woman's wealth. Dowry paid to the bridegroom.

stupa *Burma.*   Lower portion of a pagoda, a domelike mound housing the relics of the Buddha.

Suarez Doctrine *Colombia.*   Doctrine, enunciated by President Marco Fidel Suarez, 1918–21, stressing links between the Bolivarian republics.

sua-sua *Philippines.*   Muslim dance in which couples hold an open fan in each hand.

suba *India.*   A province as a unit of local administration under the Mughal Empire.

Suba *Tanzania.*   Ethnic group.

Suba *Tanzania and Kenya.*   Niger-Kordofanian language.

subahdar *India.*   1. Viceroy or governor of a SUBA in MUGHAL times. 2. Local military commandant.

Subaihi *Yemens.*   Ethnic group.

subak *Indonesia.*   Irrigation society in Bali.

subalBe (singular: cuballo) *Senegal.*   Fishermen among the TOUCOLEURS.

Subanon *Philippines.*   1. Pagan ethnic group of Mindanao. 2. Austronesian language.

Subay *Saudi Arabia.*   Tribe.

subbha *Nepal.*   Tribal official.

Subi *Tanzania.*   1. Ethnic group. 2. Niger-Kordofanian language.

Subia *Botswana.*   Ethnic subgroup.

subkha *Saudi Arabia.*   Salt flats near the sea.

sub-lema *Uruguay.*   Label adopted by a faction of a political party in order to make proportional representation operative within the constitutional framework.

sublime porte *Turkey.*   See PORTE.

subprefecto *Bolivia.*   Administrative head of a province.

subtiaba *Nicaragua.*   Indian ethnic group.

sucre *Ecuador.*   Monetary unit.

Sudari (singular: Suwaydi) *Oman.*   Tribe of eastern Arabia.

Sudra *India.*   The lowest class in the four-tiered Hindu caste system, comprising artisans.

sudreh *India.*   White cambric shirt worn by the PARSIS.

sueng *Thailand.*   Flute.

Sufi *Islamic countries.*   Mystical and ascetical sect of Islam that originated in Persia (Iran).

sufra *Iran.*   Religious session attended only by women.

Sugbunaron *Philippines.*   See CEBUANOS.

Suhul *Saudi Arabia.*   Tribe.

sujeicao *Brazil.*   Labor performed by rural peasants as a form of payment to the land owner.

suji *Koreas.*   Annual ceremony honoring ancestors.

suk *Arab countries.*   Bazaar, sometimes covered.

suk *Uganda.*   Ethnic group.

sukapiban *Thailand.*   Local sanitation and health district.

sukia *Costa Rica.*   Shaman among the TALAMANCA tribe.

sokong *Burkina Faso.*   Title of chief of Imperri.

Suku *Indonesia.*   Large kinship group among the Balinese.

Suku *Zaire.*   1. Ethnic group. 2. Niger-Kordofanian language.

Sukuma *Tanzania.*   1. Ethnic group south of Lake Victoria, subgroup of the NYAMWEZI. 2. Niger-Kordofanian language.

Sukur *West Africa.*   Afro-Asiatic language.

sukya *Honduras.*   Shaman, or medicine man, among the MISKITO and SAMBO.

Sula *Indonesia.*   Austronesian language.

Sulaymankhayl *Afghanistan.*   GHILAZAI tribe.

Sulod *Philippines.*   Austronesian language.

sulu *Solomon Islands.*   Short SARONG.

Sulubbah *Saudi Arabia.*   Tribe.

suma *Gambia.*   Leaders or lineage with large tracts of land.

sumakunda *Gambia.*   Lineage in direct succession to the throne.

Sumambu *Indonesia.*   Austronesian language.

suman *Philippines.*   Cake made from glutenous rice, sugar and coconut milk.

sumar (plural: asumar) *Ghana.*   Charm or talisman.

Sumba *Indonesia.*   Austronesian language.

Sumbawa *Indonesia.*   Austronesian language.

Sumbawanese *Indonesia.*   Ethnic group of the Lesser Sundas.

Sumbwa *Tanzania.*   1. Ethnic group. 2. Niger-Kordofanian language.

Sumo *Honduras.*   Indian tribe of the northwest.

Sumo *Nicaragua.*   Dialect of the Bocay group of Chorutegans.

Sumus *Honduras.*   Indian tribe along upper Rio Coco.

sunar *Nepal.*   Goldsmith class of untouchables.

Sundanese *Indonesia.*   1. Ethnic group of Java. 2. Austronesian language.

Sundi *Angola.*   KONGO subgroup.

Sundi or **Basundi** *Congo.*   Subgroup of the KONGO.

Sungor *Chad.*   Nilo-Saharan language.

Sunni *Islamic countries.*   Mainline or orthodox sect of Islam holding to the legitimacy of the first three CALIPHS. From *Sunna* doctrine.

Sunwar *Nepal.*   1. Tibeto-Nepalese ethnic group. 2. Sino-Tibetan language.

supari *India.*   Betelnut or arecanut chewed as a mild intoxicant.

supercaid *Morocco.*   Executive of a CERCLE.

suplente *Latin America.*   Alternate elected along with the delegate to the senate and chamber of deputies.

suq (plural aswaq) *Oman.*   Variant of SUK.

sur *Somalia.*   Well for livestock.

surakan subanum *Philippines.*   Cymbal or gong.

surau *Malaysia.*   Prayerhouse, less than a mosque.

Suri *Ethiopia.*   Nilo-Saharan language.

Surnai *Afghanistan.*   Flute with seven finger holes and a conical bore.

surra *Sudan.*   Extended family with three degrees of relationships.

surval *India and Pakistan.*   Petticoat worn by Muslim women.

susiyyat *Tunisia.*   Cloth woven from Egyptian flax.

Susu *Guinea.*   Variant of SOUSSOU.

Susu *West Africa.*   Niger-Kordofanian language.

Susu *Guinea-Bissau.*   MANDE group related to the DYULAS and SONINKE.

suudu *Senegal.*   Group of male newcomers who room together, among the TOUCOLEURS.

suyacal *Guatemala.*   Rain cape made from the leaf of the corozo palm.

Suyia *Tanzania.*   BANTU clan.

svetambara *India.*   In JAINISM, sect that favors clothing as distinguished from DIGAMBARA, which favors nudity.

svikero *Zimbabwe.*   Any SHONA medium through which an ancestral spirit works.

swa *Thailand.*   Cymbal.

swabasha *Sri Lanka.*   Native language.

swadeshi *India.*   Literally, of one's own country. Promotion of home industries and crafts as opposed to reliance on foreign goods.

Swahili *East Africa.*   1. Coastal ethnic group, partially Arabized. 2. Lingua franca of East Africa with a large admixture of Arabic words. Also, *Kiswahili.*

Swaka *Zambia.*   Congolese LUNDA tribe in Luapula Valley.

swami *India.*   1. Lord. 2. Term of respect for a Hindu priest or holy man.

swaraj *India.*   Literally, home rule. Self-government, especially as the goal of the struggle for independence from the British.

swastika *India.*   Literally, all is well. Ancient Indo-Aryan symbol of prosperity depicted on the walls and floors of Hindu temples and homes.

Swati *Swaziland.*   Niger-Kordofanian language.

swatantra *India.*   Freedom.

Swazi *Swaziland.*   BANTU-speaking people of NGUNI stock.

Sylheti *Bangladesh.*   Indo-European language.

syli *Guinea.*   Monetary unit.

taai *Burma.*   Temporary shelters built near rice fields as watch houses after harvest.

taarof *Iran.*   Elaborate ceremonies of ritual politeness.

ta'ata'afa popa'a *Tahiti.*   Person of Euro-Polynesian racial background.

taazich *Iran and Iraq.*   Highly emotional passion play on the anniversary of Husayn's death in MUHARRAM.

taba *Brazil.*   Amerindian village.

tabanca *Guinea-Bissau.*   Village as a unit of local administration.

tabareus *Brazil.*   Lower class rural people in Bahia.

tabaski *Guinea.*   Year-end festival.

taberna *Brazil.*   Roadside tavern.

Tabi *Sudan and Ethiopia.*   Nilo-Saharan language.

tabla *South Asia.*   Two drums joined together, one slightly smaller than the other, beaten with the fingers and palm.

tablado *Uruguay.*   Low street stage or platform during carnivals. Also, performances on such stages.

tablon *Guatemala.*   Square, terraced garden plot.

tabodive *Burma.*   Harvest festival held on the full-moon day of February.

taboleiros *Brazil.* Sandy tablelands of the northeast.

taburete *Nicaragua.* Leather chair in poor homes.

Tabwa *Zambia.* Congolese LUNDA tribe in Luapula Valley.

Tacacho *Nicaragua.* Dialect of basic CHORUTEGAN of Mexican origin.

tacan *North Korea.* Socialist work system emphasizing consultation and comradeship between managers and workmen.

Tacana *Bolivia.* Amazon Indian linguistic stock.

Tacanan *Bolivia.* Ethnic group in Pando and La Paz departments.

taccavi *South Asia.* Emergency credit for farmers.

Tacunbiacu *Bolivia.* Amazon Indian group in Santa Cruz department.

Taegukki *South Korea.* National flag with symbols of yin and yang.

taegum *Korea.* Bamboo flute.

taekwondo *Korea.* Martial art, similar to karate.

Tafi *Ghana.* CENTRAL TOGO ethnic cluster in the Volta Region.

tafia *Haiti.* Rum made of distilled sugarcane juice.

Tagabili *Philippines.* Pagan ethnic group.

Tagakaola *Philippines.* Pagan ethnic group.

Tagalog *Philippines.* 1. Lowland Christian group. 2. Austronesian language; national language.

Tagaydan *Philippines.* Pagan ethnic group on Mindoro Island.

Tagbanua *Philippines.* Pagan ethnic group.

tagnawa *Philippines.* Work bee.

Tagoi *Sudan.* Niger-Kordofanian language.

Taherza *Iran.* BALUCHI tribe.

tahil *Malaysia.* Unit of weight equal to 1 oz.

Tahitian *Polynesia.* Austronesian language.

tahsil *India.* Unit of local administration, subdivision of a district.

tahsildar *India.* Administrative official of a TAHSIL.

tahuna *Polynesia.* Literally, master. Skilled master craftsmen who conduct ritualized ceremonies.

Tahylandang *Indonesia.* Austronesian language.

Tai *Thailand.* KAM TAI.

taifa *Maghreb.* Guild.

taifa *Morocco.* City-states under the Almoravid dynasty.

taife *Morocco.* Party, group or guild in medieval times.

taik *Burma.* Group of monasteries under an especially venerable monk called *hsayadaw.* Also, *kyaung taik.*

Taimanni *Afghanistan.* See CHAHAR AIMAK.

taipa *Brazil.* Palm leaves used to cover the mud or adobe houses of the rural poor.

Taita *Kenya.* 1. Northeast coastal BANTU ethnic group. 2. Niger-Kordofanian language.

taj *Ethiopia.* Fermented honey beverage.

taj *India.*   Crown.

Tajik *Afghanistan.*   DARI-speaking tribe, believed to have descended from Indo-Bactrians.

taka *Bangladesh.*   Monetary unit.

Takestani *Iran.*   Indo-European language.

Takia *Papua New Guinea.*   Austronesian language.

taki taki *Guyana.*   Low-status dialect of English used among laborers.

takraw *Thailand.*   Game played with a light, woven rattan ball.

taksim *Turkey.*   Partition (of Cyprus).

Tal *West Africa.*   Afro-Asiatic language.

tala *Afghanistan.*   Flute of metal or reed.

tala *Western Samoa.*   Monetary unit.

talak *Islamic countries.*   Relatively simple divorce procedure among Muslims by which a husband may recite a formula in the presence of his wife and register the divorce with the village IMAM for a fee.

Talamanca *Costa Rica.*   Ethnic group of the Caribbean coast.

Talacote *Botswana.*   Ethnic subgroup.

Talaud *Indonesia.*   Austronesian language.

talb *Western Sahara.*   Debt acquired for inflicting a wound. Compare DIA.

taleb *Algeria.*   Koranic teacher.

taledek *Indonesia.*   Solo dance.

Talensi *Ghana.*   MOLE DAGBANE ethnic group in Upper East Region.

tali *India.*   Gold pendant engraved with the likeness of a goddess and suspended by a consecrated string of many fine yellow threads tied by a BRAHMIN around the neck of his wife at the time of marriage ceremony.

talibe *Senegal.*   Follower of an Islamic brotherhood, among the WOLOF.

talipot *India.*   The great-leaved fan palm of south India.

talla *Ethiopia.*   Barley beer fermented with leaves of the gesho plant.

tallari *Egypt.*   Coin, 1/5th of an Egyptian pound.

Tallensi *Burkina Faso.*   Ethnic group of the MOSSI cluster.

talotbot *Thailand.*   Short thin drum.

talowta *Zimbabwe.*   Small group of SOTHO speakers.

taluk *India.*   Subdivision of a district.

talukdar *India and Nepal.*   1. Chief revenue officer of a TALUK in India. 2. Village headman in Nepal.

Talysh *Iran.*   Indo-European language.

Tama *Chad.*   1. SAHELian ethnic group. 2. Nilo-Saharan language.

Tamachek *Niger.*   Ethnic group.

Tamacosi *Bolivia.*   Amazon Indian group of Santa Cruz department.

tam'aiga *Samoa.*   Chief of royal rank.

tamal *Senegal.*   Drum.

tamale *Central America.* Food made of cornmeal and ground meat seasoned with red peppers, wrapped in corn husks or plantain leaves and roasted or steamed.

Taman *Burma.* Sino-Tibetan language.

Tamang *Nepal.* 1. Tibeto-Nepali ethnic group. Also, *Murmi Lama, Dhamang.* 2. Sino-Tibetan language.

Tamasheq *West Africa.* Afro-Asiatic language.

Tamazight *Maghreb.* Afro-Asiatic language.

tambala *Malawi.* Coin, 1/100ths of a KWACHA.

Tambanua *Sabah.* Austronesian language.

Tamberma *Togo.* 1. Ethnic group of the KABRE cluster. 2. Niger-Kordofanian language.

tambo *Ecuador.* In the Inca empire, points of relay or stopover on the highways.

Tambo *Zambia.* Tanzanian ethnic group.

tambon *Thailand.* Commune or group of about 10 villages.

tambor *El Salvador.* Large drum.

tamboura *India.* Nonfretted musical instrument of the lute family, consisting of four strings and producing a droning sound, used as accompaniment to the SITAR or SAROD.

tambur *Afghanistan.* Musical instrument consisting of metal strings passing over an ivory bridge and resting on the wooden face of a resonating chamber made of gourd.

tamein *Burma.* Brightly colored silk or cotton woman's garment.

Tamenes *Guatemala.* Indian carriers who carry heavy weights on their backs.

Tamil *India.* DRAVIDIAN people of south India and Sri Lanka. 2. The language of this people.

tamimah (plural: tama'im) *Oman.* Paramount shaykh.

Tampolense *Ghana.* GRUSI group in northern region.

Tana *Central Africa.* Nilo-Saharan language.

Tanala *Madagascar.* Ethnic group.

Tanda or **Tenda** *Senegal.* Ethnic group, including BASARI, KONAGI, Ba-Jaranka, and Bedik.

Tanda *Zaire.* Ethnic group.

tandur *South Asia.* Bread oven made of half-baked clay and buried in the ground. Also *tandoori.*

tanety *Madagascar.* Cultivation of marginally productive land on a hillside.

Tangale *West Africa.* Afro-Asiatic language.

tang che *Vietnam.* Ritual mourning periods divided into five classes: *dai teng,* for three years; *co phue,* for one year; *cuu cong,* for nine months; *tieu cong,* for five months, and *ty ma,* for three months.

Tang chungang *North Korea.*   Literally, center of the party. Unofficial title of Kim Chong Il, son of Kim Il Sung.

tang kanbu *North Korea.*   Party cadres of the Korean Workers Party.

tangomaus *Guinea-Bissau.*   Literally, tattoed men. African slaves.

tang sasang *North Korea.*   Party ideology. Also, *hyongmyong sasang.*

tang sepo *North Korea.*   Party cells of the Korean Workers Party.

tanguito *Spanish America.*   Variant of the tango.

tanindrozana *Madagascar.*   Ancestral village or land.

tanka *Nepal.*   Religious wall hanging.

Tankamba *Burkina Faso.*   Ethnic group related to the SOMBA.

tanodbayan *Philippines.*   Ombudsman.

tanquay *Ethiopia.*   Sorcerer.

Tantra *India.*   See TANTRISM.

Tantrism *India and Nepal.*   Esoteric form of Hinduism emphasizing magic followed by the Shaivites, divided into the Right Hand, which follows ancient Vedic rituals, and the Left Hand, which worships female aspects of the deity. Their Scriptures are known as Tantras.

tanzimat *Turkey.*   Literally, reorganization. Political reform and modernization, 1839–1878.

Tao *Bolivia.*   CHIQUITOAN dialect spoken by Amazon Indians in Santa Cruz department.

tao *Philippines.*   Common man.

Ta'oih *Laos.*   Austro-Asiatic language.

tao quan *Vietnam.*   Chief guardian spirit of a household. Also, *vua bep.*

Taoubalt *Western Sahara.*   Small tribe.

tapa or **siap** *Oceania.*   Bark cloth made by soaking and heating the bark of the mulberry tree.

tapa de dulce *Costa Rica.*   Crude brown sugar cake.

tapadera *Mexico.*   Literally, cover or lid. Leather guard covering each of the stirrups of a Mexican saddle.

tapal *India.*   Mail service in south India.

tapalo *Mexico.*   Scarf or shawl made of coarse material.

tapaojo *Guatemala.*   Heavy leather blind placed over the eyes of a pack animal.

tapesco *Nicaragua.*   Poles used in bed construction.

Tapiete *Bolivia.*   Indian group of TUPIAN linguistic stock in CHACO.

tapisque *Guatemala.*   Grain harvest.

tapone *Thailand.*   Hand drum with two heads.

tappa *India.*   Classical vocal style of music that developed in north India in MUGHAL times.

tap tap *Haiti.*   Gaily colored truck used as a bus.

taqsim *Jordan.*   Musical instrument, originally from Turkey.

taquiari *Bolivia.* Dance of the eastern highlands.

taquiyah *Iran.* Religious dissimulation and pretended conformity in a hostile environment permitted by the Koran as a means of self-defense.

Taracahitan *Mexico.* Ethnic group.

taraghiba *Western Sahara.* Sacrifice of a camel to establish an alliance, obtain protection or as compensation for a damage or crime.

Tarahumara *Mexico.* Azteco-Tanoan language.

tarahumaras *Mexico.* Indian tribe noted for their physical stamina as foot racers.

tarai *Nepal.* Flat alluvial land below the mountain ranges.

Taraki *Afghanistan.* GHILAZAI tribe.

Tarascans *Mexico.* Indian tribe in the state of Michoacan, noted as fishermen.

Tarasco *Mexico.* Indian language.

tarea *Guatemala.* A day's work of a laborer.

tarik *Turkey.* Variant of TARIQA. Path of instruction toward spiritual perfection undertaken by a SUFI devotee.

tarikat *Turkey.* SUFI dervish order or lodge.

tarimba *Guyana.* Stringed instrument made of fleshy leaf, the skin of which is raised by a bridge or the pith.

tariqa (plural: turuq) *Islamic countries.* Literally, the way. Means of attaining spiritual perfection through mystical ecstasy and trance produced through hypnotic chanting and dancing. Also, the SUFI brotherhoods founded for this purpose.

tariqat *Islamic countries.* SUFI brotherhood.

tarjeta de control *Cuba.* Identity card.

tarkap *Cameroon.* Father of the bride wealth.

tarkhan *Pakistan.* Functional caste of blacksmiths, carpenters and artisans.

Tarok *West Africa.* Niger-Kordofanian language.

tarro *Guatemala.* Giant bamboo, used in construction.

taruma *Guyana.* Amerindian flute.

tas *Honduras.* Among the MISKITOS, a plot of one-fourth of a hectare.

Tasaday *Philippines.* Cave-dwelling aboriginals in Mindanao.

tasajo *Honduras.* Dried meat rubbed with salt and dried in the sun; jerky.

Tashilhait *Morocco.* Oral language of the SHLUH tribe.

tasseng *Laos.* Canton, a territorial subdivision of a district, or MUONG.

tassot *Haiti.* Meat preparation dired on a hot tin roof, marinated and then grilled over a charcoal fire.

tata *Senegal.* Garrisoned fort built by MALINKE rulers with earthen walls.

Tatog *Tanzania.* Nilo-Hamitic ethnic group.

Tatoga *Tanzania.* Nilo-Saharan language.

tatty *India.* Screen or mat made of fragrant grass, cuscus, watered and kept wet to keep the hot winds out.

Tauade *Papua New Guinea.* Papuan language.

Taune *Burma.* Order or sect of SHAN monks, slightly less strict than the MENGKYAW.

taungdaing *Burma.* Buddhist flagstaff in the precinct of a pagoda or monastery.

taung ok *Burma.* Revenue official.

taungya *Burma.* Fields cultivated by the swidden, or slash-and-burn method.

Taungyo *Burma.* Sino-Tibetan language.

Tau-oi *Vietnam.* Highland ethnic group.

Tausug *Philippines.* MORO group in Sulu and Zamboanga.

Tausug *Philippines, Sabah and Indonesia.* Austronesian language.

Tavara *Zimbabwe.* SHONA group occupying area between North Darwin district and the Zambezi River.

Taveta *Kenya.* Northeast coastal BANTU group.

Taveta *Tanzania.* Niger-Kordofanian language.

tavy *Madagascar.* Slash-and burn cultivation.

tawab *Saudi Arabia.* Seven counterclockwise circumambulance of the Kaabah as part of the HAJ.

Tawana *Botswana.* Subgroup of the NGWATO. Also, *Batawana.*

Tawana *Zimbabwe.* Branch of the western Sotho or Tswana speakers in central Botswana.

Tawara *Mozambique.* Ethnic group of the SHONA-Karanga cluster.

taxaua *Brazil.* TUPI tribal leader.

Tay *Vietnam.* Largest ethnic minority, in Viet Bac Autonomous Region.

tayefeh *Iran.* Clans.

tazaung daing *Burma.* Festival that follows the festival of lights.

tazi *Afghanistan.* Afghan hound.

tazkar *Ethiopia.* Forty-day memorial fast for the dead.

T'Boli *Philippines.* Austronesian language.

Tchaditude *Chad.* Authentic Chadianness, as opposed to Western culture.

Tchamba *Togo.* Ethnic group of the KOTOKOLI cluster.

tchikumbi *Congo.* Initiation rites for girls.

Tebu *Libya.* BERBER group in the south.

Tebu *Niger.* Ethnic cluster including DAZA and TEDARA.

tecnicos *Mexico.* Technicians.

Teda *West and North Africa.* 1. Muslim branch of the TOUBOU people who call themselves *Tedagada.* 2. Nilo-Saharan language.

Tedara *Niger.* Ethnic group of TEBU.

teertha *India.* Holy place of pilgrimage.

teff *Ethiopia.* Grain for making bread.

tegalan *Indonesia.* Unirrigated field.

Tegali *Sudan.* Niger-Kordofanian language.

Tegessie *Burkina Faso.* LOBI ethnic group speaking a KULANGO dialect.

tegua *Colombia.* Untrained rural medical practitioner.

tehsil *India.* Variant of TAHSIL.

Tehuelche *Argentina.* Indian language.

tejo *Colombia.* Cards.

Teke *Congo and Zaire.* 1. Ethnic group on both sides of the Zaire River. 2. Niger-Kordofanian language.

Teke or **Bateke** *Gabon.* Ethnic group.

Tekkes *Afghanistan.* TURKMAN subgroup near Herat.

Tekna *Western Sahara.* Ethnic group in the southern foothills from the Anti-Atlas to the Saguia el-Hamra.

Telugu *India.* DRAVIDIAN language of Andhra Pradesh.

Tem *West Africa.* 1. Ethnic group. Also, *Kokotil.* 2. Niger-Kordofanian language.

Temascal *Guatemala.* Sweat or water bath, housed in a low structure built of poles, mud and stones.

Tembe *Swaziland.* BANTU people of NGUNI origin.

tembefas *Uruguay.* Resin and stone ornaments for pierced lips, among Indians.

Tembo *Zaire.* 1. Ethnic group of the Eastern highlands. 2. Niger-Kordofanian language.

tem-giao *Vietnam.* Collective name for the three traditional religions: Buddhism, Confucianism and Taoism.

Temiar *Malaysia.* Austro-Asiatic language.

Temne *Sierre Leone.* 1. Second largest ethnic group in the country. 2. Niger-Kordofanian language.

temporales *Central America.* Heavy rains in June and September.

Temuan *Malaysia.* Austronesian language.

ten *Senegal.* Title of the king of Bawol.

Tenda *Guinea.* Ethnic group consisting of CONIAGUI, BASSARI, BADYARANKE, BOENI and MAYO.

tendana (plural: tendama) *Ghana.* Land priest in Upper and Northern Regions in charge of religious affairs and land.

tenencia *Chile.* Fourth-class police station.

Tenggarese *Indonesia.* Ethnic group of Java.

teniente politico *Ecuador.* Political lieutenant of a parish.

tenis-knis *Philippines.* Joking song of the SAMAL in Sulu Archipelago.

Tenkodogo *Burkina Faso.* Ethnic group of the MOSSI cluster.

tenmodi *India.* South Indian drama.

tense *Burkina Faso.* MOSSI ceremony opening the agricultural season.

tent *Mauritania.*   Nuclear family.

tente en el aire *Honduras.*   Offspring of a TORNATRAS father and a Spanish mother.

Tepehuan *Mexico.*   Azteco-Tanoan language.

Tepeth *Uganda.*   Ethnic group on the isolated mountains in Karamojong territory—Mounts Moroto, Kadam and Nepak.

teponahuastle *El Salvador.*   Drumlike musical instrument made from a hollowed section of a log.

tepuis *Venezuela.*   Massive, perpendicular flat-topped bluffs reaching considerable altitudes.

teqlay ghizat *Ethiopia.*   Provinces.

tequila *Mexico.*   National alcoholic beverage made from the maguey cactus.

terbia *Western Sahara.*   Slaves acquired through purchase or capture.

tercio *Bolivia.*   Unit of weight varying between 125 and 150 lb.

termo *Brazil.*   Administrative unit corresponding to a county.

Ternate *Indonesia.*   Papuan language.

terno *Philippines.*   MESTIZA dress with scooped neckline and butterfly sleeves.

terra caida *Brazil.*   Breakaway floating islands in the Amazon River.

terra mixta *Brazil.*   Sandy soils in the coffee growing region in North Parana.

terra teniente *Bolivia.*   Landholder

terrare *Paraguay.*   Cold MATE, drunk in summer.

terreiro *Brazil.*   Terrace of stone or mud for drying coffee beans.

tertib *Morocco.*   Tax levied during the French Protectorate.

tertulia *Spanish America.*   Gathering or circle of friends for a glass of wine or a cup of coffee in a cafe or bar.

tesaban *Thailand.*   Town council or SUKAPIBAN.

Teso *East Africa.*   Nilo-Saharan language.

Teso *Uganda.*   Eastern Nilotic ethnic group.

testur *Somalia.*   Canons of the clan custom.

Tet *Vietnam.*   Lunar new year festivities.

tet doan ngo *Vietnam.*   The double-five festival, on the fifth day of the fifth month, marking the beginning of the hot season.

Tetela *Zaire.*   1. Ethnic group. 2. Niger-Kordofanian language.

Tetete *Ecuador.*   Small, little-known Indian group in the jungle, on the Colombian border.

tet trung thu *Vietnam.*   Moon-watching festival in mid-autumn.

tetikala *Madagascar.*   System of shifting cultivation in which dry bush or grassland is burned and sorghum or corn sown in the ashes.

Tetum *Indonesia.*   Austronesian language.

teug *Senegal.*   Metal workers among the WOLOF.

Teuso *Uganda.*   Eastern Nilotic ethnic group.

Teve *Mozambique.* Ethnic group of the SHONA-Karanga cluster. Also, GURONGOCA, CHIMOIO.

Tewa Tao *Burma.* Pantheon of MON spirits.

thabeng *Lesotho.* Mountain country.

Thai *Thailand.* Core ethnic group consisting of Central Thai, or Thai Bhakklang; Thai Lao, or Thai Isan; Northern Thai, or Lana Tai; and Southern Thai, or Thai Pak Tai.

Thai Malay or **Thai Islam** *Thailand.* Ethnic group.

Thakali *Nepal.* BHOTE group.

thakin *Burma.* Term of respect, equivalent to sir.

thakur *India.* Literally, in SANSKRIT, idol or deity. Term of respect in Bengal for chief or man of rank.

Thakur *Nepal.* KSHATRIYA caste among the PAHARI.

thakurdwara *India.* Hindu temple.

Thakuri *India.* Indo-European language.

thamadi *Burma.* Village revenue assessor.

thamaing *Burma.* Prose history of a pagoda or monastery.

thammayutika *Thailand.* Buddhist reform sect initiated by King Monghut, 1851–68.

thampuran *India.* Title of honor among NAIRS of Kerala or MALAY-ALAM-speaking royal families.

thana *India.* District subdivision, such as a unit of police and revenue administration.

thana *Nepal.* Police court.

thanadar *Nepal.* Chief of a police station.

thananukrom *Cambodia.* Head of a diocese of the Buddhist SANGHA.

thang *Thailand.* Unit of weight equal to 16 kg.

thangara *Malawi.* One-string lute with a gourd resonator.

thangata *Malawi.* System of compulsory labor under British rule.

thangyat *Burma.* Poem recited in chorus alternatively by two groups, especially at Burmese new year's celebrations.

thanh hoang *Vietnam.* Patron saint or guardian spirit of a village worshipped at the DINH, or communal hall.

thap huang *Vietnam.* Act of burning joss sticks in worship.

Tharaka *Kenya.* 1. Central Bantu speaking group in Eastern Province. 2. Niger-Kordofanian language.

Tharu *Nepal.* 1. Ethnic group comprising the BHOKSA and MECHI. 2. Indo-European language.

Tharur *Nepal.* Ethnic group.

that *Laos.* STUPA, a memorial building, usually a hemispheric mound, holding a relic of the Buddha.

thathanabaing *Burma.* Head of the Buddhist SANGHA.

thaub *Saudi Arabia.* Long-sleeved, high-necked A-line garment made of white cotton.

thay thuoc *Vietnam.* Medicine man.

thebe *Botswana.* Coin, 1/100ths of a PULA.

thedingyut *Burma.* Festival of lights, marking the end of the rainy season in mid-October.

thein *Burma.* Religious building.

Thembu *Zimbabwe.* 1. Bantu-speaking people of southern Nguni origin. 2. Their language.

Theravada *Buddhist countries.* From SANSKRIT, *thera,* elder. Buddhist sect, also known as HINAYANA, or Southern Buddhism, prevalent in Sri Lanka and Burma. It considers Buddha as only a man and does not worship his image or offer prayers to him. Its Scriptures are written in PALI.

thesavalamai *Sri Lanka.* Customary marriage rules in a locality.

thet mahachat *Thailand.* Ceremonial event in WATS in mid-October.

Thien *Vietnam.* Zen Buddhist sect, also known as DHYANA.

thimkhang gongma *Bhutan.* High court.

thingyan *Burma.* New year in April, also known as water festival.

thit bo bay mon *Vietnam.* Seven dishes of beef served as one meal.

Tho *Vietnam.* KAM TAI.

Thod kathin *Thailand.* Ceremonial contribution of money, robes and durable goods to Buddhist monks in the lunar month following the end of Lent.

tho kong *Vietnam.* Guardian spirit of the kitchen.

thoma *Sierra Leone.* Secret society among the SHERBRO.

Thonga-Hlengwe *Zimbabwe.* Ethnic group.

tho phung to-tien *Vietnam.* Cult of ancestor worship.

thudong bhikku *Thailand.* Wandering monk.

thue dien *Vietnam.* Land tax.

thue than *Vietnam.* Head tax.

thug *India.* Hindu religious brotherhood of marauding robbers who generally strangled their victims as offerings to the goddess Kali. Suppressed by Lord William Bentinck from 1829–36.

thugee *India.* Brigandage or dacoity practiced by THUGS.

thugyi *Burma.* Village headman in upper Burma.

thum *Nepal.* Division of a district as a territorial unit.

thumri *India.* Lively mixture of KHYAL and TAPPA suitable for pantomime and dance.

thuoc bac *Vietnam.* Literally, northern medicine. Traditional system of medicine of Chinese origin based on roots, shoots, bark, fruits and tubers of plants and herbs.

thuoc lao *Vietnam.* Tobacco smoked with a water pipe.

thuoc nam *Vietnam.* Literally, southern medicine. Traditional system of medicine of Chinese origin based on freshly gathered herbs and medicinal plants.

thuoc phien *Vietnam.* Opium.

Thuri *Sudan.* 1. Nilotic ethnic group. 2. Nilo-Saharan language.

thu tu *Vietnam.* Custodian of a temple.

Thwala *Swaziland.* True Swazi clan.

Tiatinagua *Bolivia.* Amazon Indian group of TACANAN linguistic stock in La Paz and Pardo departments.

Tibetan *Bhutan.* Sino-Tibetan language.

Tiboi *Bolivia.* Indian group in Beni department.

ticka or **tilak** *India.* Mark on the forehead made with colored earth or unguents to denote sectarian distinctions, or by women as an ornament.

tico *Costa Rica.* A Costa Rican. From the frequent diminutive ending of the word in "ico" or "tico."

Ticomeri *Bolivia.* Amazon Indian group in West Beni department.

Ticuna *Brazil.* Indian language.

Tidjaniya *West Africa.* Islamic brotherhood, founded by Si Ahmad ben M. al Tidjani in 1781, and including the OMARIYYA and MALIKIYYA branches.

Tidong *Indonesia.* Ethnic group of Kalimantan.

Tidore *Indonesia.* Papuan language.

tiedo *Senegal.* Warriors among the WOLOF.

Tiefo *Burkina Faso.* Ethnic group.

tiempo muerte *Cuba.* Dry season in which sugarcane cannot be harvested.

tien chi *Vietnam.* The most important member of the Council of Notables in a village.

tienda *Colombia.* Store that serves as a social center for the community.

Tiene *Zaire.* Niger-Kordofanian language.

Tien Thien *Vietnam.* Sect of the CAO DAI.

tien su *Vietnam.* Patron saint of a particular profession or trade.

tierno *Senegal.* Spiritual leader among the PEUL and TOUCOLEURS.

tierra adentro *South America.* Interior low lands of the Oriente.

tierra caliente *South America.* Hot, usually coastal region.

tierra fiscale *South America.* State lands.

tierra fria *South America.* Cold region, usually in the highlands.

tierra templada *South America.* Temperate zone region.

tifinagh *Algeria.* TUAREG writing system.

tighremt *Morocco.* BERBER family or communal granary.

Tigraniyyah *Sudan.* SUFI order in West Africa.

Tigre or **Tigray** *Ethiopia.* 1. Ethnic group related to the AMHARA. 2. Afro-Asiatic language.

tihar *Nepal.* Festival of lights, or DEEPAVALI in the month of Kartik, that lasts for five days.

Tijaniya *North Africa.* One of the four major Islamic brotherhoods.

Tikar *Cameroon.* 1. Collective name for various related tribes of the Bamenda Plateau. 2. Niger-Kordofanian language.

Tikhondzi *Swaziland.* Lieges of the Swazi king, former immigrants from the southern BANTU kingdoms.

tikina *Fiji.* District as a unit of social government.

tilak *India.* Variant of TICKA.

tilensi *Western Sahara.* Well, up to one meter deep.

timars *Turkey.* Fiefs or subdistricts.

timbalan yang di pertuan agong *Malaysia.* Deputy paramount chief.

Timbaro *Ethiopia.* East Cushitic peoples.

Timbe *Papua New Guinea.* Papuan language.

timera *Mauritania.* Class of inferior peoples among the SONINKE.

Timorese *Indonesia.* Austronesian language.

ti moun *Haiti.* Adoption of peasant children for a temporary period, or until they are grown, by better-off families.

Timuri *Iran.* Indo-Iranian ethnic group in Khorasan.

Tin *Thailand.* MON-KHMER highland ethnic group.

T'in *Thailand.* Austro-Asiatic language.

tinajas *Guatemala.* Large vessel for transport of water.

tinamit *Guatemala.* Indian word for MUNICIPIO.

tindisa *Tanzania.* Ethnic group. See HADZAPI, KINDIGA.

Tinggian *Philippines.* Christian and pagan ethnic group in Abra Province in north Luzon.

tinkling *Philippines.* Pantomime dance in which couples hold a pair of bamboo poles close to the ground.

tinkundla (singular: nkundla) *Swaziland.* Rural district councils.

Tio *Zaire.* Ethnic group.

tipoy *Bolivia.* Garment of Oriente Indians, a plain ankle-length dress of homespun cotton.

Tippera *Bangladesh.* 1. Tribal group in the Chittagong tracts. 2. Indo-European language.

Tira *Sudan.* Niger-Kordofanian language.

tirailleurs *Morocco.* Regular soldiers.

Tiribi *Costa Rica.* Dialect of *Terraba* Indians.

Tiro *Indonesia.* Austronesian language.

Tirthankara *India.* Literally, stepmaker. Title of a predecessor of Mahavira, founder of JAINISM.

Tiruray *Philippines.* 1. Pagan ethnolinguistic stock in Cotabato. 2. Austronesian language.

Tiste *Nicaragua.* Drink of fresh parched corn ground with chocolate.

Titu *Zaire.* Ethnic group.

titulado *Spanish America.* Certified teacher.

titulo docente *Honduras.* Teaching certificate.

Tiv *West Africa.* 1. Ethnic group. 2. Niger-Kordofanian language.

tivasham *India.* Hindu ceremony performed on the anniversary of a parent's death.

tizi *Morocco.* Mountain pass.

tjamat *Indonesia.* Head of a subdistrict.

tlang pi *Burma.* Village council among the Northern CHINS.

Tlokwa *Botswana.* Tribe of Sotho origin, widely distributed in southern Africa.

to *Laos.* Ordinary person.

to *North Korea.* Province.

To'abaita *Solomon Islands.* Austronesian language.

Toala *Indonesia.* Austronesian language.

Toaripi *Papua New Guinea.* Papuan language.

Toba *Bolivia.* Indian group of *Guaicuruan* linguistic stock in Santa Cruz department.

Tobaru *Indonesia.* Papuan language.

Tobelo *Indonesia.* Papuan language.

Toda *India.* Pastoral and polyandrous tribe of Nilgiri Hills.

toea *Papua New Guinea.* Coin, ¹⁄₁₀₀ths of a KINA.

tojisa *South Korea.* Governor of a province.

Tojolabal *Mexico.* 1. Indian ethnic group. 2. MAYAN language.

Toka *Zambia.* BANTU tribe in south central region.

Tokelau *Tokelau.* Austronesian language.

Tokhi *Afghanistan.* GHILAZAI tribe.

toko *Indonesia.* Small Chinese store.

tokor *Senegal.* Chief of a matrilineage among the SERER.

tol *Ethiopia.* Tribe.

tola *India.* Unit of weight equal to about 180 grams, but varying widely.

Tolai *Papua New Guinea.* Austronesian language.

tolba *Mauritania.* Disciples of a SUFI MURABIT.

tolderia *Paraguay.* Native Indian village.

toldo *Spanish America.* Skin tent used by Indians.

tolitoli *Indonesia.* Austronesian language.

tolong-menolong *Indonesia.* Principle of reciprocal aid.

Toma *Guinea.* Ethnic group in Macenta region.

Tomaghera *Chad.* Teda clan of the TOUBOU.

Toma-Manian *Guinea.* Ethnic group.

Tomata *Bolivia.* Indian group in Potosi and Tarija departments.

Tombodji *Mozambique.* Ethnic group of the SHONA Karanga cluster.

tombo kalana *Madagascar.* Tattooing.

Tombulu *Indonesia.* Austronesian language.

Tomina *Bolivia.* Indian group in Chuquisaca department.

Tomini *Indonesia.* Austronesian language.

tonada *Spanish America* Music with slow-moving romantic songs and melancholy themes.

Tondanou *Indonesia* Austronesian language.

tonelada *Guatemala* Unit of measure equal to 20 quintals.

tong *Koreas.* Urban block, subdivision of a ward.

tonga *India* Light and small two-wheeled horse-drawn vehicle.

Tonga *Mozambique.* Ethnic group.

Tonga *Southern Africa* Niger-Kordofanian language.

Tonga *Zimbabwe.* BANTU speaking group between Malawi and South Africa.

Tongan *Tonga.* Austronesian language.

Tonghak *Korea.* Literally, Eastern learning. Indigenous religious movement, largely antiforeign, that spearheaded the rebellion of 1894. Later renamed CHONDOGYO.

tonguihak *Korea* Korean system of medicine stressing herbs and acupuncture.

Tongwe *Tanzania* Ethnic group.

tonnelle *Haiti.* Covered area of a VOODOO temple usually thatched with palm branches.

tono iilanero *Venezuela* Folk songs sung by cowboys of the plains.

Tonsea *Indonesia* Austronesian language.

Tontemboa *Indonesia* Austronesian language.

ton ton macoute *Haiti.* Literally, bogeymen. Francois Duvalier's secret police and informers who terrorized the population with a license to kill.

to nuu (plural: to nu wai) *Liberia* KPELLE term for wealthy man of high standing.

tooroBBe (singular: toorodo) *Senegal* Among the TOUCOLEURS, the highest stratum of society including rulers, religious leaders and free cultivators.

tope *Costa Rica* Ceiling for credit set by the Central Bank.

tope *India* 1. Grove or orchard. 2. Ancient Buddhist monument shaped like a dome.

topi *India* Hat, as a solar helmet.

Toposa *Sudan.* 1. Nilotic ethnic group of Equatoria. 2. Nilo-Saharan language.

Toradja *Indonesia* Ethnic group of Sulawesi.

Toraja-Sa'dan *Indonesia* Austronesian language.

torbellino *Colombia* Dance of the interior highlands.

tormenta *Uruguay.* Sudden swirling wind accompanied by thunderstorms.

Tornatra *Honduras* Offspring of an Albino father and a Spanish mother.

Toro *Uganda* Western BANTU ethnic group.

torodo (plural: torodbe) *Senegal.* Muslim teacher and leader.

toroguaco *Nicaragua.* Dance with 40 dancers and 17 costumed actors.

Toromona *Bolivia.* Amazon Indian group of TACANAN linguistic stock in La Paz department.

tortilla *Spanish America.* Thin, flat baked cake of cornmeal, usually prepared as a pliable dough called *massa.*

tortuga *Guatemala.* Drum made from turtle shell.

tosajo *Spanish America.* See CHARQUI.

totok *Indonesia.* Ethnic Chinese who are oriented more toward China than Indonesia.

Totonacan *Mexico.* Indian group in the central highlands.

Totonaco *Mexico.* Unaffiliated language.

totoposte *Guatemala.* Toasted TORTILLA, usually salted.

Toubou *Chad.* Literally, inhabitants of Tu or Tibesti. Collective name for various nomadic or seminomadic pastoralists in the north, especially Tibesti region. The two major tribes are TEDA and DAZA.

Toubouri *Chad.* Ethnic group in Fianga sousprefecture.

Toucoleur *Senegal and Gambia.* Niger-Kordofanian language.

Toucoleur *Senegal, Gambia and Mauritania.* Mixed SERER-PEUL group. Also, *Tokolor.*

toughu *Zambia.* Wage-earning or working woman.

touiza *Western Sahara.* Gathering of women to stitch the khalma or tent, and for any other work.

Toura *West Africa.* Niger-Kordofanian language.

toyacales *Guatemala.* Woman's headgear in the form of strands of woolen cords, twisted and braided in the hair with the ends falling down the sides of the face and the back of the head. Also, *tunkun, cintas.*

trabuco *Brazil.* Heavy shotgun used by backlands bandits.

trampolim *Brazil.* Springboard for social advancement.

tran *Vietnam.* Province.

transmigration *Indonesia.* Migration from overcrowded Java to the outer islands.

trau *Vietnam.* Mastication of BETEL, palm, lime and, sometimes, tobacco.

triangle *Southeast Asia.* Name given to a territory in eastern Burma and northern Thailand, which is a center of opium cultivation. Also, *Golden Triangle.*

Trieng *Vietnam.* Austro-Asiatic language.

trigeno *Nicaragua.* Dark brown MESTIZO.

trimpong *Bhutan.* Judicial officer in a district.

Tring *Vietnam.* Highland ethnic group in central region speaking a KOHO dialect.

Trios *Suriname.*   Amerindian tribe.

Tripitaka *Buddhist countries.*   Literally, three baskets. Collection of scriptures, embodying Buddha's teachings and oral traditions.

Tripuri *India.*   Sino-Tibetan language.

tronos *Guatemala.*   Litters for statues of saints or images carried by members of the COFRADIAS.

tropas *Bolivia.*   Privates in the army.

tropeiro *Brazil.*   Dealer in or driver of pack animals.

trotro *Ghana.*   MAMMY lorry, a truck carrying passengers and produce.

Trucial States *Middle East.*   Former name of the United Arab Emirates, so-called because they were bound by truces with the paramount British power.

Truk *Micronesia.*   Austronesian language.

truong toc *Vietnam.*   Head of an extended patrilineal family.

Tsaangi *Congo and Gabon.*   Niger-Kordofanian language.

tsahafi tezaz *Ethiopia.*   Royal scribe, keeper of the seal.

tsampa *Nepal.*   SHERPA food consisting of raw barley meal with milk, tea of GHEE, forming a gruel or mash.

tsantsa *Ecuador.*   Shrunken and dried human head used by the Jivaro Indians in their rituals.

Tshikwanga *Zaire.*   Boiled manioc wrapped in manioc leaves.

Tshong *Sikkim.*   Buddhist Nepali group.

Tsimihety *Madagascar.*   Northern ethnic group.

tsiny *Madagascar.*   Guilt or blame.

tsofo *Cameroon.*   Descendant of the companions of the founder, among the BAMILEKE.

Tsogo *Gabon.*   Niger-Kordofanian language.

Tsong *Sikkim.*   Ethnic group.

Tsonga *Mozambique.*   1. Ethnic group comprising RONGA, SHANGANA, TSWA and HLENGWE. 2. Niger-Kordofanian language.

Tsongdu *Bhutan.*   The National Assembly.

tsoro *Zimbabwe.*   Board game played with pebbles or pips in rows of holes.

Tswa or **Tsua** *Southern Africa.*   Northern subgroup of the TSONGA cluster, including *Vilankulu, Mukhambi, Hlabangwana, Masinge, Yingwana* and *Makakwa.*

Tswana *Southern Africa.*   1. BANTU-speaking people of the western Sotho group including the HURUTSHE, *Kalahari, Kgatla, Kwena, Malete, Ngwaketse, Ngwato, Rolong, Tswanam, Thlaping, Thlaro* and *Tlokwa.* Also, *Chuana.*

Tswapong *Botswana.*   1. Ethnic subgroup. 2. Niger-Kordofanian language.

tuan *Malaysia.*   Honorific used as a prefix meaning sir.

Tuareg *North Africa.* Partly Caucasoid and partly Negroid BERBER-speaking people who call themselves *Kel Tagilmus,* or people of the veil, referring to the narrow strip of cloth worn by men over the lower part of the face.

Tuba *Argentina.* Macro-Guaicuruan language.

tuba *Philippines.* Alcoholic drink made by fermenting sap of the coconut, nipa or buri palm.

tubab *Senegal.* White people or black people who adopt the white man's dress and customs.

tu dan *Vietnam.* Collective name for the four Vietnamese social classes: *si,* or scholars; *nong,* or farmers; *cong,* or craftsmen; and *thuong,* or merchants.

Tucyan *Burkina Faso.* LOBI ethnic group.

tu do tuong *Vietnam.* The four social evils: *tuu,* or wine; *sae,* or women; *ven,* or opium; and *ao,* or gambling.

tug (plural: tugag) *Somalia.* Seasonal freshet in a dry watercourse.

Tugen *Kenya.* Third largest KALENJIN group.

tugurio *Colombia.* Slum.

tui kanokupolu *Tonga.* Until 1845, the de-facto king of Tonga.

tui Tonga *Tonga.* King of Tonga.

Tukude *Indonesia.* Austronesian language.

tukul *Ethiopia.* Circular hut made of strong upright sticks set close together and struck into the ground.

Tukulor *West Africa.* Variant of TOUCOLEUR.

tul *Guatemala.* Rush or reed for making mats.

tula *Afghanistan.* Whistle flute.

Tula *West Africa.* Niger-Kordofanian language.

tuladan *Nepal.* Weighing a political or religious dignitary in silver or gold on special occasions.

tulafale *Western Samoa.* Literally, orator. Executive officer of a village.

tullal *India.* Form of MALAYALAM narrative poetry devised by Kunjan Nambiar.

tultogan *Philippines.* Bisayan bamboo drum.

tultul *Papua New Guinea.* Adviser representing local interests at the village level.

Tulu *India.* DRAVIDIAN language.

tulwar *India.* Curved saber used by the SIKHS.

tulwar *Indonesia.* Saber.

tum *Guatemala.* Indian musical instrument consisting of a section of a log used as a drum.

Tumbatu *Tanzania.* Tribe of mixed Afro-Asian origin.

Tumbuku *East Africa.* 1. Collective term for *Henga, Kamanga* and other ethnic groups. 2. Niger-Kordofanian language.

Tumbwe *Zaire.* Ethnic group.

tumo *Burma.* Village shaman among the AKHA.

tun *Central America.* 1. MAYA year of 360 days, divided into 18 months of 20 days each. 2. Percussion instrument made from a hollowed log.

tuna *Panama.* Street parade and carnival with music and dance.

Tunacho *Bolivia.* Indian group of ZAMUCOAN linguistic stock in CHACO.

tung gang *Philippines.* Alcoholic drink made from bahi palm in Manoba.

tungo *Sierra Leone.* KISSI house without walls.

Tunjur *Chad.* Ethnic group in Kanem and Ouadai.

Tunka *Senegal.* Title of the ruler of Gajaga Kingdom.

Tunni Torre *Somalia.* Non-Somali group in Brava.

tunsi *Tunisia.* Town dwellers.

Tupuri *West Africa.* Niger-Kordofanian language.

tunta *Bolivia.* Processed potato.

Tupamaros *Uruguay.* Castroite terrorists active during the 1960s and 1970s, named after Tupac Amaru, leader of the Inca revolt against Spain.

Tupian *South America.* Of or relating to TUPI, South American family of tribes and languages.

Tupi-Guarani *South America.* One of the major families of Indian languages distributed widely over Brazil, Chaco, Paraguay and the Plata estuary. In Chaco, Paraguay and Uruguay, it is identified as Guarani and elsewhere as Tupi. The former lingua franca, LINGUA GERAL, was derived from Tupi Guarani.

tur *Somalia.* Well, six to 12 feet deep, usually dug in the river sand or along the coast.

Turan *Afghanistan.* Major subdivision of the GHILZAI tribe.

Turco *Spanish America.* Any Middle Easterner.

Turka *Burkina Faso.* 1. SENUFO ethnic group in the southwest. 2. Niger-Kordofanian language.

Turkana *East Africa.* Nilo-Saharan language.

Turkana *Kenya.* Plains Eastern Nilotic speaking group.

Turke Turka *Burkina Faso.* Ethnic group of the SENUFO cluster.

Turkish *Turkey.* Ural-Altaic language.

Turkmans *Afghanistan.* Turkic-speaking nomadic people. Also Turkomans.

Turkmen *Iran and Afghanistan.* Ural-Altaic language.

Turku *Chad.* Pidgin Arabic.

Turno *Spanish America.* Parish festival for raising money with carnival, dances, MARIMBA music, bingo, etc.

Turu *Tanzania.* Ethnic group.

Tusyan *Burkina Faso.* Ethnic group of the LOBO cluster.

Tutsi *Rwanda and Burundi.*   Tall, angular, relatively light-skinned people who ruled both Rwanda and Burundi until Belgian rule and who are dominant in Burundi.

Tutura *Bolivia.*   Indian group in Cochabamba department.

Tuvalu *Tuvalu.*   Austronesian language.

Twa *Rwanda and Burundi.*   Pygmoid subgroup of Twide Pygmies.

Twi or **Twi Fante** *Ghana.*   AKAN ethnic group.

Tyapi *Guinea.*   Ethnic group in Gaoul region.

tyeddo *Gambia.*   Warriors serving a WOLOF or SERER king or chief selected from the *jam,* or slave class.

Tyefo *Burkina Faso.*   Ethnic group of the SENUFO cluster.

Tzeltal *Mexico.*   1. Indian group. 2. MAYAN language.

tzijolaj *Guatemala.*   Piccolo of cane or reed with three or four holes.

tzolkin *Guatemala.*   Sacred year of 260 days in the MAYAN calendar.

Tzotzil *Central America.*   1. MAYAN tribe. 2. MAYAN language.

Tzutuhil *Central America.*   1. MAYAN tribe. 2. MAYAN language.

tzute *Guatemala.*   Piece of decorated cloth worn by Indian women as part of the headdress, as a shawl or as a sling to carry their babies.

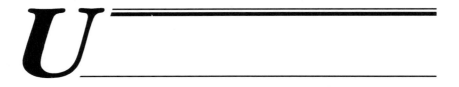

U *Burma.*   Term of address toward a man of learning or piety.

Uba *Brazil.*   Primitive canoe hollowed out of a tree trunk used by Amazonian tribes.

Ubaghara *West Africa.*   Niger-Kordofanian language.

Ubangi *Central Africa.*   Ethnic group of the Central Rain Forest.

Ubanguian *Central African Republic.*   Ethnic group including BAN-ZIRI, BOURANKA, SANGO and YAKAMA.

ubonei *Burma.*   Buddhist duty days.

ubugabire *Rwanda and Burundi.*   Clientship by which the HUTU indentured themselves to the TUTSI in a vassal-lord relationship in return for the use of Tutsi cattle.

ubuhake *Burubdi.*   See UBAGUBIRE.

ubukeberwa *Rwanda and Burundi.*   Land tenure involving free men who receive land for farming but may leave at will.

ubushikiwiza *Rwanda and Burundi.*   Obligation owed by the recipient of land for cultivation.

ubwatsi *Rwanda and Burundi.*   Pastureland or land set aside for food crops other than bananas, coffee or cash crops.

ubwoko *Rwanda and Burundi.*   Kinship group consisting of several lineages.

ud *Jordan.*   Large pear-shaped lute with a short neck and five double strings plucked with the quill of an eagle's feather. See OUD.

Uda or **Urha** *Nepal.*   Trading caste among the NEWARIS.

ude *Senegal.*   Leather workers among the WOLOF.

udekki *Sri Lanka.*   Dance of Kandy.

Uduk *Sudan.*   1. Ethnic group of Darfung. 2. Nilo-Saharan language.

Ugarano *Bolivia.*   Amazon Indian group of ZAMUCOAN language stock in CHACO.

ugas *Somalia.*   Title of chief or elder.

Uhunduni *Indonesia.*   Papuan language.

Uhuru *Tanzania.*   Freedom.

Uinal *Guatemala.*   Twenty-day month in the MAYAN calendar.

ujamaa *Tanzania.*   Literally, familyhood. National socialist ideology enunciated by former president Julius Nyerere implying collective virtues such as cooperation, respect for individual dignity, mutual consideration and common ownership of means of production.

Ukaon *West Africa.*   Niger-Kordofanian language.

Ukpe Bayobiri *West Africa.*   Niger-Kordofanian language.

Ukugidza *Swaziland.*   Communal dancing accompanied by singing and hand-clapping.

ukunywana *Rwanda and Burundi.*   Blood brotherhood.

Ukwuani-Aboh *West Africa.*   Niger-Kordofanian language.

ulama (singular: alim) *Islamic countries.*   Collective term for Muslim religious and legal scholars responsible for interpreting and determining the application of the SHARIA.

ulema *Arab countries.*   Religious leader. See MUTAWWT.

Uma *Zambia.*   Congolese LUNDA tribe in Luapula Valley.

ūmaganuro *Burundi.*   National festival of the sowing of the sorghum.

umara (singular: amir) *Persian Gulf.*   Power holders in government.

Umbanda *Brazil.*   Hybrid religion combining West African spiritism and Catholicism.

umbigada *Brazil.*   Navel-to-navel bump, a feature of butuque, forerunner of samba.

umda (plural: umad) *Egypt.*   Village headman.

umhlaba *Swaziland.*   Arable land, and by extension, people who farm such lands.

umhlanga *Swaziland.*   Week-long reed dance, an annual ceremony in June or July performed by unmarried girls.

umkhiso *Zimbabwe.*   SINDEBELE word for drizzly, misty weather.

umlisana *Zimbabwe.*   Subheadman among the NDEBELE.

umlungu *Zimbabwe.*   SINDEBELE for European.

umma *Islamic countries.*   The community of Islamic believers.

ummet *Turkey.*   Variant of UMMA.

umntfwana *Swaziland.*   Literally, child of the nation. Title of the heir to the throne following the death of the king.

umnumzana *Zimbabwe.*   NDBELE head of household.

Umr, Bani (singular: Ma'muri) *Oman.*   Tribe of Batinah Province.

umra *Saudi Arabia.*   Obligatory and prescribed rites for HAJ pilgrims, including circling the KAABAH, drinking from the sacred well of Zamzam and running between the hills of Safa and Marwa.

umrah *Saudi Arabia.*   Pilgrimage, lesser than the HAJ, which may be undertaken any time during the year.

umstakatsi (plural: batsakatsi) *Swaziland.*   Sorcerer.

umuganero *Burundi.*   National festival of the sowing of the sorghum.

umuganwa *Burundi.*   Chief or headman.

umuhamagazi *Burundi.*   Public announcer who transmits royal orders to the people.

umuhana *Rwanda.*   Local kin group.

umukungu *Rwanda.*   Head of an INZU, or group of male related families.

umulozi *Rwanda.*   Bewitchers.

umunta *Swaziland.*   Swazi older than three months, officially considered a person.

umupfumu *Burundi.*   Medicine man.

umuryango *Rwanda and Burundi.*   All married male members of a family and their wives plus their unmarried male and female children.

umushikiriza *Burundi.*   Executor of a judgment.

umusozi *Rwanda and Burundi.*   Literally, hill. Social and economic division of a district comprised of all the families living on a hill and the surrounding villages.

umutahl *Rwanda and Burundi.*   Judicial official who summons parties.

umuteguro *Rwanda and Burundi.*   Ceremony marking the passage of a chief's cattle over a pasture.

umuti *Swaziland.*   Homestead or a small village.

umutumbuzi *Rwanda and Burundi.*   Female chief or deputy chief.

umuzi (plural: imizi) *Zimbabwe.*   NDEBELE homestead.

umvuleka (plural: imivuleka) *Zimbabwe.*   Warlike spirit or rebellion.

umwami *Burundi.*   Literally, the king is dead, long live the king. Permanence of the monarchy as an institution.

umwariho *Rwanda and Burundi.*   Administrative official of a king or chief.

umwimbu *Rwanda and Burundi.*   Land tax, usually a basket of millet and two jugs of beer.

unani *Islamic countries.*   Muslim system of medicine.

undi *Zambia.*   Title of the chief.

Unga *Zambia.*   Congolese LUNDA tribe in Luapula Valley.

unpersonales *Uruguay.*   Verse drama enacted by a solo player.

unitaria *Venezuela.*   One-room school.

untfwanenkosi *Swaziland.*   Prince as a head of a SIVE.

untouchable *India.*   In Hinduism, a social outcast who is below and outside the caste system and whose presence is believed to contaminate the higher castes. Also, since independence, scheduled caste.

up *North Korea.*   Town.

upadhyaya *India and Nepal.*   Reciter and teacher of the Hindu SASTRAS, below the rank of an ACHARYA.

upanayana *India.*   In Hinduism, tying of the sacred thread around a BRAHMIN's chest signifying his twice-born status.

Upanishads *India.*   Literally, sitting close to, in the sense of a group sitting around a teacher. Philosophical treatises or speculative commentaries attached to the BRAHMANAs providing the underpinnings of Vedic religion. They consists of over 100 texts, the oldest of which antedate 500 B.C. The most important are the Aitareya and Kausitaki in Rig Veda, Chhandogya and Kena in Sama Veda, and Taittiria, Svetsvatara, Bribhadaranyaka, Isha, Prasana, Manduka and Mandukya in Yajur Veda.

uparaja *Thailand.*   Heir apparent.

upazin *Burma.*   Assistant or junior monk.

up chang *Korea.*   Town chief.

uposatha *Thailand.*   *See* BOT.

up pradhan panchyat *Nepal.*   Deputy chief of PANCHAYAT.

uqqal (singular: aqil) *Syria.*   The initiated among the DRUZES.

urad *Somalia.*   Literally, firstborn. Putative descendant of the original clan treatymakers among the SAAB.

Urdu *Pakistan and India.*   Indo-European language, derived from Hindustani, but written in Arabic script and spoken principally by Muslims.

urf *Arab countries.*   Unwritten tribal codes of conduct.

Urhobo *Nigeria.*   EDO-speaking ethnic group in Bendel State.

Urhobo *West Africa.*   Niger-Kordofanian language.

uro *Togo.*   Title of the paramount chief of the KOTOKOLI.

urs *South Asia.*   Among Muslims, anniversary of a PIR's death.

Uru *Bolivia.*   Indian group of PUQUINAN linguistic stock.

urumba *Malawi.*   Hunter's dance of TUMBUKU ethnic group.

urupfu *Rwanda.*   Rituals connected with death.

usal al din *Shiite countries.* Five cardinal pillars of Shiite faith: *tawhid,* divine unit; *nubuwwah,* prophecy; *maad,* resurrection; *imamah,* belief in imams; and *aal,* divine justice.

usarios *Colombia.* Users of government agricultural service.

usendo (plural: izinsendo) *Zimbabwe.* NDEBELE term for clan.

Ushi *Zambia.* Congolese LUNDA tribe in Luapula Valley.

usina *Brazil.* Sugar refinery.

Uspantec *Central America.* Language group, part of the QUICHEAN linguistic stock.

Uspantec *Honduras.* MAYA tribe.

utang no loob *Philippines.* Literally, debt inside oneself. System of reciprocal obligations.

Utani *Bolivia.* Social status of young AYMARAS who, upon marriage, are granted a share of the communal land.

utaybah *Saudi Arabia.* Tribe.

Utaztecan *Nicaragua.* American Indian language family including NICAROS and SIGUAS.

uteis *Brazil.* Colonial era militia units.

Utugwang *West Africa.* Niger-Kordofanian language.

Uzbek *Afghanistan.* 1. Turkic-speaking people, the greater majority of whom live in the Soviet Union. 2. Ural-Altaic language.

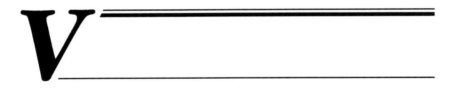

Va *Burma.* Northern upland MON-KHMER ethnolinguistic group.

vada modi *Sri Lanka.* Northern Indian drama.

vadzimu (singular: mudzimu) *Zimbabwe.* Among the SHONA, spirits representing departed ancestors.

Vagala *Burkina Faso.* Ethnic group on Ghanaian border related to GOUROUNSI.

Vagala *Ghana.* GRUSI group related to MO, SISALA and TAMPOLENSE.

vahalkadas *Sri Lanka.* Frontispiece in a STUPA.

vahiny *Madagascar.* Stranger.

Vai *Liberia.* Northern MANDE-speaking people in Grand Cape Mount.

Vai *Sierra Leone.* Ethnic group, speaking a MANDE language.

Vai *West Africa.* Niger-Kordofanian language.

vaidya *India.* AYURVEDIC physician.

Vaikino *Indonesia.* Austronesian language.

Vaiphei *India.* Sino-Tibetan language.

vairagi *India.* In Hindu philosophy, one devoid of passion.

Vaiseshika *India.* One of the six orthodox systems of Hindu philosophy founded in the third century B.C. by Kanada. It strives to explain the physical world in rational terms.

Vaishnavaism *India.* Hindu sect devoted to Vishnu, the preserver in the Hindu pantheon. It became a major force by emphasizing mysticism.

Vaishnavite *India.* Adherent of VAISHNAVAISM.

vaisya *India.* Third of the four castes in the Hindu caste system, comprising traders.

vakil *India.* Lawyer.

vali *Turkey.* A ruler of a VILAYET.

valih *Madagascar.* Harp-like musical instrument formed by stretching strings across a curved piece of bamboo.

vamachara *India.* In Hinduism, left-handed TANTRISM.

vamsavali *Nepal.* Legendary histories of dynasties.

van kieu *Vietnam.* MON-KHMER-speaking highland ethnic group in central region, extending to the Laotian border.

vannam *Sri Lanka.* Solo dance.

vaqueiro *Brazil.* Cowboy in the northeast, usually a CABOCLO. Also, *vaquero.*

var *Somalia.* Man-made pool or catchment area for collecting rainwater.

vara *Spanish America.* Unit of length equal to 32.9 inches.

Varama *Gabon.* People related to ESHIRA.

varan *Sri Lanka.* Delegation of divine authority to lesser beings in Buddhism.

varatty *India.* Cake of dry cow dung, used for fuel.

varna *India.* Caste system.

vas *Sri Lanka.* In Buddhism, evil power that affects people through evil eye *(asvaka),* evil mouth *(katavaha)* and evil thoughts *(hovaha).*

vatan *Turkey.* Fatherland.

vatapa *Brazil.* Afro-Brazilian dish with manioc powder, dende oil, pepper, peanuts, and meat or fish.

Vazaha *Madagascar.* Europeans, especially the French.

vecindaddes *Mexico.* Tenements.

vecino *Bolivia.* CAMPESINO who migrated to the city and adopted urban life-styles opposed to his Indian heritage.

Vedanta *India.* Literally, the goal of the VEDAS. The most famous of the six systems of Hindu philosophy founded by Badarayana. Its three main branches are the monism of Sankaracharya, the qualified monism of Ramanuja and the dualism of Madhva.

Vedas *India.*   Corpus of Hindu religious Scriptures including hymns, prayers, ritualistic instructions, philosophy, mythology and holy lore. There are some 100 books in all, of which the four principal ones are Rig Veda, Sama Veda, Yajur Veda and Atharva Veda. Each Veda is further divided into four parts: samhita, or collected hymns; Brahmanas, or directions for sacrificial rites; Aranyakas, or speculative texts for recluses; and Upanishads, or philosophical treatises.

Veddahs *Sri Lanka.*   Aboriginal inhabitants of the island.

Vedic *India.*   Of or relating to the Vedas, or Hindu scriptures, especially the age in which the Vedas were compiled.

Vedina or **Buduma** *Chad.*   Ethnic group.

vega *Southern Africa.*   Open tract or fertile plain.

velario *Bolivia.*   Funeral vigil.

vellala *India.*   TAMIL high-caste Hindu.

venado *Guatemala.*   The dance of the deer, lasting from one to 15 days.

venda *Brazil.*   Colonial store.

Venda *Zaire.*   1. Ethnic group. 2. Niger-Kordofanian language.

Venda *Zimbabwe.*   BANTU-speaking ethnic group.

ventimilli *Libya.*   Former Italian settlers.

venu *India.*   *See* BANSRI.

veranda *India.*   Open-pillared gallery around a house.

verano *Guatemala.*   The summer dry season from November through April.

Veracruzano *Central America.*   MAYA tribe.

Vere *West Africa.*   Niger-Kordofanian language.

verin *Maldives.*   Chief of an atoll.

ves *Sri Lanka.*   Dance of Kandy.

vestibular *Brazil.*   National university entrance examination.

vestido *Mexico.*   Formal Western dress.

veziriazam *Turkey.*   Grand vizier.

viandas *Cuba.*   Tubers with no exact English equivalent.

Vidhan Parishad *India.*   State Legislative Council.

Vidhan Sabha *India.*   State Legislative Assembly.

Vidri *Central African Republic.*   BANDA ethnic group.

Vidunda *Tanzania.*   1. Ethnic group of Kilosa. 2. Niger-Kordofanian language.

Vietnamese *Vietnam.*   Austro-Asiatic language.

Vigala *West Africa.*   GRUSI ethnic group.

vigilenga *Brazil.*   One-masted sailboat plying the Middle Amazon.

Vigye *Burkina Faso.*   Ethnic group of LOBO cluster.

vihara *Buddhist countries.*   Buddhist monastery.

vihia *Cambodia.* Buddhist temple or sanctuary in a WAT.

vihuela *Colombia.* Seven-stringed guitar.

vila *Brazil.* State-funded housing.

vilayet *Turkey.* Province ruled by a VALI.

Vili *Congo.* Subgroup of the KONGO.

Vili *Gabon and Angola.* Ethnic group.

villa *Central America.* Small town larger than a PUEBLO.

villas miserias *Argentina.* Literally, misery towns. Squatter settlements.

ville de province *Haiti.* Provincial town.

villes nouvelles *Morocco.* Literally, new towns. Modern part of an old city.

vimbuza *Malawi.* Dance to expel evil spirits among the TUMBUKU, TONGA and CHEWA.

vina *India.* Lute with seven strings, a curved neck and two large gourds used as resonating chambers, popular in south India.

vinaya *Burma.* Code of conduct for Buddhist monastic order with 227 rules.

vinta *Philippines.* MORO square-sailed outrigger canoe.

vintana *Madagascar.* Fate ordered by the position of the sun, moon and stars.

vinyao *Malawi.* Initiation ceremony of CHEWA and NYANJI boys.

Vinza *Tanzania.* Ethnic group.

Violencia, la *Colombia.* Protracted civil strife from 1948 through the 1950s, ended by the Declaration of SITGES.

viraha *Sri Lanka.* Love songs.

Vishnu *India.* The third god in the Hindu trinity, considered as the destroyer of the universe, as distinguished from Brahma the creator and Siva the sustainer.

visita *Spanish America.* Visit of a parish priest to an outside parish without a regular priest.

viss *India.* Unit of weight equal to 3 lb and 2 oz.

viviendas *Ecuador.* Housing unit.

vivientes *Bolivia.* Common laborers who perform odd jobs for ARRENDEROS.

volantes *Brazil.* Flying columns of police troops used to comb the backlands against bandits between 1920 and 1930.

vong co *Vietnam.* Type of gong used in modern theater.

vo-nghe *Vietnam.* Martial art.

Voodoo *Haiti.* Occult religion of Beninese origin, widely practiced even by formal Catholics.

voto do cabresto *Brazil.* Literally, halter vote. Voting under instructions from local political bosses or CORONELS.

Voungou *Gabon.* Ethnic group related to the ESHIRA.

Vru *Bolivia.* PUQUINA-speaking Indian group.
vua *Vietnam.* Royal title of former kings.
vuelta mani *Chile.* Strictly reciprocal exchange of labor among the
  MAPUCHE.
Vute *West Africa.* Niger-Kordofanian language.

Wa *Burma.* Austro-Asiatic language.
wa *Burma.* Rainy season from July to October, which coincides with
  the Buddhist holy season when few secular activities are openly permitted.
Waama *West Africa.* Niger-Kordofanian language.
wabenzi *Kenya.* Wealthy, conspicuous consumers.
Wa-Boni *Somalia.* Group of hunters and fishermen along the southern coast and in the Gado region.
wacha-wacha *Congo.* Native dance.
Waci-Gbe *West Africa.* Niger-Kordofanian language.
waddad (plural: waddado) *Somalia.* Religious functionary in an Islamic brotherhood, who serves as scribe, judge or master of ceremonies.
Waddar *India.* DRAVIDIAN language.
wadi (plural qwdiyah or widyan) *Arab countries.* Generally dry watercourse.
Wagdi *India.* Indo-European language.
wagan *Ethiopia.* Relatives by blood or marriage.
Wa-Gosha *Somalia.* Literally, people of the forest. Negroid people on
  the Juba River banks.
Wahadimu *Tanzania.* Ethnic group in Zanzibar.
Wahgi *Papua New Guinea.* Papuan language.
Wahhabi *Arab countries.* Puritanical Islamic sect of fundamental-
  ists founded by Muhammad ibn Abdul Wahab, known originally as
  Muwahiddun, or Unitarians. It is the dominant sect in Saudi
  Arabia.
Wahibah, Yal (singular: Wahibi) *Oman.* Nomadic tribe.
Wahidi *Yemens.* Ethnic group.

wai *Thailand.* Traditional greeting in which palms are placed together, fingers slightly bent forward toward each other and inward, in front of the chest, with head bowed.

Waigeli *Afghanistan.* Indo-European language.

Waiwai *Guyana.* CARIB-speaking Amerindian tribe.

waiyawachakon *Thailand.* Lay member or bursar in a WAT.

Waja *West Africa.* Niger-Kordofanian language.

wajang *Indonesia.* Fantasy drama in which puppets and/or people portray gods and kings. Its various forms include *wajang kulit,* with stick puppets; *wajang kolek,* with wooden puppets; *wajang oreng,* with people; and *wajang toping,* with masks.

wakf *Islamic countries.* Religious trust property administered by the state or religious institutions.

wala *Cameroon.* Descendants of servants of the FON, among the BAMILEKE.

walayat *Shiite countries.* Ability to interpret the inner mysteries of the Koran.

Walaytta *Ethiopia.* Afro-Asiatic language.

Walbe *Ghana.* MOLE-DANGBANE ethnic group.

wali (plural wulah) *Arab countries.* Representative of a ruler.

wali *Pakistan.* Preceptor in a SUFI order.

waliah *Malaysia.* Religious district.

walikoten *Indonesia.* Mayor.

walla *India.* (Person) engaged in practicing the profession of, or trading, or native of; as in competitionwalla, JUTKAwalla, Kabuliwalla. Also, *wallah.*

Wallisian *New Caledonia.* Polynesian language.

Walo (singular: walo) *Ghana.* MOLE-DAGBANE group who speak Wale or Wali.

walo *Senegal.* Alluvial floodplain.

WambaaBe (singular: bambaalDo) *Senegal.* Upper caste of GRIOTS among the TOUCOLEURS.

wamsa *India.* Caste.

Wan *West Africa.* Niger-Kordofanian language.

wananchi *Kenya.* Common people.

Wanda *Tanzania.* Ethnic group.

Wangara *Ghana.* MANDE merchants, often called DYULA.

wangara *West Africa.* Urban quarters inhabited by strangers. Also, *zongo, maro.*

Wanji *Tanzania.* 1. Ethnic group. 2. Niger-Kordofanian language.

wan khao phansa *Thailand.* First day of the rainy season.

wan phra *Thailand.* Holy days in the Buddhist calendar. Also *uposalha.*

Wapemba *Tanzania.*   Ethnic group.

Wapisiana *Guyana.*   Arawak-speaking Amerindian tribe.

Wara *Burkina Faso.*   Ethnic group of the SENUFO cluster.

Waranle *Somalia.*   Literally, spear carrier. Pastoral people with martial traditions.

Warao *Venezuela.*   Macro-CHIBCHAN language.

Waray-Waray *Philippines.*   1. Ethnic group in Visayan Province. 2. Austronesian language.

wari *Haiti.*   Draught game of West African origin.

waris or **waris jaub** *Malaysia.*   All persons related by blood or marriage.

waris dekat *Malaysia.*   Close relatives consisting of one's own nuclear family.

Warji *West Africa.*   Afro-Asiatic language.

warra *Ethiopia.*   Family among the GALLA.

Warrau *Venezuela and Suriname.*   Indian tribe.

Wasa *Ghana.*   TWI ethnic group.

washint *Ethiopia.*   Simple fife with four holes. Also, *shambako.*

Wasi *Tanzania.*   Afro-Asiatic language.

Waskia *Papua New Guinea.*   Papuan language.

Wassa *Ghana.*   Major AKAN group.

Wassalunka *Mali.*   Small ethnic group in southwest, related to the PEUL.

wat *Ethiopia.*   Thick, highly spiced sauce eaten with INJERA.

wat *Thailand.*   Buddhist temple-monastery complex.

watan *Algeria.*   Subdivision of a Turkish BEYLIK or province.

wataniyah *Arab countries.*   Nationalism.

Watumbatu *Tanzania.*   Ethnic group in Zanzibar.

wayang *Malaysia.*   Variant of WAJANG.

wayiBe (singular: baylo) *Senegal.*   Metalworker caste among the TOU-COLEURS.

wazara *Arab countries.*   Cabinet.

wazir (plural: wuzara) *Arab countries.*   Cabinet minister. Properly, adviser or confidant of a king.

Waziris *Afghanistan.*   Tribe along the Khyber Pass.

wazo *Burma.*   Festival marking the commencement of the Buddhist Lent.

wedenga *Zimbabwe.*   CHISHONA for supreme spirit.

wee *Liberia.*   Ethnic group related to SAPO in Nimba, Grand Gideh and Sinoh counties.

weina dega *Ethiopia.*   Temperate zone, including greater portion of the high plateau.

wend pous neba *Burkina Faso.*   Name of traditional animist religion.

werd *Mauritania.*   Initiation into an Islamic brotherhood.

wereda *Ethiopia.*   District.

wesak *Sri Lanka.*   Buddhist festival.

wes-kos *Cameroon.*   Variety of pidgin English along the West African coast in Senegal.

Wetawit *Sudan and Ethiopia.*   Nilo-Saharan language.

weton *Indonesia.*   Coming-out day for a baby on the seventh and 35th days after birth.

Wewewa *Indonesia.*   Austronesian language.

weyzero *Ethiopia.*   Title of a high noble woman.

white elephant *Burma.*   Term applied to imperial power and sovereignty.

wi *Burma.*   Religious practitioner among the KARENS.

wibas *Tunisia.*   Unit of measure equal to 0.35 hectoliters.

Widekum *Cameroon.*   Western highland ethnic group.

wihan *Burma.*   Hall for worship or preaching in a WAT.

wilaya (plural: wilayaat) *Arab countries.*   Province.

wilaya *Islamic countries.*   Friendship and cooperation among believers in Islam.

wilayism *Arab countries.*   Parochialism in politics, placing local interests before nation.

Wile *Burkina Faso.*   Ethnic group of the MOSSI cluster.

winyan *Thailand.*   In Buddhism, ego-soul.

Wiru *Papua New Guinea.*   Papuan language.

wiwonhoe *North Korea.*   Committee.

wizarat *Afghanistan.*   Cabinet ministry.

Wobe *West Africa.*   Niger-Kordofanian language.

woleswal *Afghanistan.*   Governor of a WOLESWALI.

woleswali *Afghanistan.*   District, or subdivision of a district.

Wolio *Indonesia.*   Austronesian language.

Wolof *West Africa.*   1. Sudanic speaking ethnic group. 2. Niger-Kordofanian language.

Wom *West Africa.*   Niger-Kordofanian language.

won *South Korea.*   Monetary unit.

Wonbulgyo *South Korea.*   Syncretic version of traditional Buddhism, founded in 1924. Also, *Round Buddhism.*

Woolwas *Nicaragua.*   Indian tribe on the eastern Caribbean slopes.

worr *Chad.*   A divinatory system using numbers, among the SARA.

woumbou *Gabon.*   BAKOTA-speaking ethnic group.

Wouri *Cameroon.*   Coastal ethnic group.

Woyo *Angola.*   KONGO subgroup.

wudang *Burma.*   KACHIN sacrificial posts of rough-hewn softwood in front of a house.

wujaq *Algeria.*   Turkish military force of Janissaries.

wulomo *Ghana.*   GA high priest.

wundanhmu *Burma.*   Any government official.

wunde *Sierra Leone.*   Secret society among the KPE MENDE and TEMNE noted for its martial training.

Wungu *Tanzania.*   Ethnic group.

wuqesa *Ethiopia.*   Skilled physician.

wura *Ghana.*   Suffix for chief in *Gonja.*

Wuthisapha *Thailand.*   Senate; the upper house of parliament.

wutmye wun *Burma.*   Commissioner of ecclesiastical lands in precolonial times.

Wuzlam *Cameroon.*   Afro-Asiatic language.

Wynanas *Suriname.*   Amerindian tribe.

Xa *Vietnam.*   Ethnic group in Tay-Bac Autonomous Region.

xa *Vietnam.*   Village.

xaca *Guatemala.*   Dark bread made from whole wheat and brown sugar.

xalifa *Senegal.*   WOLOF and PULAR term for the head of the Muslim community. Derived from KALIFA.

Xamaro *Bolivia.*   Amazon Indian group of CHIQUITOAN linguistic stock in Santa Cruz.

Xamtanga *Ethiopia.*   AGEW-speaking ethnic group.

Xanga *Mozambique.*   Ethnic group of the SHONA Karanga cluster. Also, CHANGA.

xango *Brazil.*   Afro-Brazilian VOODOO cult.

Xaquese *Bolivia.*   Amazon Indian group in Beni department.

Xariono *Bolivia.*   Amazon Indian group in Santa Cruz department.

Xaray *Bolivia.*   Amazon Indian group in Beni department.

xa truong *Vietnam.*   Village chief.

xemia *Laos.*   Priest-king of the Lao Theung.

Xhosa *Southern Africa.*   Ethnic group.

xicalancas *Mexico.*   Painted gourd bowl used by Indians.

Xirima *Mozambique.*   Ethnic group of the MAKUA-Lomue cluster.

xu *Vietnam.*   Coin, 1/100ths of a DONG.

xuxu *Brazil.*   Pale green vegetable, called chayote in English.

Yaaku *Kenya.* Ethnic group inhabiting Mukogodo forest.

Ya'aqib (singular: Ya'qubi) *Oman.* Tribe of al-Dahirah Province.

Ya'aribah, al (singular: Ya'rubi) *Oman.* Small tribe.

yabu *Afghanistan.* Pack pony of the TURKMANS.

yadu *Burma.* Form of poetic composition.

Yafa *Yemens.* Interior tribe.

yag *Guyana.* Festival of thanks for the recovery of a sick child.

Yagaria *Papua New Guinea.* Papuan language.

yagligures *Turkey.* Greased wrestling, national sport of Turkey.

yagout *Western Sahara.* One of the four TEKNA tribes.

yai *Vietnam.* See DAO.

yajna *India.* Ritual worship invoking divine blessings.

yajoka *Ethiopia.* Tribal high court among the GURAGE.

Yaka *Angola.* KONGO subgroup.

yaka *Zaire.* Ethnic group of southern savanna.

Yaka *Southwestern Africa.* Niger-Kordofanian language.

Yakan *Philippines.* 1. MORO group in Sulu and Zamboanga. 2. Austronesian language.

Yakha *Nepal.* Division of RAI ethnic group.

Yakoma *Central African Republic.* UBANGUIAN group.

yal *Arab countries.* Family, used as a prefix to tribal names.

yala *Sri Lanka.* Secondary growing season for paddy.

Yala *West Africa.* Niger-Kordofanian language.

Yalna *Chad.* Subgroup of the HADJERAY.

Yalunka *Sierra Leone.* 1. Ethnic group, branch of the SUSU. Also, *Dialonke, Jallonke.* 2. Niger-Kordofanian language.

Yaly *Indonesia.* Papuan language.

yamazat *Burma.* Puppet show.

Yamba *Cameroon.* Niger-Kordofanian language.

Yampara *Bolivia.* Indian group of Chiquisaca department.

yana *Ghana.* Paramount chief of the DAGOMBA.

yanacona *Bolivia.* Member of an urban class of servants and artisans.

Yanadi *India.* DRAVIDIAN language.

Yanamano *Brazil.* Amerindian tribe, also known as *Guaharibo* or *Waika.*

yanapero *Ecuador.* Indian permitted to shelter and graze his animals on a HACIENDA in return for services.

yancunu *Honduras.*   BLACK CARIB ceremonial dance with masks set to African music.

Yandang *West Africa.*   Niger-Kordofanian language.

yangban *Korea.*   Civil and military bureaucracy or nobility.

Yangbye *Burma.*   Austro-Asiatic language.

yang di pertuan agong *Malaysia.*   National paramount rulers elected for five-year terms from among the hereditary rulers of the nine Malay states.

yang di pertuan besar *Malaysia.*   Ruler of Negeri Sembilan.

yang di pertuan negara *Malaysia.*   Ruler of Sabah.

Yang-Mbun *Zaire.*   Ethnic group of southern savanna.

Yanomamo *Venezuela.*   Indian language.

Yans *Zaire.*   1. Ethnic group. 2. Niger-Kordofanian language.

Yao *Southern Africa.*   1. Muslim ethnic group. 2. Niger-Kordofanian language.

Yao *Thailand.*   Hill people. Also, *lu Mien.*

Yaoure *West Africa.*   Niger-Kordofanian language.

yapa *Bolivia.*   Bonus offered by a trader.

Yaqay *Indonesia.*   Papuan language.

Yaqui *Mexico.*   1. Azteco-Tanoan language. 2. Indian tribe speaking this language.

Yarahmadzai *Iran.*   BALUCHI ethnic group.

Yaravi *Ecuador.*   Sierra Indian music of five-tone scale.

yarse (singular: yarga) *Ghana.*   Itinerant merchant.

Yarse *West Africa.*   Ethnic group.

Yas, Bani (singular: Yasi) *Oman.*   Tribe of eastern Arabia.

yasana *Fiji.*   One of the 14 provinces under the Fijian Affairs Board.

yashmak *Turkey.*   Double veil worn by women.

Yatenga *Burkina Faso.*   Ethnic group of the MOSSI cluster.

yavusa *Fiji.*   Cluster of MATAQALIS united by shared inheritance from an ancient progenitor or by historical traditions or alliances.

yaylaq *Iran.*   Summer camp of the nomads.

Yazidi *Iraq.*   Religious group whose pantheon of gods includes Satan in the form of a peacock.

ye *Burma.*   Shifting cultivation practiced in dry areas.

yein pwe *Burma.*   Ballet in ZAT PWE classical drama.

yeismo *Argentina.*   Spanish accent called Rio Platense, in which vowels are thickened and "ll" and "y" are pronounced like the English "j".

Yeke *Zaire.*   Ethnic group of southern savanna.

yeke-yeke *West Africa.*   *See* ADOSA.

Yekhee *West Africa.*   Niger-Kordofanian language.

Yela *Zaire.*   1. Ethnic group. 2. Niger-Kordofanian language.

Yemba-Nwe *Cameroon.*   Niger-Kordofanian language.

yen lao *Vietnam.* Village feast or celebration in honor of senior citizens.

Yerava *India.* DRAVIDIAN language.

yerbajero *Bolivia.* Herder who tends another's flock for 10 percent of lambs born during his service.

yerbales *Paraguay.* Groves of yerba trees from which YERBA MATE is made.

yerba mate *Southern America.* Paraguay tea, national drink in Paraguay and Argentina.

Yerukala *India.* DRAVIDIAN language.

Yeskwa *West Africa.* Niger-Kordofanian language.

yeti *Nepal.* Abominable snowman of the Himalayas.

yeye *Guinea.* French-style popular music, once banned by Sekou Toure.

Yeye *Botswana.* Niger-Kordofanian language.

ygabas *Paraguay.* Long canoe made from logs, used by GUARANI Indians.

Yilo Krobo *Ghana.* A branch of the KROBO ADANGBE.

Yira *Zaire.* Ethnic group of eastern highlands.

yiri *Ghana.* Family compound in Upper and Northern Regions.

yochol *South Korea.* Ceremonies and rituals as an ingredient in harmonious social relationships.

yodaya *Thailand.* Classical music.

yoga *India.* One of the six orthodox systems of Hindu philosophy founded by Sage Yajnavalkya in the second century B.C., divided into *Karma* (work), *Bhakti* (faith), *Jnana* (knowledge), *Mantra* (spells) and three dealing with physical exercise, *Laya, Hatha* and *Raja.*

Yogad *Philippines.* 1. Ethnic group in Luzon. 2. Austronesian language.

yogi *India.* In Hinduism, practitioner of any of the YOGAS, generally an ascetic.

yoke thay *Burma.* Marionette or puppet show.

Yombe *Angola.* Subgroup of the KONGO.

yondo *Chad.* Intensely painful initiation rite of puberty for boys among the SARA.

Yoruba *West Africa.* 1. One of the largest ethnic groups in Africa divided into over 20 subgroups including *Oyo, Egba, Iketu, Obori, Egbado, Ijebu, Ife, Ijesha, Igbomina, Ondo* and *Ekiti.* Yoruba deities are important in Afro-Cuban and Afro-Brazilian cults. Also, *Anago, Nagot.* 2. Niger-Kordofanian language.

Yucatec *Mexico.* MAYAN ethnic group.

Yucateco *Mexico.* MAYAN language.

Yuddhisthiraera *India.* See KALI YUGA.

yuga *India.* One of the four ages of mankind: Kriti Yuga, Treta Yuga, Dvapara Yuga and Kali Yuga, or the present age. Four yugas make one maha yuga, or 4.32 million solar years and 2,000 mahayugas, or 8.64 billion years, make one kalpa, or day of the creator.

yuil sasang or **hyongmyong sasang** *North Korea.* The one and only (communist) ideology.

yuk *Thailand.* Large statues or sculptures of mythological giants in WATS.

Yumbo *Ecuador.* Indians descended from Panzaleo tribe on the western slopes of the Andes in the Oriente.

Yumbri *Burma* Northern upland ethnic group of Proto-Mongoloid racial stock speaking a MON-KHMER language.

Yungur *West Africa.* Niger-Kordofanian language.

Yurcacare *Bolivia.* Amazon Indian group in Cochabamba and Santa Cruz.

yurt *Afghanistan.* Light circular tent of the nomads, a collapsible frame with a door in the sidewall and a hole in the conical top to serve as a chimney, covered with light straw matting in summer and felt in winter.

Yuruks *Turkey.* Nomadic Turks.

Yusufzai *Afghanistan.* Minor tribal confederation near the Pakistan border.

yuvaraja *India.* Heir apparent.

ywa *Burma.* Village.

Zabrama *Ghana.* SONGHAI ethnic group. Also DJERMA-SONGHAI.

zacate *Guatemala.* Hay or grass.

Zadran *Afghanistan.* GHILAZAI tribe.

zafan *Ethiopia.* Literally, to balance. Various types of songs, as *zafan awarada* or high-pitched songs by women, or *zafan engurguro,* or quietly hummed chants.

zafra *Spanish America.* Sugarcane harvest.

zagat *Burma.* Public rest house.

Zaghawa *Chad and Sudan.* 1. Ethnic group. 2. Nilo-Saharan language.

zaim *Algeria.* Influential Islamic leader or political boss.

zaim *Saudi Arabia.* Brigadier in the Saudi army.

zaire *Zaire.* Monetary unit.

zakat *Islamic countries.*   Tax sanctioned by the Koran, usually about 2 percent of income, levied on all adult Muslims for charitable purposes.

zalul *Saudi Arabia.*   Racing camel.

zamad *Ethiopia.*   Blood kin.

zamba *Ecuador*   MESTIZO music with syncopated melodies.

Zambal *Philippines.*   Christian ethnic group.

Zambezi cluster *Southern Africa.*   Collective name for ethnic groups in Malawi, Zambia, Zimbabwe and Mozambique.

zamindar *India.*   Under British rule, large landholder with tax collection powers. Thus, zamindari, land held by a zomindar.

zamindari *India.*   Landed estates held by ZAMINDARS.

zamorin *India.*   Title of the Hindu MAHARAJA of Calicut (Kozhikode).

Zamucoan *Bolivia.*   Major language family in Chaco.

Zanaiki *Tanzania.*   Niger-Kordofanian language.

Zanaki *Tanzania.*   Ethnic group.

Zande *Central African Republic.*   Ethnic group whose ancestors founded the Zande Empire.

Zande *Zaire.*   1. Ethnic group of southern savanna. 2. Niger-Kordofanian language.

zanderij *Guyana.*   White sand.

Zandoma *Burkina Faso.*   Ethnic group of MOSSI cluster.

Zangberese (singular: Zangbeo) *Ghana.*   Name for the HAUSA in the northwest.

zanja *Spanish America.*   Irrigation canal or ditch.

zansi (plural: abezanzi) *Zimbabwe.*   SINDEBELE term for the south or southern people.

Zao *Vietnam.*   See DAO.

zaouia *Mauritania.*   Core territory of each of the Islamic brotherhoods. Also, ZAWIYA.

Zaparos *Ecuador.*   Indian tribe of the Oriente.

zapato *Sapnish America.*   Tap dance.

Zapotec *Mexico.*   Ethnic group of the southern highlands.

Zapoteco *Mexico.*   Oto-Manguean language.

zar *Ethiopia.*   Evil spirit.

zar *Iron.*   Unit of length equal to 100 cm.

Zaramo *Tanzania.*   Ethnic group in Dar es Salaam.

zariba *Somalia.*   Thornbush enclosure for animals.

zarzuela *Philippines.*   Kind of folk opera in three acts.

zat pwe *Burma.*   Drama based on the JATAKA stories told by the Buddha.

Zatutu (singular: Zutti) *Oman.*   Non-Arab tribe.

zawiya (plural: zawaya) *Morocco.*   Literally draw together. Lodge of a religious order identified with its founding MARABOUT.

zay *Burma.* Bazaar.

zayat *Burma.* Public shelter or resting place.

Zaydi *Yemens.* Shiite group that recognizes Zaid as the original IMAM.

Zayse *Ethiopia.* Afro-Asiatic language.

zazalahi *Madagascar.* Unmarried young men.

zbande *Afghanistan.* PASHTO for water mill.

zeffan *Ethiopia.* Secular music.

zei *Saudi Arabia.* Confederation of tribes in the Hadhramaut.

zekkat *Burkina Faso.* Tax on nomad cattle.

Zela *Zaire.* Ethnic group.

zemetcha *Ethiopia.* Literally, green. Campaign to indoctrinate the peasantry in the Ethiopian version of socialism.

Zenaga *Mauritania.* Afro-Asiatic language.

zenana *India.* Apartment of a house in which Muslim women are secluded.

Zenata *Algeria.* One of the two great BERBER confederations.

Zenet *Mauritania.* BERBER dialect.

zepaules *Haiti.* From *les epaules,* or shoulders. VOODOO ceremonial dance accenting shoulder movements.

zerbaghli *Afghanistan.* Single-headed drum with a body made of baked clay and head of goatskin.

Zerma *Burkina Faso.* Ethnic group.

zeze *Congo.* Dance.

Zezura *Zimbabwe.* Central SHONA.

Zezuru *Zimbabwe.* SHONA-speaking ethnic group.

ziara *Mauritania.* Special visit or pilgrimage to a ZAWIYA.

ziara *Somalia.* Celebration in memory of a clan ancestor.

ziarat *Afghanistan.* Village shrine of a saint or a *shaheed* (martyr).

Zigua *Tanzania.* Ethnic group, on the coast and in west Tanga.

zikert *Ethiopia.* Religious feast in the Orthodox Church.

zikr *Sudan.* Remembrance of god in SUFI orders.

zilla *India.* District as a unit of local administration.

Zimba *Mozambique.* Ethnic group of the MARAVI cluster.

Zimba *Zaire.* Niger-Kordofanian language.

zimbabwe (plural: madzimbabwe) *Zimbabwe.* Stone structure.

zimiwal *Nepal.* Village headman.

zimpen *Bhutan.* District magistrate.

Zinza *Tanzania.* Ethnic group.

Zirak *Afghanistan.* PASHTO subgroup of DURANIS made up of *Alikozais, Achakzais, Popalzais* and *Barakzais.*

ziva *Madagascar.* Joking relationship characterized by familiarity, informality and the right to insult without fear of offending others.

ziyarah *Algeria.* Pilgrimage to a religious shrine or the tomb of a MARABOUT.

Zizi *Lesotho.*   NGUNI group, also known as BAPHETLA.

znaga *Western Sahara.*   Non-Arabic nomads.

zo *Liberia.*   Traditional magico-religious healer; elder of a community in central and western regions.

Zombo *Angola.*   Unit of KONGO.

Zome *India.*   Indo-Tibetan language.

zonda *Uruguay.*   Hot wind blowing from the north in summer.

zongo *West Africa.*   Literally, strangers' quarters. Part of town or village occupied by non-natives.

zopilote *Nicaragua.*   Literally, buzzard. Folk dance in which performers dress as birds of prey singing satirical verses about politicians who are lampooned as birds of prey.

zu *Guatemala.*   Flute.

zuhur *Islamic countries.*   Manifestations of the IMAM.

Zulgo *Cameroon.*   Afro-Asiatic language.

Zulu *Swaziland.*   Ethnic group, BANTU-speaking branch of Northern NGUNI.

Zulu *Lesotho.*   Niger-Kordofanian language.

zurkhana *Iran.*   Literally, house of strength. Club for wrestlers and weight lifters.

zurron *Peru.*   Leather sack for packing cocoa beans, each holding four smaller sacks.

zute *Guatemala.*   General utility cloth used by Indians for a variety of purposes, including head-covering, baby sling or padding to balance a basket on the head.

zuyacales *Guatemala.*   Raincoats made from palm leaves.

zwagendaba *Mozambique.*   Ethnic group of the NGUNI cluster.

zwaya *Mauritania.*   Religious elite who constitute the top class of the white Moorish nobility.

zwiingo *Rwanda.*   Chief of a BABANDWA, or politico-religious fraternity.

APPENDIX

LANGUAGE FAMILIES OF THE WORLD

AFRO-ASIATIC or HAMITO-SEMITIC LANGUAGES

Berber
Old Libyan*; Guanche*; Numidian*; Modern Berber: Kabyle, Rif, Shilh, Tuareg, Zenaga

Chad
Bata-Margi group, Hausa, Kotoko group, many little known languages in Nigeria

Cushitic
Beja (Bedauye); Bilin; Galla, Saho-Afar, Sidamo, Somali; Doko, Wolamo; Burungi, Mbugu

Egyptian
Ancient Egyptian*, Coptic*

Semitic
  EAST SEMITIC
  Akkadian
Assyrian*, Babylonian*; Nuzi Akkadian*
  WEST SEMITIC
  Northwest Semitic
Aramaic: Old*, Biblical*, and Palestinian Aramaic*; Mandean*, Syriac*, Neo-Syriac

Canaanite: Old Canaanite*, Moabite*, Phoenician*, Punic*, Ugaritic*, Old (Biblical) Hebrew*, Talmudic Hebrew*, Israeli Hebrew
  Southwest Semitic
Arabic: Classical A.*, Arabian A., Egyptian A., Iraqi A., Syrian A., Western A. (incl. Andalusian* and Maltese); Southern A. (incl. Sabean* and Himyaritic)

Ethiopic: Ge'ez (Classical Ethiopic)*, Amharic, Tigrē, Tigrinya

ALTAIC LANGUAGES

West Altaic
  BULGARIC
Chuvash, Volga-Kama Bulgar (E Bulgar)*
  TURKIC
  East
Chaghatay*, (Old) Uighur* (incl. Kök

An asterisk (*) indicates a dead language. A dagger (†) represents a highly tentative listing.

	Turkic*), New Uighur, (Iranized) Uzbek
South (Oghuz)	Azeri (Azerbaijani), Turkish (or Ottoman Turkish or Osmanli), Turkoman (Turkmenian)
West (Kipchak)	Bashkir, Crimean Tatar, Karaim, Karakalpak, Kazakh, Kazan Tatar, Kipchak*, Kirghiz, Noghay
North	Abakan, Oyrot, Soyon, Tuva
East Siberian	Yakut
East Altaic	
MONGOLIAN	
East	Chakhar, Khalkha, Kharchin, literary Mongolian
	Afghanistan Mongol
North	Buryat (incl. Selenga)
West	Oirat (incl. Kalmuck)
TUNGUSIC	
Manchu	Manchurian, Udekhe
Tungus	Even (Lamut), Evenki (Tungus), Negidal

AUSTRO-ASIATIC LANGUAGES

Mon-Khmer (SE Asia)	Cham, Khasi, Khmer (Cambodian), Mon, Nicobarese, Wa
Munda (India)	Ho, Mundari, Santali, Sora
Annamese-Muong	Muong, Vietnamese (Annamese)

CAUCASIAN LANGUAGES

North Caucasian	
ABKHAZO-ADYGHEIN	Abkhaz-Abazin, Adyghe (incl. Kiakh or Circassian and Kabardian), Ubykh
DAGHESTANI	Avaro-Andi group, Dargwa group, Lakk, Lezghian or Samurian group
VEINAKH	Chechen, Ingush, Bats
South Caucasian (relation to N Caucasian uncertain)	
KARTVELIAN	Georgian, Laz, Mingrelian, Svan

An asterisk (*) indicates a dead language. A dagger (†) represents a highly tentative listing.

DRAVIDIAN LANGUAGES (mainly S India)

Brahui (NW India)
Gondi, Konda; Telugu, Tulu
Kanarese, Kodagu, Malayalam, Tamil

INDO-EUROPEAN LANGUAGES

Anatolian	Hieroglyphic Hittite*, Hittite (Kanesian)*, Luwian*, Lycian*, Lydian*, Palaic*
Armenian	Classical Armenian*, Eastern Armenian, Western Armenian
Baltic	Latvian (Lettish), Lithuanian, Old Prussian*
Celtic	
BRYTHONIC	Breton, Cornish*, Middle Welsh*, Welsh (or Cymric)
CONTINENTAL	Gaulish*
GOIDELIC	Old*, Middle*, and Modern Irish, Manx, Scots Gaelic (Scotland and Nova Scotia)
Germanic	
EAST GERMANIC	Burgundian*, Gothic*, Crimean Gothic*, Vandalic*
NORTH GERMANIC	Eastern: Old Danish*, Danish, Dano-Norwegian (Rigsmaal); Gutnish; Old Swedish*, Swedish
	Western: Faroese; Icelandic; Old Norse (incl. Old Icelandic)*, Norwegian (Landsmaal)
WEST GERMANIC	
High German	Old* and Middle* High German, standard German
	Central: Middle and Rhine Franconian, Pennsylvania Dutch, Yiddish
	Upper: Alemannic (incl. Alsatian, Swabian, and Swiss German), High Franconian; Austro-Bavarian; Lombard*
Low German	Old Saxon*, Middle Low German*, Plattdeutsch (Modern Low German)

An asterisk (*) indicates a dead language. A dagger (†) represents a highly tentative listing.

Old Low Franconian*, Flemish, Dutch, Afrikaans

Anglo-Frisian: Old Frisian*, Frisian; Old English (incl. West Saxon, Kentish, and Anglian dialects)*, Middle English*, Middle Scots*, English (British, Scottish, American, Australian, New Zealand, South African English; also various creoles, e.g., Beach-la-mar, Taki-Taki)

Greek (Hellenic)
WEST GREEK   Doric*, Tsaconian; Northwest Greek*
EAST GREEK   Aeolic*; Arcado-Cyprian (incl. Mycenaean Greek = Linear B)*; Ionic (Homeric Greek)*, Attic*, Koine*, Byzantine Greek*, Modern Greek (incl. Katharevusa and Demotik)

Indo-Iranian
DARDIC or
PISACHA
(central Asia)   Kafiri, Kashmiri, Khowar, Kohistani, Romany (Gypsy), Shina

INDIC or
INDO-ARYAN   Vedic*, Sanskrit*, Prakrits* (incl. Pali*)
  Central Indic   Eastern Hindi: Awadhi, Bagheli, Chattisgarhi (or Laria)
                          Western Hindi: Khari Boli (standard Hindustani) (literary Hindi; Urdu)
  East Indic   Assamese, Bengali, Bihari (Bhojpuri, Magahi, Maithili), Oriya
  NW Indic   Lahnda, Punjabi, Sindhi
  Pahari   Central Pahari (Kumaoni, Garhwali), Eastern Pahari (Khas-kura or Gorkhali or Nepali), Western Pahari
  Sinhalese   Sinhalese (incl. major dialect Mahl)
  South Indic   Marathi (incl. major dialect Konkani)
  West Indic   Bhili, Gujarati, Khandesi, Rajastani (many dialects)

IRANIAN   Avestan*, Old Persian*
  East Iranian   Khwarazmian*, Ossetic, Pamir dialects,

An asterisk (*) indicates a dead language. A dagger (†) represents a highly tentative listing.

	Pashto (Afghan), Saka (Khotanese)* Sogdian*, Yaghnobi
West Iranian	Baluchi, Kurdish, Middle Persian (Pahlavi)*, Parthian*, Persian (Farsi), Tajiki

Italic

(NON-ROMANCE) Faliscan*; Old*, Classical*, Vulgar*, and Medieval* Latin
Oscan*, Sabellic*, Umbrian*

ROMANCE Catalan (E Spain); Dalmatian*; Old French*, French (incl. Canadian French, Haitian Creole, Louisiana French); Galician (NW Spain); Old Italian*, Italian (dialects and standard Tuscan); Moldavian; Old Portuguese*, Portuguese (incl. Brazilian P.); old Provençal*, Provençal (SE France); Rhaeto-Romanic (incl. Friulian, Ladin, Romansh); Rumanian; Sardinian; Old Spanish*, Spanish (incl. American Sp. and Philippine Sp.), Judeo-Spanish (Ladino) (Sephardic)

Slavic

EAST SLAVIC Byelorussian (White Russian), (Great) Russian, Ukrainian (Little Russian)

SOUTH SLAVIC Old Bulgarian (Old Church Slavonic)*, Bulgarian, Macedonian, Serbo-Croatian, Slovenian

WEST SLAVIC Czech, Kashubian*, Polabian*, Polish, Slovak, Sorbian (Wendish)

Thraco-Illyrian
(uncertain grouping) Albanian (incl. Geg and Tosk), Illyrian*, Messapic*, Thracian*, Venetic*

Tokharian (W China) Tokharian A (Agnean)*; Tokharian B (Kuchean)*

LUORAWETLAN or PALEOASIATIC LANGUAGES (E Siberia)

Chukchi, Kamchadal, Koryak
Possible relation: Ainu, Gilyak

An asterisk (*) indicates a dead language. A dagger (†) represents a highly tentative listing.

MACRO-KHOISAN LANGUAGES (S Africa)

South African Khoisan

Bushman (incl. Auen, Hiechware, !kung, Naron), Hottentot (incl. Korana, Nama)

East African Khoisan

Hatsa, Sandawe

MALAYO-POLYNESIAN or AUSTRONESIAN LANGUAGES

Indonesian or Malayan
WEST

Chamorro, Formosan, Malagasy
Philippine: Bisaya, Igorot, Ilocano, Magindanao, Tagalog
Southern: Balinese, Dyak, Javanese, Makassar, Malay (Bahasa Indonesia), Sumatran, Sudanese

EAST
Aru, Savu

Melanesian
Fijian, Malo, Marovo, Mono

Micronesian
Caroline, Gilbertese, Marianas, Marshallese, Yap

Polynesian
Hawaiian, Maori, Marquesan, Rapa Nui, Rarotongan, Samoan, Tahitian, Tongan

NIGER-CONGO LANGUAGES

Adamawa-Eastern
Sango, Zande, many little known languages

Benue-Congo or Central Branch
BANTOID GROUP
Bantu

Bemba, Chaga, Chwana, Herero, Kamba, Kikuyu, Kimbundu, Kongo, Luba, Luganda, Ngala, Nyaruanda, Rundi, Shona, Sotho, Swahili, Swazi, Xhosa, Zulu

Non-Bantu
Bitare, Bute, Mambila, Tiv
CROSS-RIVER
GROUP
Boki, Efik, Olulomo
JUKUNOID
GROUP
Jukun, Kentu, Nyidu

An asterisk (*) indicates a dead language. A dagger (†) represents a highly tentative listing.

PLATEAU GROUP	Eggon, Kambari, many little known languages
Gur or Voltaic	Lobi-Dogon group, Mossi-Grunshi group, Senufo group
Kordofanian	
KATLA GROUP	Katla, Tima
KOALIB GROUP	Koalib, Laro, Otoro, Shwai, Tira
TALODI GROUP	Eliri, Lafofa, Tacho, Talodi
TEGALI GROUP	Tagoi, Tegali, Tumale
TUMTUM GROUP	Karondi, Katcha, Miri, Tumtum
Kwa	Akan (incl. Baoule, Fanti, Twi) Ewe, Fon, Gan, Ibo, Ijo, Kru group (incl. Kru and Bassa), Nupe, Yoruba
Mande	
WESTERN	Bambara, Dyula, Malinke, Soninke; Kpelle, Loma, Mende
EASTERN	Dan, Mwa, Samo
West Atlantic	
NORTHERN	Biafada, Fulani, Mandyak, Serer-Sin, Wolof
SOUTHERN	Bulom, Gola, Kissi, Limba, Temne

NILO-SAHARAN or SUDANIC LANGUAGES
(mainly E Africa)

Chari-Nile or	
Macro-Sudanic	
EASTERN	Nilotic: Acholi, Dinka, Nuer, Shilluk; Bari,
SUDANIC	Masai, Nandi, Suk
	Nubian: Nile Nubian; Kordofanian Nubian; Birked
	Dagu, Barea, and other small branches
GENERAL	Bagirmi, Sara dialects; Moru; Mangbetu;
SUDANIC	Kreish
BERTA	
KUNAMA	
Fur	Fur
Koman	Ganza, Gule, Koma, Mao, Uduk
Maban	Maba, Runga
Saharan	Kanembu, Kanuri; Daza, Teda; Berti, Zaghawa
Songhai	Songhai

An asterisk (*) indicates a dead language. A dagger (†) represents a highly tentative listing.

SINO-TIBETAN LANGUAGES

Chinese	Archaic*, Old* and, Middle* Chinese
	North: Mandarin
	Central: Hsiang, Wu
	South: Foochow, Amoy-Swatow, Kan-Hakka, Cantonese
Thai	Laotian (Lao), Shan, Thai (Siamese)
Tibeto-Burman	
BURMAN	Standard Burmese, Kachin, Karen languages, Kuki-Chin, Miao, Yao
TIBETAN	Bodo, Garo, Lepcha, Naga, standard Tibetan

URALIC LANGUAGES

Finno-Ugric	
FINNIC	Balto-Finnic: Estonian, Finnish (Suomi), Karelian, Livonian, Lude, Olonecian, Vepse, Vote
	Lapp
	Permian: Komi (Zyrian), Votyak (Urᵈ murt)
	Cheremiss (Mari), Mordvinian
UGRIC	Hungarian (Magyar)
	Obi-Ugrian: Ostyak (Khanty), Vogul (Mansi)
Samoyedic (N Urals)	North: Nganasan (Tawgi), Yenisei-Samoyedic, Yurak
	South: Ostyak-Samoyedic (Selkup), Sayan-Samoyedic

Non-Related Languages of the Old World: Andamanese, Basque, Burushaski, Elamite*, Etruscan*, Hurrian*, Iberian*, Japanese, Ket (Yenisei Ostyak), Khattian*, Korean, Ligurian*, Meroitic*, Sumerian*, Urartaean (Vannic)*, Yukaghir, each of the 96 aboriginal languages of Australia, each of the 132 Papuan languages.

An asterisk (*) indicates a dead language. A dagger (†) represents a highly tentative listing.

ALGONQUIAN-MOSAN LANGUAGES
(North America)

	Kootenai (Kutenai)
Algonquian	
CENTRAL	Algonquin, Cree, Delaware, Fox, Illinois*, Kickapoo, Menominee, Miami*, Montagnais, Naskapi, Ojibwa (Chippewa), Ottawa, Potawatomi, Powhatan*, Sauk, Shawnee
EASTERN	Abnaki, Malecite, Micmac, Mohegan*, Narragansett*, Natick*, Passamaquoddy, Penobscot, Pequot*
WESTERN	Arapaho, Blackfoot, Cheyenne
Ritwan (N Calif.)	Wiyot, Yurok
Mosan	
CHIMAKUAN	Chimakum, Quileut
SALISHAN	Bella Coola, Coeur d'Alene, Flathead
WAKASHAN	Bella Bella, Kwakiutl, Nootka

ANDEAN-EQUATORIAL LANGUAGES†
(mainly South America)

Andean	
ARAUCANIAN	Mapuche
QUECHU-MARAN	Aymará, Quechua
ZAPAROAN	Iquito, Zaparo
Equatorial	
ARAWAKAN	Arawak, Taino (Caribbean region)
TUPI-GUARANI	Guaraní, Tupí (Lingua Geral)
Jivaroan	Jívaro
Tucanoan	Tucano, Yupua

AZTECO-TANOAN LANGUAGES
(W North America and Mexico)

Kiowan	Kiowa
Tanoan	
TEWA	Hano, Nambé, Pojoaque*, San Idlefonso, San Juan, Santa Clara, Tesuque

An asterisk (*) indicates a dead language. A dagger (†) represents a highly tentative listing.

| TIWA | Isleta, Sandia; Picuris, Taos |
| TOWA | Jemez, Pecos* |

Uto-Aztecan

AZTECOID	Cora, Huichol, Classical Nahuatl (Aztec)*, Nahuatl, Tolteca-Chichimeca
HOPIAN	Bannock, Hopi
PIMAN	Papago, Pima
SHOSHONEAN	Comanche, Shoshone
SOUTHERN CALIFORNIAN	Cahuilla, Luiseño, Tubatulabal
TARACAHITIAN	Cahita, Tarahumara, Yaqui
UTAN	Paiute, Ute
Zuni (doubtful relation)	Zuñi

ESKIMO-ALEUT LANGUAGES

Aleut, Eskimo

GE-PANO-CARIB† (Caribbean region and South America)

Cariban	Carib, Quimbaya
Gê (S Brazil)	Apinage, Chavante
Panoan	Caxibo, Conibo

HOKAN-SIOUAN LANGUAGES (North America)

| **Caddoan** | Arikara, Caddo, Pawnee, Wichita |

Hokan-Coahuiltecan

COAHUILTECAN	Coahuilteco, Comecrudo*, Karankawa, Tonkawa
HOKAN	Barbareño Chumash, Karok, Pomo, Salinan, Shasta, Yana, Yuman group (Mohavi, Walapai, Yuma)
	Central America: Jicaque, Subtiaba, Tequistlatec
Iroquoian	Cayuga, Cherokee, Erie*, Mohawk, Onondaga, Oneida, Seneca, Susquehanna*, Tuscarora, Wyandot (Huron)
Keresan	Western Keresan: Acoma, Laguna
	Eastern Keresan: Cochiti, Santa Ana

An asterisk (*) indicates a dead language. A dagger (†) represents a highly tentative listing.

Natchez-Muskogean	Alabama (incl. Koasati), Chickasaw, Choctaw, Creek, Natchez, Seminole
Siouan	Assiniboin, Biloxi*, Catawba, Crow, Dakota, Hidatsa, Iowa, Kansa, Mandan, Omaha, Osage, Ponca, Sioux, Winnebago
Tunican	Atakapa, Chitimacha, Tunica
Yukian	Yuki

MACRO-CHIBCHAN LANGUAGES†
(Central and South America)

Chibchan	Boruca, Cara, Chibcha*, Paez
Misumalpan	Bambana, Miskito

MACRO-OTOMANGUEAN LANGUAGES
(Mexico and Central America)

Chinantecan	Chinanteco
Mixtecan	Amusgo, Cuicatec, Mixtec
Otomanguean	Chiapanec, Mangue, Mazatec, Otomí, Popoloca, Trique
Zapotecan	Solteco, Zapotec (several languages)

NADENE LANGUAGES (W North America)

Athabascan	
NORTHERN	Beaver, Carrier, Chipewyan, Kutchin, Sarsi, Sekani, Slave, Yellowknife
PACIFIC	Chasta-Costa, Hupa, Mattole
SOUTHERN	Apache, Kiowa Apache, Lipsan, Navaho
Haida	Haida
Tlingit	Tlingit

PENUTIAN LANGUAGES
(W North America and Central America)

California Penutian	Costanoan*, Maidu, Miwok*, Wintun, Yokuts

An asterisk (*) indicates a dead language. A dagger (†) represents a highly tentative listing.

Chinook	Chinook, Wishram
Mayan	
MAYOID	Chontal, Huastec, Itzá, Maya, Tzeltal, Tzotzil, Yucatec
QUICHOID	Aguacetec, Cakchiquel, Mam, Quiché
Mixe-Zoque	Huave, Mixe, Popoluca (Sierra), Zoque
Oregon Penutian	Alsea, Coos, Kalapuya, Takelma
Sahaptian	Cayuse, Klamath, Modoc, Nez Percé, Walla Walla, Yumatilla
Totonacan	Tepehua, Totonaco
Tsimshian	Tsimshian

Non-Related Languages of the New World: Hundreds of the languages of South America are not yet satisfactorily classified. Many of these may belong to the families already established, or the classifications may have to be considerably changed.